P9-DGR-734

THE URBANIZATION OF AMERICA

Rutgers University Press

NEW BRUNSWICK, NEW JERSEY

THE URBANIZATION
OF AMERICA

[1860-1915]

Blake McKelvey

Copyright © 1963 by Rutgers, The State University
Library of Congress Catalogue Card Number: 62–21248
SBN: 8135–0421–X
This book was manufactured with the assistance of a grant from the
Ford Foundation
Third Printing

To my Mother

Author's preface

Many cities both large and small had by 1860 won a secure place on the map of America and in the stream of its history. The federal census, which then required a minimum of 8000 residents for inclusion in its urban categories, listed 141 such places that year. Of these, ninety-three had more than 10,000 inhabitants, thirty-five more than 25,000, and nine more than 100,000. But whether defined statistically in these terms, or in those adopted at subsequent censuses, or sociologically in Professor Louis Wirth's compact phrase as "relatively large, dense, and permanent settlement[s] of socially heterogeneous individuals," the cities were destined, in the next five decades, to multiply almost sixfold in number and sevenfold in size, and to develop significant new relationships.

In this study, however, I am not primarily interested in tabulating the increased number and density of cities. That basic aspect of the urbanization process has been treated repeatedly by able scholars whose statistical analyses are readily available.[1] Nor am I seeking to establish categories that will neatly classify urban differences. These tasks are relevant, but my purpose here is to examine the character of city growth, to uncover, if possible, some of its causes, and, most of all, to explore the relationships between this development and other phases of American history during the period.

Several questions stand out. How, for example, did the cities contribute to the settlement of the continent, and how did the great westward movement influence the growth of cities? Did the commercial and industrial revolutions create the cities, or vice versa, and was the immigration movement a major influence? What bearing did the cities have on the progressive movement and on the broader developments of the nation's social and cultural life? We cannot answer all of these questions, but by raising and considering them we can hope to get a clearer picture of the history of America in this half-century.

To achieve that end we will take a close look at both the internal structure and functions and the external relationships of the cities of the period. We will discover that, just as they had earlier provided trade centers for the expanding agrarian economy, they continued after the Civil War to channel the nation's commerce, and in the process generated a new industrial society. Their increasing density and heterogeneity accentuated many internal problems and prompted institutional innovations—they were evolving new structures to embody their more specialized functions. Yet the human and material elements and the social patterns they produced varied so greatly from place to place, as well as in time, and included so much overlapping, that the categories of cities defy precise delineation.

Many scholars have tried to formulate definitions of a city, a metropolis, a suburb, a community, and the urbanization process.[2] Their inability to reach agreement reflects the fact that these are human aggregates and historic experiences, not abstractions. Even if the attempt to isolate the strictly urban factor in human affairs should ultimately succeed, and adequate techniques for its quantitative study be formulated, as one scholar has proposed,[3] the historian of cities would remain more broadly interested in the interplay of that influence with other forces affecting man's response to his environment. For the present, at least, this is as far as existing records will permit us to go.

Fortunately the records already available are illuminating. Each community, developing as a more or less unified entity, had a history of its own, as numerous studies have shown. My own four volumes on Rochester supply perhaps the most complete account of any one city's history, but Miss Bessie Pierce's three volumes on Chicago treat its history exhaustively and carry the story to 1893. Several single-volume city histories and numerous books on urban problems and developments in this period contribute much to our understanding; they will be mentioned frequently in my notes.[4]

Most of the cities started as regional market places, and a few as mining camps, industrial promotions, administrative centers, college or resort towns. Those that successfully exploited river, lake, or ocean ports, or achieved the status of rail hubs, attained commercial importance and became in some cases the central metropolis for a broad region. All these cities and many that were less fortunately situated for trade developed industrial potentials; some of the latter achieved sufficient technological proficiency or sufficient prominence by exploiting the resources of rich hinterlands to attain recognition as industrial metropolises.

This classification conforms roughly with the understanding of urban leaders of the period. I have, in fact, generally followed the contemporary terminology, using the terms *town* and *city* interchangeably to designate communities of urban proportions as indicated in the context. I have tried to recognize signs of shifting functional interests and to portray the changing character of both the cities and the metropolitan centers as they adjusted to new internal, regional, and national developments.

It was because their constant adaptation to such changes afforded leadership in the broader currents of American life that the growth of cities acquired historical significance. The rapid increase of that influence during the half-century under review reflects the fact that, beginning in the 1860's, urban population gains exceeded rural gains in size, as they had for several decades in per cent. The acceleration of this process, coupled with the progressive addition of new urban functions, enabled the cities by 1915 to absorb half the total population. I have accordingly entitled this study *The Urbanization of America.*

In order to refresh our understanding of the character and spread of American cities at the opening of the period, it seems appropriate to start with a summary of their development in earlier decades. The Introduction, therefore, presents a hasty survey of the economic and demographic forces that brought cities into being and scattered them sparsely across the continent before 1860. It also offers a brief sketch of their characteristics at that date.

I have divided the main body of the text into five parts. Four of these treat major aspects of the urbanization movement down approximately to 1910. The first deals with the economic and demographic forces that tended to multiply and scatter urban centers across the land. The second follows the internal civic and political evolution of the cities. The third and fourth parts trace the appearance of urban social and cultural innovations and their embodiment in customs and institutions. Finally, in the fifth part, I endeavor to pull the varied strands of city growth and influence together, as urban leaders in many fields were, in fact, doing in the years before the First World War. They had achieved, we discover, a new spatial and functional synthesis, based in part on an emerging metropolitan regionalism, which had already assumed a significant role in American history.

Acknowledgments

I have received generous assistance throughout the preparation of this volume from many librarians and scholars. My colleagues on the staff of the Rochester Public Library have been most helpful, especially Miss Emma B. Swift, Mrs. Margaret Hallock, Miss Sue Billings, and Miss Marion L. McGuire, and I wish to thank Mr. Harold Hacker, Library Director, and his predecessor, Mr. Rutherford D. Rogers, for their interest and backing in this undertaking. Several librarians elsewhere have responded to requests for elusive materials, and Mr. John Russell of the Rush Rhees Library of the University of Rochester has generously made its resources available.

A number of able students of urban history have given aid and encouragement. I am most grateful to Professor Arthur M. Schlesinger, long my mentor in historical study, who read and made helpful criticisms of an early draft of the manuscript, Professor Bayrd Still also read and criticized an early draft, and both Dr. Louise Wade and Professor Richard C. Wade read portions of more recent versions, making helpful suggestions. I wish to thank these generous friends and also Mrs. Mary T. Heathcote, who has made many stylistic criticisms that have considerably improved the manuscript.

For aid in assembling the illustrations I am greatly obliged to Mr. Beaumont Newhall, Director of the George Eastman House, and to his assistants Robert M. Doty and Jerry Steffani, and to Miss Marion Simmons of the New York Public Library. For her painstaking care in typing numerous drafts of the manuscript, in checking and rechecking references, and in compiling the bibliography and index, I am most grateful to Miss Meryl Frank, my secretarial and research assistant. And finally to my wife, Jean Trepp McKelvey, I give warm thanks for advice on the treatment of economic aspects of the urbanization process and for her patient perusal of successive versions of the manuscript.

Contents

THE URBANIZATION OF AMERICA

Introduction

After more than a century of gradual acceleration, the urbanization process passed, during the 1860's, into a second and more complicated stage. In addition to the commercial functions that fostered their early growth, the cities of America now acquired, as a result of technological advances and population increments, new industrial energies. These resources, coupled with the nation's geographic expansion, not only brought renewed vitality to many old centers, but also multiplied the number of cities, increased their diversity, and raised the quality of their interrelationships.

To understand the character of post–Civil War urban developments, it is necessary first to review the early history of American cities. Their rates of growth after 1800, separately and as an urban total, seem astonishing until one recognizes that they were not starting from scratch, but were emerging as strategic outposts in a rapidly developing intercontinental, almost world-wide, system. That system had attained sufficient maturity and specialization to nurture a new technology, which gave birth in turn to an industrial revolution that appeared first in England and was already spreading to the Continent and to America.[1]

The new technology caused a great speed-up, not only in industrial production at a few nascent manufacturing centers, but also in commerce by water and rail. As a result, the pressure for expansion became most acute both on the undeveloped frontier, notably in the American West, and at key breaks in trade. These latter were the points of most rapid urban growth in pre–Civil War America, and with one exception they accounted for its major cities. Moreover that exception, Boston, had early developed its port and at mid-century was organizing a metropolitan region that would serve as the pattern for a new era of national aggrandizement and increased economic self-sufficiency.

Thus, although the growth of American cities was to assume startling proportions after the Civil War, many communities already took a lusty pride in their urban dimensions. Eight of the nine cities that by 1860 had passed the 100,000 mark were thriving ports—the most striking products of an age of rapid land settlement and the commercial expansion it brought. Four on the Atlantic—Boston, New York, Philadelphia, and Baltimore—had colonial origins; New Orleans on the Gulf boasted of its French background; three, of more recent vintage—Cincinnati, St. Louis, and Chicago—stood at strategic points on the Ohio, the Mississippi, and the Great Lakes. The ninth city, Brooklyn, was a mushrooming suburb but shared the benefits of the country's greatest harbor. Three additional port towns in the interior and one on the Pacific, as well as the national capital, would each attain that size within a decade. All of these and a score more, each reporting in excess of 25,000 residents, had acquired many other attributes of a major city. The 1860 census tabulated nearly four hundred places whose residents numbered at least 2500.[2] The grand total of such urban residents had reached 6,216,518, almost a fifth of the national population, as contrasted with one twentieth in 1790.

New York, the national metropolis, had steadily surged ahead. Surpassing even Constantinople in size, it stood third in the Western world, exceeded only by London and Paris. Articulate visitors from abroad, such as Anthony Trollope, who arrived in the fall of 1861, often voiced disappointment over the structures they saw in New York, but all marveled at the bustling throngs in its streets and at the ceaseless activity in its great harbor. Their astonishment grew when they learned that a brief ferry ride over the East River would land them in Brooklyn, which at mid-century had leaped into third place among American cities. Indeed, short ferry lines linked a half-dozen towns with Manhattan, giving greater New York a population of 1,174,774 in 1860.[3]

More cosmopolitan than any of its great rivals abroad, New York was in some ways the most typically American city. Its enterprising merchants, assembled from every section of the country, took full advantage of the port's central location on the East coast. Its geographic position and spacious harbor attracted ships from all parts of the world, stimulating local efforts to make it also the chief point of export. The completion of the Erie Canal in 1825 provided a cheap route to the interior and assured New York's commercial predominance.[4]

A state project, supported alike by the merchants of Manhattan and the residents of many inland communities eager to open an outlet for their produce, the Erie Canal spawned a succession of thriving towns. By channeling the trade of the Great Lakes down the Hudson River, it made New York the Empire State and its capital, Albany, the largest predominantly administrative center in the nation. Buffalo, at the junction of the canal with the upper lakes, quickly became their leading port, though others to the west were rising rapidly. Eastward along the canal, Rochester and Troy began to develop industrial potentials as well.[5]

The advancing frontier of settlement, during the second quarter of the century, drew an ever increasing host of migrants over this water-level route into the North Central States. The practice there, as throughout most of the West, of selling land on an instalment plan forced the settlers to produce a marketable surplus to meet their annual payments. Many failed to master that requirement, sold their improvements, and moved on to break new land farther west, but others, more commercial-minded, took their places. Almost every year saw a larger output of goods descend to the New York docks. As merchants and shipwrights at each potential harbor linked forces, steamboats multiplied on the Hudson and on the Great Lakes. Other aspiring towns at a dozen points along the route prompted the construction during the late thirties and forties of lateral canals and feeder railroads. All contributed to the rising stream of produce that helped to make Manhattan a world metropolis.[6]

Of the remaining colonial ports,[7] only Philadelphia and Boston had by 1860 attained major proportions, though a younger rival, Baltimore, and Brooklyn, too, now surpassed Boston in population.

Yet Boston, like Manhattan, was already surrounded by a ring of thriving suburbs. If it had annexed them, as Baltimore and Philadelphia did, it would have maintained third place until overtaken by Brooklyn in 1855. Instead, the Bay State capital, hard-pressed by New York's superior commercial advantages, was the first to promote interior industrial towns. After 1820, its investments at Lowell and several lesser places produced the merchandise needed to maintain a fairly steady growth in Boston's foreign trade. These activities, joined with the fishing harvest and the output of its own craftsmen, created sufficient wealth to enable Boston to build a system of feeder railroads to Lowell and Worcester and Providence, tying them securely in its trade basin during the thirties, and to push on to Portland, to Springfield and Albany, to Hartford and New Haven, even to Montreal and New York before 1860.

Thus Boston had by the mid-century successfully developed the prototype of the metropolitan region that was destined to challenge the overriding sway of the national metropolis on the Hudson. Moreover, Boston sustained cultural institutions that strengthened its dominant position in New England and in several fields exerted a wider national influence than those of New York.[8]

Most visitors were eager to praise the Yankee capital, but some now found Philadelphia an overgrown village. The monotony of its checkerboard street pattern, with seemingly endless rows of two-story structures extending off to a murky horizon, canceled out the pleasant aspect of some front stoops and back yards. Even the lovely old square surrounding Independence Hall appeared lost in the morass of shops and houses. Trollope, for one, could scarcely believe this sprawling town's claim to a population of half a million. If true, he remarked, it placed William Penn's settlement ahead of all but Paris on the Continent.[9] The boast seemed more incredible in view of the city's decline from third to fourth place in value of imports and to ninth place in exports.

Yet the census of 1860 sustained the estimate, recording Philadelphia's population at 565,529. That figure represented a threefold increase during the decade and resulted from the annexation in 1854 of several vast suburbs and the absorption of a larger territory than any city but London had assembled under one municipality. With this growth, Philadelphia had dissipated its old Quaker atmosphere, losing the charm it had displayed in the early Federal period, without developing a distinctive new character. Its 6298 shops, the great majority of them relying on hand labor, produced a diversified output valued at nearly $136,000,000—a close second to that of much larger New York. Yet Philadelphia lacked the appearance of an industrial town, such as travelers who had visited the factories at Lowell or the foundries at smoky Pittsburgh now expected to find.[10] Nevertheless, in output, and indeed in internal structure and appearance, it too supplied a metropolitan prototype full of significance for the future.

To observers who overlooked its industries, Philadelphia's prospects seemed not only overshadowed by New York but seriously limited as well by the aggressive advance of nearby Baltimore. The younger port had suddenly spurted ahead in the thirties as its canal-building efforts of the previous decade began to produce results. Its decision in 1827 to build a steam railroad into the West, in order to challenge New York's water route, had threatened to isolate Philadelphia and spurred Pennsylvania to span the state with a linked series of canals and railroads. That state system reached Pittsburgh in 1835 and held it firmly, though reluctantly, in Philadelphia's orbit. Although the Baltimore & Ohio Railroad, in which the city of Baltimore invested a half-million dollars, failed at the time to gain an entry to Pittsburgh, it pushed on to Wheeling in 1852, thus tapping the Ohio Valley's trade. Reports of this venture stimulated both Philadelphia and Pittsburgh to invest still larger sums in the privately chartered Pennsylvania Railroad, which reached Pittsburgh later the same year. Yet Baltimore's increasing share of western trade and its uncontested sway over the southern Piedmont region sustained a vigorous growth that encouraged metropolitan aspirations and supported many cultural facilities.[11]

Even more astonishing urban developments were occurring on the western frontier. As Professor Richard Wade has shown, the great interior migration was accompanied by the rise of several western cities with lofty ambitions. Founded in most cases as forts and trading posts in the eighteenth century, they not only promoted land settlement but also provided vital commercial links with the markets of the East and of Europe.[12]

Yet if settlement and trade advanced together, it was not as one harmonious operation. Impatient migrants, attracted by the fertile lands and spurred by the promises of enthusiastic speculators, trooped across the mountains in increasing numbers after 1800, outstripping the wagon trains of the merchants who endeavored to supply them. In Lexington, at the Kentucky end of the Cumberland road, and in Pittsburgh, at the headwaters of the Ohio, the demand for provisions, household furnishings, and new equipment became so great that many artisans abandoned their quest for land and, particularly in Pittsburgh, laid the foundations of an industrial economy. Protected by the mountain barrier and by the long and tedious upriver haul on the Mississippi—which provided, however, an ideal route for exports—the new industrial centers prospered until technological advances back East produced steamboats and railroads to breach their defenses. Lexington's early pre-eminence disappeared shortly after the steamboat was introduced on the Ohio in 1811; with the inauguration of upriver traffic four years later, even Pittsburgh felt the challenge.

Richly endowed with mineral resources, Pittsburgh had a secure industrial future. Yet its prosperity in the pre–Civil War period also depended on commerce, and it lost to Cincinnati its early dominance over the Ohio River trade when the steamboat enabled traders to bring merchandise up the river from New Orleans, dwarfing the flow across the mountains. Cincinnati, in the heart of the "Old West," was further strengthened in 1832 by the opening of a canal which ran north to Lake

Erie, linking it with the New York trade system and stimulating some metropolitan commission merchants to open offices there. Louisville, on the south bank of the Ohio, some distance downstream, quickly established its hegemony in Kentucky, but failed to match Cincinnati's growth. Only New Orleans outstripped it in the West, and the Gulf port's great advantage as the chief export center for cotton, the king of prewar commerce, barely enabled it to hold that lead in the fifties as meat packers and other pioneer industrialists boosted Cincinnati into fourth place nationally in manufacturing.[13]

If cotton was king, the steamboat was certainly the trade queen, particularly in the West. The boom it gave to New Orleans enabled that city not only to overshadow Charleston, Savannah, Mobile, and all other ports south of Baltimore, but also to dominate the great valley above it, and even to take first place in value of foreign exports for a decade after 1834. Manhattan commission merchants and bankers supplied much of the capital, as well as the enterprise, for the New Orleans trade; they also controlled the coastal packet lines and soon brought a sizable portion of the cotton shipment to New York to buttress its foreign commerce. New Orleans contended with Philadelphia and Baltimore for second place in 1840, but fell back to sixth in size as the East Coast cities, strengthened by their railroads, surged ahead during the next decade. And by the fifties, other challengers besides Cincinnati were appearing in the interior.[14]

The 2500 steamboats that docked at New Orleans in 1855 rendered major benefits to the upriver ports they served. St. Louis, at the confluence of the Missouri and the Mississippi, became the center of the river trade of the Great West. Its growth was most dramatic during the forties and fifties, when it attracted such large numbers from abroad that its foreign-born inhabitants reached 59 per cent, the highest in the country. Its mounting population had almost overtaken that of Cincinnati, and of New Orleans, too, by 1860, and would soon bound ahead.[15]

While the migrants and the merchandise of the East and of Europe were finding access into the heart of America by way of New Orleans and the Mississippi steamboats, both were advancing even more tumultuously along the northern water-level route. Five eager lake ports sprang up west of Buffalo—Cleveland, Toledo, Detroit, Milwaukee, and Chicago. All of them organized boards of trade and enjoyed thriving prospects. Chicago, which displayed the greatest vigor in building feeder rail lines, experienced a meteoric rise. Some of its rivals joined in support of one or another of the ten major railroads fanning out from that strategic lake port, yet none profited so greatly as Chicago, which became by 1860 the hub of the world's most extensive rail network.[16]

New and significant urban alignments were thus developing. Since St. Louis and Cincinnati had established rail connections in 1855, the arrival of the Baltimore & Ohio at Cincinnati two years later provided an eastern outlet of major importance. Yet the trip eastward by rail scarcely afforded the pleasures of a ride on a luxury steamer to New Orleans and around to New York by coastal packet, nor were the freight rates so attractive. Chicago, which by 1857 also had alternate rail and water connections with New York, soon acquired competing lines to Boston, Philadelphia, and Baltimore. Each served a number of thriving cities en route and stimulated the development of new industry as well as commerce. Chicago, bursting with energy, was already projecting several of its feeder roads into major systems and would soon extend them across the trade arteries of its great rivals, threatening their regional supremacy. Few of its residents, who exceeded 109,000 in 1860, doubted their capacity to assume first place, at least in the West, within a decade or so.[17]

Another decade would, in fact, see Chicago linked with San Francisco, but a vast and almost unoccupied two-thirds of a continent separated them in the early sixties, and no place larger than Dubuque, Iowa, with 13,000 residents, intervened. The land and river trails leading West were, however, already clogged with migrants. Many of them were spurred by the quest for gold, for its discovery near San Francisco in 1848 had started a new westward movement by land and sea, and the bay settlement itself had mushroomed. Half of its 56,000 residents in 1860 were foreign-born, but that circumstance, true also of Milwaukee and Chicago as well as St. Louis, and approached in several other major towns, was less noteworthy than the presence of numerous Orientals. The additional fact that natives and immigrants shared the status of first settlers in San Francisco gave the community a strikingly cosmopolitan character. It had attracted hopeful prospectors, eager merchants, and a motley host of restless adventurers, including many talented young men whose vitality created an atmosphere of precocious sophistication.[18]

Among the newcomers at San Francisco in the early sixties was Samuel L. Clemens, a footloose aspiring writer. Mark Twain, as he styled himself, had grown up in Missouri; he had been a journeyman printer and a river pilot and knew many midwestern towns and cities firsthand. His trek across the Rockies, including lengthy stopovers at mining camps, had supplied the material which quickly won him recognition in San Francisco. Mark Twain was himself a product of the emerging urbanism of the West, and his skill in depicting some of the amusing contrasts between its pretensions and its actualities prompted the *Alta California* to send him back East as a correspondent.[19]

Mark Twain found New York in 1867 "too big" for his comfort and convenience. He felt lost in its crowds and sensed the loneliness and solitude their busy indifference created for unnumbered thousands who, like himself, lacked a fixed place in the swirling tumult of the metropolis. Yet when he hastened off for a month's visit to more familiar St. Louis and to Hannibal, his home town, the provincial eddies there proved equally disconcerting. After his tedious 52-hour ride—on a train which appeared to stop at every crossroad—westward through Pittsburgh and Indianapolis to St. Louis, he was swept by boisterous old and new friends in that rapidly growing city into a series of "sociables" that were a bit too gushing for his taste.[20]

When he reached Hannibal it seemed, by contrast, in the doldrums. Despondent because the railroad it had helped to build across the state to St. Joseph had now acquired a link with Chicago to the east, its citizens complained that the trains, like the river, passed through without stopping. Mark Twain, having noted this circumstance with a filial sigh, hastened to procure a seat on an express train back to New York. On this eastward journey he marveled at the thriving cities he sped through—Cleveland, Columbus, and others he had scarcely heard of. Their bright prospects reminded him of Sacramento, the rising capital of California, or even of San Francisco. He was not quite ready for the great metropolis toward which he was headed; like many other American urbanites, he would spend the next few decades resisting its pull.[21]

Mark Twain's unease upon his return to New York was historically symbolic. Sharp contrasts had already developed between life in a few established metropolitan centers and that in the great majority of cities and towns scattered across the continent. Many of the latter had, of course, acquired some urban characteristics and a few proclaimed ambitious plans for expansion, but often their promoters seemed as visionary as William Gilpin, who prepared a map in 1853 for "Centropolis" adjoining Independence, Missouri, and five years later transposed it to Kansas City, and still later to Denver.[22]

Most of the founders of the new western settlements, like those of the colonial period, patterned their town plans and other schemes on older urban traditions. The gridiron street layout of many ancient cities, modified by the inclusion of square parks introduced in London by Londonderry, which had influenced the planning of Philadelphia in 1682, won favor in new towns because of its efficient arrangement of house lots. Some promoters dispensed with the squares, as in the plan for the northern expansion of old Manhattan in 1811, but many towns, aspiring to become county seats, reserved at least one square for court buildings. This tradition, well established in the southern colonies, was early carried north to Rochester and west to Louisville, among other places. The public greens of New Haven and the common of Boston supplied other models for many New England and western settlements, though none of them became a major city. In contrast, L'Enfant's design for Washington, imposing radial avenues and circles on the gridiron plan, had its influence at Buffalo, Detroit, and Indianapolis, and in several other places where a single promoter held undisputed sway.[23]

Generally, however, the rival developers of several adjoining tracts each laid out a grid of streets with little regard for either the natural topography or the plats of his neighbors. They measured their success in the number and prices of the lots sold, and such gains often proved sufficient to create a boom-town atmosphere, which encouraged still wider and more speculative subdivisions.[24]

Eager to gain a march on their rivals, the promoters of each town hastened to adopt the most convenient arrangements at hand. With little deliberation they patterned their town charters and city ordinances on those familiar to the leaders. Inevitably the current of migration that bore merchants and artisans west from Philadelphia and Baltimore to found the Ohio Valley towns also carried their laws and social customs, giving that urban frontier a special character. In like fashion a combination of Yankee and Yorker traditions moved westward along the water-level route of the Erie Canal and the Great Lakes, helping to draft similar charters in a dozen cities scattered from Brooklyn to Milwaukee. These interrelationships were seldom conscious—except when a new town ambitiously proclaimed itself the Philadelphia or the Gotham of the West—for a jealous localism generally prevailed, and the professed model was more frequently distant Manchester or ancient Athens.[25]

Even the largest cities, preoccupied with the conquest of vast spheres of influence, had a raw, unsophisticated character. Their booming growth, based on the commercial exploitation of a fresh continent, received more attention than the provision of urban amenities. Not even Boston, despite the favorable impression it made on superficial observers, could escape criticism after 1840 from those who looked behind its Georgian façade. Only a few favored districts there and in New York, Philadelphia, and Baltimore retained their former homogeneity and still served the more obvious local needs. Some cities of the second rank, with populations of 10,000 to 50,000, seemed more agreeable as places of residence. Yet those in the East that elicited the approval of foreign travelers—New Haven, Albany, Rochester, Lexington, Columbus, among others—had lost their attraction for many Americans who were restlessly pushing on to more promising settlements farther west.[26]

Most of the merchant manufacturers in both small and large places were absorbed in the processing of raw materials for easier shipment. Eager for a quick turnover of capital, they reaped their profits through an exchange of such products for finished articles from abroad. Their incessant shipments nurtured a prosperous commercial class whose interests dominated the pre–Civil War cities. An increasing army of craftsmen still produced for. the most part by hand and as independent entrepreneurs. Only in a half-dozen New England towns and in a few elsewhere had opportunities for more ambitious manufacturing ventures received close attention. Such enterprise generally relied on immigrant workers, but since these newcomers were already crowding into many northern communities, the increasing abundance of this labor force promised to hasten the transformation of the American city.[27]

The successful townsman of the mid-century had a speculation, not a business. A rapid advance in real estate values provided the foundation of credit in most new or growing towns. Millers and other processors of area products gained or lost according to the price fluctuations of the raw and the finished articles. Merchant wholesalers and forwarders everywhere, but especially in Chicago, were on the lookout for a corner on the market; in San Francisco storekeepers quickly accumulated the miners' nuggets by selling scarce goods at inflated prices.[28]

The local competition was fierce, but frequently, as each city grew, a need developed for the establishment of co-operative agencies. Boards of trade appeared in thirty-odd places primarily to marshal the community's forces against an outside rival. They welcomed government aid in building canals and making other improvements, but their members relied increasingly on their own wits and some indorsed the new doctrine of laissez faire that trickled in from abroad. Most of these organizations were ephemeral, however; many faltered or dropped from view when a leader migrated or an activity collapsed. Except perhaps at Boston and a few smaller places, the emergence of a stable business class was still to come.[29]

In their haste to garner the riches of a new country, few citizens could devote more than a year or two to civic tasks. Although a democratic sharing of responsibility resulted, as the mayoralty passed annually from one to another community leader and as each scion of a leading family served his term as alderman, the accomplishments were generally meager. Some basic tasks, such as fire fighting, appealed to the lusty energies of volunteers; others often went by default. The benefits a successful waterworks offered to promoters of urban real estate hastened its construction in many cities. Nearly seventy towns built public water systems before the Civil War; eighty private companies operated water mains in these and other communities. Yet nowhere did they reach half the residences. Many places of moderate size, such as Providence, Rochester, Milwaukee, and Portland, Maine, relied entirely on private wells and water carriers. Philadelphia, the most progressive in this respect, did no more than supply water from the upper reaches of the Schuylkill with most of the silt filtered out.[30]

Less obvious civic functions were little improved, if at all, over those of the colonial cities. The cobblestone paving and open drains of that period had been redesigned to facilitate greater traffic, but such improvements failed to keep pace with the expanding network of streets, most of which resembled rural roads in construction. Boston and a few other metropolitan centers had consolidated their night and day watches into a uniformed police force; elsewhere law enforcement retained the characteristics of the volunteer period. Boards of health and similar civic agencies, except in the case of a few school boards, were temporary bodies with at best a small emergency staff. Sanitation was loosely regulated by ordinances adopted impulsively from time to time, but the collection of garbage was generally left to the pigs, which were more numerous in some towns than the human residents. Horses and cows, dogs and cats, chickens and geese were accepted members of the urban community and contributed a bucolic aroma even to the largest metropolis.[31]

Yet if the past lingered on in many sections of every town, it did not command the attention new improvements received. These were often the products of merchant manufacturers whose advertisements, generally in small type, filled most columns of the four- and eight-page dailies. The latter, too, reflected the city's progress in their number and their circulation, although even now they reached barely one in ten of all urban inhabitants. In the late fifties the appearance of the first block advertisements heralded a new era in business promotion.[32] Stove makers, offering to replace outmoded fireplaces with room heaters and central furnaces, vied with the purveyors of such novelties as bathtubs, indoor toilets, and ice chests. Only one in ten of Boston's 177,000 residents had access to a bathtub in 1860, and the number of its water closets barely approached 10,000—but this was a standard few communities could equal.[33]

Urban residential conveniences were, of course, lacking in most of the poorer districts. These areas also tended to become overcrowded as newcomers with scanty resources doubled up to save expenses. In several rapidly growing cities greedy landlords built flimsy rookeries to accommodate as many families as possible; others converted old mansions and warehouses for the same purpose. Boston and New York already had congested slum areas where the latest and poorest immigrants massed in densities unrivaled even by European cities.[34]

Wealthy residents shared the constrictions of urban space, and their patronage of boarding houses and family hotels reflected a necessary adjustment. The general restlessness of the population, with frequent migrations a common experience, also militated against the purchase of a home. Many families shunned the chores involved in maintaining private establishments. Moreover, the rapid growth of most cities during the forties had so inflated land values that only the rich could afford to buy a house lot in town. Prices remained low on the outskirts, except where speculators were active, but workmen had to locate within easy walking distance of their jobs.

Even in the largest cities, where enterprising men began in the fifties to construct street railways, progress was spotty; their horse-car lines scarcely totaled 500 miles at the close of the decade. In Boston, New York, and Philadelphia, where the new facility made its most rapid advances, the slow pace, five to six miles an hour, limited the distance a busy resident could travel. Congestion was the rule in these pedestrian cities.[35]

Other harbingers of the new urban era soon to open were the gaslight companies. Although a few of these had commenced operation in the major cities several decades before, it was only in the mid-fifties, with the introduction of improved lamps for safe use in the home, that the service became widespread. Most of the towns equipped with gas mains in 1860 were in the North, where supplies of soft coal were more readily available. Shipments of Pennsylvania anthracite were beginning to supplant wood in some urban stoves and fireplaces, and soft coal was developing a market as a furnace fuel. Yet the back-yard woodpile was still a common feature of city life, while improved kerosene lamps provided the major source of illumination in most urban houses.[36] In many of the larger places and in all those of medium and small size, one-family houses and cottages predominated, frequently adjoined by a vegetable or flower garden.[37]

Just as enterprising merchants spearheaded the advance in city services, private associations took the lead in supplying urban cultural facilities. The public schools were a notable exception, for here the cities, at least in the North, had in the forties and fifties shouldered the major burden for the education of their children, the largest single element in their populations. As in the support of the churches, provisions for higher education, for adult education, and for the arts relied on private subscriptions and associations. Often the first expressions of local pride centered on the organization of an athenaeum designed to conduct lectures and maintain a library. These bodies appeared in small as well as large towns, and although many were ephemeral they helped to foster an urban culture. If their book collections were generally meager, comprising an assortment of school texts and miscellaneous castoffs of the private libraries of their patrons, they nevertheless supplied hopeful nest eggs of such literary storehouses as the Boston Public Library, which opened with nearly 100,000 volumes in 1861.[38]

Only a half-dozen urban libraries approached Boston's in size. And only a half-dozen cities possessed art galleries, though again many boasted of small museums that housed miscellaneous collections of pictures, stuffed animals, rocks, and other curios. Natural history enjoyed greater prestige than the theater, and the traveling circuses shared some of it. The latter, with the first minstrels and troupes of musicians, supplied much of the commercial entertainment at the music halls which were already springing up in a number of cities. But recreation was not yet a major concern except in the largest metropolitan centers.[39]

Thus the differences between the social as well as the business affairs of residents of small and great cities, though often only of degree, were sometimes substantial. Among the metropolitan centers, New York, Boston, and Philadelphia each afforded a profusion of social and cultural opportunities, although the number of residents who enjoyed them was limited. Baltimore, Cincinnati, St. Louis, and Chicago were similarly alert in several respects. A few smaller cities had made earnest efforts to emulate the leaders, and places as different as Washington, Nashville, and Rochester displayed a new concern for cultural matters.[40]

Everywhere, of course, the daily involvement with material concerns commanded first attention. Yet that preoccupation, true for the great majority of the men, did not hold all women in its grasp. While domestic duties kept most of them at home, a few unmarried spinsters ventured forth as schoolteachers in each town, and occasionally a resourceful widow carried on her late husband's business; only in scattered factories, however, did young women find industrial employment. Some who could escape these responsibilities took an increasing interest in "society." In that field at least they now displaced men, who in more tranquil colonial days had shared and sometimes dominated most social functions. Exciting opportunities beckoned there, since the turmoil of urban growth and the fluidity of movement often made it difficult for the old families to hold their ranks against the aspirations of zestful newcomers who established charitable and reform societies, conducted ladies' fairs, and even staged conventions on women's rights.[41]

Perhaps the most significant aspect of these developments was the slow appearance of intercity links and co-operative services. The loosely organized lyceum circuits exerted a pervasive influence; the book trade and of course the churches were even more widely organized. Although the latter were not exclusively urban institutions, the Sabbath schools and reform societies they established had their roots in the cities and provided new if tenuous bonds between them. The forerunners of later theatrical circuits and of intercity associations in other cultural fields were also appearing. Yet these faltering beginnings scarcely foreshadowed the multitude of social and cultural strands that would increasingly bind the cities of America together in later decades.

I "THE RISE OF THE CITY":
[1860-1910]

The historic process of America's urbanization acquired new momentum and a significantly different emphasis following the Civil War. As the improved transport facilities reached farther inland, rival trading centers sprang up to serve each frontier. The discovery and exploitation of rich mineral deposits and other natural resources, increasing the national output manyfold, added tremendously to the flow of commerce in which many cities shared and over which the national metropolis on the Hudson continued to exercise a loose domination. But New York's former pre-eminence, based on the strategic location of its great port, was lessened as the rise of new factory towns transformed America, during the second half of the century, into an industrial nation. This process, which relegated exports and imports to a secondary position, created new demands for technological improvements and for organizational services. As competing cities and metropolitan centers endeavored to perform these functions, new trade patterns developed, and new civic and cultural patterns as well. Although these forces often appeared chaotic, close study reveals the presence of several basic themes.

New York City strove in many ways to maintain its status as the national metropolis. Boston, Philadelphia, and Baltimore each attained a measure of autonomy by promoting the trade facilities of its region and by developing industrial potentials. Several leading marts in the interior also discovered that local manufacturing and regional rail systems engendered rapid growth and thus strengthened their influence throughout the surrounding area. By disrupting some of the earlier trade routes and elevating industrial activity to a new level of importance, the Civil War accentuated these trends. The contest between New York and other aspiring metropolitan centers would supply a continuing theme for the complex urban drama of succeeding decades.

A second major theme can be found in the strife between neighboring cities for control over regional provinces. The competition that already flourished among a half-dozen interior commercial hubs helped to speed the planting of new towns throughout the country. Each sought to develop and expand its territory and to ward off encroachments. Unfortunately the railroads, which served for a time as the primary agencies of both aggression and defense, often required outside capital, thus necessitating an alliance with expansive metropolitan forces in the East. The threat of domination from that direction was sometimes avoided by multiplying the sources of credit or by developing sufficient local or regional industrial capacity to sustain a prosperous trade. But these and other devices were open to the promoters of rival cities; the situation became increasingly complex as dynamic new commercial and industrial centers asserted their claims to large spheres of influence.

A third major theme was the gradual evolution of a community out of the welter of conflicting individuals and groups that surged into each growing town. Generally, at the start, two or more rival cliques of town-lot promoters struggled to direct the city's growth to their private benefit. Contending commercial interests soon became eager to influence the course of trade. In many places manufacturers emerged and endeavored to break into the local power structure and shape its policies to their advantage. To strengthen their position, some men quickly formed alliances with out-of-town groups, often merging their interests in far-reaching corporations that became increasingly independent of any particular urban base. But since the impelling concerns of the great railroads and other monopoly systems frequently dictated policies that were inimical to parochial interests, their development inevitably prompted many local factions to submerge their rivalries sufficiently to acquire a new sense of community.

Few laws limited the aspirations of contending promoters or rising industrialists. In fact, it was in these years that the new doctrines of social Darwinism, as propounded by Herbert Spencer, strengthened the laissez-faire tradition and checked efforts to adopt regulations. Nevertheless, procedures appropriate in dynamic regional centers of the 1850's soon proved unsuited for either a thriving commercial hub or a busy industrial city. And while the leaders of growing towns were discovering these distinctions, determining local directions, and developing effective agencies in practice, experience also demonstrated the need for legislative curbs against some of their more reckless schemes. The struggle for suitable regulatory procedures comprised a fourth and increasingly dominant theme of urban growth, injecting the city more positively into state and national politics.

Thus the urbanization process brought a continuing reorganization and structuring of economic relationships. The first three chapters in this section describe some of these developments. As the national population trebled during the period, new towns sprang up throughout the West and in most older sections as well. I have tried to identify and briefly characterize the more dynamic ones. By 1890, practically all those destined to achieve even moderate size had appeared.[1] If a few of the 392 urban places of 1860 languished, so many others arose and prospered that at least 597 numbered 10,000 five decades later. The federal census of 1910 listed 228 of 25,000 and upward, eight of which already exceeded a half-million. Cities over 100,000 mounted from nine to fifty and comprised a larger percentage of the total population at the close of this period than had all urban places at its start. The earlier concentration in the Northeast became less striking, though the urban percentages there doubled. Every section shared in the rise of the city, most notably the Far West, where more than half the residents congregated in towns.[2]

These statistical increases were impressive, and the heterogeneity of the urban population proved equally important. The great hosts attracted from varied places by the lure of the city, as depicted in Chapter Four, supplied the diversity of needs and aspirations, talents and tastes, that differentiated one city from another and characterized the great metropolis.

1. *The diffusion of urban sites*

If the American experience in pre–Civil War land settlement taught any-thing, it was that town-lot promotion and city building offered grand prospects to ambitious men. A score of imposing cities in the Midwest demonstrated what could happen within a lifetime. An impartial ob-server could, of course, have named many settlements where hardships and frustrations had blasted the dreams of their founders; he might have noted that most of the pioneers had long since disappeared in the tur-moil of growth that marked the few successful ones. Yet the glamour re-mained. Many canny promoters chose sites along promising trade routes, preferably at the intersection of two or more such routes and in the midst of a productive region. They followed earlier promoters in this respect, but in the postwar decades the railroads supplied the major arteries of commerce, and the strategy of their advance determined the fortunes of new settlements. The discovery that this strategy could be influenced if not controlled both by the aggressive promoters of rival cities and by the land grants and restraints of government brought the urbanization movement of this period more directly into the main stream of the nation's history.

The Civil War caused a slight interruption but also provided a turn-ing point in America's urban developments. A result in part of the bitter struggle of the agrarian South to maintain political leadership over the more urbanized North, the war created a new imbalance. The closing of the Mississippi to northern trade in 1861 was a boon to the east-west railroads, benefiting especially Chicago and other cities that had devel-oped through connections. The insistent demand for war materials and other supplies spurred manufacturing in many towns. Huge profits, swollen by inflated prices, encouraged expansion and gave business leaders in many places new confidence. Although the national banking system, inaugurated during the war, designated New York as the principal reserve center, it did not establish a monopoly there, and numerous private bankers, especially in interior cities, hastened to incorporate. They developed a new sense of community solidarity with local merchants and manufacturers.[1]

It was Washington, not New York, that caught the limelight during the war. The symbolic importance of its defense or capture made it a prime objective on both sides. To the many thousand recruits who hailed from or knew any of the principal cities of the North, Washington must have appeared at first sight as an insignificant town. Short on both industry and trade, it had provided only the housekeeping services and was deficient in most of these. The unfinished Capitol, with the great dome a gaping hole, seemed to characterize the city. Many towns lacked water mains, sewers, street lights, and pavements, but their absence in Washington became acutely evident during its protracted crisis. Alternately abandoned and overcrowded, as the threats of invasion sent residents fleeing and brought an influx of soldiers, Washington suffered the ravages of repeated waves of occupants who were friendly to the North but seldom solicitous of the city. Yet Lincoln's determined efforts to complete the Capitol and to erect hospitals as well as other essential governmental structures stimulated private builders, too. A few palatial hostels arose and back-alley shacks multiplied as the city's population increased a third during the war and surged past the 100,000 mark before the end of the decade.[2]

Washington's internal changes were relatively insignificant, but as the command center its stature as a city was enhanced. The necessity of defending and provisioning the capital called for the improvement of its rail lines, linking it more closely with the rest of the country. Other cities, too, benefited from the war. The recruitment program, which required each town to meet successive troop quotas, fostered community solidarity, while the battle records of regiments identified with one or another city often kindled a spirit of civic pride. Pittsburgh, Troy, and other metal-working centers retooled to produce rifled cannon, gun mounts, and heavy plates to convert the wooden frigates into ironclads after 1862; they also met the increased demand for rolling stock. Philadelphia, convenient to but not as dangerously near Washington as Baltimore, and already abounding in skilled craftsmen, became the most active provisioning depot; it erected 180 new factories in three years, and emerged briefly as the leading manufacturing city at the close of the war.[3]

The army's huge demands stimulated other industrial centers, too. Bulk orders for shoes and uniforms, for blankets and tents, as well as for swords and guns, prompted merchants in several towns to make hasty arrangements for their production by drawing scattered craftsmen into improvised factories. With southern cotton unavailable, some New England cotton mills converted to wool in order to fill the demands of clothing manufacturers in New York and elsewhere. The production of ready-made civilian clothes as well as uniforms increased as use of the recently invented sewing machine spread more widely there and in the shoe factories near Boston. Pittsburgh built a half-dozen large foundries in one year and became the major producer of iron and steel. Much smaller New Haven also erected six large factories in one season and achieved a new distinction for firearms and locks. Cincinnati lost its standing as "Porkopolis of the West" to Chicago, but sustained itself by more diversified production. Chicago opened its Union Stock Yards and stepped up the output of its reaper factories, whose machines were much in demand on the spreading grain fields of the Middle West.[4]

Industrial growth, though modest in volume because of the labor shortage, acquired new dimensions. An increased diversity was evident as new mills sprang up at Cleveland to refine the oil lately discovered in Pennsylvania, and as new evaporating tanks arose at Syracuse to replace the salt supplies shut off in the South. Another factor was government promotion, but the national ordnance works at Springfield and the federally owned drug laboratory at St. Louis were dwarfed by many new private establishments. Among the latter was a cotton-dress factory erected at Newark to supply a market previously held by independent seamstresses. Like other such factories, it drew the productive energies of the less skillful craftsmen under the direction of managers whose experience would equip them to supply vital leadership to growing cities during the next half century.[5]

After Appomattox, many of the war's influences were suspended, but the new banking system and the increased emphasis on railroads continued. The railroad land-grant policy, launched in 1864 to encourage construction through sparsely settled territory (with the object of uniting as well as developing the country), presented expansive western cities with an opportunity to secure federal backing for their imperial schemes. The objectives of both the public and private sponsors of the transcontinental railroads made these trade arteries great colonizing agents, too.

They were, however, not the only nor indeed the first colonizers. Venturesome settlers and land speculators had preceded them, and as the land-grant railroads pushed into new districts, planting towns for their own convenience and profit, they often encountered fierce opposition from the promoters of independent settlements. Many of these towns, like the growing cities in the East, tried to build competing rail systems. These contests prompted the leaders of new communities to seek alliances with other capitalists in the East; when that strategy failed, they pleaded with state and federal governments for both favors and safeguards.[6]

The chief favor sought by urban delegations at Washington during the sixties and seventies was aid for the construction of railroads. These arteries had already emerged as the principal means of passenger travel and soon became the great freight handlers, too. As their mileage trebled in the quarter-century following the war, they gave a powerful impetus to industrialization. This period of their most rapid extension also saw the adoption of a standard gauge, and the introduction of air brakes, automatic couplers, and mechanical block signals. These improvements —all products of an urban-centered technology—contributed to the growth of individual cities and, more significantly, to the development of vital interurban relationships.[7]

These years also witnessed the formation of the major trunk systems: the New York Central, the Pennsylvania, the Baltimore & Ohio. The organization of these great corporations wrought a fundamental change in the direction and control of urban growth. Businessmen in a dozen cities scattered along their competing routes had built the rudiments of the three systems before the Civil War in the form of loose chains of independent roads. City and state grants and distant capitalists had helped to finance them and to promote their regional trade. When the inefficiencies of separate management brought moves toward consolidation, ambitious men such as Cornelius Vanderbilt grasped their helms.[8]

A former commodore of a Hudson River steamboat line, Vanderbilt typified the new commercial baron. He acquired full direction of the New York Central & Hudson River Railroad by 1869 and within fifteen years secured stock control of important regional lines reaching west from his terminals at Buffalo and Lewiston to Cleveland, Detroit, and Chicago, and north to Toronto in Canada. The new management greatly improved the freight service and the conveniences of travel, but it lost touch with local urban groups and seemed at times unmindful even of the commercial interests of its great metropolitan base.[9]

New York's leading neighbors, Philadelphia and Baltimore, received only slightly better treatment from their railroad magnates. J. Edgar Thomson, who dominated the Pennsylvania Railroad in the early years, developed it into a great trade system. He secured control of lines extending west from Pittsburgh to Chicago and St. Louis, but he also pushed a line northeast to New York City, thus making Philadelphia, like others along the route, a way station. John W. Garrett, who performed a similar feat of empire building for the Baltimore & Ohio, adopted the most competitive techniques in his battle for western trade. When, in retaliation, the Pennsylvania blocked his entry into New York, he endeavored to build up the port at Baltimore. Other cities, however, especially those along the main line, soon felt the penalties of their position as price cuts on long-haul freight had to be made up from the short-haul traffic.[10] The trunk-line pool of 1877 brought a truce to the price war, but spread to other systems the blight on intermediate towns.

While the trunk systems were threatening several regional market centers with way-station fate, they were competing vigorously at all western points of contact. By 1880, Chicago, St. Louis, Cincinnati, and Cleveland had emerged in that order as the dominant inland marts, with undisputed metropolitan status. The fierce rivalry between St. Louis and Chicago in extending trade arteries farther west demonstrated a keen awareness among their leaders of the fact that their own prosperity and that of their towns depended on the breadth of their commercial spheres. Thus the rail networks became active though by no means subservient appendages of the great cities. The less stable empire of the Erie and the varied efforts to consolidate New England's many roads into unified systems similarly influenced the economic fortunes of the places they served.[11]

All the older cities of the Northeast watched these developments with interest. Many of their capitalists promoted new lines, and often the town councils voted generous appropriations for stocks or bonds to help push some locally important road to completion. The desire for a competitor to the Vanderbilt monopoly prompted Syracuse to back two lines and Rochester three, with bonds totaling $1,000,000 apiece; both secured, as a result, direct access to the Pennsylvania coal fields, but ultimately saw the hoped-for competition vanish as the major systems absorbed their independent companies. Nearly three hundred other New York State municipalities extended such aid to railroads before 1875. Buffalo, though served by three major systems and endowed with an unrivaled position at the eastern end of the upper lakes trade, invested nearly a million in another road and numbered over 100,000 residents by 1870.[12]

Similar efforts marked urban developments throughout the Northeast and North Central States. Most of the advantageous sites had already been settled, but the order of their precedence depended increasingly on the improvement of rail connections. The Reading and the Pennsylvania railroads "made" Reading and Altoona by the location of shops at these formerly quiet towns; only a few cities, such as Buffalo, Cleveland, and Chicago, could rely in large part on their natural positions to bring the steam roads begging to their door.[13] Chicago's period of vigorous railroad promotion ended in the sixties; St. Louis, after a late start, endeavored in the seventies to recoup lost ground.[14] Toledo and Milwaukee had to take the initiative in building lines, as did St. Paul, at the headwaters of the Mississippi, and many another ambitious community in the Midwest.[15] Cincinnati and Louisville both attracted northern roads eager to share their Ohio Valley trade, but each strove to outdo the other by extending lines through Chattanooga and Nashville, respectively, to Atlanta and Birmingham and other centers of the New South.[16]

Neither the railroad builders nor the cities of the East and South could rival the enterprise of their counterparts in the West. There, ambitious promoters, generously aided by government grants,[17] completed the first transcontinental line in the late sixties and launched three more within another decade. The Union Pacific and Central Pacific not only gave a great spurt to San Francisco, it also started booms at Omaha and Salt Lake City en route. Other hopeful towns made great efforts to secure the main roads and, when that hope faded, opened connecting links. Kansas City, St. Paul, Fort Worth, Denver, and Spokane in the interior, Los Angeles, San Diego, Portland, Tacoma, and Seattle on the West Coast, each based its future on the iron horse.[18]

Kansas City, a cow town in the late fifties, had already discovered that its advantageous situation at the apex of the great bend in the Missouri River would not assure dominance over the western trade. An eager rival, Leavenworth, was bidding for a connection with the Hannibal & St. Joseph Railroad and its link to Chicago. Kansas City, which had focused its major effort on securing the Pacific Railroad of Missouri, now captured the Hannibal & St. Joseph by building the first bridge across the Missouri. Its opening in 1869 assured competing main-line connections with both St. Louis and Chicago. Two roads already reached westward, and within a decade the vigorous promotions of land jobbers

and commercial leaders, spurred by the editorials of the visionary pub-
lisher Robert T. Van Horn, from Cincinnati, had given Kansas City ten
rail spokes in its hub. As it became the leading trade center of the
prairie states, the 4000 residents of 1859 increased fourteenfold in two
decades; by the end of the century they would number 163,752.[19]

The new western railroads, built far ahead of population, hastened
to promote land sales and, like the Illinois Central and other midwestern
roads before them, founded many towns en route. Most of the construction camps and other settlements languished as their original activities
declined, but Cheyenne, Butte, and Reno, among many others, survived
by developing new functions. Several older Mexican towns, like El Paso,
Santa Fe, and Albuquerque, were also sustained by rail connections.
The vast expanse of the plains and the lofty grandeur of the mountains
stirred some men to found towns as pleasure and health resorts, notably
General William Jackson Palmer's Colorado Springs, handsomely laid
out in 1871 on a 10,000-acre tract at the foot of Pike's Peak. An
imaginative promoter of several other communities and many railroads,
Palmer also encouraged the ubiquitous Nathan C. Meeker in the establishment of his co-operative colony, named after Horace Greeley, a
reclamation venture that became the model for many to follow.[20]

Denver achieved urban leadership throughout the Rocky Mountain
region by the exploitation of its central location and of fortuitous miners'
"strikes." A raw frontier settlement founded by two parties of claim
jumpers in 1858, it thrived as a supply depot for gold miners until by-
passed by the first transcontinental railroad in the late sixties. Threatened
by Cheyenne, the Union Pacific's contender for the mountain trade,
Denver's several thousand residents refused to accept defeat; they organized a board of trade and raised $280,000 to build a spur line from
Cheyenne, drawing the Union's trains to its door. The completion of the
spur in 1870 coincided with the opening of a new road from Kansas
City, which assured Denver a competitive advantage and brought it a
fivefold growth during that depression decade. The rapid development
of the Rocky Mountain territories, whose population climbed from
600,000 to 1,000,000 during the eighties, gave their chief trading center
another threefold increase, and the discovery of a rich gold field at nearby Cripple Creek sustained Denver during the depression of the mid-
nineties. Goaded on by the indomitable David H. Moffat, formerly a
promoter of Omaha and Des Moines, its business leaders projected new
railroads, erected splendid hotels and theaters, devised schemes to attract
traders as well as miners, and again doubled Denver's population, making it by 1910 the undisputed metropolis of a vast region.[21]

None of the eighteen mountain towns of 10,000 or more in 1910, not

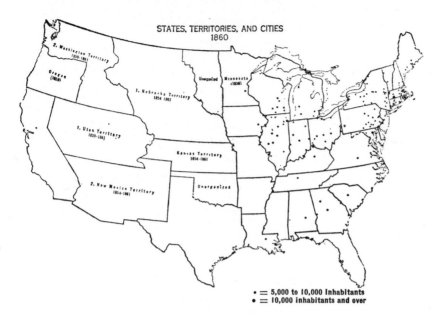

1. Map of States, Territories and Cities, 1860. *Paullin* Atlas, *Plate 64, Courtesy of the Carnegie Institution of Washington*

2. Map of Railroads of 1870. *Adapted from Paulin* Atlas, *Plate 141, Courtesy of the Carnegie Institution of Washington*

even Denver, which had reached 213,381, could match the promotional efforts of the new coastal cities. San Francisco not only won its place among the country's first ten by 1870, when it numbered 150,000 residents, but also attained a metropolitan character rivaling that of New York and Boston.[22] Even more spectacular was the rise of Los Angeles. Surviving the collapse of its first speculative boom, which started in the sixties and petered out in 1876 when the first railroad failed to provide the expected bonanza, Los Angeles embarked on a second orgy of town-lot promotion a decade later, when the newly arrived Santa Fe precipitated a rate war that cut transcontinental fares to as low as forty dollars, and for a day or two reduced the Kansas City rate to an even dollar. Exciting auction-excursions and lavish advertisements pushed lot sales to $10,000,000 a month in the summer of 1887. Over 1000 subdivision plots were laid out that year, a third of them within the corporate limits. San Diego, Pasadena, and other southern California cities shared in this great land boom, the most extravagant in American frontier experience. Although scores of ghost towns resulted, California's urban population mounted until by 1910 it ranked sixth among the states.[23]

No one city could dominate the Northwest, but Portland made a determined attempt. The importance of transport advantages was recognized from the start, and the Oregon Steam Navigation Company, organized in 1862, endeavored to secure them all for Portland, conveniently located where the Willamette enters the Columbia River. Local efforts to develop rail connections, sparked by several large landholders, soon drew the attention of promoters of the great transcontinental systems. Ben Holliday, Henry Villard, James J. Hill, and Edward H. Harriman each left his mark on the city, but their bickering and the advantages of its northern rivals denied Portland the trade supremacy it coveted. Tacoma, child of the railroads, dated its beginning from 1873, when the Northern Pacific, a land-grant road promoted by New England interests and based at Duluth, on Lake Superior, chose its site on Puget Sound for a western terminus. A decade later the Northern Pacific completed its tunnel through the Cascade Mountains, starting a Tacoma boom that prompted Villard to invest in its future. Jim Hill of the Great Northern, a St. Paul promoter enjoying British and Dutch credit connections, chose to back Seattle instead, thus leaving Tacoma dependent on the mercies of one road.[24]

Seattle avoided such a fate when its local promoters, again headed by great land jobbers, not only captured the Great Northern but also secured a branch line of the Northern Pacific, which soon carried more freight than the main line to Tacoma. Seattle's increasing advantage over all rivals on Puget Sound came in part from its more favorable location for trade with Alaska, brought suddenly onto the map by the discovery of gold at the Klondike in 1897. If its geographic location was important, so also were its natural resources, for the northern port enjoyed easy access to nearby coal fields and to some of the best timberlands of the West. Its speedy action in establishing a third link to the East, by way of Vancouver and the Canadian Pacific, enabled it to surpass Portland in population by 1910. Only Los Angeles, which saw the opening of oil wells in its vicinity, exceeded Seattle's almost sixfold growth in two decades.[25]

Few places could match that rate, and those few were southern cities. Most of the lusty towns of the South were, however, still modest in size, and their rapid advance at the turn of the century reflected the energies of the New South awakened a half-century after those of the North. If the Civil War did not retard urban developments in the South, it certainly did not accelerate them.[26] Southern trade with Europe declined after the war, and many of the old ports languished. A few that acquired new rail connections in the eighties, such as Norfolk, Mobile, and New Orleans, enjoyed a moderate expansion, but they did not equal the vitality displayed by new rail hubs in the interior—Atlanta and Nashville at first, and later Louisville, Memphis, and Dallas. Northern investors took a special interest in Atlanta, hastening its reconstruction and promoting its development as the regional metropolis of the Southeast. Yet it was the new rail centers on the southwestern frontier—Oklahoma City, Fort Worth, and San Antonio—and Birmingham, the new industrial city in Alabama, that made the most rapid spurt toward the end of the period.[27]

Of course the vast majority of towns in every region experienced no such growth. Some promoters with grandiose dreams were disappointed, but many founders who hoped merely to outstrip neighboring rivals were content to see their community emerge as the principal market for a township or county.

Owatonna, which has been studied in useful detail, was typical of many modest places. Established in Minnesota a few years before the Civil War, it prospered with the settlement of its rich farming hinterland. Though only 949 in number, its residents secured a city charter in 1865 in anticipation of the arrival of a railroad—two railroads in fact—the next year. Owatonna already had two banks, rival weekly newspapers and hotels, numerous competing stores and shops, and several forwarding merchants; it soon had a flour mill and other modest ventures, but its location at the intersection of two railroads failed to give it the expected boom. The rich produce of its agricultural hinterland sustained a slow growth to 3849 by 1890. Several small industrial plants and two strong co-operatives centered in Owatonna, yet the city barely numbered 5600 at the end of the period. Some impatient and ambitious residents left for larger places; those who remained built a prosperous community and won it a measure of fame by commissioning Louis Sullivan to design and build a new bank in 1907.[28]

Such towns as Owatonna contrasted sharply with many restless and unstable ghost towns left desolate on the successive frontiers of American expansion. Some communities were poorly located from the start; others were overshadowed by vigorous neighbors more fortunate in attracting railroads or other advantages. Some mining towns disappeared when their mineral resources became exhausted; other settlements languished when their promoters failed to develop useful functions or lost earlier activities as improved transport facilities drew them into nearby cities. Like many towns, Canon City, Colorado, bid for a state institution; when successful, Canon City chose the penitentiary in preference to the more uncertain university. Thaddeus S. C. Lowe built a scenic railroad and an astronomical observatory in order to dramatize the clear skies of Pasadena and assure it resort status. In the expansive American economy, a local specialty was becoming increasingly essential to community prosperity, for no town could live to itself.[29]

Meanwhile the railroads, which had begun as urban tentacles, had now become autonomous systems eager to extract advantages from the cities they served. Inevitably they inspired criticism from those adversely affected. Towns that were either by-passed or forced, as in the case of Los Angeles and many others, to make large contributions for rail services, protested vigorously when the rates were jacked up after the inhabitants began to produce for export. Farmers and townsmen alike cried out for protection against the iron-limbed octopus.[30] The first effective reaction came in Illinois, when the merchants of Chicago, unable to control the operations of the grain warehousemen through the Board of Trade, encouraged their customers in rural areas to demand a provision in the state constitution of 1869 authorizing the regulation of warehouses. The aroused farmers gave the legislature (rather than the Board of Trade, as proposed in Chicago) such authority over railroads as well as warehouses, and the general assembly took prompt action the next year.[31]

Although the farmers, experiencing a revival of spirit through their wide-spreading Granges, forced the passage of similar laws in a half-dozen other midwestern states, urban commercial groups frequently supplied leadership there and generally dominated the movement in the East. In Massachusetts, in 1869, Boston businessmen secured the creation of the first permanent railroad commission—a fact-finding body with only advisory powers. In New York City a leading wholesale grocer, Francis B. Thurber, rallied fellow wholesalers, commission men, and other merchants in a long battle for a state railroad commission.[32]

Earlier antimonopoly movements had, in fact, sprung up there among businessmen crowded out of the telegraph field by Western Union or frustrated by other developing combinations. The widely circulated addresses and pamphlets of the National Anti-Monopoly Cheap Freight Railway League of the mid-sixties, together with news of British and Continental railroad regulations, helped to alert men in far-distant cities to the threats presented by large-scale corporations. When the first regulatory laws in the Midwest, though finally sustained in the courts, were popularly discredited by the depression of the mid-seventies and largely repealed by men chanting the slogans of laissez faire, it was the unflagging agitation in New York and other commercial centers that revived the movement and finally led it to victory.[33]

The New York merchants were caught in a squeeze between the four trunk lines to the West. Vanderbilt of the Central was seemingly ready to sacrifice their interests in order to achieve peace among the rival systems and maintain interest payments on his inflated capital. His agreement to a slightly higher rate on western shipments to New York, as contrasted with those secured for Philadelphia and Baltimore by their rail magnates, under the trunk-line pool of 1877, infuriated the Manhattan merchants. They supported Thurber's Cheap Transportation Association, later renamed the New York Board of Trade and Transportation, and backed its drive for state and later federal regulation.[34]

These merchants, despite the endorsement of their Chamber of Commerce, needed additional support from upstate towns. To win them over, Thurber adopted the pro rata clause they demanded, although this jeopardized the cheap rates to the West desired in the metropolis. Even then the battle for a state railroad board proved inconclusive. Finally a New York–inspired National Anti-Monopoly League corralled votes from the Farmers' Alliances, Granges, and others who suffered from the special privileges that some merchants in key cities enjoyed.

The Hepburn investigation of 1879 in New York had meanwhile uncovered such startling evidence concerning railroad stock manipulations, special rates, and similar inequities, that antimonopoly movements in other states were greatly strengthened. Thurber and his associates marshaled the National Board of Trade behind the larger and, for them, more essential drive for congressional legislation. Furthermore, since fifteen states had created railroad commissions before the New York one was organized, the conflicting measures they applied and the recurrent troubles involved in maintaining the trunk-line pool helped to persuade even some railroad magnates that federal regulation would be advantageous. Although the Interstate Commerce Commission, when eventually created in 1887, failed to correct all discriminations between cities, its establishment marked the end of an era of freebooting railroad building and town planting.[35]

The I. C. C. did not itself exert such far-reaching influence. The great westward movement of settlers had practically run its course; as Frederick Jackson Turner was to observe a few years later, the American frontier was virtually closed by 1890. Much unoccupied land remained, and later migrations, filling in the unsettled pockets, would found many new villages, but few of them were destined to achieve major proportions. The total of incorporated places increased nearly 80 per cent during the next two decades (as contrasted with a jump of 120 per cent in the preceding two), yet less than a score of the new listings would attain populations of 30,000 by 1930, and most of these few were suburbs or satellites of the great cities. Unlike so many of their predecessors, born of ventures into vast undeveloped areas, the new towns represented for the most part either the accretion of an old agrarian neighborhood or the overflow of a nearby metropolis.[36]

Less than a fifth of the 6236 new incorporations after 1890 had attained by 1910 even the minimal urban requirement of 2500 residents. Moreover, the first category of towns, those with up to 10,000 inhabitants, barely retained its proportionate share of the urban total; it was in fact losing significance as a meaningful classification of the population, for the urbanization movement was beginning to exert a greater influence on settlements within the radius of expanding metropolitan centers than on isolated communities. A few new boom towns appeared, such as Miami, a neglected site on the east coast of Florida brought to life by the arrival of a railroad in 1896, and Tulsa, Oklahoma, in the middle of newly discovered oil fields. These, however, were the exceptions; it was the unexploited potentialities of established cities, or of old hamlets near them, rather than the prospect of founding new ones, that supplied an enticing substitute for the American frontier after 1890.

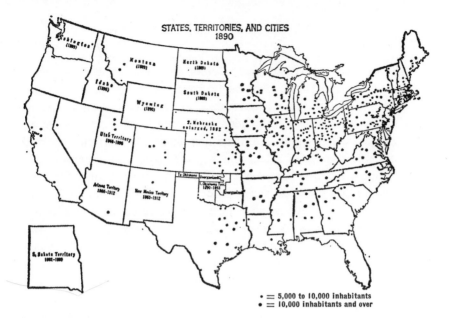

3. Map of States, Territories and Cities, 1890. *Paullin* Atlas, *Plate 65,
Courtesy of the Carnegie Institution of Washington*

4. Map of States, Territories and Cities, 1910. *Paullin* Atlas, *Plate 66,
Courtesy of the Carnegie Institution of Washington*

:

The founding and promotion of cities had been an integral part of the westward movement from its beginning. New urban centers provided leadership on successive frontiers, yet ambitious commercial hubs back East generally gave direction and supplied much of the energy needed to push the great railroads and other trade arteries forward. Often it was a group of restless but vigorous men from an eastern city who planted the new towns of the West. A canny instinct for trade prospects helped the more successful ones to choose the best sites. Their knowledge of city ways enabled them to organize effective promotional ventures, and their quick grasp of the larger strategy of urban growth prompted them to seek advantageous connections with metropolitan centers in the East. In no case did either geography, local enterprise or resources, or outside promotion alone suffice; a combination of these factors provided the foundations for most of the thriving urban centers of the West and brought added strength to many older places in the East.

The building of new towns was, of course, only a preliminary stage in the urbanization of America. And although many venturesome men engaged in this exciting activity, the great majority preferred to locate in places already securely established and possessing some tangible improvements. These brighter prospects tended to draw the more enterprising residents of each region into its trade centers. There some promoted and built new railroads into distant portions of the hinterland; others undertook to mill or to process in other ways the products of the region. Always eager to extend their town's influence, they became jealous guardians of its local trade arteries, commercial privileges, and industrial prospects, when outside threats arose.

Greatly quickened after the Civil War, especially after the depression of the mid-seventies, these centrifugal forces produced a reaction, around the turn of the century, toward a more closely integrated galaxy of cities. The monopolistic drives of struggling railroads, almost essential to their survival, threatened the well-being of many communities and stirred another reaction, this time toward government control. As tensions arose from the basic contests between New York and competing metropolitan centers, between these giants and their regional rivals, and between warring factions within each center, the dilemmas inherent both in free enterprise and in government control began for the first time to trouble urban leaders in America.

2. The emergence of industrial cities

So many ambitious towns sprang up in the early days on each frontier that many were threatened with atrophy when the railroads enabled a few to stake out broad hinterlands at the expense of their neighbors. Only through industrial enterprise could most cities hope to prosper. Some enjoyed special opportunities as a result of the timely discovery of mineral resources nearby or at points easily reached by cheap water transport. A few achieved industrial leadership through the exploitation of local water power or by the invention of machinery to process regional products more efficiently. Others escaped a way-station fate because a steady flow of immigrants spurred residents to develop new industries based in part on cheap labor and to produce for a national market. Still others prospered through the manufacture of patented or specialty articles. Several combined these tactics, and all labored to produce a marketable surplus.[1]

The rise or decline of an individual town was of major concern only to its promoters and its more settled residents; others could and did move elsewhere without loss. But the widespread survival of many threatened communities by means of industrial enterprise was of primary significance. A few such towns became the prototypes of the industrial city and endowed it with special characteristics. Several others pressed the advantages their manufacturing activities brought and did so with such vigor that they achieved metropolitan status; a few of these, notably Minneapolis, acquired regional hegemony. Moreover the emphasis they gave to industry forced their commercial rivals also to accord it increased attention. To promote these efforts, the business leaders of most communities reorganized old boards of trade or established new associations. By the turn of the century the industrial output of American cities had so outstripped that of any foreign country that the character of international trade was transformed, and with it the services performed by the great ports.

The industrialization of America is a separate story, but the impetus given to that development by the rise of the city cannot be overlooked.[2] The impetus given to industrialism by the rapid discovery and exploitation of the country's natural resources is more fully documented and understood, and so also is the effect of the great influx of immigrant workmen in this period.[3] Here, however, we are interested in the converse side of these historic movements—the contributions that new sources of energy and raw materials, new supplies of labor and industrial skills, new machines and techniques of production made to urban growth.

Because of their glamour, the successive gold rushes have long had a place in American history, yet their product never compared in value with that of the silver and copper mines and appeared insignificant when measured against the output of the iron and coal fields. Similar contrasts marked their respective towns. Gold-mining towns such as Virginia City were more pretentious than those based on silver and copper, but their permanence depended on the discovery nearby of "baser" metals. Not even the iron- and copper-mining camps became major cities (Butte, Montana, was a possible exception). Only where abundant supplies of coal or other fuels were found was manufacturing encouraged and urban growth maintained.[4]

Even in the coal fields, few mining towns became major cities. In the hard-coal region of Pennsylvania, where the ore deposits extended over several counties, numerous settlements or "patches" sprang up about many colliery shafts, creating a density of as much as 1300 persons per square mile without achieving the integration essential for urban status. By 1900 only Scranton and Wilkes-Barre had exceeded 100,000 and 50,000 respectively, and this chiefly because they were not as exclusively occupied with mining as, for example, neighboring Hazelton, which barely numbered 25,000 a decade later. In fact Scranton, at the turn of the century, had more industrial workers than either miners or tradesmen.[5]

Generally a nearby commercial or industrial city supplied the marketing, banking, and other urban services for mining districts, thus strengthening its claim to regional leadership. Sometimes a mining town developed a new industry to convert the products of neighboring collieries, as in the coke district around Uniontown and Brownville, only to see its control absorbed in time by a regional capital, in this case Pittsburgh.[6] Most mining communities, victims of absentee ownership and constricted by their specialty, failed to develop the internal leadership necessary to attract competing transport arteries or to tap new sources of credit.[7]

Other fuel strikes brought dubious benefits to communities at their sites, but presented great opportunities to the commercial marts that acquired control. The oil towns of northwestern Pennsylvania, which displayed great vitality during the seventies, were soon checked as monopoly control over refining and marketing siphoned the profits of the industry into the hands of Rockefeller and his colleagues in Cleveland and other processing centers.[8] Natural gas brought a sudden boom to several communities, notably Findlay and Toledo, Ohio, but their fortunes ebbed with the arrival of outside control.[9] Toledo, already an important railroad hub and advantageously situated for lake trade, remained primarily a regional market until civic leaders, reasserting the town's rights to its power resources, enabled industry finally to pull ahead of commerce and boost the city into the 100,000 bracket by the close of the period.[10]

Some cities prospered as processors of regional farm products. Minneapolis, a small neighbor of St. Paul in the seventies, captured leadership in the wheat belt of the Northwest during the eighties by developing mills able to produce a better flour from the spring wheat of that area than St. Louis or other rivals could mill from winter wheat. Kansas City won its independence from St. Louis and Chicago by building up its meat-packing industry. Milwaukee ventured with less success into each of these fields but achieved its greatest triumph in the brewing industry, likewise based on products of the area. Memphis competed with many other places in lumber milling but excelled in the production of cotton-seed oil. Each of these and several like them strengthened their positions by developing accessory industries and by extending urban economic services to a hinterland which they constantly endeavored to expand. All attained metropolitan status chiefly because of their manufacturing services.[11]

Many cities, even when overshadowed by near neighbors, prospered through the employment of cheap immigrant labor.[12] The shoe industry, in which the introduction of machinery after the mid-century tended to supersede old craft skills, lent itself to this use. Lynn and Haverhill had developed a reputation for shoes in earlier decades, and after the Civil War Cincinnati and Rochester, among others, began to specialize in this field. New York and Philadelphia, because of their large markets and abundant supply of newcomers, became shoe producers, although not as important as the older New England centers, where the earlier crafts-men supervised a new work force of immigrants.[13]

But cheap labor, even when supplied from abroad, did not long re-main content in America, and the shoe industry produced some of the most determined union-organizing drives of these decades. Unfortu-nately, from the viewpoint of the cities involved, when union demands mounted in one town, many firms (except those engaged in quality pro-duction) sought new sites, such as Milwaukee, Chicago, or Manchester, New Hampshire, where the organizers had not yet penetrated. The migration of shoe companies, facilitated by the practice of leasing rather than purchasing the machinery, presented a constant threat to cities in this field. It also provided an extreme example of the industrial mobility that contributed to both the diffusion and the fluidity of Amer-ica's urban development.[14]

The textile industry, too, displayed an intense interest in cheap labor, but the range of its migrations was limited. Originally established at water-power sites in New England, where textiles nurtured several of the country's first factory towns, notably Lowell and Manchester, this industry quickly replaced its early native-born labor from the first influx of Irish and other immigrant groups, thus speeding the urbanization as well as the cosmopolitan transformation of the Yankee homeland. Dur-ing the post–Civil War expansion, when steam began to supplement water power, Fall River pulled into the lead among textile centers be-cause of its easy access to water-borne coal and its cheap immigrant labor, including that of women and children.[15] Some textile towns added other specialties; Chicopee developed tool shops and began to produce bicycles; Holyoke became a paper city; Lowell ventured into woolens, carpets, knitted products, and other enterprises. Successive waves of new immigrants—Polish, French Canadian, and Portuguese—enabled management to fight off many union demands; yet pressure from the workers and the restraints of labor legislation in America's second most urbanized commonwealth presented Massachusetts textile firms with an increasing disadvantage in competition with the new cotton mills of the South.[16]

The development of the textile industry in the South had a substan-tial economic basis. The slow spread of cotton factories in North and South Carolina and Georgia during post–Civil War years uncovered a new supply of cheap labor in the poor whites of the Piedmont area and began in the eighties to attract northern capital, some of it from the New

England firms themselves. Advances in technology—the Northrop automatic loom and the ring spindle, which eliminated the skilled mule spinners who had formed the backbone of textile unions in the North— enabled the southern mills to employ unskilled labor and to defeat the first effort at organization around 1900. Since many northern firms hesitated to make the fresh investments that new machinery required, New England textile cities saw the greater part of the expanding market after 1890 pass by default to new towns in the South.[17]

A major reason for the embarrassment of some of the New England towns was the defection of their absentee entrepreneurs and the failure to replace their talents from among the immigrant workers.[18] On the other hand, some cities prospered because of the enterprise and skills that waves of newcomers brought. British and Dutch glassmakers strengthened the economy of Pittsburgh and Toledo and gave economic vitality to Corning, New York, La Salle, Illinois, and many other towns. German brewers helped to build up Cincinnati, St. Louis, Rochester, Chicago, and especially Milwaukee; despite some opposition from local temperance forces, they ultimately won acceptance and influence in each place.[19] Skilled mechanics and technicians from England, Germany, and elsewhere received a more immediate welcome and financial support in developing enterprises ranging in one town from buttons to optical instruments; [20] the classic example of immigrant enterprise, however, was the clothing industry, and many cities fattened upon it.

When the ready-to-wear clothing trade appeared at mid-century its most enterprising leaders were German Jews. Many who had gained a footing as tailors or peddlers or retail merchants now expanded their operations by employing some of their more recently arrived fellow countrymen. Several of these firms, which sprang up in the more populous centers and engaged the talents of vigorous salesmen, installed the newly invented sewing machines, employing women and girls to operate them. As cutting machines were perfected and the specialization of tasks increased, some of the shops blossomed into factories. Others, particularly in New York and Chicago, where the largest influx of a new wave of Eastern European Jews occurred, developed a contract system that enabled the recent comers to work under men of their own group and in neighborhood lofts where they could speak their native tongue.[21]

This activity spread widely and unobtrusively, helping to sustain sizable colonies of Eastern Jews in Boston and Baltimore, in Cleveland, Cincinnati, Rochester, and a dozen smaller places. Every member of the family lent a hand, but it soon became evident that only the contract bosses were prospering. Again a union movement developed and brought long years of bitter strife, with both the owners and the organizers seeking to gain an advantage by playing one city against another in regional lockouts and boycotts. Nevertheless the industry, responding to the rapid urban growth, continued to expand, and the companies, closely dependent on their labor supply, could not migrate freely. Wages remained low, and the wide use of sweatshops helped to foster living standards that were among the worst in America—so wretched, in fact, that the public conscience was pricked. Soon local, state, and federal investigations began to study the problem. New pressure for governmental supervision developed, and a resurgence of union effort occurred among the workers as the period closed.[22]

If the classic example of immigrant enterprise was the clothing industry, that of the native was the commercial bank, though foreign-born bankers increased in number after the seventies. Each new settlement boasted one or more of these institutions, which quickly multiplied as the towns grew. By 1880, 6532 banks with national, state, or private charters—one to every 2000 urban residents—served a variety of functions, among them the promotion of city growth. Although the accumulation and use of private savings was still a minor feature, as was investment banking, the facility these establishments brought to commercial transactions, and the concentration they effected of fluid capital in the sixteen cities designated as redemption centers under the National Banking Act of 1863–64, strengthened the leading marts within their respective regions and tied their economy to the great central reserve capital in New York.[23]

It was not the banks, however, but enterprising men who determined the direction of a city's industrial development. Sometimes an influx of newcomers with special skills transformed a town's activity. Thus at Rochester after the mid-century, when flour milling and canalling had passed their apogee, a host of immigrant craftsmen created the clothing, shoe, nursery, brewing, and woodworking industries that gave it a new burst of growth, placing it in the 100,000 bracket by 1885. The lack of convenient coal, iron, and other natural resources had threatened to blight the "Flower City's" manufacturing prospects, but the new industries depended less on raw materials than on human skills and on the excellence of their products. Such varied and specialized instruments were designed and built that they again transformed Rochester, within three decades, into a center of technical industry. A young bank clerk, George Eastman, discovered that the photographic laboratory he set up in his mother's kitchen held more fascination than a teller's cage, and the city soon shared his rewards.[24]

Enterprise in abundance characterized most cities throughout these decades. Growth itself created a rich market, not only for food and apparel and building materials but also for a variety of new articles that promised urban convenience. Ingenious men perfected the telephone, the elevator, the trolley car, the bicycle, and the automobile—to name only a few that contributed to the ease and speed of communications in cities, thus increasing the momentum of their growth. Energetic promoters extended the use of these products widely through the towns of America and at the same time greatly benefited those where the factories were located.[25]

The widespread technological advance frequently prompted independent inventors to work on similar problems at the same time. Occasionally a city assembled so many skilled craftsmen in a particular industry that it generated innovations and attracted experts from distant places. The Edison shops at Harrison, New Jersey, the Brush Electric Company at Cleveland, and the Thomson-Houston works at Lynn drew proficient electrical workers to these centers; Eastman attracted to Rochester rival photographic and optical companies eager to share its concentration of specialized skills. Although many manufacturers, impelled to acquire patent rights that might obstruct the development of their products, hastened to absorb competitors, the formation of new firms almost in the shadow of the expanding companies often continued unabated. Some of the new concerns developed subsidiary articles which they produced for the major distributors—speed shutters for cameras in Rochester, lamp stems for incandescent globes at Harrison—thus contributing to the integration of major community industries while retaining the enterprise many restless but talented craftsmen desired.[26]

The upsurge of inventiveness flooded the patent office with applications as the 120,000 registered before 1870 mounted by 1910 to well over a million.[27] Promoters who helped to develop the new mechanical devices generally enlisted support from local capitalists. The limited-dividend corporation, freely available under the general laws of most states, proved especially attractive, and such incorporations, almost non-existent in manufacturing in 1860, numbered over 40,000 at the close of the century. Although they comprised barely a tenth of all establishments, they produced 60 per cent of the value, and almost completely dominated the metal and technical branches. The flexibility of these economic "persons"—their capacity for expansion or consolidation, for a shift in leadership or a change in product—fitted them admirably for growing cities faced with problems of economic integration.[28]

The most rapid increase among giant corporations occurred at the turn of the century, as they mushroomed from twelve in 1896, each valued at $10 million or more, to fifty that exceeded $50 million by 1903.[29] Even after the move for consolidation began and strong, often monopolistic groups took hold, a rapidly expanding market and more effective sales promotion frequently enabled the trust to keep all its affiliated plants in operation, at least for a time. Sometimes a new factory site was selected, as in the case of the General Electric Company, a consolidation of Edison and rival concerns, but the new beginning it made at Schenectady in 1886 could not absorb all the work in process at Harrison, Lynn, and Cleveland, among other places. Several of the old centers prospered, while Schenectady became an industrial city of high quality.[30]

Numerous towns, though not the majority, enjoyed similar benefits. The typewriter brought life to Ilion, New York, and new vigor to Syracuse; telephone factories clustered for a time at Boston and Chicago, but soon spread out; the cash register placed Dayton on the industrial map. A score of cities manufactured elevators, and many more contributed to the production of trolley cars and their equipment.[31] Bicycle companies sprang up in a host of towns during the early nineties, but shortly after 1899, when the American Bicycle Company absorbed forty-eight of them, production was centered in ten plants at Springfield, Massachusetts, and Hartford, Connecticut, each of which suffered a severe blow when the trust collapsed a few seasons later. Several former cycle factories had meanwhile shifted to the manufacture of automobiles, in which Detroit quickly took the lead. Its surplus of capital from an expiring lumber trade, together with an overabundance of skilled marine-engine mechanics, welcomed the new industry.[32]

So many cities suffered from the migration of old companies and other effects of consolidation that the antitrust forces won general approval. The long battle for the regulation of railroads had spread antimonopoly doctrines, nurturing a strong faith in competition, and prepared the way for the speedy adoption of the Sherman Anti-Trust Act in 1890. Yet its vague provisions left many issues undecided. In the courts, where the rising trusts had much more effective representation than in the legislatures, the legal curbs atrophied and almost disappeared. Protests against government interference with "free enterprise," on which the welfare, particularly of industrial cities, seemed to depend, enlisted

support from most business groups and discouraged efforts to halt con-
solidations. Only the more flagrant invasions of local community interests aroused effective action, such as the Standard Oil Company's
stranglehold over the fortunes of Toledo and other Ohio towns in the
early nineties, or the Trans-Missouri Freight Association's attempt to
control the traffic of the Southwest a few years later. Champions of the
efficiency of large-scale enterprise multiplied, and in 1889 New Jersey
provided a corporate form for the holding companies that widely superseded the old trusts.[33]

In most cities new firms quickly replaced those absorbed or otherwise
lost, and many small market towns grew into promising industrial centers. The number reporting at least 10,000 factory workers increased
from thirty to fifty-four during the last two decades of the century; those
listing 5000 or more rose from forty-five to eighty-one. After 1900
many factories migrated to the suburbs, and this presented the parent
city with new problems of economic integration. All growing towns
felt an increasing need for local leadership.[34]

Boards of trade and chambers of commerce sprang up in city after
city as rallying points for their businessmen. Only a few of the thirty or
more such organizations formed before the Civil War had survived,
notably those of Chicago, Buffalo, Pittsburgh, and New York. Now the
extension of the telegraph and the laying of the Atlantic cable in 1866
opened new possibilities for long-distance trade negotiations and stimulated the formation of organizations to conduct local exchanges and disseminate trade information. Most of the new crop of business clubs
were, like their predecessors, chiefly concerned with commerce, but in
1869 the Milwaukee Chamber of Commerce raised a fund of $860 "to
promote the city's industrial growth." Its list of the town's advantages
for trade and industry, published in 1871 and widely circulated, heralded
a new, more industrial approach. A few years later, the same body
initiated an industrial exposition patterned after the Centennial in Philadelphia. Its building, erected at a cost of $300,000 and opened in 1881,
supplied facilities for annual exhibitions during the next two decades
and inspired businessmen in St. Louis, Chicago, and Minneapolis to
similar efforts.[35]

The most forthright move in this direction occurred at Philadelphia
in 1894, when the city council organized a Commercial Museum and
provided it with a building and equipment to display local industrial
products and to promote foreign trade. San Francisco, St. Louis, and
Boston established similar museums. Not to be outdone, an Association
for the Advancement of Milwaukee urged real-estate men to grant free

sites or free rent to new industrial ventures and collected subscriptions from capitalists to back them. The association, which also proposed tax concessions, boasted after two years that its efforts had attracted a score of new industries to the city, helping it to reach fifteenth place by 1900.[36]

Some of the post–Civil War boards of trade declined after a few seasons, but new organizations generally appeared in response to urgent business needs. Several midwestern towns formed promotional bodies similar to Milwaukee's. In 1892 the Cleveland Board of Trade created a committee for the promotion of industry, which led in turn to the reorganization of the board as a Chamber of Commerce a year later, when a full-time secretary was engaged to handle such activities and to develop new civic and welfare functions. Other chambers, too, were seeking competent secretaries, and in 1913 as their activities became standardized the newly established Harvard Business School organized a course for them.

The effort to provide free sites or other subsidies for new industries lost favor in some chambers after concerns of questionable merit accepted such benefits only to move on when a higher bid arrived. But the promotional value of numerous trade conventions, industrial exhibitions, and publications that featured local advantages gained wide acceptance among the several hundred boards and chambers of the early 1900's. If the annual reports often sounded a bit boastful, even to local observers, such growing industrial cities as Milwaukee, Cleveland, Pittsburgh, Detroit, Buffalo, Columbus, and Rochester—not to mention several of the newer towns of the West—all gladly supported active groups.[37]

Although the basic philosophy of most of these chambers involved unfaltering support for "free enterprise," especially after events in the nineties sharpened the issue, some of their committees did try to establish voluntary standards of production and fair dealing. Their resolutions generally opposed state and federal regulations, but many were quick to appeal to the I. C. C. or to an appropriate state authority when a long-haul railroad rate schedule or some other monopoly practice seemed prejudicial to the locality. Their concern for the city's welfare often aligned them against freebooting utility combines and high-handed industrial giants. Leadership in the continuing attack on trusts and corporate monopolies generally came from other sources, but the chambers were exponents of community business interests.[38]

Most growing towns had, of course, developed a sense of the community's interest long before organizations to promote it emerged. An informal leadership, which later sociologists would call the power structure, generally directed important aspects of the development of each city. The promoters of town sites and urban subdivisions, who frequently joined the merchants to support and direct the expansive projects of the commercial centers, seldom gave effective leadership to the industrial cities. There the initiative more frequently came from ambitious craftsmen, often men with inventive talents, whose struggle to produce and market new products transformed them into captains of industry. They were the most alert developers of each town's external economy. Newcomers from abroad, and others from small towns nearby, rose in this fashion to positions of influence.

Many industrial cities developed specialties based on the skills of their workers or the inventive talents of their technicians. On the other hand the mining towns and some others largely dependent on one industry frequently lost control to absentee owners who opposed the development of independent enterprise. The widespread reaction to, or fear of, that fate strengthened the antimonopoly forces of the commercial centers, plagued by railroad pools, and hastened the triumph of the progressive movement.

The most important contribution of the industrial cities was the mounting output of their factories. Statistics show that the value added by manufacturing doubled between 1859 and 1879 and more than doubled again in the prosperous eighties, and yet again, despite two depressions, by 1909. The value added by manufacturing increased tenfold in the half-century, almost trebling the increased value of farm products. Moreover the portion of the national income derived from manufacturing mounted from 16.6 to 20.8 per cent during the last three decades, while that derived from agriculture held steady and the contributions of both trade and transportation declined.[39]

In this period, at least, industry rather than commerce was the chief source of urban growth. Over nine-tenths of the industrial production occurred in urban factories, and as their output increased a surplus for export developed in some fields. Shipments abroad of manufactured foodstuffs and of finished industrial products mounted steadily after 1876 until, by 1898, even the latter exceeded comparable imports. As American factories progressively crowded European products out of the domestic consumer trade, the American farm was relieved of the burden of balancing foreign payments. The export of foodstuffs, both raw and manufactured, declined after the turn of the century, but the exports of other manufactured products more than took up the slack, maintaining a sufficiently favorable balance of trade to liquidate some of the foreign investments. Thus urban industrial growth freed the national economy not only from dependence on European factories, but also from reliance on foreign banks for new capital. That, however, was only a minor aspect of the industrial city's accomplishment, for the value added to its products exceeded the total value of all imports almost seven to one by 1899, as contrasted with a ratio of five to two, four decades earlier. As foreign trade diminished in relative importance, domestic trade mounted, and the industrial worker produced material goods in sufficient volume to raise the standards of consumption throughout the country.[40]

3. The transformation
of the metropolis

Inevitably, as the industrial towns multiplied in number and increased their output, the character and functions of the commercial centers became progressively more complex. Eight of the nine leading cities of the pre–Civil War period, all situated at major breaks in the natural trade routes, experienced a shift in rank and a decrease in territorial sway, yet each nevertheless doubled or trebled its population by developing new functions and by serving its remaining district more intensively. Even Chicago, which vastly extended its domain during the sixties and seventies and bounded from ninth to second place by 1890, was already at that date witnessing the split-up of its empire as several outlying provinces developed a measure of independence under local leadership. The new regional hubs—Minneapolis, Kansas City, and Denver, among others—still depended reluctantly on Chicago and St. Louis for some metropolitan services at the turn of the century, while those two great centers sought to strengthen their position by wresting additional functions from New York, still the overshadowing national metropolis.

This struggle for regional economic autonomy had its antecedents, as we have seen, at Boston, Philadelphia, and Baltimore before the Civil War. Each had discovered that its own or some nearby industrial growth added greatly to its strength. Most of the leading marts in the interior also followed this pattern, but a few developed specialties, such as Chicago with its stockyards, that gave them a still broader influence. A half-dozen industrial cities with restricted territorial basins—including Pittsburgh, Cleveland, and Milwaukee—based their growth on the predominance they achieved in particular fields of manufacturing. As national headquarters for their specialties, they challenged New York's supremacy and compelled it and other commercial centers to cultivate

specialties of their own. All these cities developed metropolitan characteristics, and the metropolis itself thus became a much more complex
type of community than its antebellum predecessor.[1]

Businessmen of many cities contributed in various ways to the transformation of the metropolis. Some founded new institutions, such as
clearing houses and department stores, to perform particular functions
for the great cities; others developed new uses for old organizations—
boards of trade, for example—or applied existing techniques more effectively, notably in the fields of promotion and advertising. Many small
cities copied some of these innovations; indeed, several ambitious towns
in the West proved especially apt and even produced innovations of their
own. The great cities welcomed imitation, and their leaders hastened to
promote the adoption of the latest urban facilities throughout their hinterlands. They took the initiative in founding adjacent suburbs, some
with functional specialties, such as dormitory and factory towns, cultural and recreational centers. They also devised methods of control to
bind regional neighbors more firmly as co-operating satellites. But they
could not check the growth of a dozen other commercial hubs and several industrial cities into metropolitan centers, each of which established
its claim to a regional hinterland.

A major development at the turn of the century was the invasion of
several old commercial centers by factories. As a result, of the fifteen
leading cities of 1910, which all enjoyed natural trade advantages, fourteen had become major industrial cities as well. Except for New Orleans,
each of the great towns was absorbing a commanding share of the output
of one or more industries. New York, the chief banker and printer, was
even more busy manufacturing clothing and cigars.[2] Chicago, which
by 1870 had become the leading butcher and packer and the leading
grain and lumber mart, was now taking the lead in steel fabrication.
Philadelphia, which after 1905 lost top place to Lawrence in the production of woolen goods, stood second or third only to New York or
Chicago in other important industries. All but two of these first fifteen
cities in population ranked among the first fifteen in industrial output.
One of the exceptions, San Francisco, would have needed only to add its
suburban factories to qualify.[3]

The high industrial rank of the leading cities resulted in most cases
from their size rather than from the intensity of their manufacturing
activities. In several the number employed in trade and commerce exceeded those in industry, although this did not hold true in 1900 of the
four largest—New York, Chicago, Philadelphia, and St. Louis. Yet the

slight predominance of industrial workers there could not compare with the ratio of two or three to one in such specialized factory towns as Lawrence, Lowell, Fall River, and Manchester in New England or Paterson, New Jersey, or even with the industrial cities among the top fifteen, notably Pittsburgh and Cleveland. Old Boston, unable to annex its industrial suburbs, was, like most of the rising metropolitan centers of the West, predominantly commercial; Baltimore, unchecked in territorial expansion, achieved a close balance.[4]

Much of the industrial activity of the great cities was of the housekeeping or service variety—carpentering, baking, and the like—merely reflecting their local population growth. Another large portion stemmed from the character of the particular population, as in New York, where the flood of immigrants chiefly explained the rise of both the clothing and the tobacco industries. Yet each metropolis developed additional factories that successfully won a national, sometimes an international market. Such products helped to balance the incoming and outgoing shipments by rail or water and secured for their towns a measure of economic individuality and independence.[5]

None of these types of enterprise could by themselves assure metropolitan status. Several small cities became dominant in one or another industry—Grand Rapids in furniture, Waltham in watches, Naugatuck in rubber shoes—without attaining that status. Some, like Rochester, were widely diversified as well but lacked a sufficiently broad regional hinterland to achieve major metropolitan rank.[6] Five even among the first fifteen were so heavily committed to industry—Pittsburgh, Milwaukee, Buffalo, Detroit, and Newark—that in the opinion of N. S. B. Gras (who several years later made the first attempt to define a metropolis in functional terms) they did not properly merit such a classification. Other functions took precedence in his analysis, notably mercantile and financial services, with the result that a regional center like Kansas City or Atlanta superseded much larger Newark, which lacked an independent hinterland.[7]

Professor Gras notwithstanding, the metropolitan status of Pittsburgh was secure. Despite some decline in its river trade after the Civil War, Pittsburgh had developed its rail facilities and, located in the midst of rich iron and coal fields, had outstripped its old rival, Cincinnati. It had mounted from seventeenth to eighth place during these decades. The crucial importance of steel in the expanding American economy gave men like Carnegie, Frick, and Mellon power to dominate the economy as well as the political and cultural life of their own region, and to check lesser rivals in Birmingham and elsewhere. Steel also made Pittsburgh *the* national industrial metropolis. Pittsburgh's leaders joined with others to promote railroad construction, steel fabrication, and related enterprises throughout the country. They retained their economic influence long after Chicago surpassed Pittsburgh in steel output, for they had acquired a national perspective similar to that of the New York financiers, as at least Carnegie revealed in his writings and philanthropies.[8]

Although some industrial towns, hemmed in by more advantageously located commercial marts, lacked expansive hinterlands, a few nevertheless developed other metropolitan attributes. Only those threatened by absorption, such as Brooklyn, Newark, and others that adjoined growing core cities, failed to develop their own milk sheds, farmers' markets, vacation resorts, and newspaper zones. Often the conflict between neighboring cities for the wholesale trade and huckstering services of intervening hamlets became intense. For example, the leading dailies of Rochester and Buffalo ran competing columns of village news to attract readers from western New York towns for their advertisers. Their merchants staged special farmers' days; their railroads announced excursions to bring country folk into the city for annual festivals and bargain hunts; their chambers of commerce scheduled good-will tours, in the nineties chartering a special train or boat and a decade later motoring through great clouds of dust into back-country villages in quest of new trade possibilities.[9]

Historically the American metropolis thus had a multiple origin. Cities located at natural breaks in trade and surrounded by vast territories had the most favorable prospects. Cities less fortunately situated for trade but possessing large hinterlands could, by promoting numerous railroads and developing industrial services, achieve the necessary regional leadership. Others, overshadowed by regional rivals but possessing dynamic industrial energies could, by attaining national pre-eminence in special fields and by intensively developing their restricted environs, also win metropolitan status.

Despite their varied origins, these great cities had much in common and grew progressively more alike. Their impact on the residents of their adjoining countrysides increased steadily with growth, transforming nearby farms into truck patches or dairies; when these later gave way to subdivisions or cheese factories, the search for milk and vegetables reached farther out. Each expanding city required a watershed and sought other special privileges in its surrounding territory. The great commercial marts endeavored in these decades to develop productive factories to stabilize their trade; conversely, most large industrial cities began after 1890 to show a more rapid increase in tradesmen and white-collar workers than in factory hands. This double reversal of trends revealed that the economy had become industrialized to such an extent that its administration demanded an ever larger force of clerks, salesmen, and accountants, while improved machinery began around the turn of the century to reduce the ratio of manpower required for production. Yet differences, though relative, persisted, preserving a distinction, as in the case of cities, between the commercial and the industrial metropolis.[10]

Metropolitan developments had, in fact, many aspects. The federal census first recognized the new urban categories of suburb and metropolitan district at New York in 1880, but did not apply them more generally or record their development in its tables until 1910.[11] The census definition was, of course, statistical, with geographic overtones, and identified twenty-five major metropolitan districts ranging down from New York (including Newark), with its 616,927 acres and 6,474,568 people, to Portland, Oregon, with 43,538 acres and 215,048 residents. The suburban population exceeded 10 per cent of the total in sixteen of these districts and amounted to 55 per cent at Boston. Old and formerly independent places were combined in some of these statistical units, as their economic activity had in part already been integrated. The twin cities of Minnesota, those on San Francisco Bay, and on the Missouri-Kansas border, were merged, as were the numerous communities around New York, Boston, Philadelphia, and Pittsburgh. Most of the appendages of these latter core cities had developed as, or into, industrial or dormitory suburbs whose independence consisted chiefly in local government.[12]

Rapidly growing cities had ever been spilling over their borders. Most of them had recaptured the overflow by periodic annexations, but suburban opposition often developed in towns separated by bodies of water or, in more recent years, merely by local pride and prejudice. Some early dormitory suburbs, such as Brooklyn before the Civil War, were invaded by industry and finally merged with the parent city. The consolidation of the boroughs of Manhattan, Brooklyn, Queens, Richmond, and the Bronx into Greater New York in 1898 produced a metropolitan total of 3,437,202, more than twice Chicago's size. In both cities, however, improved transport facilities spread business activity and tenement houses, prompting wealthy residents to seek new homes still farther out—on Long Island, in Westchester and the Oranges about New York; in Evanston, Forest Park, and Riverside about Chicago. Rapid transit speeded this outward movement after the turn of the century, and the high tax rates and other attributes of the central cities strengthened the determination of some residential suburbs there and elsewhere to resist annexation at all costs.[13]

The industrial suburb was generally a more deliberate creation. Several began as satellite towns, born of the idealistic desire of an industrialist to remove factories and workers from the congestion and squalor abutting his city's wharves and freight lines. A new beginning on a larger and cheaper site also offered many advantages, as towns like Pullman, Leclaire, Vandergrift, and Barber revealed.[14] Unfortunately, such domination of all economic activity proved as unsound with an industrialist in charge as it had been a few decades earlier under idealists in the utopian communities. Independent businessmen generally shunned these one-man creations. In them the normal conflicts between labor and management, though suppressed for a time, often erupted in violence, as at Homestead, near Pittsburgh, in 1892 and at Pullman, near Chicago, two years later. Even where industrial peace was maintained, the satellite failed to develop the economic diversification of normal urban places. Its products and markets contributed to the parent city, and it generally ended as a suburb.[15]

The great metropolitan centers spawned other satellites, too. The Coney Islands of the sixties and seventies could not satisfy the total recreational needs of the increasing number of urbanites, nor could the old aristocratic spas expand rapidly enough to accommodate all who sought a week or two of relaxation. New camping sites on the ocean or on an inland lake—Ocean Grove, Falmouth, Saranac Lake, Chautauqua —sprang into being, and earlier watering places such as Atlantic City and St. Petersburg mushroomed into thriving resort cities.[16]

The establishment of new college towns, like Palo Alto in California, and the vitality brought to Ithaca and Evanston, among many such villages, reflected other colonizing energies of the urban giants whose capitalists endowed educational institutions for city youths away from home.[17] One might almost say that most of the state capitals, now increasingly overshadowed by the rising commercial and industrial cities, had become administrative colonies, although they were by no means subservient to the metropolis. Boston and Providence, Denver and St. Paul were exceptions, since other activities predominated there. Yet along with Washington itself, several state capitals acquired a new animation toward the end of the period, both in their rates of growth and in the performance of useful functions.

:

Most of the rising metropolitan centers served as both regional and national marts. All the ports contended at Washington for increased appropriations for harbor improvements. New York's towering advantage, accentuated by the Civil War, suffered a percentage drop during the freight-rate battles of the seventies, yet its trade mounted steadily in volume as its early preponderance compelled all major eastern railroads to seek access to its cargoes. Rival Atlantic ports, served only by one or two roads, tried to equalize New York's assets. Philadelphia and Baltimore secured a slight rate differential on grain shipments from Chicago by the agreement of 1877 among the major carriers, which the trunk-line pool enforced by various means until 1898 when the I. C. C. gave its official endorsement.[18]

Baltimore and Boston developed belt railroads to serve a majority of their docks, following the more complete systems installed at San Francisco in 1891 and at New Orleans in 1904; they thus avoided much of the confusion resulting from competition between shipping areas in the New York harbor. Their improved efficiency brought additional trade.[19]

Yet none of its rivals could keep pace with New York's drydock improvements or match its wide choice of anchorages and piers. Boston fought to retain the services of the Cunard Line; both Philadelphia and Baltimore established independent steamship companies to assure regular sailings and won a slight advance in their percentages of total imports. Nevertheless, the preference New York enjoyed as the immigrant gateway, even before the federal government made it the headquarters for inspection and registration in 1890, assured it an unending succession of incoming vessels whose owners were eager for quick export loads. Foreign as well as American mail subsidies favored New York, too, and many ships that served other ports discovered a need to put into the Hudson as well, in order to fill their holds.[20] Despite the relative decline of foreign trade, when contrasted with the growth of internal commerce, its volume increased enormously, and New York continued to serve as the great hinge, to use Jean Gottmann's graphic term, linking an expanding America with Europe and the Western world.[21]

New York retained its virtual monopoly over foreign trade, yet the establishment after 1880 of inland customs offices, to which bonded imports could be delivered by rail under seal, greatly facilitated the commerce of many interior places. The number of customs districts rose in two decades to 126; with the progressive channeling of trade through the larger cities, however, that trend was reversed, so that a reorganization in 1912 reduced the number to 49 customs districts.[22]

Inland metropolises won their greatest advantages, not in foreign trade but as regional marts. The vast hinterlands of western centers represented potential rather than tangible assets, since the density of settlement was so much greater in the East, but the challenge of that potential and the absence of entrenched interests and traditional methods often encouraged a small western metropolis to adopt the most recent eastern innovations. Thus it was that Chicago in the sixties, when only ninth in population, ventured to experiment with the new department-store pattern of merchandising imported from Paris. Shortly after Lord & Taylor and Macy's in New York began to add new departments to their drygoods stores, Marshall Field's new store in Chicago boldly combined all the new features: the fixed-price system of Macy's, the large display advertisements in the daily papers which Wanamaker had developed, and more departments than any one store had previously housed. Soon comparable stores appeared in San Francisco, St. Louis, New Orleans, and lesser cities. Passenger elevators, electric lights, inter-department telephones, cash registers, and in 1893 a pneumatic-tube system at Marshall Field's marked the rapid evolution of this new metropolitan institution.[23]

Another mercantile innovation of still wider and somewhat opposite effect was the chain store. One of the first, the Great American Tea Company, organized at New York in 1864, became five years later the Great Atlantic and Pacific Tea Company and soon had branches scattered across the land. The five-and-ten-cent store, opened by Frank W. Woolworth at Lancaster, Pennsylvania, in 1879, quickly established a branch at Harrisburg and another at Scranton and spread widely in the next decade. Grocery, drug, and cigar store chains linked large and small towns in a new commercial economy that brought them more efficient service, often cheaper prices, and goods of a more standard if not always an improved quality. The mail-order firms, which first appeared in the seventies, made possible by mass production of consumer products, extended urban services even farther into the rural areas.[24]

Improvements in merchandising occurred in many cities. N. W. Ayer & Son established an advertising agency in Philadelphia during the seventies that marked a considerable advance over its prewar predecessors in Boston and New York.[25] The publication of the first newspaper directory in 1869 provided advertising agencies with an accurate list to work with, and several of them followed a Milwaukee pioneer in supplying syndicated ads to small-town papers. The number of industrialists who advertised on a large scale increased rapidly after 1890; among them was George Eastman, whose "You press the button, we do the rest" not only made the Kodak famous, but also spawned a brood of catchy slogans. The development of the lithographic half-tone reached a stage in the late eighties that permitted a wider use of illustrations and greatly enhanced the effectiveness of newspaper and magazine advertisements, thus helping to extend the market area for patented and trademark products. As a result of the new promotional techniques, the country's advertising budget, predominantly urban in character, increased, according to one statistician, tenfold between 1865 and 1900.[26]

Another characteristic metropolitan feature was the expanded use of insurance, which spread the risks of large-scale enterprise. Although numerous local companies had appeared before the Civil War, it was shortly after its close that the Equitable Life Insurance Company of Des Moines, Iowa, developed the new, low-cost, tontine insurance. This, with industrial insurance, which was introduced in the mid-seventies, vastly enlarged the market for policies and compounded the funds until they exceeded $3 billion by 1905, tempting speculative investors to exploit these gushing pools of credit.[27] Public indignation against the reckless use of these funds, drawn from the people themselves, contributed, as we shall see, to the reaction that expressed itself in the progressive movement.[28]

Since neither these funds nor those of the commercial or savings banks were available to the average consumer, pawn shops and other dispensers of small loans multiplied. One of the earliest of these shops appeared at Chicago in 1869 advertising modest loans on chattel mortgages. The demand proved so great and the interest rates so lucrative that similar establishments opened in a dozen midwestern cities before 1881, when Boston produced one that offered loans on assignments of wages. Some of the more successful of these ventures opened branches even in small places. Although the opportunity to negotiate modest loans helped some people get ahead, the exorbitant interest charges, ranging to 200 per cent and more a year, trapped many poor folk in a vicious form of bondage. Protests against the money sharks burst forth in many towns, particularly during the depression of the mid-nineties. Investigations of the abuses in Philadelphia and elsewhere inspired a number of state laws; charitable substitutes failed, however, to satisfy the wide demand for small loans, and the rich profits the trade offered gave rise to ingenious schemes to circumvent these regulations. Renewed protests after the turn of the century produced a group of more practical remedial loan societies in most large cities.[29]

Improved grain elevators and huge warehouses supplied other metropolitan services in aggressive commercial hubs. Wholesale jobbers appeared, dealing in lumber, grain, and cattle at first, later in the products of eastern factories. Mail-order, chain, and department stores, making their purchases at regional or national centers, substituted traveling supervisors and buyers for salesmen; still the salesmen multiplied, representing the rising industrial firms or fanning out from regional warehouses. Wholesale and retail districts sprang up in all the great cities, the wholesale offices near railroad sidings, the retail stores at focal points of the local transit system and lining its heavy passenger routes. Regional produce markets, creameries, ice barns and refrigeration plants, lumber and coal yards, employment offices, trust companies, banks, and insurance offices, each found a place, generally in a specialized district, of every expanding metropolis.

Corn exchanges, organized by the earliest business groups in Cincinnati, St. Louis, Chicago, Milwaukee, and Minneapolis, provided a pattern for efforts to systematize other regional economic activities. Significant among these were some twelve independent regional stock exchanges.[30]

Of these, the New York Stock Exchange overshadowed all rivals in volume of business. Its pre-eminence dated from the sixties, when a merger of two older groups assumed that name. The opening of the Atlantic cable and the introduction of the first ticker machines at this time brought an increase of Exchange members to 1060 and prompted the creation of a governing committee of twenty-eight to supervise operations. Trading declined during the depression of the mid-seventies, when the ferocity of the railroad pools discouraged independent brokers, but activity revived after 1888 as industrial shares began to appear on the Exchange board. By 1911 fully one-third of the shares listed were industrials, and the fate of many factories in distant cities hung on the fluctuations in Wall Street. [31]

The operation of the market passed through several stages. When Western Union acquired control of the New York Stock Exchange telegraph services in 1871, it opened quotation boards in numerous cities, most of which persisted after the Stock Exchange re-established supervision over such facilities two decades later. The New York Exchange limited its hours of operation and forbade members to engage in an evening exchange, but did not penalize trade on the so-called curb market or at other outside centers within the prescribed hours. The need for a more efficient method of handling the actual delivery of shares prompted three abortive efforts to organize a stock clearing house before its final establishment in 1892. Demands for a check on the call-loan system multiplied as speculation soared after the turn of the century, and the "rich man's panic" of 1907–08 provoked Governor Charles Evans Hughes of New York to order an investigation of the Exchange and its relation to savings and investment banks.[32]

New York's loosely organized but tightening control over the investment market was only one aspect of its domination over the American monetary system. The pre-Civil War situation, with strongly entrenched Boston and Philadelphia bankers holding their own against their Manhattan rivals, had disappeared after the National Banking Act of 1863 made New York the reserve capital for deposits of currency. Soon afterward these and other established cities, despite their early opposition to the national system, acquired a major share of the bank-note circulation and, as redemption centers, resisted the drive of expansive new towns in the West and the South for a liberalization of these privileges.[33] Despite the authorization of additional bank-note circulation in 1870, protests against the system continued since bullion drained steadily into the eastern metropolis. The designation in 1887 of two new central reserve cities, Chicago and St. Louis, and the extension of redemption privileges to a total of forty-six others by the close of the period failed to check the concentration of banking strength in New York.[34]

Unfortunately the centralization of credit services had developed without a clear definition of responsibility. As the reserves from outside banks soared far above the local deposits in New York's national banks, the proportion of the nation's currency maintained in liquid form for emergency use declined; moreover, the practice of extending credit to stock speculators and that of making call loans against these funds further threatened stability. The increased productivity of the urban economy had stimulated a rapid growth in the volume of savings throughout the country, sufficient to force a wide reduction of interest rates during the eighties and nineties. The reckless use of these funds by some bankers prompted an effort after the panic of 1893 to regulate the use of savings-bank resources. Yet the unchecked powers of private bankers and trust companies, whose surpluses likewise funneled into New York and who depended in large part on foreign capitalists to meet unusual demands, enabled such men as J. P. Morgan to assume effective leadership during the minor crises that arose each summer and fall, when interior demands shot up, but rendered the system vulnerable in times of major crisis when the European credits withered. Since the assets of all American banks multiplied sevenfold in the last three decades of the period, the continued dependence on the now relatively small flow of foreign capital, even in normal years, proved precarious, as 1903 and 1907 demonstrated.[35]

The mounting criticism of the inadequate national currency alarmed bankers, especially those in the interior. In 1897 the Indianapolis Chamber of Commerce called a convention to devise reforms, and when action on its recommendations was deferred, eastern bankers in 1900 secured the adoption of a more stringent Gold Standard Act. The minimum capital required for the chartering of a national bank was reduced to $25,000 that year, and the number of such institutions almost doubled within a decade. As this expansion failed, however, to satisfy growing urban needs, the total of state and private banks and trust companies rose from 9519 to 13,317 during the same decade, almost twice that of the national banks, though the resources of the former were barely half as great.[36]

Some of the clearing houses organized in aspiring banking centers as they developed—five before the Civil War, forty-four by 1890, and 141 by 1910—sought earnestly for a formula that would insure flexibility and expansion as well as security. Originally designed for the convenient exchange of checks, many of these institutions devised procedures that benefited their members in normal times and helped to maintain banking operations within the district during unsettled periods. One such device was the loan certificate first tried out at New York City during the Civil War. Seven clearing houses issued such certificates for brief periods in the panic of 1873; fourteen in the more acute crisis two decades later. Despite repeated affirmations of the gold standard, over fifty of these bodies resorted to loan certificates again in 1907. The need for a more flexible and yet secure currency prompted renewed efforts to attract private bankers and trust companies into these associations; the continued reluctance of some independents to accept such regulation finally strengthened the demand for new legislation. The Aldrich-Vreeland Act, adopted in response to this movement in 1908, tended also to underscore the pattern of widely spaced metropolitan regions.[37]

Yet the New York bankers maintained their dominance and, in fact, proceeded to extend it alarmingly. With J. P. Morgan in the lead, they had completely reorganized the corporate structure of several of the major railroad systems since the mid-nineties and achieved similar feats in the industrial field. Morgan and his associates took the initiative in the formation of the United States Steel Corporation, the International Harvester Company, the General Electric Company, the American Telephone & Telegraph, and numerous other giants. The National City Bank of New York, with Rockefeller's backing, organized the Consolidated

Gas Company, which operated in many cities, the Amalgamated Copper Company, and other large monopolies that obtained a stranglehold on mining communities such as Butte, Montana. Two additional New York banking groups played similar roles in the rapid consolidation of industrial enterprise into other great trusts centered at the metropolis.[38]

The hostility which had developed toward the railroads during the seventies, and toward all out-of-town monopolies as they appeared in subsequent years, now shifted to the great corporation bankers who were taking them over. Despite the effort of responsible bankers to safeguard small investors from forced manipulation of the market by the creation of a Stock Exchange Clearing House in 1892, it provided little protection during the panic of the following year. The free use of insurance-company funds to bolster trust companies and launch vast promotional ventures around the turn of the century helped to precipitate the crisis of 1903–05. Though such manipulations were checked in 1905 by the Hughes investigation and partially corrected by a new law, the dramatic spectacle presented late in 1907, when Morgan and his partners secured permission from President Roosevelt to acquire the Tennessee Coal, Iron & Railroad Company, in face of the antitrust laws, as their price for stabilizing the stock market, scarcely lent confidence to the law's defenders. Both public and private investigations documented the widespread protests against the banking control exercised at New York, and also played their part in the progressive movement.[39]

Although American urban developments failed to produce clear-cut divisions between industrial and commercial cities or between regional and national centers, there is merit in retaining these distinctions. Many dynamic places shared most of these attributes; yet all differed in local circumstances and in leadership emphasis. Individuals and groups in each town, seeking to promote and sometimes to dominate an industry or a field of trade, were increasingly impelled to reach beyond the city's boundaries for control of the source of supply, the technology, or the commercial and marketing agencies. These forays brought them into contact with similar forces in neighboring or distant places. The economic relationships that resulted were sometimes co-operative, sometimes fiercely competitive. By helping to breach old city boundaries, they reshaped the emergent urban society into a metropolitan regionalism which would soon take more permanent form; they also stimulated creative innovations as each community endeavored to outstrip its rivals.

But, since no city or metropolis was self-sufficient, and since the American economy and indeed its human life line were still linked closely to Europe, the need for a great commercial and immigrant entry port continued. New York, which had comprised 16 per cent of the country's urban population (the total of all places over 8000) in 1860, plus another 7.1 per cent in its four suburban boroughs, suffered but a slight diminution in its preponderance. The Greater New York of 1910 gathered within its expanded borders 4,766,883 residents, or 13.3 per cent of the nation's urban total, with another 4.7 per cent in the outer reaches of its urbanized district.[40] Yet America was building an urban constellation, not a solar system, or isolated cities, and New York, now the world's second city in size, no longer ranked undisputed as the national metropolis.[41]

The rise of many cities not only created a new spatial pattern for the nation, but also transformed the daily experiences of most urban residents. The manifold services which the larger towns rendered in their efforts to co-ordinate the economy had brought a host of new organizations and business practices and tremendously accelerated the national output. The competitive system, which encouraged and, in fact, depended on aggressive enterprise, rewarded some people with wealth and power, but blasted the hopes and fortunes of many others.

There seemed, for a time, to be no clear standards of business ethics. The relentless drive and greed of some of the triumphant captains of trade and industry, who had achieved a scope of operations that freed them from any one urban base, aroused widespread indignation and inspired pleas to the state and federal authorities for regulatory safeguards. Moreover, the Robber Barons, as they were called by a later generation, could never agree on the division of the spoils, and their incessant struggles frequently brought shattering panics and economic breakdowns. Although they had begun to recruit administrative and legal aides as bureaucratic successors, these new men seemed unable to resolve the dilemma of conflicting social and private interests.

In opposition to such men, numerous advocates of visionary panaceas arose and attracted a following in many cities. But as none of these radicals engendered wide confidence, the spirit of reform assumed a moderate course.[42]

4. The lure of the city

Of course this astonishing upsurge of cities and metropolitan centers, with its unprecedented release of economic energies, reflected the joint efforts of the founders and of the multitudes who flocked into towns across the land. The total population growth west of the Alleghenies during any fifty-year period of the westward movement, including the cities newly built there, never quite matched the national urban increase of 35,000,000 between 1860 and 1910. Yet the two movements were complementary, for urban developments closely followed—indeed, sometimes preceded—and in most cases promoted land settlement. The productivity of each frontier, in forest, farm, or mineral products, created cities and maintained them.

The thrill of founding a new town was but a transitory aspect of the lure of the city. If perhaps several hundred men shared in the early excitement of establishing each of the 2000 urban centers that arose during these decades, the great host that came after the founders responded to quite different lures. Most of them sought better economic opportunities. Not pioneers in the traditional sense, they nevertheless were venturesome enough to break loose from a rural or small-town heritage and seek their fortunes in larger communities. Many others came from distant lands, and although their destinations were not often of their choosing, or always to their liking, a combination of forces drew them into the great cities. In fact, it was the rising metropolitan centers whose attractions proved most enticing, as their rapid growth demonstrated. They presented the widest appeal and evoked the most diversified response.

Although many of the new towns remained relatively insignificant throughout this period, they performed a primary service in the urbanization movement. Content at first to market the produce of their regions, they increasingly became a market themselves for that produce and a haven for the surplus population as well. This process repeated itself on each new frontier, as the rural areas reached saturation and then remained static—or in some cases experienced a slow decline—as the lure of a nearby city, or, in the early days, of a new West, drew off at least the surplus.[1] The earlier depopulation of Vermont townships spread to other rural communities in New England during the sixties and to rural counties in New York, Pennsylvania, and Ohio in the seventies and eighties. It reached farther west as crop changes permitted a less intensive cultivation or the introduction of farm machinery released workers from the field. By the eighties, the lure of cities in the Northeast had checked the westward migration of many natives of that region and had begun to stimulate an eastward backwash from western farms.[2]

When some new blight, or a change in climate, or, more frequently, a drop in prices resulting from overproduction brought disillusionment, hundreds of thousands flocked to the city. Many drifted there in defeat, only to accentuate urban problems. Others came with eager anticipation, among them Hamlin Garland, who recalled years later his first arrival in Chicago with his brother: "Everything interested us . . . Nothing was commonplace, nothing was ugly to us."[3] Garland's confidence was buttressed by his possession of a handicraft learned on the farm. He could shingle houses if necessary, and growing towns presented the best opportunities. Thus the cities absorbed the shinglers, the seamstresses, the shoemakers, and many other half-trained artisans from rural areas. These men, with the peddlers become merchant-manufacturers, helped to develop industries that balanced the agricultural advance and stabilized the national economy.

Spokesmen for rural areas frequently bemoaned the loss of many of the farm's ablest youths to the towns.[4] Yet it was by no means an overall loss, for the rural areas continued to grow and doubled in population in the half-century. Their productivity increased approximately fivefold, creating a hazardous market situation. Fortunately the sevenfold growth of American cities more than balanced the exchange and saved the farmers from a slow deflationary slide into penury. The steadily mounting urban population, with increases that exceeded those of rural areas in every decade except the 1870's, enabled the towns not only to consume most of the increased output of the farms, but to produce material goods in sufficient supply to equip and enrich the farms and the new cities as well. The excitement they afforded and the opportunities they offered quickened the urban migration.[5]

The move to the city was seldom made in a single jump. Even Garland had his taste of small-town life before heading for Chicago. Although statistical studies of such migrations are lacking for this period, other evidence indicates that most rural migrants tried their luck in regional hamlets before venturing to a bigger town.[6] The percentage of American-born residents in cities under 25,000 exceeded that for larger ones in each decade. And since many born in small places migrated to the metropolitan centers, the influx to small towns from the countryside must have been large. As a result, the native-born increased their proportion of the total population of cities under 25,000 from 53 to 58 per cent between 1890 and 1910.[7]

Estimates of the cumulative volume of this migration are at best inferential. While the urban totals almost trebled between 1880 and 1910, reaching 42,000,000, rural residents, though still most numerous, increased barely one-third. Yet the children born in rural homes (which comprised the great majority throughout this period) represented perhaps two-thirds of the 30,000,000 increment among the native-born. They contrasted with the 7,000,000 added to the foreign-born totals. Although the census neglected to tabulate the rural contribution, a rough calculation is possible. If we subtract from the total urban gains the approximately 10,000,000 born in urban families and the 7,000,000 immigrants, we get a round figure of at least 11,000,000 urbanites of 1910 who came from rural American homes after 1880. How many of their predecessors also hailed from that source is uncertain, yet it seems clear that well over a third of all city residents in 1910 were natives and of rural origin.[8]

A major portion of the urban growth in these decades represented the overflow of a fecund countryside, and another major portion came from Europe. The American city presented an inviting prospect to many men and women abroad, who hastily packed their belongings and joined the swelling stream of humanity bound for the promised land. The 5,248,568 immigrants who came in the 1880's exceeded the sum of any two consecutive earlier decades, and although hard times in the nineties temporarily checked the flood, it surged to 8,202,388 during the ten years following 1900. The great majority of these later immigrants settled in cities, helping to man their commercial and industrial activities and to enrich their social and cultural life. Many, of course, were temporary residents, moving on quickly to other communities, like their restless American neighbors, and many soon returned to the home country; but they left a net total of 9,635,369 foreign-born in American cities in 1910.[9]

These migrants contributed significantly to the economic as well as the population growth, particularly of the manufacturing cities. The major stream, entering through New York and Boston, gave a great surge of energy in the eighties, to these busy centers, to their suburbs and satellites, and to the extended file of industrial cities stretching inland along the water-level route. By 1890 the foreign-born comprised 45 to 50 per cent of the residents at Fall River and four other New England textile towns and at Duluth in the Midwest. They exceeded 40 per cent in two great cities, Chicago and San Francisco, and comprised more than a third of the populations of a dozen major towns of the Northeast and North Central regions. In some of these and in older manufacturing centers, such as Philadelphia, Pittsburgh, Cincinnati, and Rochester, the children of earlier migrants now exceeded the foreign-born in number though not as yet in the work force. Even in the South, immigrants were staffing some industrial places, like Wheeling, West Virginia, and San Antonio and Galveston, Texas. They comprised a major share of the increment at West Coast cities.[10]

Few immigrants reached their final destinations without assistance, which of course was not always disinterested. Official state bureaus and consular agents worked with the American Immigrant Company in the 1860's and later with land-company and railroad jobbers who in turn helped shipping agencies in foreign ports to fill their holds with steerage passengers.[11] On disembarking at Boston or at Castle Garden in New York—or, after 1891, on Ellis Island—most of the newcomers needed to re-establish their earning capacity immediately. If not already provided with a ticket to some farther destination, they welcomed the advice of friendly fellow countrymen or, in the later decades, of an immigrant aid society. The congestion that inevitably developed at the ports of entry prompted efforts by humanitarians there and by leaders of certain nationality groups to assist willing migrants to reach less crowded destinations inland. The Castle Garden Labor Bureau found jobs, many in the West, for over 400,000 between 1868 and 1886. Catholics, Jews, and several Protestant sects maintained such programs and helped to populate several Irish, German, and Jewish colonies in western states. Many even of those initially settled on the land soon gravitated to the cities; after 1880 this westward stream was predominantly an urban one.[12]

Although neither the immigrants nor the migrants from rural America comprised a majority of the urban population in any decade, together they supplied much of the new enterprise and most of the workers throughout this period, for they were chiefly young adults. In contrast, most of the urban-born residents, in the early postwar decades, were children, though many were scattered in all age brackets. Since in the cities marriage was frequently deferred, the number of urban-born children of both native and foreign parents mounted slowly until the late 1880's, when a trend toward earlier marriage developed. As the number of youthful parents increased, they quickly raised a generation of city-born offspring who by 1910 comprised the largest segment of the urban population.[13]

The census reports failed to give a very clear picture of this development. Although the crude method of calculating births from the number of children of one year or less, plus the deaths in this group, supplied useful data, the irregular recording of deaths proved a source of error. Nevertheless, a determined attempt to tabulate and check all deaths in selected registration cities in 1880 and in later censuses revealed a large surplus of births in every place.[14] At the turn of the century, despite widespread alarm over declining birth rates, the surplus was increasing as improvements in sanitation and other health measures reduced the death rates.[15]

Perhaps the most startling cumulative figure was the urban total of 12,346,900 natives of foreign or mixed parents in 1910—most of them born in cities. They numbered nearly 30 per cent more than the foreign-born living there. Until 1900 these Americans born in immigrant families crowded the lower-age brackets, where they generally outnumbered the children of native parents in cities of 25,000 and upward; less than 8 per cent of all under fourteen were foreign-born. Despite the great influx of adults during the eighties and their deferred marriages, the number of children was sufficient in 1890 to keep the median age for such cities at slightly under twenty-four years. The median rose to twenty-six or twenty-seven as this generation matured during the next two decades; by 1910 the age distribution of the offspring of the foreign-born closely resembled that of those born of native parentage, among whom their own children were now counted. That year the second-generation Americans outnumbered natives of longer standing, even among adults, in most cities of 100,000 or more, though they did not as yet equal the foreign-born adults there or in smaller places.[16]

The study of urban census data received greater attention as the period drew to a close, but no statistical analysis could depict the rich complexity of the human elements that peopled the American city.[17] As the decades advanced, the immigrant tide became increasingly diversified. By 1880 Germans had displaced the Irish as the dominant minority in most of the great cities, and these two groups continued for another decade to hold first or second place in all but Boston and Detroit, where Canadians, taking second place, outnumbered the Germans and the Irish respectively, and at Minneapolis, where Canadians took second place to the Swedes, with Norwegians a close third. This was only the beginning, for the next decade saw eastern and southern Europeans crowding the poorer districts of all major cities. By 1900 the Poles had become the second largest minority in Buffalo and Milwaukee; the Austrians held that position in Cleveland, the Russians in Baltimore, the Italians in New Orleans, and the British in Los Angeles.[18]

The increased representation of these later arrivals became more striking after the turn of the century. Many of their predecessors were achieving positions of influence not only in such centers of concentration as St. Louis, Chicago, and Milwaukee, but in a host of other places. In San Francisco the wide diversity from the start deprived any one group of a leading role and gave the community a cosmopolitan character. In Minneapolis, on the other hand, the Scandinavians were sufficiently numerous to overshadow other immigrant groups; they played an active role in the city and made it, in effect, the Scandinavian capital of America, the center of Swedish and Norwegian papers, churches, and seminaries.[19]

In most cases, however, the immigrants, who generally arrived after the city's development was well launched, crowded into the poorer districts, where lodging was cheap, or built sprawling settlements on the outskirts. These ethnic colonies, whether large or small, served as magnets for latecomers from each land. There the weary migrant could find friends able and willing to listen to his story and to help him find a job and a home. An element of chance had no doubt brought the first small groups of Poles to Buffalo, Milwaukee, and Chicago in the seventies, but within a decade these attracted thousands of their fellow countrymen, who hastily established numerous institutions and erected congenial if crowded homes often in their native style. By the end of the period Chicago's Polish district ranked next to Warsaw and Lodz in size. Several other foreign neighborhoods in the great metropolitan centers achieved a similar distinction, which encouraged the establishment of old-country churches and other institutions and fostered a nostalgic revival of native handicrafts and customs.[20]

The Russian Jews and Italians, who took first and second place from the Germans and the Irish in New York City after 1900, also crowded the work benches and labor gangs of many other places. Newly industrialized towns of modest size—some of which, like Burlington, Vermont, had escaped earlier migrations—now attracted a fresh influx from abroad. The challenge these newcomers presented to old customs often proved startling in such communities, but most northern cities had long since become familiarly patched by nationality settlements. Foreign travelers who wandered off Main Street had frequently to remind themselves that this was America and not some European country.[21]

These often quaint and sprawling "towns" which grew up within most of the larger American cities, not only accelerated urban expansion but also complicated the task of integration and created other knotty problems. The heavy concentration of immigrants in the larger cities, increasingly evident after the eighties, provided another mark of urban differentiation. Neglecting the smaller towns, which became more exclusively the home of older Americans, these newcomers converged on cities whose industrial or commercial prospects had already attracted 25,000 or more residents. They promoted, as a result, the rapid growth of both the manufacturing cities of median size and the great metropolises.[22] They also helped to blur the clear distinction between these two kinds of cities by presenting them with similar social problems.

But if foreign-language districts were not unusual in most northern cities throughout these decades, in the South and most of the West the older Americans held undisputed sway. At no time did immigrants and their children together approach in number the native populations of southern cities, which relied for their growth almost exclusively on migrants from their rural hinterlands. Most of the rapidly growing western towns welcomed newcomers from any source, but only on the Pacific Coast did the foreign-born continue to predominate among urban adults until 1890. There a small strain of Orientals added an exotic note, exciting the curiosity of European visitors and introducing grave problems of social adjustment.[23]

The increased heterogeneity of American cities created numerous problems. That immigrants made positive contributions to America's urban and industrial growth cannot be questioned, but frequently, in periods of depression or labor-management strife, their great numbers seemed to pose a serious threat in many cities. Clashing cultural traditions aggravated the situation and helped to produce occasional outbreaks of violence in which race and color were issues.

Charitable folk deplored the hardships newcomers suffered in the slums of New York, Boston, and elsewhere. They had secured the establishment of the Castle Garden reception center before the Civil War, and they continued to promote improvements in its record-taking and inspection techniques, generally with the object of safeguarding the migrants as well as the community. They organized the Castle Garden Labor Bureau in 1867 to serve immigrants and employers alike.[24]

Many other urban groups voiced demands for immigrant restrictions. Both the Knights of Labor and the Federation of Organized Trades and Labor Unions circulated petitions in the early 1880's against the importation of workers under contract. They helped to secure the passage in 1885 of the Foran Act, curbing that practice; unfortunately its terms also raised ethnic and racist issues. Anti-Catholic and anti-Jewish bodies, some open and others secret, carried on a persistent agitation, but only in times of stress did they muster much popular support. Even then their strength was insufficient to enact effective restrictive measures, for the heterogeneity of the population of most cities inhibited any widespread repression of one group.[25]

Indeed, the immigrants performed so many and such vital roles in most growing cities that they could not easily be dispensed with. Urban business groups generally opposed the first movements for restriction, and most political leaders, conscious of the importance of the naturalized voter, hesitated to advocate a closing of the gates. Possibly there were elements of greed and corruption in the early defense of the immigrants' right to enter the country, but the civic leaders and labor reformers, who at first viewed the hordes of ignorant voters and cheap laborers with trepidation, ultimately swung around to their defense. Meanwhile, the violence incited by some of the more radical immigrants turned many business leaders against all foreigners in the late eighties and early nineties. But by then a number of settlement-house workers had appeared who were able to persuade many civic reformers of the beneficial potentialities of the immigrants.[26]

The West Coast secured a check on Chinese immigration in the national act of 1882. Despite occasional disturbances, earlier migrants from the Far East had by this date settled into colorful Chinatowns in San Francisco and elsewhere. The population of these colonies remained fairly constant, while that of the surrounding cities mushroomed. As a result the Chinese, many of whom gradually shed their foreign dress and cut off their queues, acquired an accepted place as laundrymen, restaurant keepers, merchants, even bankers. Unfortunately the hostility they had encountered during the sixties and seventies flared up again in the nineties, when the arrival of a wave of Japanese peasants stimulated renewed anti-Oriental demonstrations. The sudden upsurge of this movement after 1900 accentuated the antiforeign agitation in Washington and gave it a new racist flavor. Although Theodore Roosevelt lulled the furor in Japan and on the West Coast by negotiating the Gentlemen's Agreement of 1908, a deep fissure had appeared in American democracy that threatened to mar the peaceful growth of urban communities, particularly in the Far West.[27]

Still graver problems of this kind already confronted the cities of the South. After the brief sway of Black Republicans in a few southern capitals ended in the late sixties, many uprooted Negroes drifted back to the land, thus helping to check the growth of the older towns. But as new cities arose, Negroes joined other rural migrants to develop them. By 1890 southern urban places of over 10,000 inhabitants included 700,000 Negroes, who represented 42.6 per cent of their total. More rigid restraints on their activities after that date turned many to the North, chiefly to New York and Chicago, where by 1910 Negroes comprised about 2 per cent of all residents. In border cities, such as Baltimore, Louisville, and Washington, Negroes supplied from 15 to 28 per cent of the population; in Atlanta, Birmingham, and Memphis, the new commercial and industrial centers of the South, their numbers ranged from 33 to 40 per cent. The average for all southern towns was 37 per cent.[28]

Few cities escaped incidents of friction between one ethnic group and another. In the North sharp conflicts sometimes erupted between rabid nativists and a broad assortment of foreigners; in border-state and West Coast towns, between racial groups. The cities were growing so rapidly that many newcomers, from nearby farms as well as from distant lands, jostled each other in the crowded business districts and in many residential quarters.

Several of the more strident spokesmen of the anti-immigration societies were recent comers themselves whose shouting called attention to their imperfect adjustment. Some other advocates of restriction boasted a longer American ancestry, however, and a staunch if not a very profound devotion to its traditions. It was a small body of youthful Brahmins in Boston who organized the Immigration Restriction League in 1894; their campaign for safeguards against the foreign menace posed another crucial issue to progressive civic leaders after the turn of the century.[29]

Of course the older native white stock, whose leaders had dominated the pre–Civil War cities, North and South (although from one-third to one-half of the residents of twenty-one of the larger northern towns were foreign-born in 1860),[30] had not been idle. Everywhere they had supplied direction for the great revolution in transportation and for the huge task of founding cities throughout the West. Although many felt recurrent impulses to migrate, those who sank their roots in any town, together with the recruits from rural areas, maintained an active leadership in its affairs down at least to the depression of the seventies.[31] By the end of that decade, however, when the number of places over 8000 had doubled, they had spread themselves very thin, particularly in the Northeast. As a result energetic men of Irish, German, or British birth or parentage who had founded new commercial and industrial enterprises were hastily named trustees of shaky banks, or directors of struggling corporations, to help restore the economy. Their successful efforts set a precedent for the involvement by 1910 of Jews, Scandinavians, Italians, and representatives of almost every European background in the leadership groups of one city or another.[32]

We need further data on this crucial process of leadership recruitment. By 1910 the native Americans had become such a conglomerate of ethnic stocks that no statistician could compute the formula of their origin. But whether, as some students have contended, the channels of advancement had been narrowed to favor those with "proper" family inheritances, or broadened, as others have implied, to reward individual talent wherever found, has yet to be determined.[33] Apparently some of the largest corporations, whose structure held secure over many decades, gave preference, at least in the front office, to men with antecedents in the company. This also held true of the numerous enterprises established by immigrants. Nevertheless, the sharp competition between rival firms maintained an active if not always an open market for managerial as well as technical skills, absorbing many ambitious newcomers who oftentimes supplied old companies with leadership for new commercial and industrial ventures.[34]

This receptivity to new leadership was enhanced by the mobility of all classes of Americans and of many industrial firms as well. Even successful business leaders in most cities saw their sons and daughters scatter in search of independent if not always better prospects elsewhere. Restless entrepreneurs and workers alike moved quickly, generally to larger towns, and for similar reasons. Rochester, located on major east-west arteries, may for that reason have been exceptional, but the fact that, despite its continued growth, barely 51 per cent of those listed in its 1864 Directory reappeared in that of 1869 suggests the fluidity of movement. That stability ratio fluctuated upward in Rochester, but very slowly, in successive five-year periods, to a high of 66.2 per cent for the 1899–1904 span. In 1890, when birthplaces were first tabulated, all major cities, North and South, contained persons from practically every state in the Union.[35]

Yet despite the incessant migrations to and from most American cities, many of them developed a core of stable families who acquired a disproportionate influence over their affairs. A recent study of the historical process that gave rise to "the Philadelphia Gentlemen" discloses the increasing advantage established families enjoyed as they developed traditions and institutions to conserve their economic and social fortunes. Nevertheless, even the "Proper Philadelphians" were constantly recruiting talented newcomers. And if a rising entrepreneur from another city had a better chance to break into the exclusive circles than one whose plebeian antecedents were locally known, that standard of selectivity accommodated and perhaps encouraged the mobility of the urban populace.[36]

Thus the power structure, at least of dynamically growing cities, remained open and expansive. Around the turn of the century, the parallel development of corporate monopolies and financial syndicates, and of exclusive private schools and other social institutions, tended to create an intercity patrician class which gradually absorbed the "upper uppers" of the major metropolitan centers. Yet its domination over the life of each community and its influence in the nation remained marginal. The continued emergence of a *nouveau riche* supplied a new elite, which so outnumbered the established leaders in some cities that they formed rival power structures of their own. The disdain with which most patricians regarded politics left an important urban field open to the leadership of men to whom the rough-and-tumble ways of democratic communities were more congenial. But the first efforts of many newcomers to seize power were often marked by corruption, and this situation provoked a revolt among the middle, not the upper, brackets of society, which injected a new vitality into the civic affairs of many cities.[37]

New divisions had meanwhile developed between the entrepreneurial elements of whatever origin and the now sharply distinguished wage-earning class. The fact that immigrants had from the start been more numerously represented among the wage earners gave labor a foreign tinge, but this distinction faded as their American-born offspring took their places. Only among unskilled workers, where the new immigrants still predominated, was the ethnic factor so clearly apparent as to inject issues of nationality into the economic conflicts between management and labor or between rival labor groups.[38]

In this study of the wide diffusion of urban centers we have noted the economic vitality they drew in large part from the private enterprise of their residents. Not only did the cities build the railroads and the railroads the cities, but the latter also encouraged, almost compelled, their trade arteries to develop far-reaching monopoly systems; they then fought for preferred service and, failing that, for some form of governmental control. Again, not only did the cities develop the industries and the industries the cities, but the latter also supplied the market for agricultural expansion and battled fiercely for domination over regional hinterlands. Strengthened by railroads and factories, the burgeoning urban giants developed spheres of influence where they challenged New York's control, thus contributing to the development of a new pattern of metropolitan regions. All towns shared in the increasingly integrated commercial and industrial economy which thus evolved, but each occupied a special place, not always of its choosing, in the complex urban system. Some drew strength from agricultural or mineral resources, or from an advantageous commercial location, only to find their economy controlled by outside capital or by the fluctuations of a world market. Others fattened on the stream of immigrants from abroad, or prospered as local inventors and entrepreneurs joined to exploit a profitable specialty. In either case their promoters soon discovered a necessity to apportion, if not to surrender, leadership to vigorous newcomers. The lure of the city affected every segment of the American population; stimulating a migration that exceeded all expectations, it created unprecedented densities and new civic and social problems.

II BUILDING AND GOVERNING THE CITIES

The economic and demographic forces that scattered urban centers across the map of America and hastened their growth equally affected their structure and government. As the spreading network of steam roads influenced the geographic distribution of cities, technological revolutions in communications and construction transformed their physical character. Monopoly trends that troubled commerce and industry posed a more immediate crisis in local utilities. The strain placed on municipal authorities, preoccupied by state and national political rivalries and sorely tried by the city's increasing complexity, often caused a breakdown in morale. Crude masters of political machines arose in some places, matching the Robber Barons in power and in disregard of basic democratic traditions; the flagrancy of their actions in turn helped provoke local and nation-wide movements that effectively challenged both the machines and the Barons after the turn of the century.

Meanwhile, the urban rivalries that played such a dramatic role in the economic arena acquired a more benign aspect in many civic realms. The contest for municipal excellence often inspired and sometimes assisted laggard towns to improve their services. The co-operative associations that sprang up among reformers and administrators respectively often seemed poles apart, but their conscientious strife nurtured a new democratic leadership and raised the standards of public service throughout America. Other disagreements sprang from the different and sometimes conflicting interests of expanding cities on the one hand and their smaller neighbors on the other. The economic tensions produced by the emergence of great metropolitan centers thus had their counterpart in the civic and political fields. Municipal elections acquired a new relevance that was often crucial in state party battles and became progressively more influential in national politics.

Among the more insistent civic problems was public versus private control. The question arose in respect to health, education, and social mores, as well as in the utility field. It also challenged the prerogatives of private contractors, especially the city builder. It was in the 1890's that a vision of the city beautiful appeared; and although it had some of the characteristics of a mirage, it quickened the civic spirit of many places with hopeful aspirations and launched the city-planning movement.

5. From horse cars to rapid transit

As in former decades, the forces active in building and extending the cities were private, though after the Civil War they became increasingly corporate in character. Whether a town's economy was commercially or industrially based, its business leadership generally stemmed at first from real estate interests and included representatives of old families with land holdings that dated in some cases from the first settlement. These local groups frequently controlled the banks and promoted the horse-car lines and other early schemes to encourage urban expansion. Rival factions already existed in some places and soon arose in others; investors from distant metropolitan centers increasingly vied for control over the lucrative aspects of each city's promotion.

The horse cars, which had won an established place in the streets of New York and three other American cities during the fifties, came into wide use and played a significant role in urban growth. The necessity to confine town limits to a convenient walking area disappeared, and with it the excuse for row houses and block tenements. Further technological improvements brought cable cars, trolleys, bridges, elevated railroads, and subways. These facilities made it possible to transport increasing numbers of workers and shoppers into restricted factory or retail districts every day and spurred the development of such areas in old and new cities. Improved transit also stimulated the erection of taller buildings, the consolidation of stores and factories, and the provision of great administrative hives. The resultant transformation of the central business district was hastened by the development of the telephone, the elevator, and other technological improvements that spread widely throughout the cities of America.

The rapid growth and reconstruction of cities called for the development of new techniques of government. Old building codes, concerned primarily with fire hazards and party walls, had to be redrafted to cover the new structural materials and methods. Public health advocates in a few great cities urged that standards of air space and light be included in the codes and that nuisances of height and use be banned. In the utility field, the multiplicity of conflicting bids for franchises and pleas for special favors inevitably involved many officials in shady transactions. Advantages derived from the consolidation of services weakened the public's traditional reliance on competition, but the rival advocates of public ownership and public control raised a doctrinal controversy that postponed action in many places.

Horse-car lines appeared in all large cities during the sixties and in most of those over 50,000 by 1880.[1] Not only did they encourage tradesmen to build homes one or two miles out from the center, but the increased volume of business they brought downtown also stimulated the reconstruction of the central district for commercial use and the replacement of old tenements with factories or warehouses. Brick or stone commercial blocks three to five stories high, some with the newly introduced cast-iron fronts, many with mansard roofs, arose in the downtown districts even of small cities.[2] Modest frame houses, often with the currently popular Gothic trimmings, spread over the outer wards of cities on the Great Lakes; brick or stucco houses, each in its separate yard, rivaled those of wood in other growing towns and predominated where lumber was scarce. Building-and-loan societies, having demonstrated their utility at Philadelphia before the Civil War, numbered 5485 in 1900, when their average assets exceeded $100,000.[3]

Only a few of the larger ports and some inland cities whose terrain limited the use of horse cars, such as Cincinnati, Pittsburgh, and Jersey City, continued to erect tenements or row houses. Philadelphia and Baltimore specialized in the latter and, despite the monotony of their streets, spreading out endlessly over the former suburbs, attracted praise for their high percentages of home ownership. Other old towns, notably Boston and Newark, had evolved a rival pattern for congestion before the Civil War—the four-story "three-decker." These buildings, constructed of wood or brick on the balloon frame, with upper-story porches decking the front or rear, stacked families vertically in more-or-less airy structures that now found a place in many growing communities. The forerunners of later apartment houses, they seemed especially appropriate along busy horse-car lines where a conversion of the first floor to commercial use often increased the owner's revenue. St. Louis and

Chicago, hard-pressed for space before their new transit improvements arrived in the nineties, erected two- or three-deckers in almost solid rows of city flats that approached New York in density.[4]

The men who directed a town's real estate and transit developments often influenced the course of its expansion as well. At Rochester, for example, a nurseryman on the southeast border joined with a town-lot promoter on the northwestern outskirts to build and operate the first horse-car line in 1863. Although that pioneer transit company proved unremunerative, its chief backers sold many house lots and diverted the city's growth from an earlier east-west direction. When competing promoters joined the company during its financial crisis, they quickly added other lines to serve their subdivisions, and the organization of several building-and-loan societies fostered the construction of hundreds of modest cottages on the outskirts. Meanwhile, a banker, Daniel W. Powers, erected a five-story business block at the central four corners, building it (1865–70) of cast iron as a safeguard against fire. When "Powers' Folly," as it was described at first, proved a sound venture, rival investors erected six- and seven-story blocks farther north and farther east, but Powers added first one and then a second and third mansard roof to his block and retained top place on the city skyline and a firm hold on its business center.[5]

Boston, hemmed in by the arms of Massachusetts Bay, needed land more desperately than horse cars, and found it with a great reclamation project which by 1870 had filled in much of Back Bay and permitted a broad extension of its residential area. Horse-car lines raced into the new territory and carried many migrants from the formerly pleasant South End and West End to the popular three-deckers of a new South Boston or to the finer homes of Back Bay. The old South End and West End were quickly inundated by an overflow of immigrants from the still older North End. Once-elegant houses, made over to accommodate several families, sprouted additions that crowded their lots and gradually deteriorated into wretched slums. Fortunately an opportunity to clear the Fort Hill section in South Boston for commercial expansion presented a hopeful solution.[6]

New York City was much too large to escape congestion, and few of those directing its expansion had any such a goal in mind. Several of its twelve horse-car lines in operation at the close of the Civil War, were backed by men interested in promoting real-estate holdings. The extension of these or new lines into the "Shantytown" above Forty-second Street, where a miscellaneous horde of squatters had appropriated undeveloped acres, brought a rapid construction of solid rows of three-

and four-story flats. Soon only those who commuted by ferry or by the steam trains could enjoy the luxury of a secluded villa, for the built-up district extended too far for daily trips by horse car to the outskirts. Instead, along upper Broadway and newly favored Fifth Avenue, fine houses shouldered each other in solid ranks of brownstone fronts. Residents of more modest circumstances tended to live near their work, since the city's three most important industries, clothing, tobacco, and retailing, were widely dispersed and encouraged the development of the distinctive neighborhoods for which New York became famous.[7]

Despite this industrial and commercial decentralization, New York's increasing population and business created such an acute demand for speedier transit that during the seventies two companies finally overrode all obstacles and built four elevated railroads. The fortunes to be won or lost through the operation of these facilities precipitated bitter legislative and court battles and gave rise to numerous scandals. Embarrassed by boodling city officials, the advocates of public ownership lost out to those who still hoped to preserve competition in the transit field.[8] The first Rapid Transit Commission, created in 1875 to supervise their operation, finally saw the elevateds completed but could make no beginning on the proposed subways.[9]

The tardy progress of New York's transit facilities was reflected in the congestion of its built-up sections. A survey by a Citizens Association in 1864 inspired the adoption of the first tenement-house law three years later. But its standards proved so inadequate and its enforcement so lax that renewed agitation for better sanitary arrangements in new housing produced a second law in 1879 requiring windows in every room and other minimal provisions. Unfortunately, the four- and five-story tenements, later described as dumbbell apartments, that arose on New York's narrow but deep lots, though they provided shallow air shafts in compliance with the law, set a pattern of urban density unrivaled elsewhere and spread, as Christopher Tunnard has put it, like a scab across most of Manhattan.[10]

Brooklyn, which shared so many of Gotham's problems as well as its potentialities, pinned its hopes in these years on the construction of the Brooklyn Bridge. After long battles for legislative approval and municipal support and the seemingly endless years of construction, interrupted by the death of its designer, John A. Roebling, and the illness of his son and successor, the great span, the longest suspension bridge in the world, was completed in 1883. The vast crowd at its dedication on May 24 foreshadowed the throngs that crossed and recrossed it daily by foot, private vehicle, or on the public railroad that soon connected with the first elevated in Brooklyn. The latter steamed through the heart of the city, challenging horse-car lines that already exceeded Manhattan's in length.[11]

So many American cities had grown up at advantageous river sites that bridges and ferries had become vital to their internal as well as their external traffic. Railroad bridges were the first to span the major rivers—the Ohio at Cincinnati, the Missouri at Kansas City and Omaha, and the Mississippi at St. Louis. The Mississippi bridge, the last of these to be completed, was opened in 1874. In Philadelphia the first major bridge built with city funds carried Chestnut Street over the Schuylkill in 1863 and remained for many years the longest and most elegant cast-iron structure in America. Boston spanned the Charles River, Pittsburgh the Allegheny, Rochester the Genesee Gorge, St. Paul and Minneapolis the Mississippi; New York and Brooklyn built several more bridges across the East and Harlem rivers. Other cities crossed lesser streams in great number with newly designed cantilever, wrought-iron or steel arch, and concrete bridges. By 1909 there were 365 that exceeded 500 feet in length.[12]

San Francisco relied on ferries to cross the Bay to Oakland, where the railroads from the East terminated, but it took the lead in solving a problem facing many hilly towns when in 1872 it scaled Nob Hill with cable cars. Their success spurred the construction of other hill-climbing cable lines, and a decade later Chicago built one that turned corners. Soon forty cities, eager to reduce the congestion of horse-drawn traffic in the business district, followed suit, notably Philadelphia and New York.

The great cost of the cable cars stimulated a search for substitutes. Although a compressed-air motor installed at Rome, New York, failed to attract backers, Thomas A. Edison and his associates successfully developed an electric motor (following an earlier one in Berlin) and demonstrated it at Menlo Park, New Jersey, in 1881. Edison was soon diverted to electric lighting, but Frank J. Sprague, one of his early technicians, continued the search for a practical electrical engine and formed an independent company. Several experimental installations followed, and Richmond, Virginia, which gave Sprague a contract in 1887, gained the credit of opening early the next year the first extended electric-trolley service. Twenty-five other electric lines commenced operation within a year. Investors looking to the future began to take a new interest in the franchises and management of the old horse-car companies.[13]

Fortunately the trolley, whose greater speed permitted longer trips, arrived in time to check the renewed congestion that threatened many cities. Whereas the horse-car lines totaled only 4060 miles by 1890, the electrics reached 15,000 within their first decade (when 909 companies reported nearly 48,000 cars, twice the number of passenger coaches on all steam railroads).[14] In some cases even this extension proved tardy. Commuters by steam roads exceeded 5,000,000 annually in each of the ten largest cities by 1890; moreover, despite the flight to the suburbs which this traffic indicated, as many as one-fourth of the wards in seven of these places showed densities that year of 100 or more per acre. Eight wards in New York exceeded 200 per acre; one had 543.[15] Only Chicago among the largest cities escaped such congestion, but its apparent good fortune arose in part from the fact that commercial and industrial enterprises used many acres in most of its crowded residential wards, thus reducing their statistical densities.[16]

Chicago's rapid growth, based on a vigorous exploitation of its commercial and industrial potentials, not only brought a host of competing railroads to its center but also scattered stockyards, lumber yards, foundries, and machine shops, and other miscellaneous industries along their routes and the river docks. The pattern of its industrial growth, more chaotic than that of cities with fewer transport facilities, foreshadowed the fate of many others. Detroit, for example, experienced a similar dispersal of factories and warehouses in the early 1900's. The trolley lines likewise spread the downtown commercial districts of many towns, pulling them out in endless shoestring extensions along the major arteries.[17]

The blight these uncontrolled land uses cast over residential properties was especially severe at Chicago, where the steel bands of crisscrossing rail lines entrapped whole neighborhoods. A Citizens' Association was organized there in 1880, comparable to earlier bodies in New York and Boston, but its effort the next year to insert standards of light and ventilation into the building code proved futile.[18] Yet as evidence of worsening slums in Chicago, as well as in New York and Boston and a few other cities, began to command the attention of local and national leaders, Congress ordered a special investigation of urban blight in 1892. Nevertheless, the continued extension of trolley lines and the construction of elevateds in Chicago (1892) and Boston (1894), relieved the pressure in most places; many promoters, assisted by hundreds of building-and-loan associations, undertook suburban home-building projects that diverted attention from the slums.[19]

American building programs were more powerfully influenced in these decades by technological than by humanitarian advances. The first passenger elevator, installed in a store on Broadway in 1857,[20] had been too slow and costly for wide use, but the hydraulic elevators introduced from England in 1866 proved more serviceable and, with the addition of safety devices, began to spread to inland cities a decade later. Their early use in large business blocks, such as the Powers Block in Rochester, was extended to the more luxurious hotels and apartment houses after the substitution of electricity for hydraulic power in the late eighties simplified operation.[21]

The elevator permitted the erection of taller buildings, but the most powerful impetus for them came from the engineers who introduced cast-iron and steel-frame construction. Cast-iron fronts and interior piers had spread from New York in the sixties; the use of iron piers in the walls commenced at Chicago, where the great demand for new construction after the fire of 1871 stimulated experimentation. William Jenney first erected a complete metal skeleton for the ten-story Home Insurance Building (1883–1885). Among others, Louis Sullivan had previously employed weight-bearing piers of brick, together with cast-iron window bays; he now quickly switched to iron columns and steel girders, sheathed in fireproof materials, in order to gain both a lighter appearance and greater height. Sullivan's ten-story Wainwright Building, in St. Louis (1890–1891), not only incorporated all the new techniques but also achieved architectural style.[22]

These great structures, made practicable by the transit facilities that brought huge throngs downtown, further stimulated such developments and increased the tension over their control. They also raised problems for other urban services and posed new zoning issues.

The skyscrapers, technological triumphs themselves, incorporated many smaller triumphs, for improvements in heating and lighting as well as in sanitary facilities found a ready market in such structures. But perhaps no new equipment rivaled the telephone in importance. Its invention and development during the late seventies attracted enthusiastic promoters in many cities, but the 148 companies they quickly formed had acquired barely 48,000 subscribers by 1880. During the eighties, as many of the pioneer concerns failed or merged, the subscribers increased fivefold; the telephone became a familiar accessory in most business establishments. The number of users became ten times larger in the next twelve years, when urban householders joined the subscribers. This increased demand for the service encouraged the telephone companies to boost their tolls. A subscribers' strike, such as that staged at Rochester between 1886 and 1888, could help to put an independent competitor on its feet, but the inconvenience of having to subscribe to more than one system ultimately demonstrated the merits of unification. It also underlined the need for regulation.[23]

:

The search for suitable controls was becoming an increasingly urgent aspect of urban growth. The rich profits that electric transit promised those in charge attracted a new type of investor who sought to escape old franchise restraints by means of consolidation and reorganization. When some city officials, endeavoring to retain competitive services, resisted these moves, the impatient promoters would sometimes hasten to buy the necessary votes on the council or the judicial bench.[24] The advantages of free transfers and more efficient operation favored the advocates of consolidation, while lower operating costs, resulting in part from increased passenger loads, enabled the new managers to "water the stock" without immediate protest from the public. Local directors, who hesitated to fleece their neighbors, could not resist the offers of outside magnates to buy them out. Soon a number of syndicates, headed by P. A. B. Widener, Thomas F. Ryan, W. C. Whitney, Charles T. Yerkes, and others in Philadelphia, New York, Chicago, and elsewhere, acquired control over scores of transit systems in the more populous centers.[25]

Seventy holding companies appeared, many with interlocking affiliations, all with stock to distribute and support. Not only did the pressure on local councils increase, but pleas for special favors also flooded the state capitals. Interested parties pressed a law through the Ohio legislature permitting towns to grant fifty-year franchises and hastened to procure one in Cincinnati. Similar moves in Illinois and elsewhere paled before the bold grab of 999-year franchises in Buffalo, Pittsburgh, and other boss-ridden towns. Detroit, under the alert leadership of Mayor Hazen S. Pingree, was almost the only American city to secure good service at low rates before the close of the century.[26]

Chicago's experience with its transit companies had spectacular features, but it was not atypical. Local men had taken the lead in building three major systems and several lesser ones before Yerkes arrived in the early eighties. Although an ex-convict, he soon became a vigorous agent for Widener and Elkins and other Philadelphia investors who sought an interest in Chicago's cable cars. Yerkes first acquired stock control of a North Side company and persuaded it to lease its properties to a new concern that he established. He enlisted local support for that firm in order to electrify the lines and then induced it to grant a big contract to a construction company organized by his Philadephia backers. Having thus paid them off with fat profits, Yerkes proceeded to capture control in his own right of the West Side lines. He could not so easily acquire the prosperous South Side system, but he blocked the efforts of its local investors to invade the West Side by himself securing a controlling interest in the elevated road erected there in the early nineties. His bid for a city-wide monopoly was thwarted at a crucial moment through a fearless exposure of his objectives by John M. Harlan of the Municipal Voters League. Frustrated in their struggles for domination over a unified monopoly, Yerkes and his rivals reached out and secured control of the transit lines of distant cities—Indianapolis, Los Angeles, and many in between. Again their construction companies received the modernization contracts and saddled each community with inflated capital costs.[27]

As the number of competing transit systems declined, city after city turned to the legislature or to the courts in search of lower fares, improved service, or a greater return from their franchise taxes. Massachusetts gave its railroad commission control over these companies and succeeded at least in preventing overcapitalization; elsewhere the states were slow to grant their railroad commissions jurisdiction over urban transit. New York City, after long legislative and court battles, finally reduced all fares to five cents in the late eighties, boosting the passenger totals on the four elevateds, now consolidated under the Manhattan Railway Company, to a high of 219,621,017 in 1892–93. The company not only met all debt charges but paid a handsome return on its stock, described a few years before, in a special investigation conducted by the State Railroad Commission, as a "pyramid of water." [28]

New York was more troubled by the need for increased transit services. The expansion of the cable-car system and the electrification of some of the horse-car lines brought the streets only temporary relief. Agitation for a subway revived, and a referendum under a reorganized and strengthened Rapid Transit Commission gave popular assent in 1894 to a plan for its public construction. Although litigation again delayed action there, Boston pressed ahead and three years later completed a subway approximately one mile in length under Tremont Street, thus greatly relieving congestion in its business district. Boston built two more short subways and Philadelphia one before 1910. New York opened the first stretch of its more ambitious system in 1904; when opposition from the surface and elevated companies, which had recently completed their own electrification, delayed its extension, Governor Charles Evans Hughes introduced legislation in 1907 replacing the old State Railroad Commission with a Public Service Commission that received much broader powers. Under its direction the elevated and surface lines were reorganized, and the subways reached 100 miles in length by the close of the period.[29]

The need for supervision became more urgent as the absorption of local companies into large traction systems progressed. The construction of transit lines into the suburbs and the building of interurban electric roads speeded this development. Fanning out from expansive communities, particularly in the Northeast and Midwest, these "electrics" spread urban influences through the hinterlands and threatened the trade of many steam railroads.[30] Soon several of the latter began to acquire stock control or complete ownership, not only of the interurbans but of the city trolleys as well. Communities such as Rochester, which had eagerly welcomed the new roads, hoping that such competition would compel the transit company to make improvements, found themselves in the grip of a larger monopoly. Fortunately, in Rochester's case, an appeal to the Public Service Commission, whose second division had jurisdiction over upstate utilities, became possible in 1907. Wisconsin created a similar board at this time, and thirteen other states followed during the next five years.[31]

In sum, American cities, responding to the larger opportunities of an expanding commercial and industrial economy, developed and made eager use of technological advances for internal communication and construction. But as these ingenious improvements were devised and promoted, each advance tended to create an imbalance elsewhere in the community's complex growth. Thus the horse cars and later the trolleys not only extended the living space available to growing cities of median size, enabling them to preserve the small-town pattern of detached houses, but also spurred the development of specialized factory and business districts, which permitted the reconstruction of many shabby old districts. In large and long-established metropolitan centers, on the other hand, the same facilities tended to spread the traditional pattern of tenements or row houses; the heavier traffic brought by longer lines added to the congestion of the older streets, further blighting the dwellings of their teeming residents. Yet the need for housing codes and improved sanitary regulations, first discovered in New York and Boston, received scant attention as builders and investors in these and smaller cities hid behind the principle of free enterprise.

The technological advances not only created new problems with each practical solution of an older one, but also engendered further advances in other technical fields. Transit improvements thus spurred the erection of larger and taller structures at focal points of their systems. Again a few men took the initiative, building skyscrapers that concentrated the more lucrative business function within a narrower frontage, casting an economic as well as a physical shadow over surrounding properties. But skyscrapers also brought better elevators and other technical advances and, together with the telephone, greatly improved the efficiency of the business community. They pierced but did not immediately shatter the traditionally horizontal urban skyline.

The promoters in each community seldom reached full accord on its development, and their controversies became more intense as one faction or another sought the assistance of, or sold out to, an outside syndicate. Aggressive investment groups in several metropolitan centers extended their influence widely by acquiring control of the transit and other utility services of many lesser cities. Their demands for franchises and special favors, often supported by lush bribes, broke the morale of numerous officials. Most urbanites still cherished earlier concepts of free enterprise, but many now discovered a need for regulatory authorities, not only to safeguard local interests against predatory groups from outside, but also to assure a more democratic direction of the city's growth. Free competition no longer seemed to supply the answer in the transit field and threatened to produce chaos in construction; whether the civic officials or the state could provide suitable controls remained uncertain.

6. "The shame of the cities'

Most of the individual and corporate entrepreneurs who so vigorously promoted urban growth took only an occasional interest in the traditional civic services. During the post–Civil War years they readily yielded control over such functions to local party chiefs, but the political leaders, preoccupied with state and national contests, often neglected their municipal responsibilities. Yet the rapidity of the city's rise created a host of new civic problems and so greatly intensified many old ones that fresh approaches became necessary. Early makeshift water and sewer systems had to be replaced in most towns. Police services had to be reorganized on a full-time basis and more efficiently equipped. Public health and welfare demanded greater attention, particularly in the metropolitan centers, as population density and heterogeneity increased.

So many complicated tasks awaited action by the city councils that some impatient citizens began to question their efficiency. Pleas to the legislatures brought the creation of special bodies to reorganize and direct the police, to construct and operate the water works, or to erect public buildings. This division of authority sometimes speeded action, but it also tended to dissipate responsibility and to weaken the democratic process. A widespread breakdown in civic morale occurred. Its manifestations, whether in the form of official corruption or in the laxity and even the debauchery of many citizens, were most striking in several great metropolitan centers; they also appeared in many lesser places. They gave rise to city bosses, but fortunately these in turn stimulated a counteracting civic response.

The optimism that animated economic leaders during the late sixties had almost no counterpart among civic officials. Confronted by a host of knotty problems, many of these men thought only of the end of their terms and a resumption of private life. Most communities had deferred normal improvements until after the war, not foreseeing, of course, that postwar inflation would add greatly to the cost. Some had assumed new responsibilities during the conflict, replacing their volunteer firemen with paid companies and expanding the police force because of unsettled conditions. Several towns had bonded themselves for bounties to encourage enlistments; others had pledged relief to war widows and orphans.[1]

These and other burdens increased when the end of the war released the soldiers, thousands of whom, maimed in body or spirit, formed a floating population that tramped from place to place, a constant threat to law and order and to the feeble welfare agencies. Indeed, all urban facilities seemed feeble and inadequate during the early postwar years, as growing cities endeavored to make up for lost time (or in some cases to repair wartime destruction) and to keep pace with the demands of expansion. The horse cars, pushing steadily outward, necessitated street extensions, additional lamps, and wider police and fire protection. The steam railroads, reaching into new territory, demanded local backing. New schools were required, and additional civic buildings; some communities needed new bridges, others new markets or docks. Everywhere, demands for the construction or extension of water works, the opening of sewers or additional cisterns for fire fighters, plagued the authorities.[2]

Few city councils, which shared responsibility in some places with boards of aldermen, could meet these demands promptly or cheaply. Taxes and debts mounted, and citizen tax leagues sprang up to plead for relief. Yet since many civic needs could not be postponed, other groups drafted petitions to the legislatures requesting special commissions to build new public buildings, as in Philadelphia, or new water works, as in Milwaukee. State boards were created to reorganize and supervise the police in Chicago and a dozen other towns. The resultant loss of self-government in American cities was graphically portrayed by a British scholar who calculated that the special municipal acts passed by the New York State Legislature in its 1867 session exceeded the total in England during the previous three decades.[3]

Such legislation was often beneficial in purpose and sometimes in immediate result, but its cumulative effect was to destroy responsible local government and cause chaos in urban finances. Many of the state-established independent boards had bonding powers without clear provisions for revenue, and the city debts they piled up during the postwar inflation became doubly onerous after 1873, when the value of the dollar rose as the price level declined one-third during the next five years. The fifteen leading cities, which added 71 per cent to their population in the decade following the war, experienced debt increases totaling 271 per cent in the same years.[4]

During the depression many citizens forgot their desire for improved urban services and focused on tax relief instead. Again they resorted to the legislatures, this time demanding constitutional limits on the taxing powers and bonding privileges of cities. Nine states followed New York's lead in this respect during the seventies. Many more prohibited municipal aid to corporations, including railroads; Illinois required all towns to adopt annual budgets and, except in emergencies, to adhere to them unless released by a special referendum. This system quickly attracted imitators. Some places faced bankruptcy; Memphis, a notable example, lost all powers of self-government when the state took over the task of restoring its solvency after the town's spirit was broken by a severe yellow fever epidemic in 1878. Others retrenched so drastically that corrupt politicians were able to exact their price before granting renewed demands for municipal services.[5]

Efforts to by-pass the ineffective city councils by creating bipartisan boards of public works sometimes hastened the development of boss rule. The officials on these executive boards, especially the men selected for administrative skill, were so eager to press ahead with street paving, sewer construction, and the like that they quickly learned to play politics with jobs and contracts. Some were contractors themselves, attracted into municipal service partly out of self-interest. They were often the only enterprising men willing to take such posts in the expanding towns. Other businessmen proved increasingly reluctant to sacrifice even a year from private activities as many had done in former decades. Experienced in the work at hand and knowing its necessity as well as its cost, such commissioners frequently awarded lucrative contracts to their own or friendly firms. "Rings" developed among these executives, the councilmen, and the legislators to pass the necessary bond issues and expedite action. Most citizens, though demanding improvements, were slow to accept the additional cost of urban services; their resistance to increased taxes or full assessments forced those in charge to resort to short-term notes and other devices that multiplied the total outlays.[6]

But if the costs of urban expansion were often staggering, many of the improvements were real. Street paving, usually of the old macadam type, was welcomed in the new low-density subdivisions where advancing lot values easily carried the special assessments, but heavily traveled thoroughfares required more durable surfaces. Although cobblestones answered that need, they proved difficult to clean and created a nerve-racking din. In 1869 New York introduced granite blocks, six by eighteen inches in size, and soon other cities, such as St. Louis and Rochester, had paved their main streets with this expensive but durable surface. Many western towns, lacking convenient quarries, resorted to wooden blocks and, when the first pavements of pine or spruce decayed, replaced them during the eighties with cedar or cypress. Brick pavements, introduced from Europe in the seventies, quickly became popular in the cities of West Virginia and Illinois, and were used in Philadelphia and Omaha a decade later.[7] Asphalt, also introduced in the seventies following earlier use in Europe, seemed at first too light for heavy traffic and too costly elsewhere, but after Washington had laid 400,000 square yards of it by 1882, Buffalo and other cities turned so rapidly to its use that its promoters tried to establish a monopoly over the supply.[8]

The maintenance of adequate pavements was complicated by the demand for other urban services. Most towns successfully laid their water mains ahead of the street improvements, though a few, such as Rochester, were tardy in this effort; but practically all soon discovered a need to tear up the streets again and again for sewers, for gas lines, and later for electric conduits. When a series of great fires at Boston, Chicago, and elsewhere speeded the efforts of lax cities to build and extend their water works during the seventies, public ownership superseded private enterprise in this field, particularly in the newer towns of the West, where the demand for improvements ran far ahead of available private capital.[9]

Most of the boards of health serving the larger cities at mid-century were emergency bodies whose activities subsided during intervals between epidemics of cholera or smallpox. However, the work of the U. S. Sanitary Commission during the Civil War and the reports of similar groups in British cities created a new interest in public sanitation. Unfortunately the discoveries during the sixties and seventies by Pasteur in Paris, by Koch in Berlin, and by Lister in Glasgow, concerning the relation of micro-organisms to various diseases, did not greatly influence the public health movement, either in Europe or America, for another decade or so.[10] Nevertheless, the joint efforts of the Sanitary and Citizens associations in New York, which conducted a wide survey of housing conditions there under the direction of Dr. Stephen Smith in 1864, finally secured the creation of a Metropolitan Board of Health free of Tammany control. Some of its medical leaders and those of the Massachusetts Board of Health began to apply a few basic sanitary principles shortly after the war.[11] Plumbing inspectors, milk inspectors, and scavengers appeared on the payrolls of several of the twenty-five cities with active health boards in 1877, but less than half even of these places had sanitary sewers, and some of those sewers emptied into streams from which other communities drew their water. Thus a local sanitary expert described Boston Harbor as "one vast cesspool, a threat to all the towns it washed." [12]

In their search for good water, most communities followed the earlier plan of tapping an upland stream, and the mounting demand increased the radius of search and the cost. A few great cities performed engineering miracles in bringing fresh water from valleys many miles distant, but most towns could not afford such works as the Sudbury, Gunpowder, and Catskill aqueducts that served Boston, Baltimore, and New York. Poughkeepsie first experimented with a filtering technique imported from England in 1872; although it successfully cleaned Hudson River water, its slow operation discouraged adoption elsewhere. The frightening spread of a typhoid epidemic from city to city along the Merrimac in Massachusetts during the eighties prompted Lawrence to install a new type of sand filter that did attract imitation. Numerous improvements followed as other towns built sand or mechanical filters within the next decade.[13] Providence established the first municipal bacteriological laboratory in 1888 (the year the Pasteur Institute was founded), and New York City introduced chlorination five years later. Over 10,000,000 American urbanites received filtered water by 1910, which helped to cut the death rates at least a fifth in New York, Philadelphia, Boston, and New Orleans, all of which had reasonably reliable statistics, and to increase life expectancy at all ages.[14]

Demands for sanitary sewers and for the treatment of their discharge followed inexorably on the completion of the water works and presented equally formidable engineering and financial problems. Ten municipalities had tried to cope with this civic need before the Civil War, and a hundred joined them before 1875, though most of their early sewers emptied into the nearest stream or bay. The cost of trunk sewers to reach a suitable discharge basin at first seemed prohibitive, but as protests against foul odors multiplied and gave rise to damage suits, and as observant health authorities in Massachusetts and elsewhere began to relate typhoid and other diseases to contaminated water supplies, citizens in many towns developed a new perspective on costs. As a result, trunk mains were built to reach an outlet beyond the city limits, sometimes a sewage farm, as at Los Angeles, more frequently a large river, or far out under a lake or bay.

Ellis S. Chesbrough, sent by Chicago to Europe in the late fifties to study the sewer and water systems of its great cities, helped in the next decade to launch an effort to reverse the flow of the Chicago river, into which the Chicago sewers emptied. With the aid of pumps and ditches, he endeavored to discharge it westward into the Illinois River in order to safeguard the lake from which the city drew its water. Although that system would have to be replaced several decades later by the broad and deep Sanitary Canal to the Mississippi, constructed at a cost of $33,000,000, Chesbrough's fame brought him a call from Boston, in 1875, to help design a system to discharge its sewage more safely into the bay.[15]

When these early engineering schemes created nuisances elsewhere, a new generation of sanitary engineers began in the eighties to devise filters and to build treatment plants that incorporated new chemical and biological discoveries.[16] As many cities assumed their responsibilities in this field during the eighties and nineties, sanitary bathrooms and kitchens with running water became standard features in new urban homes, and plumbing was installed in the better dwellings of many older districts. Lawrence adopted the first plumbing code during its struggle to curb typhoid, and other municipalities quickly followed its example. By the close of the century several communities were waging vigorous campaigns against backyard privies, and the collection of night soil had ceased in many places; yet Baltimore, for example, still had 90,000 earth closets.[17]

The health authorities, which often shared these responsibilities with the city engineers, were more directly involved in the supervision of urban milk supplies. The first inspectors appointed during the seventies, chiefly in Massachusetts, sought only to detect and prevent adulteration —a practice that increased alarmingly as the mounting city populations stimulated dealers to import milk from distant farms, often watering it generously en route. Producers who kept large herds in urban stables, feeding the closely confined cows on the mash from nearby breweries, elicited criticism from temperance advocates and prompted efforts to inspect such barns. In the eighties the discoveries of Pasteur and Koch became generally known and strengthened the demand for a careful check of all herds. Yet the first moves to inspect outlying farms, in order to guard against unhealthy cows and assure other sanitary conditions at the source, met resistance because of the city's limited jurisdiction. Another decade passed before several states, following Minnesota's 1895 example, granted urban authorities more ample powers. Meanwhile an organized attempt by some progressive farmers to protect and certify the quality of their milk achieved improved standards during the mid-nineties, notably at the Fairfield Dairy in the New Jersey sector of the New York milk shed. The earlier appearance of practical bottles and the use of steam to sterilize them, as well as the use of ice during shipment, further safeguarded consumers of the certified product, though only the rich could afford it.[18]

Technological advance came with disturbing rapidity in the lighting field. Gas lamps were already replacing those using oil in most streets and many private homes before the Civil War, and the high prices encouraged competitors, some promoting natural gas, others a new water-gas patent. The struggle for franchises to rip up the streets and for lucrative lamp contracts exerted new pressures on the councilmen. Prospects of large profits again attracted groups interested in monopoly control. The absorption of local companies into syndicates began in the eighties and soon confronted many cities with challenges to their civic and economic autonomy. Attempts in some places to halt rate increases by chartering a competitor brought inconvenience and expense as the streets were torn up for new mains; frequently, as at Rochester, the companies would merge shortly before competition commenced, and the new mains would be abandoned. Meanwhile, the development of practical electric lamps offered a new solution. These light plants, introduced at Cleveland in 1879 and at Wabash, Indiana, in 1880, multiplied as the decade advanced and not only challenged the gas companies but shadowed busy downtown streets with colonnades of poles bearing festoons of wires above the treetops. Again the pressure for franchises and street-lighting contracts, as well as the invasion of monopoly groups, compounded the difficulties of municipal government.[19]

The pressures of urban expansion alone were not responsible for the corruption that blackened the record of many growing cities during these years. Numerous moralists have depicted the city as the breeding place of vice and crime. Certainly the backwash of the Civil War and the hardships of successive depressions converged there. The outbreak of violent strikes, the appearance of local and intercity criminal gangs, the pickpockets and gamblers who followed the races from place to place, all baffled the inefficient police of the day.[20] Even in the eight cities which in the mid-sixties boasted a uniformed police force headed by a chief, conditions became so bad that appeals to the legislature brought police reorganizations under commissioners appointed by the governor. As additional towns established police departments, flagrant bursts of crime or, more frequently, shifts in political control caused administrative overturns—ten times within five decades at Cincinnati, six times at New Orleans. When, as in other civic fields, the state-appointed board gradually became a less popular solution, many of the newly drafted home-rule charters substituted an individual commissioner named by the mayor and responsible to him.[21]

Although the police multiplied, and at a faster rate than the urban population, the crime ratios mounted almost as rapidly. Few of the statistics were reliable, yet no observer could doubt the increase in crime. Only in homicide did some urban centers, particularly in the Northeast, enjoy a respite, in contrast with the frontier West and the South, where both rural and urban murders abounded. The industrial Northeast had outbursts of violence during periods of economic crisis, and numerous crimes of violence in certain immigrant neighborhoods, but it suffered most from the mounting number of offenses against property. The situation became so serious in some districts, particularly in the "little Italies" and Chinatowns of the great cities, that many merchants bought protection from the gang that seemed dominant in the area.[22]

Occasionally a corrupt police force provided such "protection" at a price, compelling the reformers to declare open war on the authorities in order to achieve a basis for good government. Thus the Reverend Dr. Charles H. Parkhurst, as president of the New York Society for the Prevention of Crime, blasted the police captains, not the saloonkeepers or the madams of the red-light district who paid them tribute. But even after Parkhurst and his colleagues, with the aid of the Lexow Commission, had exposed the extent of official corruption and had ousted the Tammany overlords, Theodore Roosevelt and his successors in charge of the revamped department, as well as conscientious police heads elsewhere, found their responsibilities baffling.[23]

Some officials began to suspect that too much was demanded of the untrained and poorly paid policemen. The introduction of alarm telegraphs in the seventies, and subsequently of police telephones; the development of specialized detective forces in the eighties; the use of mounted officers to control crowds and, in the nineties, of bicycle squads to catch speeders; the wide adoption after 1887 of Bertillon measurements for aid in identifications—all helped in the struggle of wits against the new breed of professional lawbreakers. But for every such crime there were numerous offenses by residents easily identified on the beat, and the conflicting pressures for and against arrests in these cases appeared on every hand. Even the courts generally refused to convict more than a small fraction of those apprehended.[24]

Boston discovered a constructive approach to the problem when it began in 1878 to experiment with probation. The new scheme, intended only for first offenders, soon proved so superior to either a jail sentence or a lenient discharge that several other large cities applied it informally, in co-operation with charity organization societies, before the turn of the century. Twenty urban states adopted probation laws applicable to both juveniles and adults within the next decade.[25]

The older and more widely practiced custom of handing out periodic fines against keepers and inmates of illegal brothels and gambling dens had gradually evolved in most towns into a more-or-less formal license system. Citizens who wished to eradicate these evils frequently pressed stringent laws through the legislatures, or the local councils, only to see them repealed or modified a year or so later. When the federal census tabulated brothels in 1880, their number in eighteen cities ranged from 104 in Buffalo to 517 in Philadelphia. Only four large towns displayed a clean record. Even Dr. Parkhurst doubted New York's ability to stamp out all such establishments, though his crusade against police connivance made it extremely uncomfortable for honest as well as dishonest officers who sought to take an equally reasonable stand.[26]

The arguments favoring a concentration of prostitution within carefully watched red-light districts prevailed in practice in many places. St. Louis and Cleveland experimented briefly with both registration and periodic health tests for prostitutes. In New Orleans the authorities spelled out the boundaries for such an area. That action, in 1897, came in response to the protests of many residents against the brothels and cabarets springing up in all parts of the city. An ordinance introduced by Alderman Story prohibited prostitution outside a specific section of the French Quarter; this area, soon known as Storyville, achieved fame for its sporting houses, cribs, gambling dens, and saloons, and simultaneously as the birthplace of jazz.[27] Several other ports and metropolitan centers which also attracted floating populations of travelers and pleasure seekers developed unofficial districts rivaling that of the Crescent City. One of the worst appeared in Chicago, where Gypsy Smith, the revivalist, launched a new anti-vice crusade in 1909 and instigated the first of a long series of vice commissions.[28]

The control of the saloon proved still more troublesome. Despite the persistence of temperance movements in rural and small-town areas, most earlier prohibition laws were repealed shortly after the Civil War, and subsequent attempts to incorporate temperance bans in state constitutions met defeat in all the industrial states except Ohio. A high-license plan, initiated as a compromise at Lincoln, Nebraska, in 1881, seemed promising, and numerous urban states adopted it. Some also passed Sunday-closing laws, banned music and games in saloons, forbade the hiring of female bartenders, and tried in other ways to limit the saloon's activities. Yet the high-license fees, ranging from $250 up to $1500, gave birth to a class of "speakeasies," in which liquor dealers operated nefarious dives behind closed doors, frequently with police connivance. As many as a thousand such dealers were reported at Philadelphia in 1896, when New York had four thousand who paid federal taxes on liquor sales but held no local saloon licenses. The boodle thus made available to obliging officials helped to corrupt city administrations; the New York ban against Sunday sales except in hotels transformed many saloons into makeshift brothels.[29]

A low state of public morals, springing in part from a narrow conception of individual responsibility; a resurgence of partisan politics with its frank acceptance of the spoils system; the rapid enlargement of citizen rolls without an adequate introduction to democratic principles —all helped to reveal the deficiencies and weaknesses of urban government. Several of the bosses who took over in New York during the sixties and in other troubled places a few decades later (while "the better element" pursued its private affairs) were cruder perhaps than most of the captains of industry, but close observers also found them warmer at heart.[30]

Years later a study of the characteristics of twenty city bosses described them as not only warm and often sentimental in spirit but also true to their friends and generally gay and optimistic and highly social in temperament. Springing in most cases from poor immigrant families, they surmounted many obstacles in their rise to power but seldom trampled their fellows in the process. Though they loved display and sported flashy clothes, they were not social climbers. They retained the confidence and support of early neighbors, of their boyhood gangs, and of the militia or fire brigades of their youth, as well as that of the political clubs into which they rose. At least 50 per cent Irish, Catholic, and Democratic, they were all native urbanites and generally confined their careers to their home towns.[31]

William Tweed, perhaps the worst and certainly the most notorious city boss, had eighteen years of rough-and-tumble political experience behind him when he became Grand Sachem of Tammany Hall in 1868. He had perfected the system of political rings to secure action during his early legislative terms and had helped to round up votes for important metropolitan bills that incidentally benefited his friends and swindled the public treasury of an estimated $200 million. When Samuel J. Tilden, the *New York Times,* and *Harper's Weekly* discovered and exposed the extent of his graft, Thomas Nast's ruthless cartoons aroused sufficient indignation among the voters to drive Tweed from power. He was tried and sentenced to prison. Although a few still-faithful supporters helped him flee to Europe, he was eventually recaptured and died in jail. "Honest" John Kelly, who succeeded Tweed, endeavored to remodel Tammany and at least rooted it firmly among the rank-and-file Democrats of New York City, an achievement that none of the other political clubs of the day—the Pilgrims of Philadelphia, the Choctaws of New Orleans, and similar groups elsewhere—could match.[32]

Although no other city bosses enjoyed such wide popular support as the Tammany chiefs, or needed such vast revenues to hold their organizations together, all had greedy henchmen to satisfy. Most bosses derived a steady flow of petty funds from gamblers, prostitutes, and others who sought protection. James McManes of Philadelphia and Christopher Magee of Pittsburgh both tapped such sources, but their chief boodle came through the franchises they granted to the gas and traction companies they controlled; Magee also did favors for certain railroads. The rewards the transport and utility corporations offered for special privileges and the sums they were prepared to pay to head off competition pushed some of the urban bosses to such extremes that popular protests became inevitable.[33]

Philadelphia discovered that sporadic protests accomplished little. A decade of earnest reform efforts finally deposed McManes and the Republican gas ring in 1881, but only with the aid of the state boss, Matthew G. Quay, who soon installed David Martin as the new city leader. A morass of petty corruption spread over the community; even the campaign of young Boies Penrose for a new charter to strengthen the mayor proved but a device to permit easier control by the state boss, a position Penrose coveted and later attained.[34]

The pattern of graft, as Lincoln Steffens was to discover after the forces of reform had begun to rally, revealed much concerning a city's character. Sometimes, as under "Doc" Ames in Minneapolis, its dominant feature was the corruption of the police and of degenerate citizens at the bottom. Sometimes it developed more directly from greedy citizens at the top, as Joseph W. Folk revealed after his heroic investigations in St. Louis. Sometimes it grew out of a labor movement misled by a clever demagogue like San Francisco's "Abe" Ruef, who fattened

on the pervasive moral laxity of the port city and on the slush funds
of the utilities. Sometimes it sprang from race prejudice, as at New
Orleans.[35]

It was seldom easy to uncover convincing proof of official corruption.
Such charges were exchanged so freely during election campaigns that
the public often had difficulty in distinguishing an honest and forthright
candidate from a designing tool of some vested interest. Even the noted
British scholar, James A. Bryce, learned the danger of accepting
superficial evidence of corruption. The case was clear against the
American city, and his indictment was resounding: "There is no denying," he wrote in 1888, "that the government of cities is the one con-
spicuous failure of the United States." [36] But when he became specific
and included the Honorable A. Oakley Hall, Mayor of New York City
during the reign of Boss Tweed, in his charges against the latter, Bryce
faced a suit for slander.

The incident arose two decades after Tweed's overthrow and long
after Hall had successfully defended himself in three protracted trials.
That much-bludgeoned man had repented of his earlier official complacency and had commenced in far-off London to rebuild his personal
reputation when the appearance of *The American Commonwealth* revived the old scandals. His ten-thousand-pound damage suit dragged on
for several years, to the discomfiture of both parties, and never reached
settlement. It demonstrated one significant fact, however. Hard as it was
to prove charges of corruption in court, the evidence was so widespread
that it had become equally difficult for even an innocent official (if we
grant Hall the customary benefit of the doubt) to vindicate himself. Only
forthright protests at the time could safeguard an official's reputation
and help to assure the public well-being.[37]

Alert citizens as well as officials could perhaps have avoided most of
the evils that shamed the cities of the early post–Civil War decades. Unfortunately, men with civic consciences were few in number. Those who
did give some attention to the city's affairs were generally absorbed
with the details of a specific problem, and there were more than enough
tasks to keep many men occupied. Some creditable advances occurred
in the paving of streets and in other practical aspects of the city's services. New ideas and techniques emerged in the health and safety departments of the more progressive cities; their application, however, was
still limited in practice at the turn of the century. There was little hope
for forthright civic progress while the great majority of a city's residents
remained content with boss rule.

Bosses arose most readily where democratic leadership was deficient. Some places avoided the scourge, but wherever the boss appeared he hastened to supply special services to those ready to pay for them. Yet he also provided for the community an element of continuity, if not genuine leadership, during a period when many forces worked at cross-purposes. The influx of immigrants with strange customs challenged some early American folkways that were by now incorporated into law, such as the quiet Sabbath. Growing towns also attracted a host of young unmarried men and women whose adjustment in the unsettled conditions of the period violated other laws that could not easily be enforced. The boss was not responsible for these situations, but his temptation to take advantage of them was as great as the temptation to peddle franchises. And despite the benefits he sometimes rendered in specific instances, the boss tended to pervert the powers of government.[38] Fortunately, a resurgence of democratic energies was already occurring in several cities and would soon bring widespread reform.

7. Civic renaissance

Rumblings of discontent, often free of political bias, resounded from city to city throughout these decades. Samuel J. Tilden's battle against Tweed broke out within the Democratic Party in 1871 and won success with some bipartisan support. The Citizens Municipal Reform Association, organized that same year in Philadelphia, sprang from the Republicans dominant there; although few achievements marked this effort, the seed thus planted bore fruit in 1880 in the nonpartisan Committee of One Hundred. Reform associations appeared under various names at Chicago in 1874, at Milwaukee a year later, and in numerous other places during the next decade. Their inspiration was broader than that of earlier or contemporary tax leagues, but their chief protests were directed at exorbitant outlays and other spectacular raids on the public treasury. Yet their negative approach stood little chance of permanent success in expansive towns where new civic needs constantly arose. Only in New York and Chicago had such leaders as Tilden and Franklin Mac-Veagh, envisioning wider objectives, urged before 1890 the assumption of local democratic responsibility for all municipal affairs.[1]

The local civic reformers required and progressively achieved broader support. As they sought the co-operation and encouragement of like-minded men in other places, they picked up new ideas and widened the scope of their programs. Yet they could not all agree either on principles or on objectives. Some sought technological improvements or stressed refinements in procedure; others advocated higher standards of morality or emphasized the theoretical analysis of government; still others played on popular emotions in their bid as journalists for readers or as politicians for votes. The circumstances differed in every city, and the debates that frequently broke out between dissimilar groups of reformers helped to clarify the issues and to formulate a broad program for progressive leaders whose experience in their own cities prepared them for wider responsibility in later years.

Since the city governments were chartered agents of the states, both pleas for special favors and demands for reform descended on the capitals. The decisions reached there were often based more on party strategy than on an informed appraisal of municipal needs. This tended to aggravate rather than dispose of the issues; it also impelled men of divergent interests to reconsider the democratic forms necessary and proper to growing cities.

Protests against special legislation increased after the Civil War and developed a positive objective—home rule for cities. Illinois took the initial step when its new constitution of 1870 restricted legislative interference with cities. Missouri was the first to grant complete home rule to its largest town, a move inspired by a vigorous drive in St. Louis, which adopted its home-rule charter in 1876. Agitation by a Workingmen's Party in San Francisco prompted California in 1879 to give its large cities the power to draft their own charters, subject to legislative approval. Two other western states adopted similar measures by 1892, but in the East the practice of state control through general legislation for different classes of communities prevailed. Since most states had only one city with the population stipulated for first rank, Class A legislation was special legislation, often with a vengeance, as New York City discovered. The constitution of 1894 in the Empire State did provide that no local act would take effect, if the council or mayor vetoed it, unless repassed by the legislature; few such bills were subsequently enacted, as it turned out, but many bills desired in the metropolis never received approval at Albany.[2]

The fact that urban reformers had to carry their battles beyond the city limits ultimately strengthened the movement by making it nationwide. News of a victory by the Philadelphia Committee of One Hundred in 1881 inspired similar groups to adopt that name in Albany, Milwaukee, Cincinnati, New Orleans, and elsewhere. A desire to discuss common problems with men from other towns prompted the call of a State Municipal Convention at Des Moines, Iowa, in 1877 and again in 1884. The organization of the American Institute of Civics at Boston in 1885 attracted members from several large places, and although its efforts, led by scholars, centered on the publication of a quarterly, increased attention to urban problems marked the pages of its magazine after 1894.[3] The announcement that year of the creation

of a lectureship on municipal government at the University of Pennsylvania, the first in the country, further revealed the awakening concern.
More articles discussing the conditions of city government found a place
in *Poole's Index* for the years 1882–1892 than during the preceding
eight decades.[4]

But the movement for municipal reform sprang more directly, both
literally and figuratively, from the city streets. The boodle that accompanied many paving contracts and facilitated franchise grabs focused the
attention of alert citizens on construction projects. In 1893 the local
need to rally support from other communities and the desire to compare notes prompted two simultaneous moves for a conference of civic
reformers. The Municipal League of Philadelphia, successor to the Committee of One Hundred, got its invitations out before those of the Minneapolis Board of Trade, and the convention at Philadelphia the next
January attracted delegates from twenty-nine similar organizations in
twenty-one cities.[5]

The men and women drawn together on this occasion, and to the
annual Conferences for Good City Government that followed, repre-
sented widely dissimilar movements at the start. The Baltimore and
Milwaukee groups were chiefly tax-conscious; those of Detroit and
Camden sprang from the efforts of churchmen to combat vice; in Cleve-
land and Minneapolis they represented businessmen's associations; the
Rochester reformers sought educational improvements. Only in New
York, Philadelphia, and Chicago could certain groups boast of several
years' experience, and only in the last was there a paid executive,
George E. Cole, the redoubtable leader of its Municipal Voters' League.
Yet the stimulus of the first conference prompted the organization of a
National Municipal League whose secretary, Clinton R. Woodruff of
Philadelphia, increased the number of affiliated societies from 16 to 180
by 1895. When some branches expired, new groups took up the work
in the same or neighboring cities. The annual conferences, led by such
men as James C. Carter of New York, Charles J. Bonaparte of Baltimore, Franklin MacVeagh of Chicago, Horace E. Deming and Theodore Roosevelt of New York, provided a rich educational experience
for old and new members alike.[6]

The conferences enjoyed a good press, both in the leading metropolitan papers and in home-town dailies eager to report the participation of local delegations. Several reform periodicals offered to serve the
league as its official organ and, failing that, printed lengthy articles discussing its programs. The league published the proceedings of its annual
conferences and issued several pamphlets, of which it distributed 24,000

copies in one year.[7] When the delegates rejected a plan to found a journal, the Reform Club of New York established *Municipal Affairs,* which it launched, in March 1897, with a comprehensive bibliography on the subject running to 224 pages. This first quarterly devoted exclusively to civic affairs reprinted many addresses delivered at the good-government conferences as well as the secretary's annual review of the progress of league affiliates throughout the country. The *Nation, Outlook,* and other leading journals followed these developments with interest, and local good-government clubs, reinforced by this publicity and profiting by examples and ideas from other places, tackled the problems in their own communities with renewed vigor.[8]

The delegates soon discovered that full agreement on a program for reform would be difficult. Leaders from eastern cities, where the strong-mayor plan had won favor, were surprised on their visit to Minneapolis in 1895 to discover the confidence displayed by westerners in the common council; many from both northern and western sections were embarrassed in Baltimore, two years later, to hear only optimistic reports of conditions in southern cities. Advocates of civil-service examinations for municipal employees, of government ownersihp for urban utilities, of complete home rule and other reforms, met opposition from critical delegates. Each convention rejected some of the resolutions hopefully advanced by men seeking an endorsement of their schemes. Since scattered votes could not settle the matter, the league determined, at its Louisville meeting in 1897, to create a committee to study the problem and submit a model program, including a working plan for its advancement.[9]

This program, as worked out by the committee headed by Horace E. Deming of the New York City Club, received thorough discussion and detailed criticism at the Indianapolis meeting a year later. The delegates made additional proposals and again debated and finally accepted the revised model at the Columbus conference in 1900. It incorporated much of the best municipal experience of the preceding decades. The program favored a large measure of local home rule but under state administrative supervision. It provided for a separation of powers between the council and the mayor, with the latter fully responsible for administration but directed to make minor appointments through a civil-service board. The plan placed a comptroller, chosen by and responsible to the council, in charge of an independent finance department and, more significantly, limited the taxing and bonding powers (except as used for capital expenditures on revenue-producing services) to fixed percentages of a city's assessed valuation. It restrained the council from granting franchises of more than twenty-one years' duration and required a four-fifths vote and other precautions. It called for the personal registration of all voters, a secret ballot, and the separation of local from state and national elections.[10]

Many of the ideas embodied could be traced to British or German precedents, yet almost all had previously received the endorsement of one or another American city; it was on the basis of this experience that the committee made its recommendations.[11] The evils of legislative interference had been too widely demonstrated to require debate, but the advantages of state administrative supervision were already appearing, notably in education, public health, and fiscal matters. The separation of powers, deep in the tradition of American state government, offered the pattern of a responsible executive as superior to that of inefficient council committees or of independent boards. Indeed, most of the hopeful reforms in eastern cities during the preceding two decades had endeavored to strengthen the mayor. Brooklyn had taken the most dramatic step in 1882 when it gave the mayor power to appoint his department heads without council approval. Boston and several other towns had followed this example in charter revisions during succeeding years, and some of the most creditable administrations were those of the early "strong" mayors, notably Seth Low in Brooklyn and Josiah Quincy in Boston. Both of these and Mayor Sam M. Jones of Toledo had helped to break the partisan tradition. Jones and a few others had campaigned successfully without any party backing.[12]

Similar chapters of experience supported the other proposed reforms. New York and Massachusetts had pioneered in extending the merit system to some municipal posts, and by 1897 more than a hundred cities had state or charter provisions of this sort, though the application was still limited in practice. The battles against franchise grabs had been widespread, none more determined than that of Detroit Mayor Hazen S. Pingree, whose inability to check the council's irresponsible actions had impelled him to seek the governor's chair in 1896. There he was working for just such a reform as the league now endorsed. In Chicago both the Civic Federation and the Municipal Voters' League had campaigned earnestly for franchise safeguards. In New York the Board of Estimate, though a product of Tweed's scheming, had proved its merits, but the less cumbersome independent-comptroller system, introduced at Philadelphia in 1879, had gained favor in the East. In fact, most of the model program reflected eastern experience, for it was there, where the evils of corruption had made their earliest inroads, that the most hopeful reaction had occurred.[13]

The model program exerted wide influence on subsequent charter revisions in many cities, but while the reformers were thus engrossed in the theory of good government, less idealistic politicians were capturing several of their early strongholds. Philadelphia and New York had been centers of reform effort, though neither became a stronghold. Minneapolis, on the other hand, had long considered its government a good one, and St. Louis had been the first to write its own charter. Each had its active reform club, and although the best the clubs could do was to sound an alarm after the franchise was stolen, that was often sufficient to rally support and turn the rascals out. So it proved in Minneapolis, St. Louis, San Francisco, and numerous other places. This time the story was front-page news, and when Lincoln Steffens finally pieced the details together for *McClure's Magazine* in 1902 and 1903 the whole country became aroused.[14]

The exposure of urban corruption by the popular magazines broadened the movement for reform. The muckrakers, as they were called—Steffens, George K. Turner, Josiah Flint, and David Graham Phillips, among others who specialized in aspects of urban corruption—stressed moral rather than technical issues. Their sensationalism, although disparaged by some reformers, stirred up many citizens unmoved by the sober advocates of charter revisions. Some good-government clubs whose business and professional leaders acquired additional responsibilities grew conservative and opposed the efforts of such reform mayors as "Golden Rule" Jones in Toledo and Tom Johnson in Cleveland. Others reached working agreements with the local boss, as in Rochester, where George Aldridge's promise to keep hands off the schools brought a truce that seemed for a time preferable to the preceding stalemates.[15]

Many practical problems demanded increased attention, both from city officials and from their reformer advisers. Although most officials hesitated to attend the annual conferences of the National Municipal League, their need for contact with other urban officials prompted the organization in 1897 of a League of American Municipalities. One of its early actions was to endorse a move by the older league to standardize municipal accounting systems. Both groups created committees to work with the U. S. Department of Commerce and Labor, which was endeavoring to compile such statistics; by 1902 they had prepared a model schedule, which Baltimore, Boston, Cambridge, and Chicago promptly put to use. Ohio and other states required reports to state auditors, and a National Association of Comptrollers reinforced the drive a year later. Soon more than a fourth of the cities over 30,000 in size had brought their fiscal reports into conformity with the recommended standard.[16]

Other practical reforms promised additional benefits. A standardization of assessment practices was widely advocated though with little effect, but the action of the League of American Municipalities in creating a bureau of information to serve as a clearing house for all cities proved useful and made Des Moines, where the bureau was located after 1903, a center of stimulation for several years.[17] The National Board of Fire Insurance Underwriters drafted a classification schedule to guide local boards in rate fixing; during the nineties the schedule helped direct official attention to the need for specific fire precautions and for more exacting building codes. The spread of the Universal Mercantile System after 1902 hastened these developments, but permitted the growth of local rating practices that provoked state regulation in Kansas and New York before the close of the period.[18]

In many cities the development of efficient fire departments was a double boon. As full-time companies replaced volunteers, the riotous disturbances and political scheming that characterized the earlier clubs abated. More responsible men operated the expensive steamers that began to appear in a few large places during the sixties and spread rapidly in the next decade. Other improvements in equipment followed: swinging harnesses to speed hitching at the sound of an alarm, first used at Allegheny, Pennsylvania, and Louisville in 1870; fire boats for waterfront towns, following the lead Boston set in 1872; the alarm telegraph of 1876; the water tower invented that year and used in New York and Boston a few seasons later; the chemical engines introduced at Chicago, Milwaukee, and elsewhere in 1886. The Holly system, first installed at Lockport in 1863, required a major investment for high-pressure mains and stationary engines, but when its efficiency as a fire fighter was demonstrated in the business districts of Buffalo and Rochester during the seventies, other large cities adopted it, especially those lacking an ample supply of potable water, since any source would serve. The mechanical-ladder truck, likewise invented in the early seventies and widely adopted, was motorized in a few places along with the fire engines, as the period drew to a close.[19]

Inevitably, even the plainest practical problems often touched vested interests or involved contracts that drew the most disinterested specialists into the turmoil of politics. The simple task of cleaning the streets could require a thorough cleansing of the Augean Stables, as Colonel George E. Waring discovered in New York. After the forthright commissioner had eliminated partisan influence, he began to rebuild the morale of his men by dressing them in white and by initiating in 1896 the first public parade of New York's "White Wings." He also pressed the search for a more suitable method of garbage disposal than dumping it at sea. New York had built one of the first incinerators in America a decade before, but that costly operation on Governor's Island had been abandoned. Several other cities had experimented with reduction plants during the intervening years; and Buffalo, St. Louis, and Philadelphia derived a financial return from by-products. Waring ordered more sanitary collection carts and new dumping boats to carry ashes and sweepings into the harbor, but he decided to "reduce" the garbage. By 1902 at least ninety-seven cities (two-thirds of all over 30,000) had one or more such plants.[20]

The duty of cleaning the streets and removing garbage was shouldered slowly during post–Civil War decades. Most cities still continued in 1890 to rely on licensed scavengers or on a single contractor. After that date an increased share of the costs of street cleaning went for snow removal, since the use of trolleys in place of horse cars made it impossible to shift, as in the past, to sleighs in winter months; the public had to assume a major part of the cost. The large outlays for street sprinkling during the eighties were curtailed somewhat as the wider use of asphalt diminished the extent of macadam surface; during the nineties numerous places followed San Francisco in oiling dusty streets. The volume of night soil declined as more water and sewer mains made it possible to eliminate privy vaults and cesspools from large sections of most towns (though many persisted long after the need vanished). The resultant disappearance of scavengers threw their less lucrative services, the collection of garbage and refuse, upon the municipal officials, and more cities accepted the tasks of waste disposal.[21]

Like Waring, who in an effort to free his department of politics stood clear of partisanship, other reformers seeking a free hand in education and public health, or in municipal engineering and finance, often leaned backward to avoid political disputes outside their field of responsibility. George Aldridge quieted the opposition in Rochester by surrendering control of the schools and public health to reformers, and found that some of these men became conservative as they acquired programs to conserve; other astute bosses made similar discoveries.[22]

Some political leaders who practiced the tactics of a "good boss" learned the value of an active program of public works. The prosperous late nineties made citizens less tax-conscious than before and rekindled their desire for improvements. Those bosses who responded quickly to the changing moods of business leaders held their power more securely than such forthright mayors as Jones and Johnson, who often pressed ahead despite protests when convinced that the city's good required it.[23] Thus "Golden Rule" Jones lost his respectable backing during his second term when, despite a current hysteria against crime, he refused to have his officers beat confessions out of suspects. He won his third and fourth terms through popular support as an independent. When his opponents in the legislature drafted a bill to place the Toledo police under a state commission, Jones fought it in the courts and secured a decision setting aside all legislation for classes of cities as unconstitutional.[24]

The good-government leaders might have succumbed to their growing conservatism in most places had not the expanding empires of out-of-town monopolies challenged local independence by absorbing one utility after another. The successive stages of this development in public transit —closely paralleled in the lighting field, as Louis D. Brandeis revealed in Boston—appeared again in the case of the telephone, and other monopolies threatened to take over such public functions as street paving. Even city bosses could be infuriated by these intrusions, though their opposition disappeared when the new companies they sometimes helped organize were bought out at a profit.[25] Many of his opponents suspected that Tom Johnson had such a motive in his battle against the traction monopoly in the early 1900's, but the Cleveland mayor had read *Progress and Poverty,* and Henry George's passion had imbued him with a zest for civic righteousness. In his ten-year regime, Johnson fought for and finally secured three-cent fares for transit patrons, the largest publicly owned electric light plant in the country, and a reassessment of urban property that incorporated many of the principles of Henry George.[26]

Local telephone systems, after a slow start in the late seventies, rapidly extended their lines in the next decades and by 1902 reached over two million subscribers, mostly in cities. This growth, by facilitating communication, spurred urban expansion; but it presented new and difficult problems for municipal authorities. The American Bell Telephone Company, organized in 1880 after an agreement with Western Union, successfully absorbed most of the early licensees, yet new independents quickly sprang up. Promoters from Chicago, Cleveland, St. Louis, and elsewhere built competing local systems, most of which offered cheaper rates. Nevertheless, the more limited range of the independent companies put them at a disadvantage, especially after the Bell company successfully linked its scattered units during the eighties, and in 1899 reorganized the vast network into the American Telephone & Telegraph Corporation. Since most of the local Bell companies had received relatively unlimited franchises in the early years, the independents, organized later under charters that guaranteed cheaper service, pressed the city councils for more favorable terms in order to maintain competition. But their failure, after several vigorous attempts, to form a nation-wide network—as well as the inconvenience of having two or more local systems—emphasized the value of monopoly in this field and forced citizens to turn to the states for the regulation of rates and services.[27]

Although franchise battles and rate boycotts captured the headlines, the telephone provided a variety of municipal services that helped to transform the city. Noteworthy examples were the electric fire-alarm installations, which totaled 764 by 1902, and the police telephone units, which that year numbered 148. Meanwhile, the early practice of attaching the wires to poles erected in the streets began in the late eighties to present serious problems. The increased array of competing telephone lines, electric-light wires, and high-voltage trolley cables created hazards that brought numerous fatalities. Several companies experimented with underground cables during the early eighties, but the prospect of having their pavements torn up for competing conduits prompted a number of towns, led by New York in 1889, to plan conduit tunnels for all wires under their principal streets.[28]

This scheme, which again followed precedents in England and on the Continent, where the municipalities built the tunnels, raised anew the debate over public ownership. Since tax and debt limits generally blocked such enterprise by American cities, new franchise battles erupted in the councils. In some places competing light companies, fearful of the controls an independent tunnel company might exert, hastened to consolidate and build the facility as a unit. But such construction was costly, and at least fifteen towns, impatient to repave their principal streets, had to build the underground conduits themselves. Thus, by either public or private effort, many progressive communities cleared their major streets of poles and wires by the end of this period. And as the work advanced, the officials extended the distribution of electric street lights, which finally exceeded gas lamps in the totals reported in 1909 by the 158 cities over 30,000.[29]

The complexity of urban problems divided the good government forces into several, sometimes hostile, camps, but all contributed to the rising demand for reform, which now became a national movement. The antivice forces, led by Parkhurst in New York, formed a National Law Enforcement League in 1883. Strengthened by disclosures of the connection between vice and municipal corruption, they pressed their campaigns in many cities; in some instances they merged with the temperance crusade.[30] The tax-conscious groups, discovering the need for more accurate knowledge of the cost and value of various materials and for more efficient procedures, found a new instrument in the bureaus of municipal research established with business support in New York in 1906, in Philadelphia and Cincinnati in 1908, and in a half-dozen other places within the next few years.[31]

Many academic reformers, appalled by the corruption they discovered in both city and state legislatures, where the graft offered by utility magnates won the necessary votes from men of all parties, pinned their hopes on government ownership of essential urban facilities. They publicized the achievements of public water works and analyzed the advantages enjoyed by towns with municipal lighting plants, both gas and electric—of which there were several hundred by 1910—and the less numerous experiments in municipal transit service. A few large cities, notably Chicago, Cleveland, and Detroit, ventured into one or more of these fields, but generally it was only in the smaller places, where limited opportunities failed to attract private investment, that municipal leaders promoted the town's growth by providing urban services at public expense, as in Holyoke, Massachusetts, and Duluth among many others in the West.[32]

Yet most municipal reformers viewed public ownership with suspicion, and their fears mounted when active socialist groups or strong labor organizations developed. Advocates of municipal enterprise met little opposition when they proposed new public markets, docks, and harbor improvements, on which huge sums were spent in these years—generally with matching federal funds—for these outlays stimulated rather than supplanted private investment.[33] But when Tom Johnson pressed for public transit and public power in Cleveland, he so antagonized the business groups that they successfully blocked his bid for the governorship, although his objective in that race was one they favored—more home rule for cities. In California the good-government forces in both San Francisco and Los Angeles were frankly antilabor; to head off the rising tide of socialism they redoubled their efforts to capture control of the local governments, and of the state as well, in order, as they frankly declared, to remove a major cause of revolt by ousting the machines dominated by traction and railroad monopolies.[34]

The rival protest movements were seldom so sharply divided and often, in fact, stimulated each other. When municipal reformers, such as Joseph W. Folk in St. Louis, Charles E. Hughes in New York, Louis D. Brandeis in Boston, and Judge Ben Lindsey in Denver, among others, decided to carry the battle against corrupt machines and monopolies to their state capitals, much of their support came from men who feared that, if reforms were not effected, more serious revolts would occur. With few exceptions the leaders had come to regard state regulation as the only safeguard for the traditional democratic forms. Many drew support from the earlier Populist groups, in the cities as on the farms, and from the rising middle class whose indignation the muckrakers had awakened.[35]

It was necessary, Brandeis discovered in Boston, to muster support from every conceivable source, in order to safeguard the public interest. The strategy and generally the programs differed with each contest. When in 1900, as a self-appointed "People's Advocate," he endeavored to block the Boston Elevated's attempt to build a second subway and thus assure itself a permanent franchise, Brandeis enlisted the aid not only of the Public Franchise League but also of the Board of Trade and the Merchants' Association in behalf of public ownership and limited-term franchises. Yet after that two-year battle had been won, and other utility interests hastily pushed a law through the legislature permitting a consolidation of eight competing gas companies, Brandeis rejected the counsel of those who urged a drive in this field for public ownership. Again he marshaled support from his old allies and from new groups interested instead in preventing an exorbitant capitalization of the gas monopoly. And when the prospect of victory faded, Brandeis, sensing the need for a new approach, proposed the adoption of a sliding-scale rate, patterned after one recently devised in London, to permit both the utility and the consumers to share in the benefits of more efficient service. Although this compromise shook the confidence of some of his former backers, it weakened the utilities' opposition and won their agreement to a reasonable capitalization. That figure, when finally determined, was a compromise, too, but Brandeis maintained that he was less interested in cheap gas than in good and fair governmental techniques. The sliding-scale rate later found wide use in other progressive cities.[36]

With such men as Brandeis in their ranks, it is not surprising that progressive civic leaders refused to accept any one limited course. Henry D. Lloyd failed to merge the municipal reformers, right-wing socialists, and trade unionists into the People's Party at Chicago in 1895, yet labor often endorsed programs for urban betterment, and some good-government leaders prided themselves on maintaining cordial relations with unions. In Milwaukee, where the right-wing socialists Victor Berger and Emil Seidel had built a responsible Social Democratic Party with strong labor backing during the preceding decade, the reformers finally contributed to its first triumph in 1910. That situation, however, was practically unique. Although a sudden reversal in the monetary cycle had brought steadily mounting prices after 1898, in effect shifting economic pressure from the farmers to the wage earners, the discontent of the latter generally found other outlets. The votes that swept the progressives to victory in several strongly urban states at the close of this period came largely from the middle class.[37]

The appeal to state authority and the support for state administrative supervision ran counter to the older drive for home rule, which continued strong in the West, but many urban problems so overlapped local jurisdictions that the old formulas no longer sufficed. Cities warring against grade crossings, to cite one example, had to resort to the legislatures or the courts to compel railroads to elevate or depress their tracks or to construct bridges or underpasses, yet more than a fifth of all grade crossings in towns over 50,000 (and nearly half in all such towns in the East) were eliminated in these years.[38]

As state regulatory commissions offered substitutes for competition in the utility field, state authority answered the need of the large urban clusters for metropolitan boards to supervise the integration of water and sewer districts, port and park developments, and other services involving two or more places. Some of the first regional boards, formed in earlier years when resistance to annexation first developed, were superseded when the consolidation of cities in some cases or of city and county governments in others (a practice general in the South) provided unified administration. But soon even that wider area did not encompass all interdependent municipalities, and new appeals to the legislatures brought metropolitan authorities to supervise specific functions about New York, Boston, Chicago, and a few other core cities.[39]

Several metropolitan districts straddled state boundaries, and all towns had functions that involved them increasingly with the national government. Special federal agencies, such as the Bureau of the Census, the Bureau of Labor Statistics, the Weather Bureau, the Immigration Service, and a score of others, provided by 1900 new services especially useful to urban communities. Additional functions undertaken toward the close of the period included those of the Food and Drug Administration and the National Bureau of Standards.[40]

Among the important federal contributions in these later years was the check that President Theodore Roosevelt's Bureau of Corporations and the resurrection of the Sherman Antitrust Act placed on monopolies. More immediate relief came from the failure of unsound combines, such as the asphalt trust, which collapsed in 1902, than from specific antitrust actions, since few cases directly involved municipalities or their utilities. Yet the assertion of federal authority no doubt deterred some corporate giants from excessive predatory policies and served, like the state regulatory boards and the Interstate Commerce Commission, to safeguard local interests.[41]

Despite the increased importance of federal and especially state administrative services, the major urban advances came from local groups. Those reformers who merged with the broader progressive movement and helped to carry it to success sometimes won the initiative and the referendum for legislation affecting cities; more frequently they secured direct-primary laws, a secret and eventually a short ballot, and other safeguards against boss rule. Those who followed more conservative lines, seeking efficiency first of all, launched surveys, founded research bureaus, introduced courses on municipal administration into many colleges and even a few high schools, and promoted adult citizenship classes.[42] Others established new professional associations on national as well as regional levels, for sanitary engineers, police officials, recreation directors and the like, and supported new journals that endeavored to keep them abreast of significant developments, notably the *Review* issued quarterly by the National Municipal League after 1904.[43] Best of all, the reformers became interested in such a variety of new services and so eager for improved standards in old functions that they convinced themselves, and often the public as well, of the need for more liberal budgets, higher taxes, and more generous provisions for the city's well-being.[44]

This renewed civic vitality found expression in a surge of administrative experimentation as represented by the commission and city-manager forms of government. Galveston, Texas, introduced the former when a disastrous flood in 1901 revealed the weakness of its old council system. Though it broke with the prevailing trend toward a separation of powers, the commission plan often achieved striking results. Its adoption by one hundred communities within a decade revealed a widespread dissatisfaction with the old councils and a desire to get things done quickly. Increased emphasis on efficiency gave birth to another governmental form, that of the city manager—an expert administrator hired by a council or commission to carry its policies into action. Again, towns of modest size blazed the trail—Staunton, Virginia, and Lockport, New York, in this case—but charter revisions to permit the appointment of a city manager were under consideration in larger places as the period drew to a close. Already the National Municipal League was beginning to debate a new model program.[45]

Resort to the states for protection against predatory monopolies after the turn of the century contrasted sharply with the situation a few decades earlier, when special-interest groups had besieged the legislatures for favors. A change had come over many legislatures, and another over the cities—closely related changes. The trek to the city had been both intensive and extensive. The five northeastern states whose urban populations exceeded 50 per cent of their totals in 1870—Rhode Island, Massachusetts, Connecticut, New York, and New Jersey—ranged between 75 and 96 per cent urban by 1910; their legislatures inevitably gave major attention to city problems. Places over 8000 had also attracted a majority of the residents in nine other commonwealths scattered from Maine to California, while eight additional states approached that status.[46] Urban representation did not increase so rapidly; in fact, a deep-seated rivalry developed in several commonwealths between the leading metropolis and the rest of the state (which could include, as in New York, many upstate cities). But it was now the metropolis and not the typical urban center that was held up, and the holdup was more frequently a road block than a robbery.[47]

If the sheer weight of urban numbers helped to change the attitude of some state legislatures, it was through the earnest efforts of citizen reform groups that this was accomplished. Municipal reformers had not only captured control in many towns from more experienced politicians; they had also devised new methods of handling the troublesome issues of the day. Although inevitable compromises often induced complacency, an almost unending succession of challenges repeatedly revived the progressive citizen's ardor and enabled him to build an effective movement after the turn of the century.

Yet the businessmen, who comprised the bulk of the civic reform groups, accepted public ownership with great reluctance. They preferred to rely on private enterprise, and only in such areas as water and sanitation did they readily resort to municipal action. As a result, theoretical reformers, who saw government ownership as a means of eliminating the corruption and inefficiencies of competing utility franchises, received support only when private promoters failed to supply the desired services. Nevertheless, the persistent advocacy of public ownership reconciled business leaders to a reluctant dependence on regulatory bodies. The extension of municipal or state supervision and rate controls over utility services, and into the fields of public health and safety, represented a major response to the complexities of city life.

8. Planning the city beautiful

The civic awakening found another dramatic expression in the city-planning movement. Again its roots reached back to early beginnings, and its character reflected much foreign inspiration, for many of the leaders, like the municipal reformers, had traveled or studied abroad. Yet its nourishment, like that of the broader movement, came from the vital forces building American cities. Imaginative architects and citizen groups took the initiative and, except in the case of public parks, achieved most of the limited advances of this period. As the popular demand for parks developed, public officials responded with enthusiasm and in some places with generous appropriations.

Home-building operations, however, remained largely in private hands. Here the owners of large blocks of urban real estate vied for the preference of the affluent groups or endeavored to extract the maximum return from buyers and renters of lesser means. The old custom under which most residents built their own houses gave way with the emergence of building trades and contractors. Despite improvements resulting from this specialization, standards of workmanship fluctuated, and shoddy materials were sometimes used. The first efforts to prescribe construction codes and other regulations met strong resistance; nevertheless a vision of the city beautiful began to win official endorsement after the turn of the century.

The movement had a slow beginning. Most townsite promoters and land speculators who laid out new communities after the Civil War were interested solely in quick profits. They divided the land into the convenient lots of a simple rectangular pattern. Subdivisions plotted along the highways radiating out from the more expansive cities followed a similar scheme. The speed with which these street plans were registered left many irregular plots undeveloped and broke the symmetry of the gridiron pattern. As a result many new residential neighborhoods retained open tracts where lads could play or their parents could plant truck gardens or pasture a cow. These breathing spaces did not last long in the larger places, where expanding industries, forced to move from downtown lofts, appropriated the more accessible plots for new factory sites. A few communities, notably Indianapolis, avoided some of this haphazard growth by extending official street plans on paper, but even in such cases absentee ownership and other circumstances retarded the improvement of large sections and gave most American cities an "unfinished" appearance in the eyes of foreign visitors.[1]

The unfinished appearance was not so disturbing as the prospect that all the land would soon be occupied. New York, alerted to that danger during the early fifties, had created a park commission to acquire and plan Central Park. The fortunate appointment of Frederick Law Olmsted as park superintendent had placed an imaginative disciple of A. J. Downing and an admirer of Liverpool's Birkenhead Park in full charge. As the romantic charm of his informal design and natural planting became evident with the passing years, Olmsted's reputation spread. A trip to the West Coast in 1864 brought commissions to design a cemetery at Oakland and a park at San Francisco; the next year found him back in New York planning Prospect Park for Brooklyn. Groups in a dozen cities were pressing for public parks and Olmsted received invitations to help with such developments in Newark, Albany, Buffalo, and Chicago, among others, and to advise on street layouts in Cambridge and several new suburban towns. It was during these years that Olmsted and the Central Park Commission drafted the plats for street extensions north of 155th Street to the Yonkers city line in Westchester, and in 1871 provided for the elimination of all railroad grade crossings in the area, the first such plan in America.[2]

While Olmsted continued to accept new commissions, other men appeared who shared some of his inspiration and skill. Calvert Vaux, brought from England by Downing, worked closely with Olmsted until 1872 and served as consultant to the New York parks in later years. H. W. S. Cleveland of Boston prepared plans for Chicago and Minneapolis parks; J. Weidermann, a landscape architect from Switzerland, designed one for Hartford. Philadelphia's Fairmont Park, started decades before as a modest preserve for the municipal reservoir, was vastly extended and developed, with the advice of Olmsted and others, by the Fairmont Park Art Association organized in 1872. Schemes for connecting boulevards lined with trees, sometimes with a mall down the center, won approval in several places as links between two or more parks, notably at Chicago. Detroit in the eighties laid out an encircling driveway patterned somewhat after the great boulevards Haussmann had built around Paris a few decades earlier. The most ambitious project of this sort evolved slowly at Boston, where Olmsted began in 1878 to devise plans for Back Bay Park that served as the nucleus for the Fenway Park System organized under the Metropolitan Park Board of 1895. Kansas City commenced that year to redesign a neglected cliff area, to clear two nearby slums for parks, and to connect them by tree-lined boulevards.[3]

Fortunately the enthusiasm for trees developed before some of the principal highways leading out from many expanding towns were closely built up. Improvement associations in most of the larger cities hastened to embellish one or more such avenues with elms or other shade trees. Commonwealth Avenue in Boston, laid out over new ground with a broad park strip down the center, was the most spacious, but Euclid Avenue in Cleveland, Delaware Avenue in Buffalo, East Avenue in Rochester, Prospect Avenue in Milwaukee, Summit Avenue in St. Paul, Canal Street in New Orleans, each won fame during the late sixties and seventies for the elegance of its mansions and the promise of its foliage. Other streets, aspiring to local residential favor, planted trees, too, and when the city park commissions appeared a decade or so later they generally assumed responsibility for such plantings. By the close of the century many places large and small could boast of the trees that shaded their residential streets.[4]

Except for Commonwealth Avenue, where the promoter's building restrictions and the pressure of eager and wealthy residents produced an architectural development comparable to that along the boulevards of Paris,[5] the great American avenues displayed a profusion of styles as each mansion strove to outrank its neighbors in the number of turrets, dormer windows, pillars, or mansard roofs.

The landscape architects and their backers were experimenting in a few exclusive suburbs with unified designs rich in promise for the future. Llewellyn Park, laid out in South Orange, New Jersey, in 1853 and built during the next fifteen years in the romantic Downing-Gothic style largely by Alexander J. Davis, seemed an impractical model. Yet Riverside, designed by Olmsted for a 1600-acre tract nine miles from the heart of Chicago, displayed the same romantic spirit, and when the first homes by Calvert Vaux began to appear there in 1870, the charm of its gently curving residential drives inspired a few other suburban planners to abandon the gridiron pattern. The passion for the picturesque evident in these lavish plans slowly gave way to a more practical conservation of the natural landscape, especially where an irregular terrain offered possibilities. Nevertheless promoters of subdivisions for the wealthy, such as the Country Club District in Kansas City, or of exclusive suburbs like Tuxedo Park near New York, continually strove for display.[6]

Of course these expensive plans had little influence on contemporary building for the wage-earning class. The older mill-town pattern of large dormitory tenements had lost favor in the North and failed to invade the new company towns in the southern Piedmont or elsewhere. In their place, modest single or semidetached houses, with occasional stretches of row houses, squatted endlessly along bleak hillsides or crowded into close patches of checkerboard streets. A few companies, as we have seen, broke boldly with this tradition and established carefully planned towns for their workmen. Pullman, the most famous, was built south of Chicago in the mid-eighties by a single architect who borrowed his pattern from the Krupp works in Essen, Germany. Vandergrift, near Pittsburgh, another satellite modeled on Essen, escaped, through Olmsted's advice, some of the monotony and congestion at Pullman; but the sections assigned to unskilled workers in each of these and similar places scarcely excelled the meanest miner's patch in facilities and fell far below in light and space. Only after the turn of the century did a few industrialists or groups of residents launch tree-planting and gardening campaigns that brought a degree of charm to such company towns as Peace Dale, R. I., and Hopedale, Mass.[7]

Except for street trees, trends toward landscaping had less effect on urban residential patterns at this time than the newly introduced "French flats," which stimulated the development of the apartment house. The Stuyvesant, erected in 1869 at 142 East Eighteenth Street in New York (where it stood until 1958) was the first of many residential structures that sprang up in cities across the land as the popularity of apartment-house life increased with the improvement of elevators and plumbing fixtures.[8] These multiple dwellings for the upper middle class of large towns supplied models that could be simplified for their poorer neighbors. Alfred T. White's Homes Buildings and Tower Buildings, erected in Brooklyn and New York in 1877 and 1878, inspired other limited-dividend projects there, at Boston, and elsewhere; but the movement gained little headway compared with similar developments abroad. Except in small places, where many workmen still built their own homes,

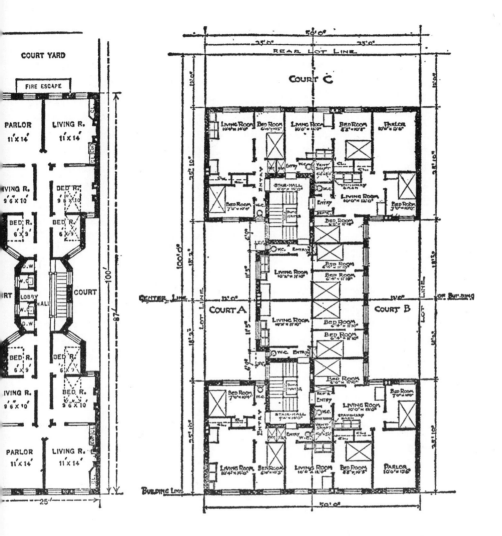

5. (LEFT) The Dumb-Bell Tenement Plan, 1879. *De Forest and Veiller,* The Tenement House Problem, *Courtesy of The Macmillan Co.*

6. (RIGHT) New Law Tenement House Plan, 1901. *De Forest and Veiller,* The Tenement House Problem, *Courtesy of The Macmillan Co.*

most urban residents of low or modest incomes had to share the houses and tenements abandoned by the more affluent migrants to the suburbs.[9]

New York was most severely afflicted, of course, and most conscious of its problem. So rapid was the city's growth that improved transit served only to spread congestion; moreover, the elevateds helped to blight endless miles of new construction on the approved dumbbell pattern. The 15,000 tenements despaired of in the late seventies more than doubled within a decade, as Jacob Riis discovered, and housed over a million residents. The first state Tenement House Commission of 1884 secured a new revision of the building code in 1887, abolishing privy vaults and requiring fire escapes, but even these obvious measures could not be enforced. A second and then a third commission tackled the problem. Robert W. De Forest, as chairman of the latter, finally secured the passage of a greatly improved housing law in 1901, which slightly reduced the density and required a bathroom in every dwelling apartment, in old as well as new tenements. By the close of the period vigilant inspectors had reduced the 350,000 dark rooms in old-law tenements to 76,324. But if 87 per cent of all tenement dwellings now included bathrooms, as De Forest reported, the practice of crowding two or more families into many units had erased much of the gain. The unrelieved density, as all sites were built up to an average of four stories, so intensified the demand for playgrounds that the authorities finally cleared a few of the most wretched slums for that purpose.[10]

An unfortunate result of New York's limited achievement was the adoption of its high-density building code in Jersey City, Newark, even Rochester, where conditions would certainly have permitted more spacious requirements. Boston and Chicago (and, of course, Brooklyn) shared most of New York's slum problems, and their reformers early sounded an alarm, but again the first warnings proved ineffective. A thorough investigation by Dwight Porter in Boston, sponsored by the Associated Charities in 1888, served merely to prompt further studies that led finally to a conservative tenement-house law in 1902 and a commission a year later to enforce it.[11] In Chicago, too, the authorities dawdled. The city, cleared of its nascent slums by the fires of 1871 and 1873, hastily rebuilt vast districts of shanties and two-decker flats, many with scarcely a dog path between them. The rich, who erected substantial new homes, only to see them blighted by the spreading network of railroads, soon abandoned many of them to immigrant tenants who often rented but one room per family. Although the health and building officials secured inspection powers in 1880, their supervision was lax until they were prodded by Hull-House and other Chicago settlement houses.

The first building code of 1898 was less stringent than that of New York; even the revised code of 1902 remained ineffective until the appointment of Charles B. Ball as head of the bureau five years later opened an era of vigorous enforcement. Already deterioration had spread north, west, and south, so that each "Gold Coast" had its neighboring slum.[12]

Yet the contrast between the slums of Chicago and New York in 1894 induced a complacent report on the former by federal investigators, who found those of Philadelphia and Baltimore still less congested.[13] Some local citizens, however, unacquainted with New York's horrors, were sufficiently shocked by what they discovered on public-health assignments or social-gospel missions into the byways of these cities, or those of Boston, St. Louis, Pittsburgh, Washington, San Francisco, and several lesser towns. Housing committees of their civic leagues and chambers of commerce devised model building codes, notably that for Columbus, which sought to preserve the single-family home and to assure it ample space; unfortunately, most of the ordinances failed to pass or suffered modifications that destroyed their effectiveness.[14]

A dozen cities, spurred by local charity-organization societies or by the publicity accorded to model-tenement competitions, chartered nonprofit housing companies before 1910, yet only in New York, Philadelphia, Boston, and Chicago was this work commenced. Most towns relied for housing improvement on the incentive speedier transit gave to new suburban construction, where building-and-loan associations were active. Many large cities endeavored in addition to secure improved sanitary provisions in their older districts by raising the health standards. (The early efforts of its board of health to weed out bad housing in Washington, D. C., curbed by Congress in 1880, were only partially revived after the turn of the century.) Nevertheless, the few scattered advocates of model housing gathered at New York in 1910 to organize the National Housing Association with great hopes for the future.[15] Here, as in so many other fields, a new national leadership was welling up from the city streets.

For several decades American architects had been searching for a fresh native expression. Many of the leaders, trained abroad, made varying attempts to reinterpret the historic styles in American brick and stone. Henry H. Richardson of Boston made the most significant contributions, and his expressive masonry in round arches and massive towers, though revealing a Romanesque spirit, gave dignity and grace to several churches, public and commercial buildings, and railroad stations. Through his most noted works, Trinity Church in Boston and the Marshall Field Wholesale Store in Chicago, Richardson's influence spread widely during the eighties. Meanwhile, Richard M. Hunt of New York was decorating several lavish châteaux with varied Gothic forms, while a rival New York firm, McKim, Mead & White, developed an adaptation of the French Renaissance style. The limestone and marble mansions the latter firm erected on upper Fifth Avenue and elsewhere attracted fashionable approval in the East during the late eighties.[16]

The growth of many inland cities offered rich opportunities for all architects and styles and focused attention on Chicago's Columbian Exposition of 1893, where the contest for preference reached a climax. Since the men who planned the World's Fair conceived of it as a great coming-out party to mark their city's emergence as a metropolis of the first rank, they invited the leading architects of the country to participate in its construction. A battle royal might have resulted, but Olmsted supplied a unifying ground setting, and Chairman Daniel H. Burnham of the leading Chicago architectural firm backed the proposal of eastern architects that the principal structures be designed in either Classical or Renaissance style. Although Sullivan's Transportation Building (which deviated somewhat from the pattern and received an inconspicuous position) and his recently completed auditorium downtown attracted the highest praise of some foreign critics, the impact of the full spectacle of the "White City" awakened its several million American visitors to the possibilities of city planning. Many returned home not only with a new conception of what a city plaza should look like, but also with new metropolitan aspirations for their town. The Cleveland Architectural Club, formed two years later, hastened to recommend a civic center with municipal buildings grouped around a lagoon—one of the first of a long series of repercussions from the fair.[17]

Local architects organized clubs in several places to consider the needs of their towns. The Municipal Art Society of Baltimore called a conference in 1899 which featured papers on municipal art, the city beautiful, and the need for city planning. *Municipal Affairs* gave its entire issue to the subject that December. The National Municipal League, the new American Parks and Outdoor Art Association, and the Architectural League of New York each held sessions on planning; popular journals turned from tributes to the fair to articles on the potentialities of other cities.[18] Charles M. Robinson of Rochester, author of several of these papers, published his first book on the subject in 1901 and became a leading spokesman of the city-beautiful movement.

As Robinson declared, "The city that would make itself magnificent has the whole world to draw upon." Soon the pervasive atmosphere of the Renaissance swept over America. New state capitols in Providence, Madison, Harrisburg, and St. Paul revealed the Beaux-Arts background of their architects. New libraries and art galleries in a dozen cities from Boston to San Francisco borrowed façades from French or Italian Renaissance palaces or from Greek or Roman temples.[19]

An important aspect of this movement was the emphasis it gave to the preparation of city plans for metropolitan centers and capitals. In Washington the McMillan Commission formed in 1900 and headed by Burnham, with John Charles Olmsted, McKim, and the sculptor Augustus Saint-Gaudens as members, brought a revival of the long-neglected L'Enfant design for the capital city. The enthusiasm that greeted its reports helped the commission to persuade the Pennsylvania Railroad to remove its tracks from the mall and join with the Baltimore & Ohio in building a central station. Its commanding location not only contributed handsomely to the plan,[20] but also recognized Washington's increasing services to the nation as a whole.

The concept of civic-center planning took hold first. Groups in Cleveland, San Francisco, Chicago, and other aspiring metropolises engaged the services of Burnham, the younger Olmsted, Robinson, or some other representative of the new profession to help design suitable arrangements of their municipal buildings. Study of the plans of Paris, Rome, Vienna, and other European capitals broadened this interest to include street patterns as well. Several cities discovered that one or another of the surviving turnpikes of their early days offered unexpected opportunities for radial avenues, if only an authority could strip away the ramshackle store fronts built out to the sidewalks in front of converted houses along these busy routes. Others opened their eyes in time to recapture their river banks, as at Harrisburg, or their lake fronts, as at Chicago.[21]

The local committees that blithely ordered and paid for these early plans frequently disintegrated when the experts recommended developments that threatened the private interests of influential members. But if most of these projects soon found their way into the archives, their appearance stirred sufficient interest to prompt the donation of historic monuments in some cities, memorial buildings in others. Most city councils, on the other hand, remained unresponsive to the new movement, though a few ordered more artistic lamp standards for their principal streets and made other minor embellishments.[22]

:

Many of the planners and the committees that backed them had derived their inspiration from the great plazas of European cities or second-hand from the World's Fair. They envisioned civic buildings of five or six stories with an occasional tower or dome adding interest to a skyline otherwise pierced only by church steeples. But although the fair diverted attention from the tall office buildings recently built in Chicago, St. Louis, and a few other cities, it was the depression of the nineties that temporarily checked their construction. Toward the end of the decade new business blocks began to rise to unprecedented heights in every large metropolis and in some lesser places as well.

Unfortunately the creative genius of the Chicago school, which had developed the skyscraper a decade before, had largely spent itself. Louis Sullivan produced a second fresh form, emphasizing the horizontal expanse of space, with the Carson Pirie Scott Store (1899–1904) in Chicago, and in the early nineties Clinton J. Warren improved the design of tall apartment hotels, but the influence of these and other innovators had succumbed to the fashions of the fair. Although their interior and structural patterns met urban needs and spread widely, most of the architects and builders felt it increasingly necessary to decorate the new skyscrapers with classical pillars and cornices, or with Gothic arches and towers.[23]

By 1910 more than fifty such structures, ranging in height from ten to thirty stories, had arisen in Manhattan; indeed, one already soared to forty-one and one to fifty floors. The congestion they created in the streets, plus the economic blight their shadows cast over surrounding buildings, particularly in cities of moderate growth, where all the best-paying tenants moved into the new quarters, created more problems than any of the paper plans had endeavored to solve.[24] Congress prescribed height restrictions for Washington, and in 1904 Boston followed that lead in an effort to preserve its skyline; elsewhere, except for Chicago's generous height limit of 260 feet, the use of zoning regulations applied only to traditional nuisances, such as slaughterhouses, or the storage of explosives, and still awaited judicial approval.[25]

Yet the need for responsible city planning was receiving increased recognition. New York and Boston had each attempted comprehensive street and park planning under municipal or metropolitan boards, and several legislatures followed Congress in creating committees to supervise the embellishments of their capitals. Hartford advanced a step further when it secured permission in 1907 to create the first city-planning commission. Chicago followed two years later, Baltimore and Detroit in 1910, and seven additional municipalities in the next year, as the new function achieved wider recognition.[26]

The planning function received its broadest and most realistic embodiment at Chicago. There Burnham and some of the men who had helped to design the World's Fair began in 1905 to consider the city's urgent need for improvements. A lakeside parkway, diagonal avenues, river beautification, a metropolitan park system, an integration of downtown and regional developments—all gained attention in this first comprehensive plan, which Burnham and his advisers submitted to the Commercial Club late in 1908. After much deliberation, the club moved the next June to secure its adoption, and the city council finally passed a resolution in November empowering the mayor to appoint a commission to study and promote the plan. The commission, comprised of 328 leading citizens, took seriously the job of educating the public. Its propaganda exceeded anything in urban-planning experience and achieved basic improvements in the street pattern and on the lake front. The scheme's failure to recognize the problem of the slum proved, however, a major deficiency as the years passed.[27]

This serious weakness of the city-beautiful movement was slowly becoming evident. Fortunately the depression, which had cast a shadow over the last months of the fair, had awakened other groups of citizens to the misery and squalor that darkened large sections of many growing towns. A few of the humanitarians who endeavored to tackle these problems took the initiative in calling the first conference on city planning at Washington in 1909. The problems of inadequate housing were soberly debated there, and again at the second conference a year later at Rochester, where note was taken of the garden-city movement in England. Delegates from New York, Chicago, Philadelphia, and Boston discussed the causes of congestion as it had developed in each of these and other great cities and urged the need for improved housing codes, zoning ordinances, and more basic planning.[28]

Thus the interdependence of cities so evident in the economic sphere appeared again, though with a different effect, in the civic realm. The tendency of ambitious firms in scattered places to draw together into great commercial and industrial monopolies also had its close parallel among utilities, where it aroused an even more vigorous and effective drive for regulatory controls. The incessant struggle in each large town for economic leadership had its counterpart in local political rivalries, and with increasing frequency these separate contests tended to merge. The rise of powerful city bosses, who often formed corrupt alliances with vested-interest groups, injected a moral issue and spurred the development of a good-government movement that gave birth to a new sense of community welfare. The formation of intercity associations of urban reformers, municipal officials, and town planners strengthened the civic cause and fostered the development of professional standards.

The recruitment of urban reformers and civil servants from various middle-class groups gave a practical as well as a conservative tinge to the movement. Not only did American cities, in contrast to many abroad, turn their backs on municipal socialism—except in cases where private enterprise saw no adequate returns or proved inefficient—but a major aspect of their development in these decades lay in the ingenious perfection of new civic conveniences. The inventive technology displayed here brought rising standards of safety and comfort to urban dwellers. But the drive with which utility combines based in a few great metropolitan centers seized and exploited the public-service opportunities of their own and lesser cities created problems of supervision and control often beyond the competence of the local elected officials.

The multitude of such problems increasingly commanded state and federal action. The battle to free and protect local democratic processes from political corruption joined with the protest against economic monopolies to create the progressive movement after the turn of the century. Even in less controversial matters, such as public health, the city received an enlarged share of both state and federal legislative and administrative attention; the new semiofficial associations and bureaus also helped to project local urban problems onto the national scene. Although it would be difficult to demonstrate that specific civic movements either hastened or retarded the growth of individual cities, all the movements stemmed from that widespread development, and most of them had much to do with its nature and with the volunteer spirit of American democracy. Moreover, they foreshadowed if they did not quite usher in a new era of metropolitanism and city planning.

III URBAN INSTITUTIONS AND SOCIAL TENSIONS

In addition to new problems of construction and control, the rise of the city also brought dramatic upheavals within the social fabric of most communities. The progressive transformation of the national economy as commercial and industrial revolutions swept across the land, building more and ever larger towns, challenged all citizens but especially city dwellers. Old residents and new had to battle constantly for a footing in the rapidly changing urban scene. As familiar social, economic, and even religious attitudes and relationships became outmoded, the struggle of the various classes and groups simply to maintain themselves was intensified.

Since most of the participants in the widespread urban upsurge were aggressively eager to better their positions, new and conflicting organizational patterns seemed to rival groups both desirable and necessary. Whereas merchant-manufacturers became industrialists with little change in function, craftsmen, who in the mid–nineteenth century had still expected as masters to own their own shops, had to make an entirely new adjustment after the rise of the factory system. The old unions they revived had to develop policies to meet the inrush of green hands, the introduction of improved machines, and the ruthless power drives of great pools of wealth and credit. Those who, by one route or another, entered the entrepreneurial ranks faced a many-sided conflict with their rivals, with burgeoning monopolies, and not least with the demands of their employees. Though a full analysis of this situation belongs to economic history, the rising industrial city, which we are here examining, both provided the setting and emerged as the chief product with the marks of strife deeply etched on its face.[1]

Yet the city was more than a factory or market place, and when, as frequently occurred in these decades, clashing economic forces brought widespread disaster, panic, and depression, other community forces rallied to meet the emergency and transformed themselves in the process from quasirural to urban institutions. Thus private charity, goaded by successive depressions and by numerous problems stemming from heterogeneous immigration or from urban congestion, developed new services and a clearer sense of community-wide responsibility. Protestant churchmen, beset by new scientific doubts and increasingly surrounded by agnostics or by members of rival faiths, evoked a social gospel, and many strove earnestly to work with Catholics and Jews, even with socialists, for the redemption of the city. Sometimes the initiative and the leadership came from the latter groups. The urgent need for reform, aggravated and highlighted by recurrent waves of unemployment and by the miseries of spreading slum areas, became more acute as the turmoil of city life brought an increase in crime and debauchery. Fortunately the varied and often hostile groups worked together sufficiently during emergencies to keep the social tensions on an evolutionary rather than a revolutionary plane.

Still another institution, the public school, felt the city's impact and helped to effect a progressive adjustment to its mounting complexities. Despite its many shortcomings, no other agency reached a wider segment of the urban population, or drew so many representatives of all groups into its basically democratic fold, and no other made in the course of this half-century a more effective response to the many challenges of its new situation.

9. *The workers and their unions*

The rapid growth of cities was reflected in the rising percentages of those employed in industry, trade, and the professions. Indeed, the ratio of those listed in the successive censuses under manufacturing to those engaged in agriculture climbed from less than one to two in 1870 to nearly nine to ten by the end of the period. The number in manufacturing quadrupled and waxed from 21.4 to 28 per cent of the total of those employed. Those in trade and commerce, and in the professions, too, increased even more rapidly and practically doubled their proportion of the total during these decades. These gains, made at the expense of agriculture and of domestic service, failed to reveal the more dramatic increase in wage earners as distinguished from the self-employed, particularly in the more industrialized states.[2] It is the slow emergence of this essentially urban situation and the reluctant adjustment of craftsmen to the status of employees that best explains the shifting philosophies and programs of the spokesmen for organized labor.

Of course the economic patterns of the industrial city were still undetermined in the 1860's. Neither the limited-dividend company nor the factory, the wage earner nor the union, had as yet begun to supersede the older occupational organization. Just as the rival schemes of ownership and control offered by co-operatives often seemed as promising as those of the corporation, so the workingman's party vied with the trade union as the instrument for labor action. The decision was a gradual one and hinged on the efficiency and drive of various groups in the community. The particular character of America's industrial evolution reflected not only the technological revolution and the flood of immigrants from abroad, but also the contest between the rival objectives of freedom and security, efficiency and democracy, community welfare and individual gain. These goals were not incompatible, but the devotion each inspired often made them appear so. The rapid growth of cities intensified these conflicts.

The Civil War provided a dividing line in labor trends as in other economic fields. Though there were numerous factories before the war, few of them employed as many as 300 "hands." The great majority of workshops in the sixties were small, averaging less than ten workers per establishment, with most of the men sharing the same tasks and hours as their bosses and some still living in the master's house. Even in the factories the owners knew many of their employees by name, and the latter, mostly young men or women, looked forward confidently to establishing a shop of their own (or, in the case of the 60 per cent who were women, hoped to escape the mill through marriage). But in the textile industry, as in the mines and on the railroads, this prospect of individual advancement had begun to fade because of the capital required, and there the companies were forced to rely increasingly on immigrant workmen.

Most of the craft unions organized in the early fifties or before were associations of journeymen, who expected soon to become masters, or of masters who joined for mutual benefit and to maintain standard prices and other conditions on the job.[3] For centuries their predecessors had been *the* industrialists; although the small-shop or master-journeyman system was already passing, few workmen foresaw its fate. When some craft unions disbanded at the outbreak of war, as their members enlisted or accepted wage offers far above union standards, rising prices soon placed old and new wage earners alike at a disadvantage, prompting a revival of old unions and the formation of several new ones. In a further effort to combat inflationary prices, particularly those of the coal merchants, trades' assemblies were organized, beginning at Rochester in February 1863, and spread to twenty-nine other northern cities within two years. The printers, hard-pressed themselves despite the incessant demand for war bulletins and the increased number of dailies, adopted the strategy in several large towns of compiling local family budgets, which approximated $18.50 for a family of six in New York in the summer of 1864 and generally ranged two dollars or more above the maximum wage.[4] United pressure on employers brought numerous pay boosts; the unions in a dozen places also sponsored co-operative stores to sell at cost. As the complexities of the monetary situation began to emerge, the Trades' Assembly of Louisville invited those elsewhere to send delegates to a convention in that city, where, in September 1864, a resolution favoring an increased circulation of legal-tender notes, or "greenbacks," was debated and adopted.[5]

The unions in this instance swam with the tide, but when, at the close of the war, the sudden release of thousands of veterans prompted labor leaders to propose an eight-hour day in order to share the work, the current ran strongly against them. The pioneer mechanics' ten-hour bell, located near the water front in Manhattan since 1844, had actually rung on an eight-hour schedule for a brief period during the war, but 1865 brought back its old regime (which most workmen still vainly sought).[6] Since the regulatory efforts of the craft unions, though based on an old tradition of self-discipline, ran counter to the dominant trend, they inspired the formation of local and national employers' associations to combat wage and hour demands.[7] As only a few of the trades had established national unions, leadership still came from the local assemblies where the hardships of unemployment were most apparent. This time the Baltimore assembly issued the call for a Labor Congress held there in August 1866. A dozen other city assemblies and three national unions sent delegates, as did fifty independent locals and a few friendly societies.[8]

The Baltimore congress met a month before the first International Labor Congress convened at Geneva, Switzerland, but the two bodies had little in common. Whereas the Europeans, under the leadership of Karl Marx, accepted the class struggle as a basic premise, the Americans debated practical reforms. They considered the relative merits of a political drive for an eight-hour day, advanced by Ira Steward of Boston with the object of assuring jobs for all, as against those offered by Edward Kellogg's earlier scheme for legal-tender notes, a flexible paper currency to be issued by the government in response to current labor needs. Advocates of the Kellogg proposal saw in it a means to finance co-operatives and other efforts to frustrate the monopoly power of bankers and merchant capitalists. Although the congress failed to reach a clear decision between the two plans, their proponents felt encouraged to work on a local level for both causes. The National Labor Union, set up as a permanent body at the last session, prepared to consider these and other reform schemes at annual conclaves in succeeding years.[9]

The entrepreneurial spirit of some labor leaders in the late sixties was best displayed by William H. Sylvis, who had made the shift from journeyman to master craftsman to president of the strong International Iron Molders Union. When faced by a fresh wage cut and a refusal of recognition in 1866, Sylvis initiated a dozen co-operative foundries, scattered from Troy to Louisville, and promoted other efforts to free workers from the wage system.[10] Meanwhile the Knights of St. Crispin, a secret society of shoemakers, formed at Milwaukee in 1867 and organized on a national basis at Rochester a year later, endeavored to protect their old handicraft from the dual threat of new machinery and green hands. They continued to cherish the hope of self-employment and found one manufacturer in Boston and another in Worcester ready to experiment with profit sharing. But elsewhere capitalists developed a factory system in bold disregard of old craft traditions, and the Crispins, who bucked this trend, succumbed in 1873 after several disastrous strikes.[11]

Labor was still uncertain of its course. The eight-hour movement relied on politics, but even in the Massachusetts stronghold of the Grand Eight-Hour League the results were meager. Successive congresses of the National Labor Union at Chicago, New York, Philadelphia, Cincinnati, and St. Louis looked with increased hope to political action in behalf of currency reform, which helped to prepare the way for a merger of these forces with the Patrons of Husbandry (of 1868) in the Granger movement of the seventies. The establishment by a group of clothing cutters in Philadelphia of the secret Knights of Labor in 1869 brought still another opponent of monopoly and champion of the workingman onto the urban scene.[12]

Some of the harsh realities of current economic trends were coming more clearly into view. One achievement of the labor reformers in Boston was the establishment by Massachusetts in 1869 of the first State Labor Bureau. Its statistical reports and informational studies shed new light on many subjects.[13] The European International, dominated increasingly by Marxian socialism, moved its headquarters to New York in 1872 and endeavored to strengthen its thirty scattered "sections" in America. Yet a doctrinal split within its ranks commanded such close attention from the leaders that they failed to influence a series of Industrial Congresses convened by the labor unions at Cleveland, Rochester, and Indianapolis in the early depression years. Representatives from the local trades' assemblies predominated and again devoted most of the time to a discussion of co-operatives and monetary reform. A report by the Boston delegate describing the work of the State Labor Bureau inspired a resolution in 1874 favoring such bureaus for every state as well as at the federal level. These gatherings also debated and approved voluntary arbitration; but motions to organize a political party or to affiliate with the Sovereigns of Industry, recently established at Worcester, met defeat, and the final congress in 1875 adjourned amidst great uncertainty.[14]

:

Labor's uncertainty was widely shared in the middle seventies. The spectacle of 20,000 business failures within the first three years of the depression so paralyzed the remaining enterprises that most of them sharply reduced their staffs, throwing hundreds of thousands more onto the street. A movement for co-operative stores and for other methods of pooling the resources of working people spread widely; but the hard times stifled most of these efforts and submerged many trade unions as well. In a few cities, among them Indianapolis, the trades' assemblies and other groups pleaded for work relief; the results, however, were meager.[15] An attempt by the socialists to unite the various labor factions and related protest movements at a convention in Pittsburgh in 1876 failed to attract the trade unionists; when the Knights of Labor delegates swung the vote on crucial resolutions against an independent labor party and for greenbacks and other piecemeal reforms, the socialists withdrew to form a separate Workingmen's Party, which disdained strike methods and all efforts to amend rather than supplant the capitalist system.[16] Yet the workers, finally driven to desperation in city after city by repeated layoffs and wage cuts, walked out in spontaneous strikes in textiles, coal mining, railroading, and many other occupations.[17]

Most of the strikes in these depression years failed, but since other efforts to relieve the plight of workingmen proved equally sterile, the stoppages continued and grew in intensity until, in 1877, violence at Baltimore, Pittsburgh, and other railroad centers brought the intervention of state and federal troops at several points.[18] When the soldiers, aided by a new force of company detectives, suppressed union resistance, the workers swung to the more radical advocates of political action. Local parties led by socialists polled several thousand votes in a number of cities recently torn by strikes and elected one or two candidates in Milwaukee, St. Louis, Chicago, and Cincinnati. Greenback-Labor nominees received an impressive vote in many other towns. In San Francisco the Workingmen's Party, strengthened by an anti-Chinese movement, won control of the state constitutional convention and soon captured the mayoralty as well. When most of these protest movements subsided, after the economy began to revive in 1879, the socialists split again. Some of the immigrant zealots, disillusioned by political defeats, withdrew to form the "Black International," a band of anarchists pledged to revolutionary deeds. In San Francisco, Henry George, shocked at the capital gains derived by the owners of urban land in rapidly growing communities, advanced his single-tax scheme to recapture for society the value it had added to the land.[19]

The protest movements generally reached their most extreme expression in cities that suffered a sharp check or recession. San Francisco, Los Angeles, and other western towns, which had enjoyed early booms with the approach of the railroads, turned violently against them as the new magnates endeavored to milk local resources. Thousands of Chinese, imported by the railroads as construction workers, formed a pool of cheap labor in California that threatened the standards of all workers.[20] The transport of several hundred of these Orientals across the continent to replace striking Crispins in North Adams, Massachusetts, alerted workmen generally and made union leaders, even those of foreign birth, more attentive to rank-and-file complaints against immigrant competition. When mill owners in Fall River broke a protracted strike there by importing French Canadians en masse, the potential threat of contract labor became a graphic reality. Wide protests against such actions of manufacturers and of the American Immigrant Company, organized several years before to supply cheap labor to employers, gradually brought the passage, during the eighties, of state and federal laws prohibiting immigration under contract, at first only of Chinese laborers, but finally, through united labor pressure, of any such workers.[21]

A major factor in the urban economy was the steadily rising proportion of women workers. Their total gainfully employed, other than in agriculture, multiplied fivefold between 1870 and 1910, while the number of men in this bracket increased barely four times. The women averaged five years younger than the men, and six-sevenths of them were unmarried in 1890, though the percentage of married women at work advanced in each decade and reached 10.7 by 1910, when they supplied a fourth of all employed women. Together they comprised a fifth of all nonagricultural workers at that date; their chief gains had occurred in the clerical, commercial, and professional divisions; those in domestic service declined. Only about 20 per cent were now engaged in manufacturing, but as these had concentrated in a few industries, the generally low wages and weak union traditions of women depressed standards in clothing, textiles, shoes, and certain food-processing plants. The plight of women workers had already elicited public concern, and by 1890 six states, led by New York in 1867, had adopted laws regulating their working conditions.[22]

Labor unions had meanwhile revived, establishing trades' assemblies in twenty-seven cities and thirty national or international associations during 1879. Since most of the latter were weak alliances, the assemblies continued to provide leadership. Their most effective weapon was the boycott, for a simple threat of such action by all local workmen frequently persuaded intransigent employers to negotiate.

Vigorous local unions produced several new organizing techniques. The union label, introduced by the cigarmakers of San Francisco in 1875 to combat Chinese-made cigars, proved a useful device. Unions in St. Louis and several eastern cities adopted labels and persuaded their national bodies to do likewise during the eighties. Some unions in large towns, notably the carpenters, engaged special agents to check on the presence of nonmembers at scattered construction projects. These walking delegates or business agents, the first local professionals in the movement, became a standard feature of the labor market by 1890.[23] The stronger trade groups won a restoration of predepression wage rates, which represented a positive gain because of the continued price decline; others barely maintained their standards and saw green hands take over the machine work in the new factories.[24]

Efforts by the craft unions to limit the number of apprentices left the unskilled to the more inclusive Knights of Labor. That body, abandoning its secrecy in 1881, sent organizers into the shoe, clothing, furniture, and other industries that were shifting from handicraft to factory production. Terence V. Powderly, labor mayor of Scranton in 1877, became Master Workman of the Knights two years later and, disparaging strikes, chose the boycott as his preferred weapon. By applying it on a national level, the Knights soon won concessions from several large industrial pools, but such boycotts of the products of rival producers often brought them into conflict with the local trades' assemblies. The latter established the Federation of Organized Trades and Labor Unions at a Pittsburgh conference in 1881, welcoming the participation of the Knights as well as of the national unions. But the Knights soon withdrew and devoted their energies instead to lectures, publicity programs, and huge rallies of unorganized streetcar men, freight handlers, railroad workers, even laborers in city road gangs. The Knights, unable to maintain their antistrike policies in many situations during the dislocations of the mid-eighties, developed a practice of stepping in to organize men engaged in spontaneous strikes, as in the case of the lumber-mill workers at Saginaw, Michigan. Yet their dramatic success in forcing concessions from Jay Gould on his far-flung railroad system in 1885, though it brought a sudden rush of new members to the order, relied so largely on popular support that when, a year later, a member of the Black International hurled a bomb during the Haymarket riot at Chicago, thus suddenly turning public sentiment against all labor, the hopes of the Knights collapsed.[25]

The decline of the Knights also reflected their failure to grasp several basic urban trends. The more firmly rooted local organizations of the craft unions, the benefit funds their larger dues provided, and the emphasis they placed on written trade agreements, enabled many, particularly in the busy building trades, to secure reductions in hours to nine and even eight a day without cuts in pay. And whenever the Knights successfully organized a majority in a local industry, their members began to demand independent trade-union status.[26] Many of the 700,000 or more workers swept into the order in 1885 quickly developed into trade unionists. When, at their Richmond Congress the next year, the Knights virtually declared war on the national unions, defections to the latter increased. The federation, which held its own meeting a few months later, revised its charter, simplified its name to the American Federation of Labor (A. F. of L.), and elected as its president Samuel Gompers of the cigar makers.[27]

Bitterness mounted and produced lasting divisions during the next few years. The two labor bodies, hurling invective at each other, proclaimed boycotts against products bearing each other's label. Doctrinal differences splintered the socialist movement. A semblance of unity achieved during Henry George's campaign for mayor of New York in 1886, when many socialists, single-taxers, and unionists co-operated, quickly disappeared. Though a few socialist candidates tasted minor victories in succeeding years, notably at Lynn and Haverhill, in Massachusetts, their principal effect was to precipitate a fusion of all hostile tickets, as in Milwaukee and Chicago, which strengthened the opponents of government ownership of utilities and other reform planks. The crossfire suffered by industrialists, brewers, and shoe manufacturers among others, as the rival labor federations fought over their workers, prompted a reorganization of employers' associations for more militant action and brought the "iron-clad oath," the lockout, the blacklist, and the injunction more widely into use.[28]

Yet the laboring class as a whole and the A. F. of L. in particular achieved sufficient strength during the eighties to maintain their ranks in face of the rising power of trusts and the ravages of the depression that followed. The frank acceptance of the wage system by Gompers and his fellows, who were content to work patiently for day-to-day improvements, enabled them to develop practical relationships with management. Thus the dramatic conflicts of the early nineties occurred in coal, steel, and railroading, where nascent industrial unions clashed with the great monopolies assisted both at Homestead and in the Pullman struggle by federal troops. Industrial unionism was checked; disillusioned leaders, such as Eugene V. Debs and Vincent St. John, became socialists; but men on the job turned increasingly to the trade unions. Labor tightened its belt as a result of wage cuts, and many hundreds of those made idle marched to Washington in a frustrated protest against unemployment. Yet the unions did not, as in earlier depressions, surrender their charters.[29]

Even political defeats did not prove final, for the major parties slowly adopted reforms that provided some safeguards at least to the most defenseless workers. After twelve states had followed Massachusetts in creating labor bureaus, the federal government organized one in the Department of the Interior in 1884. Soon their investigations and reports revealed conditions that could not be tolerated. Shocked at the number of children employed in certain industries, the public demanded and secured laws establishing a minimum age in seven states and maximum hours in twelve by 1890, and further improved and extended this legislation within the next decade to all the heavily urban states. Laws in thirteen states limited the hours of work by women, though only three proved enforceable. After many adverse rulings in the lower courts, the Supreme Court finally upheld the state's power to regulate hours of working women in *Muller vs. Oregon* (1908). A total of seventeen states had also, by this date, adopted some curbs on working hours for men, most of which applied only to labor on public projects.[30]

The A. F. of L. and most of its constituent bodies were less interested than the Knights or earlier groups in this restrictive legislation. The initiative for most of these measures, and the powerful backing, too, came from numerous welfare organizations: the Associated Charities, the Society for Prevention of Cruelty to Children, and the Consumers League. The league grew out of a movement to limit the hours of female clerks in stores and spread from city to city during the late nineties. Florence Kelley, its dynamic executive director; the representatives of urban settlement houses, and Ralph Easley and Seth Low of the National Civic Federation, often had to plead for labor's backing for crucial bills.[31]

Most A. F. of L. leaders, convinced that their best hope lay in a conservative business unionism, took little part even in the drive against monopoly. Labor's caution in supporting such legislation sprang from a fear, not unjustified as events soon proved, that the antitrust measures might be applied to restrain their own efforts to secure labor unity. Not only did some of the strong national unions develop techniques for dealing with a broadly extended management, they also became staunch defenders of the American system. All witnesses before the U. S. Industrial Commission in 1899 agreed that the workers they employed or represented were better off than those in European countries and that their situation had improved over that of their predecessors two or three decades before.[32] A painstaking "Inquiry by the Board of Trade of London, England," revealed, a decade later, that the wages and hours in twenty-eight of the leading industrial centers of America compared very favorably with those in British cities.[33]

State and federal investigations disclosed that the best conditions were to be found in the large factories. Almost without realizing it, labor and the reformers had shifted from attacks on to praise for the factory system. The better light and air and other sanitary provisions of the many new structures erected by the expanding industries of the eighties and nineties helped to create a new social atmosphere.

Some managers developed an enthusiasm for workmen's amenities. Introducing rest rooms, dining facilities, first aid, recreation—even shower baths in one Brooklyn factory—they made it difficult for labor unions to gain a foothold and stimulated other companies to undertake similar improvements. A few firms, notably the National Cash Register Company of Dayton, and the Westinghouse Air Brake Company in Pittsburgh, achieved model factories before 1900, and a few men, such as N. O. Nelson of St. Louis, who established suburban Leclaire, and the ironmaster George McMurty, who founded Vandergrift near Pittsburgh, made comprehensive and imaginative efforts to create ideal industrial communities. A number of others adopted profit-sharing schemes, such as those of the Pillsburys in Minneapolis and Eastman in Rochester, or signed arbitration agreements and experimented with various methods of promoting industrial peace.[34]

If model factories were still a rarity in 1900, the prevailing standards had risen high enough to stimulate the remodeling of many old mills and to justify the popular condemnation of makeshift sweatshops in scattered lofts and rookeries in the congested parts of several cities. These degenerate offspring of the old master-journeyman system had acquired their strongest hold on the clothing industry, which had been inundated by successive waves of German, Jewish, and Italian immigrants whose poverty had compelled each group to battle the others by accepting reduced wages and progressively worse living arrangements.[35] Although the unions failed to develop disciplined organizations among these workers until the close of this period, popular indignation over their plight, as revealed by official investigations and other reports, gave incentive to the humanitarian movement that was beginning to sweep through the cities of America at the turn of the century.[36]

The great labor battles of this period, over the open versus the closed shop and other issues, ravaged individual cities, notably Los Angeles, Chicago, and Pittsburgh, but failed to alter the basic relationships evolved by capital and labor during the preceding decades. Some local unions and trades' assemblies surrendered leadership to their national bodies, yet the familiar trades' policies of nonpartisanship and business unionism prevailed. In the building trades, however, the carpenters took the lead in forming city-wide councils to settle differences between their associated unions in order to present a united front in local negotiations. When the introduction of factory-made building materials challenged the old handicrafts and gave birth to rival woodworking unions, the carpenters repelled the invasion and established their supremacy in the industry.[37] The task of organizing the new machine workers received national as well as local attention; jurisdictional committees appeared on both levels as the unionization drive spread, enrolling approximately a fifth of all urban wage earners by 1904, the banner year of this period, which saw unions active in all large and many small places.[38]

Yet the transformation this upsurge might have brought to the urban economy did not occur, for a reaction had already commenced in several small, recently industrialized cities. Dayton and Fremont in Ohio, Bloomington, Illinois, Beloit, Wisconsin, Los Angeles, and other towns where new mechanical factories, as distinguished from heavy industry, had taken root, formed citizens' alliances and other agencies to combat unionization. The Dayton Employers' Association, headed by John B. Kirby, Jr., an implacable foe of organized labor, launched its antiunion drive in 1901 with two catchy slogans, an "open shop" and a "classless America." A similar movement in Sedalia, Missouri, produced the first citizens' alliance that year. Soon numerous towns and a few large cities each had its alliance pledged to the restoration of "American principles." The movement spread to St. Louis, Kansas City, Chicago, Pittsburgh, even Scranton. In 1903 the National Association of Manufacturers, organized in 1895, swung its influence to the cause. Its president, David M. Parry of Indianapolis, a vindictive but persuasive speaker, helped to found the Citizens' Industrial Association of America, with representatives from 124 employers' associations and citizens' alliances. Though the National Board of Trade and most local boards and chambers of commerce shunned active participation in the conflict, business groups, especially in small places, rallied to check if not to oust all unions, forcing a slow retreat and in some cases a complete rout of organized labor. Even the valiant efforts at conciliation initiated by the National Civic Federation, which sprang in 1900 from business leaders formerly active in the Civic Federation of Chicago, failed to halt the drive.[39]

Nevertheless the National Civic Federation exerted a moderating influence during many industrial conflicts and frequently helped to launch successful negotiations. It, too, organized branches in Pittsburgh, Detroit, Milwaukee, and Denver, among other cities, and conducted national conferences that brought prominent industrialists, such as Carnegie and Charles M. Schwab, into friendly association with union chieftains like Gompers and John L. Mitchell. Ralph Easley, the federation's untiring director, enlisted the aid of Senator Mark Hanna of Ohio and Seth Low, former mayor of New York. Serving successively as chairmen, they not only inspired the creation by Theodore Roosevelt of a Federal Conciliation Service in 1903 (a move endorsed by the mayors of 139 cities threatened by coal shortages) but also pressed a campaign to free unions from Sherman Act restraints. The federation advocated, among other legislative measures, workmen's compensation and social insurance plans already applied widely in Europe.

In 1898 the Reform Club of New York drafted a workmen's compensation bill, which labor rejected as inadequate. Similar bills failed to pass in several industrial states, though after the turn of the century Maryland and three others adopted embryonic measures, which were shortly held unconstitutional. Many new factories installed safety devices, yet industrial accidents continued, and their victims had to resort to the courts for indemnities. The only benefits available were those supplied by voluntary funds, mostly local in character. Thirty-five industrial benefit societies, 84 national unions, and some 461 local sickness funds extended partial coverage to over a million members. In contrast with the situation in the great cities of Europe, where by 1910 the vast majority of industrial workers were covered, only those who needed it least participated in these plans.[40]

The socialists, meanwhile, achieved a shaky political organization and waged a persistent educational campaign, but failed to capture any wide support from working people. A continued influx of refugee intellectuals from abroad helped to replenish socialist losses and also kept the doctrinal controversies at fever heat. Dissension within their ranks, even during the depths of the depression, defeated the efforts of Henry D. Lloyd to develop a labor coalition party in Chicago in the mid-nineties;

that fiasco speeded the socialists' break both with the Populists and with the A. F. of L.[41] The Socialist Labor Party likewise soon split, as its less radical faction joined with the previously expelled and still more moderate Social Democratic forces to found the Socialist Party in 1901. In spite of a few scattered victories, notably at Milwaukee in 1910, the major impact of the socialists was an indirect one exerted through the ministers and other humanitarians they influenced but despised.[42] The more radical De Leon faction of the old Socialist Labor Party joined the Western Federation of Miners and other dissident groups in 1905 to found the Industrial Workers of the World, which soon espoused revolutionary doctrines. Partly because of its activity in western mining and lumber centers, the I. W. W. became a symbol of violence even in eastern cities, where the hostility of most trade unionists, as well as that of municipal officials and other citizens, blocked effective intrusion.[43]

Only the right-wing socialists continued after the turn of the century to dream hopefully of co-operatives. Labor leaders accepted not only the wage system, but factories and improved machinery, too, as their drive for safety regulations, accident compensation, and shop committees demonstrated. In fact, even their demand for shorter hours had acquired a new objective—to extend the worker's leisure for personal enjoyment rather than to spread the jobs. Although neither unions nor management responded quickly to the piece-rate system and other efficiency schemes developed by Frederick W. Taylor at Philadelphia and elsewhere after 1895, both sides hoped to gain from added production.[44] If the term scientific management still seemed a bit pretentious, cost-of-living studies were increasing in number and in documentary value as the wage earner acquired not only a recognized status but also an implied right to a decent standard of living. Even the clerks in the expanding commercial stores, whose self-appointed champion was the Consumers League, began toward the close of the period to organize committees and to conduct widespread campaigns in many cities for a half-day holiday once a week during summer months. The immigrant worker monotonously tending a machine in some vast factory, though still in the majority of cases unorganized, had become, in the eyes of many humanitarians, if not yet an equal partner in the industrial world, at least a citizen endowed with potentialities that could not be disregarded.[45]

The rise of the city not only brought a great increase in the number of wage earners but also confronted them with new economic and social problems. In their efforts to secure a satisfying share of the products of their labor, the urban workers formed a variety of organizations. The trade unions, gradually emerging as the favored bodies, developed new techniques of influence and established a firm base in specific urban centers; only then did they weld bonds of unity between the workers of various industries and many cities. These trends, continuing throughout the half-century, injected another power struggle into the complex urban maelstrom and spurred the development of combative management responses.

Despite the violence that sometimes erupted in this field, the workers generally chose a moderate course in the political arena. The great productivity of their labor, in conjunction with an abundance of enterprise capital and vigorous management, achieved a steadily rising standard of living, which weakened the arguments of Marxist socialists and other extremists. Moreover, although the steady influx of newcomers from abroad continually replenished the ranks of labor and gave it a foreign tinge, the fact that many individual workers or their children still found an entry into the entrepreneurial or professional groups blurred in American cities the distinctions that prevailed abroad. Yet the strife between these broad economic divisions, though it seldom dominated local or national political contests, represented a new and potentially dangerous fissure in urban society, one that aggravated many other city problems.

10. From charity
to community welfare

Urban workingmen, despite their organizational initiative, would have faced a harder task and would perhaps have followed a different course had it not been for the activities of sympathetic fellow citizens. Although most labor leaders condemned charity and were critical of religious institutions, the character and welfare of the emerging working class was considerably influenced by the development of middle-class charities and churches. On the other hand, the workingman's hostility spurred philanthropists to found new welfare institutions designed to alleviate the hardships of the city's poor. Moreover, the socialists, as scornful of charity organizers as of bread-and-butter unionists, unwittingly stirred a countereffort to avoid the threat of class-divided communities. The measures adopted never fully relieved the misery of the unfortunate, but the spirit of good will persisted, and despite their frustrations many humanitarians displayed a sincerity and resourcefulness that eventually won the co-operation of some labor leaders.

The charities of the mid-century were as unprepared as the workingmen's associations for the changes brought by urban growth. The New York Society for the Prevention of Pauperism and similar bodies in the other leading cities had often declared that the assistance they gave should promote social adjustment, but almost the only practical work of that nature was the shipment of orphans to farm homes in the West. The orphan asylums maintained by denominational groups in eighty-one towns, as well as the homes for destitute widows, faced increased responsibilities during the Civil War. The 112 hospitals in some fifty places were similarly strained; scattered communities opened additional asylums and hospitals during the war, as well as at least twenty-five homes for disabled soldiers.[1]

The Civil War inspired the formation of several new relief agencies. Ladies' Aid Societies appeared in practically every northern city. Their members wrapped bandages, prepared kits for the soldiers, and welcomed troops passing through town; some assisted soldiers' dependents and comforted the bereaved. These groups soon drew together under the direction of the U. S. Sanitary Commission to administer service to the men in camp. Money was needed to support this work, and Lowell, Massachusetts, held the first of a long series of sanitary fairs through which the women of many cities collected a major share of these funds, which totaled $7,000,000 throughout the North before the end of the war. Meanwhile the frightful reports of the first battles challenged the energies of local Y. M. C. A.'s and moved their leaders to volunteer as temporal and spiritual counselors to the wounded. Their efforts prompted the organization of the Christian Commission, chiefly staffed by "Y" men, which ministered to soldiers in hospitals and camps. Although aid societies were less numerous in southern cities, much relief was distributed there by individuals and spontaneous groups. The "Y's" of Richmond and Charleston were especially active and organized more units among southern troops stationed nearby than appeared in all northern regiments.[2]

These humanitarian efforts, sustained by an aroused community spirit, suffered a loss of interest during the early postwar years. Some homes for disabled soldiers closed their doors within a decade, and several hospitals languished. The larger towns, however, soon discovered urgent needs for more hospitals, and philanthropic residents made generous bequests to many new ones in order to accommodate practitioners of three rival medical systems (the allopathic, the homeopathic, and the followers of Dr. Hahnemann) and three religious faiths. Even more important was the public-hygiene movement which attracted support from most of the thirty-six city health boards during the early seventies.[3] That development reflected scientific as well as humanitarian stirrings. Meanwhile the humanitarians in a number of cities established local industrial schools where the women and children left destitute by the war could find shelter and some vocational training. By 1876, when the U. S. Commissioner of Education first surveyed such activities, he collected reports from 20 industrial schools, 130 "homes for the friendless," and 200 orphan asylums.[4]

Most of these institutions served only women or children, but during the depression of the mid-seventies, when thousands of men lost their jobs, the problems of the homeless male and the destitute family commanded attention. Since the old poor laws held the towns responsible for those able to meet certain residence qualifications, local overseers of the poor distributed large sums in these depression years, though the effect was not always apparent. In growing cities, where the most recent arrivals were often the first to lose their jobs, their cries for relief presented additional difficulties. Throngs of idle men appealing for work relief spurred efforts at Boston, Chicago, and elsewhere to initiate public work projects, but their extent was limited. Several benevolent societies, organized to check excessive distributions by the overseers, found their own volunteer visitors approving unprecedented outlays and hastily disbanded. As men abandoned their families to seek jobs in distant places, a vast army of homeless migrants began tramping from place to place, challenging both the vigilance of the police and the understanding of humanitarians. Mrs. Josephine Shaw Lowell headed a New York committee to investigate the problem of the able-bodied pauper or tramp. Both public and private agencies opened soup kitchens and lodging houses in the larger cities. In New York the Affiliated Societies served over 7000 a day during the hard winter of 1873–74.[5]

Fear that these charitable activities would demoralize the "respectable" poor and encourage pauperism stimulated efforts on both local and state levels to organize private charity on a more systematic and constructive basis. Two early state boards of charity had provided useful supervision of local relief in Massachusetts and New York and in the sixties six other states created similar boards. A multiplicity of charitable societies, especially in the largest cities, also prompted moves at New York, Philadelphia, and Boston to organize a central agency where the records of all could be filed and other measures be taken to avoid duplication of effort or conflicts of policy. The Bureau of Charities in New York City secured the endorsement of 158 societies at its start in 1873 and compiled a registry of 14,000 names, but criticism by some of its affiliates brought all operations to an end within two years. Similar bureaus in Boston and Brooklyn also succumbed to internal friction. Only a Germantown bureau, which organized one Philadelphia ward that same year, persisted. The first permanent city-wide society for the organization of charity appeared at Buffalo in 1877.[6]

These developments had their antecedents in Europe. In fact both the Germantown and Buffalo efforts reflected the inspiration of the original charity-organization society founded in London in 1869. The Reverend S. H. Gurteen had participated in that pioneer venture, headed by Octavia Hill, before he came to Buffalo. His leadership there and the circulation of his reports as well as those of London helped spread the movement to New Haven, Brooklyn, Boston, and at least six other places within two years. By 1883 there were twenty-five charity-organization societies and a dozen more with similar objectives serving most of the large cities of the northeastern and north central states.[7]

Their purpose, as Miss Hill put it, was to supply "not alms but a friend." They even hoped to reduce the volume of almsgiving and all forms of outdoor relief by means of "friendly investigations" to determine the real nature of each applicant's need. The Buffalo scheme divided the city into eight districts (later four) and enrolled volunteer investigators to visit needy families within these areas. Since the society did not plan to distribute relief, it required only modest funds to support a central index. Although a few of the early organization societies did administer emergency assistance in communities lacking such agencies, the gradual revival of economic activity in the late seventies soon enabled the new bodies to report a sharp reduction in relief costs in most places. Special needs appeared, however, and Gurteen introduced, again from Europe, the penny-bank saving system to encourage thrift, the crèche or nursery for the day-care of the children of working mothers, and the provident wood yard to enable Buffalo charities to separate "the needy sheep from the shiftless goats." [8]

Buffalo and other towns of moderate size readily expanded their welfare services under the leadership of organization societies, sometimes called associated charities, but the profusion of institutions in the larger metropolitan centers made the task of integration there both more difficult and more essential. Emergencies often spurred the establishment of new agencies; when the functions were clearly defined and threatened no duplication they frequently won adoption elsewhere. Thus Societies for the Prevention of Cruelty to Animals spread rapidly following a lecture tour by Henry Bergh, founder of the first at New York in 1868 chiefly for the defense of overloaded horses. A comparable movement, beginning in 1874, to organize similar bodies for the protection of children elicited wholehearted support, though in some places the leaders sought to economize by combining the two functions in a Humane Society.[9] Homes of the Good Shepherd and juvenile reform schools increased in number.

Several organization societies issued periodicals to promote their programs. Philadelphia's *Monthly Register* appeared first, in 1880, followed by the *Bulletin* (1884) and *Lend-a-Hand* (1886), both in New York, and by Chicago's *Reporter* (1888). Most of these flourished only briefly, but the New York *Charities Review* and Baltimore's *Charities Record* (both 1891) continued into the next century. Absorbed by their major function of co-ordinating institutional activities, several organization societies neglected their visiting services, which seemed less urgent during the generally prosperous eighties.[10]

If the need for relief declined, the complexity of urban life increased and hastened the establishment of new institutions designed to work with special groups in the community. In some fields an aggressive national organization assumed the initiative, as in the case of the Y. M. C. A., whose International Committee, set up largely through the efforts of the New York "Y" in 1864, encouraged the revival of earlier associations and planted new ones in towns across the land. The fact that its leadership came in large part from New York gave the movement the broader physical-culture emphasis developed there, where the new building of 1869 featured a gymnasium and a residence for transients, yet the fervent evangelism engendered by Dwight L. Moody at the Chicago "Y" helped to animate the drive for expansion. By the mid-eighties "Y's" in nine of the ten largest cities had erected buildings equipped with a gymnasium, baths, and bowling alleys, as well as an auditorium, offices, meeting rooms, and residential dormitories; many lesser "Y's" provided some if not all of these features. Full-time "Y" secretaries increased from 14 to 111 during the seventies and included a growing number of men from business, though many still came from the clergy; the first two training stations opened in 1880.[11]

The somewhat comparable Y. W. C. A.'s multiplied without the aid of a national body. Inspired in part by British antecedents, the first groups established a young ladies' boardinghouse at New York in 1860 and six years later at Boston. The rapid increase in the number of young women who found employment in cities prompted the organization before 1875 of twenty-eight such societies under various names in America and Canada. Approximately half of them maintained boarding homes, posted job opportunities, and opened small libraries; seven offered instruction in sewing, and practically all conducted religious services. The eight cities represented at the first Y. W. conference at Hartford in 1871 increased fivefold by 1893, when thirty-two college groups also responded; most of the former associations maintained rooms and nine had gymnasiums, the oldest dating from 1884.[12]

The emphasis on evangelical affiliations that characterized some though not all of these bodies left the field open in such places, notably Boston and Buffalo, for the establishment of still another institution, the

Women's Educational and Industrial Union. Welcoming the co-operation of Unitarians, Jews, and Catholics, as well as evangelical Protestants, it sought to provide secular benefits for women in cities. Mrs. Abby Morton Diaz, who inaugurated this work at Boston in 1877, included in her program classes in English, sewing, and stenography, lectures on practical as well as cultural subjects, social entertainment for working girls, an employment agency, and a legal consultant. The union provided downtown facilities for noon lunches, with adjoining rest rooms, and opened a women's exchange where the unemployed could make articles for sale. Several Buffalo ladies, who launched the second such union in rooms rented in 1884 from the Society for the Organization of Charity, soon acquired a building of their own. At least a dozen other large towns, scattered from Providence to San Francisco, established similar unions; scores more founded women's exchanges.[13]

None of these organizations was prepared to cope with the emergencies created by the depression of the mid-nineties. A real crisis developed as the panic of 1893 brought many industrial enterprises to a halt, spreading unemployment throughout the land. Estimates of the number made idle ranged from over a half-million in sixty cities to approximately 800,000 in a second and broader urban survey; the unemployed in the three largest places on both lists exceeded 50,000 each. Public outlays, long considered too lavish, quickly proved hopelessly insufficient. The campaigns of independent relief-giving societies and, where they were lacking, the drives of the associated charities failed miserably. Subscriptions of a few thousand dollars in many communities, even of more than $100,000 in each of five metropolitan centers, seldom exceeded the total of the unemployed, including dependents; they demonstrated, in city after city, the utter inadequacy of charity as a cure for economic depression. As a result, many businessmen, as well as representatives of the Y. M. C. A.'s and the ministerial associations, joined for the first time with labor leaders in calling mass meetings to recommend action. They drafted petitions to the municipal authorities, not for charity, but for work relief; they created committees to interview industrialists and to canvass householders for part-time jobs for the idle. Efforts to stimulate employment, both public and private, occurred in cities from Boston to Denver; a few achieved noteworthy results.[14]

More new societies for the organization of charity appeared in 1893 than in any previous year. Several older ones endeavored to revive their visiting services, but most of the volunteers quickly became discouraged. Buffalo devised a new church-district plan, assigning specific visiting areas to each congregation, yet only in Boston and Baltimore, where the volunteers had developed sufficiently high standards of training to win respect, did the citizen investigators prove useful. Numerous towns established provident loan societies (based on a model in Paris), opened coffee and soup depots, and rescue missions and other cheap lodging-houses; some, following Buffalo's earlier practice, maintained wood yards or stone piles to test each relief applicant's good intentions. Mayor Pingree in Detroit plowed several vacant lots to provide potato patches for poor families, a scheme that quickly spread to other places. Indianapolis opened a public store to make relief payments in kind. Boston societies raised $136,568 to finance work-relief projects that for a time employed 7460 men at 80 cents a day. Still the hardships of the urban poor continued to increase as additional families exhausted their meager resources and joined the ranks of the destitute. Slowly the more conscientious leaders of the charity-organization societies broadened their study of pauperism into an effort to understand and remove the evils of poverty.[15]

The most fruitful centers of the new approach during the 1890's were the social settlements. These institutions, a dozen of which had already appeared in five American cities, likewise traced their antecedents to British sources, for it was Toynbee Hall, founded at London in 1883, that supplied the inspiration and the basic pattern for these ventures. The American leaders, mostly young college graduates, had also developed a strong sense of mission at home. Stanton Coit, from Amherst, heard of Toynbee Hall while studying in Europe. After a few months as the second American "resident" there, he returned in 1886 to organize the first Neighborhood Guild in the New York slums. Two of his assistants, both Smith graduates, soon joined their fellow alumna, Vida D. Scudder, an instructor at Wellesley who had visited Toynbee Hall, to open the College Settlement on New York's East Side in 1889. That venture quickly attracted the support of the five eastern women's colleges and led to the establishment of similar centers in Boston and elsewhere.[16]

Jane Addams, from Rockford College, Illinois, who also visited Toynbee Hall during a trip abroad, returned to found Hull-House on Chicago's South Side that same year. The Northwestern University Settlement in Chicago, Andover House in Boston, the University of Chicago Settlement, and Chicago Commons, all appeared in quick succession, marking the awakening concern of college and seminary groups for the urban problems at their door. Other early centers established by Episcopal, Jewish, and Presbyterian leaders included East Side House and Henry Street Settlement, both in New York, Kingsley House in Pittsburgh, and Whittier House in Jersey City. Ten more appeared during the next two depression years in these cities and at Philadelphia, Cleveland, and Buffalo, and the first Catholic settlement was established in Cincinnati.[17]

The object of the new institution was to bridge the widening gap between the classes in American cities. By sharing some at least of the everyday experiences of slum dwellers, the settlement residents hoped to lay the foundation for mutual understanding and to launch a co-operative attack on community problems. Thus Jane Addams quickly opened a music hall, an art gallery, and a kitchen at Hull-House, organized clubs for neighborhood children as well as adults, and joined eagerly in local campaigns for better garbage collection, for a playground, even for the recognition of unions and the arbitration of labor disputes.[18] Mary McDowell, the first kindergarten worker at Hull-House and first president of its women's club, soon received a call to organize the University of Chicago Settlement, where she developed these and other activities, notably a neighborhood bath house, a children's garden, and a school of citizenship for recent immigrants. Lillian D. Wald, who as a young nurse conducted a mission class on New York's Lower East Side, discovered the need for regular visiting nurses and made a nursing service a major feature of the house she opened on Henry Street.[19] Professor Graham Taylor of the Chicago Theological Seminary made Chicago Commons a field-work assignment for his students and developed such a sensitive hold on the community that the settlement's neighborhood council was able to control its political selections and convert the ward into a bastion for civic reformers.[20]

The warm friendliness that characterized most of these efforts helped to restore a sense of neighborliness in many depressed urban districts. Some of the middle- or upper-class residents, who increased from two to twenty-five at Hull-House within a decade, and similarly at other settlements, gave all their time to the cause; they became the pioneers of the new profession of social worker. In addition to those they organized, other local groups soon took advantage of the settlement-house facilities. Ethnic clubs, religious societies, even unions, responded to the unexpected hospitality of these neighborhood centers and learned a new sense of comradeship with those of different backgrounds and aspirations. The problems did not disappear, nor did easy solutions emerge, but a spirit of hopeful co-operation developed. Many citizens not identified with the movement gained a new view of poverty by reading the flood of articles that soon issued from settlement-house experience. Most of the leaders were too busy to write books in the early years, but in 1898, Robert A. Woods, director of Andover House in Boston, brought out *The City Wilderness,* a revealing account not only of wretched conditions but also of the historic origins of one of the many depressed urban neighborhoods where 115 centers already employed nearly 500 staff members and housed over 700 residents.[21]

Some settlement leaders became active in broader civic fields. A few, such as Mary McDowell, had had earlier associations with the organization societies, and she now co-operated with non-settlement leaders in organizing the Women's Trade Union League in 1903 and with Jane Addams in persuading President Roosevelt to launch a federal investigation of women in industry. Miss Addams played a prominent role in the Chicago Civic Federation and with Julia Lathrop, one of her residents, led the fight for the first juvenile court in the country, which was established in 1899; she also campaigned with others for a state child-labor amendment, successfully passed in 1903. Within the next ten years at least twenty states established juvenile courts, chiefly for their large cities. Lillian Wald and Florence Kelley prodded Roosevelt to call a national Children's Conference at the White House in 1909, out of which a few years later came the Federal Children's Bureau.[22]

The increased concern for children directed attention to the family. When the tendency to late marriage declined in the nineties, the percentage of homes broken by divorce began to mount. Although the average incidence for urban counties in the several states surveyed in 1908 was only 10 per cent higher than that of the rural districts, the trend was upward, which indicated that the growing complexity of city life had aggravated the problem. The rising proportion of women gainfully employed, even married women, made marriage easier, despite the fact that many men now found it harder to support a family on their own wages; but the monetary responsibility women assumed rendered them more independent and less willing to prolong unhappy marriages. Whether the net result was good or bad, the organization of family-welfare societies in sixty communities during the early 1900's demonstrated widespread concern over the situation.[23]

Revitalized by the work of the settlements and by the new energies welling up through the churches, the charity-organization societies, many of them renamed associated charities, broadened their coverage and increased to 150 by 1904. The number of benevolent institutions had doubled since 1890, as children's nurseries, hospitals and dispensaries, industrial schools, and employment bureaus appeared in many cities;

moreover, both Catholics and Jews provided additional facilities for their own dependents, particularly in the great city slums. The St. Vincent de Paul Society took a lead in this work among Catholic charities, and the Baron de Hirsch Fund trustees provided aid and inspiration to the Jews. Both endeavored around the turn of the century to promote local co-operation with those organization societies that offered services in the crowded immigrant areas. At the same time, to safeguard their parochial interests, the Catholics formed local associations, similar to the United Hebrew Charities established a decade before in a dozen places.[24]

Long before the nationality groups and the social reformers began to direct their attention to the slums, a lonely group of pioneer health officials had opened the attack on this Achilles' heel of the American city. Unfortunately their number was so small and other problems so great that they were constantly diverted into fields where progress seemed more feasible. The need for an ample supply of safe drinking water, for sanitary sewers and garbage disposal, for programs of vaccination, quarantine enforcement, and hospital segregation of contagious diseases, for milk and meat inspection and the regulation of nuisances—all pressed on the health authorities of rapidly growing towns. Only as the work in several of these fields advanced did the basic housing deficiencies regain attention. Meanwhile a number of private health agencies rallied to the officials' support.

Concern for the welfare of infants in poor homes soon brought another advance. When it was discovered, in 1890, that the infant death rate in the New York slums had raised the city's child mortality to nearly one in ten, humanitarians hastened to establish depots for the free distribution of milk to the mothers of children under five. Determined to use only pure milk, Nathan Strauss, who maintained several of these stations in 1893, introduced pasteurization in this country. After a lengthy battle with the backers of certified milk, he secured the acceptance of his product as fully equal in quality to its expensive rival. Barely 5 per cent of New York's supply was pasteurized in 1900. As the merits of pasteurization became evident, however, it spread within a decade to dealers handling a fourth of that city's consumption and made even more rapid progress elsewhere.[25] Public milk stations, first established by the city health officer at Rochester in the summer of 1897, won favor at New York and other places. As the standards in urban markets improved, with the wider use of refrigeration and pasteurization, many of these stations, staffed by nurses, became child-welfare clinics, which further helped to reduce the infant death rate before the close of the period.[26]

Thus the new concern for child welfare, slowly developed by urban charities since the Civil War, received official support. The use of medical inspectors for an annual check of all school children commenced at New York, Boston, and Chicago during the early nineties and spread to sixty cities within a decade. Child-labor laws won approval in many industrial states after Massachusetts blazed the way in 1888. Day nurseries and similar charities multiplied, and children's wards appeared in the major hospitals. The organization of child-welfare societies promoted the formation of divisions or departments of child hygiene within the official framework at Detroit, Buffalo, and a few other large towns, while educational exhibits in twenty-six states publicized the movement.[27]

Trailing these advances came improvements in hospitals both public and private. The early isolation depots, maintained by all towns during recurrent sieges of smallpox, were little better than their popular name suggested—pest houses. Though Boston, Worcester, and a few other centers in the East began building decent quarantine hospitals during the nineties, another decade passed before many cities had met this need. Even the search for sites was blocked in most places, since few neighborhoods welcomed such institutions in their midst. Fortunately the rapid advance in medical knowledge after the turn of the century increased public confidence in the hospital's ability to control the spread of infection. As a result, the number of municipal hospitals rose to 164 by 1910, when the total of all hospitals approached two thousand. Together they admitted two million patients during the year, while 574 health dispensaries treated another 2,440,018 persons, most of them urban residents.[28]

Of course each hospital had its origin in a movement that stemmed from some local situation. Thus when a tornado ripped through Rochester, Minnesota, a town of some 6000 residents, on August 21, 1883, Dr. William W. Mayo and his sons organized relief work in an improvised hospital supported by generous donations from neighboring hamlets and cities. The Mayos enlisted volunteer nurses from a local convent of Sisters of St. Francis. Together they not only restored community confidence but also inspired the mother superior to plan the erection of a permanent institution. St. Mary's Hospital opened in 1889 with the three Doctors Mayo in charge; its Catholic sponsorship was a serious handicap in that predominantly Protestant community, but the superior skills of the Mayos and their daring surgical feats attracted wide attention and silenced local prejudice. Soon that hospital, expanding with the reputation of its great physicians, drew numerous students, interns, and practicing surgeons from distant places and gave the little city a new functional specialty.[29]

Many additional advances occurred in the field of public health. Campaigns against spitting on the sidewalks, on the trolley floor, or in other public places wrought a transformation in the personal habits of most urbanites and greatly improved sanitary conditions. As the antituberculosis movement, which commenced in the Trudeau Sanatorium in 1885, gained momentum, numerous associations established private or in a few cases public sanatoriums on the outskirts of cities, where patients could enjoy pure air and escape the shattering confusion of urban life.[30] Public baths, long common in European cities, began to reach America in the nineties. Both the low repute of some of the commercial bath houses and their opposition to publicly owned competition checked the movement. Nevertheless, as home bathtubs became more prevalent in middle-class housing, popular concern for cleanliness increased, and the campaign to provide public bathing facilities in the congested districts finally triumphed in many metropolitan centers.[31]

Urban complexities baffled many individuals, converting some into hopeless derelicts. Charity visitors uncovered shocking conditions in most of the lodging houses for single men. They discovered thousands in New York sleeping on "tiers of narrow shelves" or, as in many cities, taking "hot-bed" turns in closely packed rooms. Although New York's Organization Society commended the Mills Hotels, erected by a philanthropist to house homeless men at a modest fee, it found most accommodations of this sort sadly deficient and launched a campaign for public inspection.[32] The same body took the initiative in founding the first Legal Aid Society in 1890. Various groups had previously extended such services to special cases in New York, Boston, and Chicago, and the two latter places as well as Philadelphia and Pittsburgh now hastened to form city-wide societies for this purpose. Legal-aid committees of the associated charities or Women's Educational and Industrial Unions gave similar help before the turn of the century to needy women and minors in several smaller places.[33]

The associated charities and like bodies had many objectives. They sought to check the political use of outdoor relief by channeling public assistance through asylums, clinics, and other functional institutions, and they supported broad movements for housing reform, playgrounds, and public health. But their sponsorship of schools for social workers brought more immediate results. Boston had started the first training program for volunteer visitors early in 1892, and Mary E. Richmond, secretary of the movement in Baltimore, shortly undertook similar work with the visitors of that city. The organization society in New York offered a slightly broader course of lectures two years later and in 1898 established a six weeks' summer program that soon became the New York School of Philanthropy. It extended its work to the full academic year in 1903–04 and several seasons later conducted a two-year course. Graham Taylor of Chicago Commons and Julia Lathrop of Hull-House taught special classes in 1906 at the University of Chicago, which launched the School of Civics and Philanthropy a year later. Harvard and Simmons had already collaborated in founding the Boston School of Social Work, and similar efforts began at Philadelphia and St. Louis before the close of the period.[34] Meanwhile, an Institute of Social Service, organized in 1898, endeavored to collect and disseminate knowledge on the subject from all parts of the world; the *Survey,* launched in 1909, quickly absorbed several local charity publications and provided a constant source of information and stimulation.[35] The new urban-born profession of social workers was achieving permanent form.

The broadening welfare program was a positive response to the mounting problems of urban life. The growth of cities had dislocated old resident families and attracted so many uprooted newcomers that earlier forms of charity no longer sufficed. Many groups founded institutions to care for the needy, but the multiplicity of appeals raised demands for economy and stirred fears of pauperization; forthright leaders in many cities made repeated efforts to check the mounting outlays of public and private relief. Periodic breakdowns in the economy intensified the search for more fundamental remedies. As a result, new functional institutions and a new professional leadership developed, particularly in the great metropolitan centers, where the increased heterogeneity made volunteer visiting by charitable matrons disagreeable to both parties. The appearance in many such places of social settlement staffs engendered a humanizing spirit and transformed the economy-minded organization leaders into a devoted group of professional workers. Although the charity movement was to some degree, in both purpose and effect, a middle-class defense against socialist doctrines, it also served to refute the extreme beliefs of some Spencerians. Strengthened by the proponents of social Christianity, it helped to leaven the impersonal materialism of the city.

11. The emergence
of the social gospel

A major impetus for the charity movement had come from religious forces in the community. Although the older Protestant churches in many cities were less well attended in the nineties than a few decades earlier, they too experienced a transformation that made them in many respects more responsive to urban needs. Tall business blocks often blotted their steeples from the skylines; clanging trolley cars and the general hubbub of the increasingly boisterous Sabbath so absorbed the sound of church bells that visitors ceased to complain, as George Sala did at Baltimore in 1879, of the excessive tolling of bells on Sunday. Yet, as James Bryce observed a decade later, the influence of the church ran deeper and stronger in America than in European communities; neither the charity movement nor the labor unions could escape its effects. The urban impact molded new religious institutions, and the city was likewise reshaped in the process.[1]

The three dominant religious groups, Catholics, Protestants, and Jews, performed separate and fairly distinct roles in the emerging city, and the rivalries their separate growth engendered strongly influenced their course. Nevertheless, as urban problems mounted in the late nineties, a spirit of co-operation began to draw some leaders of each group together.

Although the Catholic Church was still in the 1860's a minor force in most American communities, it maintained an effective hold over large numbers in Boston, New York, and Baltimore and rapidly increased its strength in Cincinnati, St. Louis, and Chicago, among other interior cities, as its leaders made the first concerted response to several urban problems. Its social program gave close attention to the needs of its members, who included, in addition to a few substantial citizens, a host of the poorest and most uncultivated immigrants.[2] To retain its hold on this rapidly increasing class of urban residents, the Church promoted a number of "combative benevolences" that endeavored to supply its followers with adequate substitutes for worldly attractions. To enforce its ban against secret societies, the Church strengthened its own benefit and ethnic clubs and developed activities designed to sustain interest in them. To head off loss of members through non-Catholic philanthropies, the Church established its own Society for the Protection of Destitute Catholic Children and founded manual-labor schools as adjuncts to its orphan asylums. Other Catholic bodies opened industrial homes for young men, Homes of the Good Shepherd, clubs for young men, even reformatory institutions in a few large cities. The development of St. James' House and St. Stephen's House in congested Manhattan parishes in the late sixties followed earlier evangelical Protestant missions, such as that of Jerry McAuley in Mulberry Street, but anticipated by two decades the later settlement houses. Yet despite the exhortations of John Boyle O'Reilly in the Boston *Pilot* and the efforts of a few other lonely Catholic critics of urban deficiencies, it was the proliferation of societies within each church that did most to build Catholic strength in the immigrant neighborhoods of rapidly growing cities.[3]

In similar fashion, the first response of the Jews to urban social problems was made through their synagogues and affiliated societies. Although still limited in number in the 1860's, the Jewish residents of several large eastern cities already supported three or more synagogues, each the product of the distinctive European origin of its members. New York, with 80,000 Jewish residents in 1870, already maintained twenty synagogues. In Boston, the Polish, the Dutch or West German, and the South German Jews each had their synagogue, and each synagogue accepted charitable responsibility for its members and for strangers in the community. In Baltimore, Cincinnati, and Chicago the German Jews had achieved a secure position, and many began in the seventies to make a conscious adjustment to their American environment. They established English-language journals and opened schools to teach English as well as Hebrew. Some of their less successful fellows, on the other hand, joined with newcomers from abroad to maintain separate and more traditional societies and synagogues. In Buffalo and other cities of a median size, two synagogues proved sufficient in the seventies, but each had its separate charities, fraternal orders, and clubs.[4]

The widening gap that separated the Reform or Americanized Jewish temples, especially after their convention at Pittsburgh in 1885, from the various orthodox synagogues defeated early efforts in several cities, in Buffalo as well as in Boston, to make the United Hebrew Benevolent Associations representative of all groups. Yet if each successive wave of newcomers had to work out its own cycle of adjustments in a new land, and if the multiplicity of national and linguistic bonds created additional divisions, the challenge of establishing a secure place in the American city brought a movement in the nineties toward co-operation. The need to maintain orphan asylums, homes for the aged, industrial schools, settlement houses, and immigrant aid societies—which could be met effectively by separate groups only in a great metropolis such as New York—created increased pressure for joint action in these community endeavors.[5]

The rising tide of Jewish immigration in the nineties hastened this development. A strong impetus came from abroad in the form of the Baron de Hirsch Fund established by an Austrian philanthropist in 1891 to assist Jewish refugees fleeing from the Czar's pogroms. It not only helped to transport many Jews to America but, as the waves of refugees funneled into Castle Garden, the de Hirsch trustees made New York the hub of its varied enterprises. When their first plan to develop farm and village settlements as an alternative to the East Side ghetto proved unworkable, the trustees shifted their emphasis to industrial education and enlisted the co-operation of Hebrew welfare agencies in a dozen metropolitan centers in a campaign that resettled over 64,000 Jews in some 1400 cities and towns during the first decade of the century.[6] The interdenominational Educational Alliance, founded at New York in 1887 to promote the assimilation of immigrants from eastern and southern Europe, won support from the fund, and the de Hirsch trustees soon reorganized that body as the North American Civic League, which brought Jews of several origins into a close working relationship not only with their co-religionists but also with Gentiles. It enlarged the classes for immigrants already functioning in nine cities and organized new classes elsewhere; it opened foreign-language libraries in sixty neighborhoods and established several housekeeper-training centers. Old hostilities faded under its vigorous leadership.[7]

More oriented towards the city than any other ethnic group, the Jews often pioneered in significant urban movements. As individual Jews, notably Samuel Gompers, provided effective leadership in labor unions, and others such as Abraham Cahan, editor of the Jewish *Forward,* in the socialist movement, Dr. Felix Adler, who founded the Society for

Ethical Culture at New York in 1876, became a creative forerunner of the social gospel. Alert to the needs of working people, he not only opened the first free kindergarten in Manhattan and a school for talented but poor children on the Lower East Side, but also organized the Tenement House Building Company in 1887 to erect model dwellings and campaigned for improved housing regulation. His influence quickened many civic causes and helped to inspire young Rabbi Stephen Wise to launch the Free Synagogue movement which in the early 1900's adapted the institutional church to Jewish neighborhoods.[8]

The progressive advance of Catholics and Jews in number and institutional equipment helped to alert Protestant leaders to the city's challenge. Their first effort, following the Civil War, to tackle urban problems through the American Christian Commission did little more than measure their failure. Although several ministerial clubs in large eastern towns formed an American branch of the Evangelical Alliance in 1867, its concern over urban sins proved less gripping than its alarm over Catholic progress until, two decades later, Josiah Strong and Samuel L. Loomis showed how the neglect of the first contributed to the second. As its new president, Strong reinvigorated the Alliance. Hebrew Christian Brotherhoods, organized in New York and Chicago in the sixties to proselytize among the Jews, made little headway. Most city churches remained unaware of these issues, though some reacted to urban growth in another way, by migrating from the congested center in the wake of their middle- and upper-class parishioners who were likewise moving to less crowded neighborhoods.[9]

Many Protestant clergymen, trying to serve their own congregations, responded in the seventies to the new currents of thought spreading through the colleges and into literary societies. After a period of hesitancy they began to expound a modified interpretation of Darwin's theories and to accept some of the findings of historical research on the origins of the Bible. Not only the Free Religionists and the Ethical Culture groups, forming in a half-dozen cities, but also clergymen of more orthodox sects came to regard urban society as an evolutionary outgrowth of more primitive forms. As they gave closer study to city problems, some became pioneers in social work; others, whose sermons sounded more radical, occasionally found themselves out of step with their congregations or their neighborhoods.[10]

The Protestant response to the city's challenge took varied forms. When their early charity societies faltered during the depression of the mid-seventies, a vigorous temperance drive welled up from the rural backgrounds of most urbanites to close many saloons and fill some churches with new members who had never heard of Darwin. The moral-reform revivals of the seventies organized blue-ribbon and red-ribbon clubs, as well as W. C. T. U.'s, and established rescue missions in several places. Though most of these efforts disappeared with the return of good times, the recession of 1886 and the progressive disruption of old handicrafts by the factory system brought a revival of both movements in the late eighties and again in the depression of the mid-nineties, when many additional cities acquired rescue missions.[11]

With the saloons often averaging one to every hundred or so residents, even some temperance advocates began to reassess their programs. The Anti-Saloon League was formed to campaign for prohibition, but a few of its supporters joined with the less adamant leaders of the social gospel in the search for suitable alternatives. A Committee of Fifty, headed by Seth Low of New York, studied the liquor problem in seventeen cities and in the course of ten years published several reports, one entitled *Substitutes for the Saloon.* One reformer, reasoning that a better home life was the first need, urged American communities to provide housing for the poor similar to pioneering projects in Scotland. Lunch and recreation rooms in factories, equipped with magazines and a Victrola, had served to close saloons across the street in one town, he reported, urging unions, too, to run their headquarters as social halls. Scattered coffee houses, neighborhood canteens, and sports clubs were praised. New York City's action in opening numerous schoolhouses to adult and youth clubs during evening hours in 1903 and Rochester's more systematic social-center program launched five years later, each provided wholesome outlets for community expression and supplied models for similar efforts in other cities.[12]

Another group of Protestant leaders made a more direct response to the immediate needs of the workingman. The hardships confronting the cotton-mill workers of New England in the early seventies brought several religious and labor leaders together into the Christian Labor Union, founded at Boston in 1872. Led by Jesse H. Jones, Congregational minister at North Abinton, Massachusetts, the union attacked the complacency of the church and the inhumanity of the capitalist system. It defended labor's right to organize, and Jones helped to form Knights of Labor districts in Boston. Its short-lived publications, *Equity* and *Labor-Balance,* urged the eight-hour day, arbitration, and co-operatives, and even gave publicity to the platform of the new Socialist Labor Party in 1878.[13]

Few clergymen accepted the Marxist doctrine, but many, repelled by its materialism, felt challenged by their urban experiences to seek a more humane social order. The problems of intemperance, of vice and crime—all aggravated by the rise of the city—commanded attention, along with the evils of proverty. The Union for Christian Work, established by Unitarians at Providence in 1868, maintained a school, a library, a club room, and a lecture series. While Unitarians in seven other towns were opening such centers, Episcopal churches founded a dozen brotherhoods and workingmen's homes to shelter the numerous poor craftsmen migrating from England in these years. Lutherans, Methodists, and other church groups also opened homes for needy immigrants and other destitute folk; thirty nondenominational missions appeared, as well as numerous tabernacles, and several of their leaders founded institutes to enlist and train volunteer workers.[14]

The new concept of Christian responsibility for the welfare of man received its most dramatic expression in the ministry of Washington Gladden at North Adams and Springfield, in Massachusetts, and later at Columbus, Ohio. His warm humanitarian spirit reacted quickly to the hardships of workingmen during successive strikes and depressions. His earnest efforts to understand and sympathize with both sides in recurrent disputes made him an effective mediator and enabled him to conduct pioneer labor-management conferences at Columbus and Toledo. His article "The Cosmopolitan City Club" outlined a program for citizen participation in local affairs that inspired the organization of city clubs and civic associations in many places, including one at Columbus in which Gladden himself took a lead. He ran for the common council in order to break the hold of a political ring there and devoted two years to the study of franchise questions and other practical civic matters.[15]

Widely hailed as the father of social Christianity, Washington Gladden helped to awaken church leaders to their responsibilities in relation to labor and other urban problems. He did not stand alone, however, for while he was introducing Henry George, Richard T. Ely, and Carroll D. Wright, among others, to his Congregational brethren, R. Heber Newton at All Souls Church in New York was performing a similar function among the Episcopal clergy. With J. O. S. Huntington, Newton brought some of them together in 1887 to form the Christian Association for the Advancement of the Interests of Labor.[16] The more numerous Methodist and Baptist churches, whose members generally belonged to the middle class, were chiefly concerned with other urban problems, notably intemperance and vice, and with the well-being of their own young people, but the formation by Walter Rauschenbusch and his Baptist associates of the Brotherhood of the Kingdom in 1893 introduced many of the leaders of these and other evangelical bodies to the social gospel.[17]

Social Christianity stressed God's immanence rather than His transcendence, and several able volumes discussed the theological origins of the social gospel. In practice, most of its followers received their inspiration after a rude awakening in the city streets. Sometimes a vivid description of the conditions there, such as Charles Loring Brace's *The Dangerous Classes of New York* (1872), or Wendell Phillips' *The Labor Question* (1884), or Josiah Strong's *Our Country* (1885), sent a young minister tramping through the slums to see for himself. But usually his constructive thinking commenced after he had become identified with some good cause and met a sudden check or disillusionment. Thus when Graham Taylor's effort to conduct a joint mission for poor working folk in Hartford encountered resistance from his fellow clergymen, Taylor explored the needs and the methods used elsewhere and became acquainted with early examples of the institutional church.[18]

The Reverend William S. Rainsford had begun his pioneer venture in this field at old St. George's Church in New York in 1880, after most of the original members had moved out of that congested district. Determined to make it a home of the people, Rainsford inspired several of his wealthy vestrymen to provide funds for a parish house where neighborhood clubs, classes, and other activities, supervised by some twenty-six divinity students who volunteered for the job, set a new pattern for church work. Soon a dozen other city churches were building parish houses or institutes and engaging assistant pastors, deaconesses, and educational directors.[19]

The harsh challenges of poverty and violence in the Chicago of the mid-nineties spurred Taylor, now a professor at the Chicago Theological Seminary, to lead his students into the slums about the Chicago Commons and then progressively into political and labor disputes. A similar experience at a parish in South Boston prompted W. D. P. Bliss to join with other sympathetic clergy in establishing the Society of Christian Socialists in 1889 and a Brotherhood Mission of the Carpenter; the latter served as a model for socialist churches or Sunday schools in other large towns.[20] Walter Rauschenbusch tried in the late nineties to steer the more radical elements among the religious and labor groups in Rochester away from the materialism of Marx. But it was only after he had directed a survey of that city's social conditions for the Y. M. C. A. in 1904 (discovering a need for legitimate outlets for youthful energies, for higher wages to encourage earlier marriages and check illicit sexual activity, for increased opportunities to enjoy nature and to take part in intellectual and aesthetic activities and other positive substitutes for the liquor evil) that his thoughts and emotions found expression in a seminal book, *Christianity and the Social Crisis* (1907).[21]

Rauschenbusch, like Taylor and Gladden among others, saw the fate of the urban church as linked with the welfare of the laboring classes. Salvation will be achieved, he reasoned, when men became more concerned for a realization of the Kingdom of God on earth than for the afterlife of their individual souls. He founded a local Brotherhood of the Kingdom in Rochester and participated for years in a Sunday Evening service for working people held in a downtown theater where many of his "Prayers for the Social Awakening" were first delivered.[22] Ever ready as he was to pit the spiritual power of the social gospel against the materialism of either capitalism or socialism, his writings and teachings helped to revitalize many city churches, to foster their social-work programs, and to rekindle a spirit of evangelism in the "Y's" and other welfare agencies.[23]

Of course, neither the settlement movement nor the denominational and rescue missions and institutional churches could fully meet all needs of the dwellers in congested areas of metropolitan cities. These efforts did, however, awaken many churchmen to the problems of the slums and improved the enforcement of sanitary and child-labor regulations. The vivid description by Jacob A. Riis of *How the Other Half Lives* (1890) supplied material for innumerable sermons and prompted investigations in many towns. House-to-house surveys of church members, first undertaken on an interdenominational basis in four New York City neighborhoods in the late nineties, became popular after the turn of the century and provided the stimulus for church extension programs and other efforts, notably foreign-language Sunday schools, designed to reach non-churchgoers.[24]

The discovery that Boston's 54,000 lodgers of 1895 had increased to 80,000 by 1905, with approximately a third of them crowded into single rooms or garrets in the neighborhood of South End House, revealed the inadequacy of the facilities provided. The disappearance of the boardinghouse, so prevalent in earlier decades, sent lodgers into the streets in search of cheap dining rooms. Although half the single women over fifteen years of age in twenty-two cities were listed as self-supporting, their meager wages and desolate surroundings often brought them into the streets, too, but for other purposes.[25] The "Y's," now widely distributed, served principally those of a middle-class background. Day nurseries, kindergartens, fresh-air funds, and playgrounds relieved the plight of many children; homes, shelters, and clinics aided many destitute folk and helped to make New York, in Riis's opinion, "a hundred fold cleaner, better, purer city than it was even ten years" before; yet the life of most workers had been little improved. Even the unions enrolled their members chiefly from the skilled trades and, except during periods of strife when large numbers of laborers were hastily organized, failed to reach the mass of transients.[26]

Both the shiftless and the industrious, both young men seeking a start and old men shuffling about, mingled with thousands of migrating newcomers on the crowded downtown streets, unable to find a place to rest. Often the saloon seemed the only resort. The Salvation Army, introduced from England in 1880, endeavored to supply a better haven by establishing huts and shelters in the blighted districts of every metropolis and near the center in many lesser places. In 1896, when Ballington Booth and his wife Maud resigned, to found the somewhat comparable Volunteers of America a few years later, the Army numbered almost 2000 officers and approximately 25,000 "soldiers," who maintained seventeen rescue missions, twenty-four lodging houses, and three farm colonies. Its program of visitation by "slum brigades," introduced in 1889, was but one of several practical social services that sought out the needy and lonely and offered friendly counsel and assistance.[27]

The Salvation Army enjoyed increased support from many established churches during the nineties, and other efforts to meet the urban challenge multiplied. As the dimensions of the problem became more widely apparent, able leaders of all faiths developed a new spirit of tolerance. The American Protective Association, founded in 1887 to curb the influence of Irish mill workers in Clinton, Iowa, had swept through many midwestern towns and invaded a number of cities there in the early nineties. It reflected Protestant fears of Catholic domination, which became especially acute during the panic of 1893; yet it won little influence in larger places in the Northeast. Though it boasted a secret membership of over 2,000,000 by the mid-decade, the popular reaction against such nativism brought its decline.[28] The widely publicized collaboration of a leading Methodist and a Catholic bishop in the establishment of a national Anti-Saloon League in 1895 revealed that men of different beliefs could work together for the city's redemption. Moreover, the support that Pope Leo XIII's *Rerum Novarum* of 1891 gave to the more liberal Catholic clergy in their efforts to reach workingmen brought new vitality to the social program of that church, which now overshadowed all its denominational rivals in most large cities. Only the Jewish synagogues and temples served a greater proportion of the residents of the worst slum areas. The co-operation between the staffs of the settlements, industrial schools, nurseries, and missions of the three leading faiths in the nineties contrasted in many places with the internal doctrinal divisions that still troubled each group.[29]

The need for concerted leadership on both local and national levels became increasingly insistent. The earlier attempt of the Evangelical Alliance to unite the churches had excluded Catholics, Jews, and Unitarians; nevertheless, Josiah Strong was able, by emphasizing its positive program, to obscure the limitations of the Alliance. Its three national conventions—especially the third one, which was held in Chicago during the World's Fair—served as preparatory institutes of the social gospel. Yet not all could assent to its restrictive pledges, and in order to cultivate wider associations the leaders of various missions and tabernacles met together at annual Conventions of Christian Workers after 1886 and increased their number to 2500 by the turn of the century. Liberal theologians, eager to bridge the gaps between the sects, organized the Brotherhood of Christian Unity in 1891 and the League of Catholic Unity four years later. Both developed strong local chapters; when some of these faltered, Unions for Practical Progress sprang up in a few cities, notably Philadelphia and Baltimore, and Christian Social Unions elsewhere.[30]

The desire for a more inclusive organization prompted the formation of the National Federation of Churches and Christian Workers in 1900. In order to increase its representation and strengthen its leadership, the federation invited delegates from comparable local bodies and from all religious denominations to a conference at Carnegie Hall in New York, where in 1905 a charter for a new Federal Council of the Churches of Christ in America was drawn up and approved. When after many months some thirty-two denominational bodies and numerous city associations had indorsed the plan, the first regular session convened at Philadelphia in 1908. The council pledged itself to a program of social reconstruction in industrial, civic, and social fields. A preliminary report on "The Churches and Organized Labor" received its early attention. After some debate, the council indorsed resolutions favoring the recognition of unions, the wide use of arbitration, and other conciliatory methods to obviate strikes and lockouts; it also recommended a constructive approach to the problems of the saloon and to other urban evils. A Commission on the Church and Social Service, organized by the council shortly after its first meeting, assembled a library of publications on social questions and boldly undertook to investigate a steel strike in

Pennsylvania; it recommended that church bodies in each city make careful surveys and give thoughtful deliberation to the interests of all parties in local conflicts; this, it declared, was an essential part of their responsibility as religious leaders in the community.[31]

The most striking example of the desired approach was the Pittsburgh Survey, already in process. The establishment of the Russell Sage Foundation, pledged to "the improvement of social and living conditions" by the promotion of research and publications, had attracted wide publicity; its decision to back the pioneer social survey of a city, previously undertaken on a modest scale by Paul U. Kellogg in Pittsburgh, focused national attention on its expanded study of a key industrial city which suffered from an acute phase of all known urban maladies. When the six-volume report was published, it shed new light on many problems that were becoming endemic in American society.[32]

The Pittsburgh Survey probed deeply into standards of living, vice and crime, sanitation and housing, the status of women, and the family. These were not uniquely urban problems, nor peculiar to the steel capital; yet, as with the industrial system, labor unionism, charity and religion, the rapid growth of cities had brought so many radical changes in these special fields of "human engineering" that they had acquired almost an urban character. It was in the cities that new approaches to each of these situations developed.

This was especially true in religion. There the increased heterogeneity of peoples and creeds challenged the expansionist desires of many sects and persuaded some of their leaders to develop co-operative techniques in order to pursue their fundamental goals. For a time the mounting strength of Catholics in the great urban centers spurred the efforts of divergent Protestants to unite, but that combative strategy proved less significant in the long run than the church's response to the crying needs of the city's poor and its unchurched multitudes. The social gospel evoked by the expanding but troubled metropolis gave fresh inspiration to its followers, and their larger vision awakened new hope for a broader harmony among city dwellers. This vision quickened the efforts of the pioneer social workers and of other emerging professional groups as well.

Yet the city's growth far exceeded the reach of any one group. The influx of newcomers brought a host of new sects, many with strange and brittle orthodoxies that shunned all bids for tolerance or co-operation. The hope for agreement on fundamentals disappeared as that word itself assumed an emotional significance among great numbers of city dwellers whose nostalgia for their rural antecedents acquired a religious fervor. Although the social gospel brought many urban issues into sharper ethical focus and contributed a dynamic force to municipal reform, to be truly effective the movement needed a more understanding audience. Only the schools could supply it; fortunately these, too, had been alerted to the needs of the city.

12. The pervasive vitality of city schools

We are not today surprised that the schools played a major role in the country's evolution, but in the 1860's less was expected of them. Even the better city schools of a century ago still functioned primarily as conservators of the traditional classical culture, and the widespread check placed on their development by the Civil War and the disorders that followed jeopardized even that function, particularly in the South. But a fresh inspiration animated the educational authorities in several northern towns, where their varied responses to the joint challenge of industrialism and the progeny of a rising tide of immigrants launched significant new beginnings. The influence of pedagogical philosophers abroad (and already a few of native origin) should not be overlooked, but it was largely through the practical leadership of superintendents and teachers in a dozen places from Boston to St. Louis that the new theories were sifted and the educational patterns for America formulated. Original ideas and fruitful adaptations of ideas came from such men as Superintendent Parker of Quincy, Massachusetts, Dean Calvin M. Woodward at St. Louis, and Edward J. Ward in Rochester, to name only three whose response to urban needs started widespread reforms. The success these and other men achieved was conditioned by the rapid urban growth, which not only compelled and supported new efforts but also challenged the adequacy of each program. Few static traditions could endure amidst the maelstrom of these transition years.

The first important innovation came from Oswego, where in the early sixties, following its period of rapid growth, Dr. Edward A. Sheldon, former superintendent at Syracuse, developed a practical application of the theories of J. H. Pestalozzi. Though not the first American to endorse the great Swiss educator's ideas, Sheldon devised a program that trained teachers to substitute sense perception for memory work and brought zest to both teachers and students at a critical period. Teachers who attended the normal school founded by his enthusiastic backers in Oswego refused to be daunted by the wide neglect of schools during the tragic sixties; they dispersed to cities and towns across the country and helped to rekindle educational efforts.[1]

After the oral- and object-teaching methods perfected at Oswego freed classes of much routine drill, the systematic arrangement of lessons by William T. Harris, superintendent at St. Louis from 1867 until 1880, opened the way for a wide introduction of elementary science courses. Harris took another forward step when in 1873 he added the kindergarten to the public schools. First proposed by Froebel and imported in 1857 for private-school use, this program applied the child's play instinct to the learning process. Another disciple of Froebel and one of the first Americans to appreciate the priority J. F. Herbart in Germany gave to child development, as against subject matter, Francis W. Parker, superintendent at Quincy from 1875 to 1880, introduced art and manual work to encourage the expression of individuality among children. Parker later went to Chicago, where he eventually collaborated with John Dewey and helped to promote the doctrine of "learning by doing." His emphasis on useful knowledge and meaningful courses, as well as his championship of free instruction for all children, extending into the secondary-school level, resolved some of the dilemmas of expansive cities and prepared them for Dewey's still broader conception of the social function of education.[2]

This receptivity to European inspiration, so characteristic of the American city, was heightened by the multiplicity of problems confronting school men. Not only was the child population mounting rapidly, greatly overtaxing the schools, but the influx of pupils from dissimilar backgrounds also disrupted earlier methods. The increased demand for teachers exceeded the supply of young men who in previous decades had taught for a term or two while studying law or seeking a business connection. Young women, many of whom lacked the classical foundation often boasted by their predecessors, responded eagerly to the call for replacements; their invasion of the upper grades, however, prompted an urgent quest for new techniques of instruction to take the place of male discipline. Faced with a shortage of teachers, many states founded additional normal schools, multiplying the twenty such institutions of 1860 four times within two decades. Numerous cities, following the example of Oswego, established their own institutes, partly to shorten the training period and offset the low salaries and reduced budgets. These and other considerations encouraged the adoption of methods designed to reduce emphasis on the quantity of knowledge to be transmitted and to stress techniques of understanding. Thus the principle of learning by doing won favor for teachers as well as pupils.[3]

The school crisis became more acute as proponents of compulsory attendance obtained laws in six states by 1871 and in twenty-six—all in the North and West—by 1890. This was primarily an urban movement; while neighboring rural districts lagged, many city councils exercised the full powers granted by the legislatures, though rural schools generally reported higher percentages of pupil enrollment than the cities, which excelled in days attended. The pressure for enforcement, for a lengthening of the school term, and for an extension of compulsory attendance both downward and upward in ages, came most frequently from the cities. There the desire to remove children from the streets, and after 1900 from the labor market, strengthened the hand of those who sought mass education. Numerous towns appointed truant officers, but the average attendance in the early years trailed a third below enrollment; among seventeen cities over 75,000 that reported in 1880, only eight reached better than 50 per cent of those eligible. The ratios for the smaller places in the Northeast were somewhat higher, and conditions improved throughout that area and in the West when several states, following the example of Massachusetts in 1875, authorized the taking of an annual school census. At least twenty cities established disciplinary schools for truants, but a major aggravation in each instance remained the inadequacy of the regular facilities.[4]

Although many large cities, inhibited by the prevalence of child labor, were slow to pull student enrollments up to the regional average, urban public schools conducted longer terms than their rural neighbors, waged a more effective battle against illiteracy, and generally carried the torch for educational reform. They were the first to adopt graded classes, anticipating most of the private institutions in this respect, and they progressively extended their classes down into the dame-school or primary field and up to the academy level. Some northern communities had made a start in each direction before the war, and the forty high schools of 1860 increased ten times by 1886, the first year their enrollments equaled those of the private academies. The public enrollment continued to soar, advancing sixfold during the next fifteen years, while that of the academies held fairly constant. This growth, greatly exceeding the urban population increment, reflected the wider assumption of civic responsibility.[5]

The urban schools in the North moved with similar speed into the kindergarten field. That innovation, effectively introduced to private schools with the organization of the American Froebel Union by Miss Elizabeth Peabody at Boston in 1867 and incorporated in the public program by Harris at St. Louis six years later, spread to ninety-three cities by 1880; two decades later the country had 250 kindergartens serving a total of 130,000 children, or approximately a fifth as many as the high schools had enrolled by 1900. A hundred additional towns joined the movement during the next five years, and a few opened a kindergarten in every public school. This was much more than a quantitative extension of services, for the application of Froebelian methods and a recognition of the merits of directed play as a teaching device revitalized all primary grades and brought a new spirit to many city schools.[6]

The expansion of a city's educational functions was facilitated when the development of parochial schools relieved the public officials of part of the burden. With the rapid growth of Catholic parishes (as migrants from Germany, and later from Italy and Eastern Europe, joined the Irish in northern cities), pressure developed among church leaders for the establishment of a separate system. Most of the early Catholic academies were either charitable or select institutions, similar to those maintained by other sects, but many parish schools appeared during the seventies, and in 1884 the Third Plenary Council at Baltimore determined that each church should provide as quickly as possible for the educational needs of all its children. It was a herculean undertaking. The first hasty provisions were often sadly deficient, yet a number of devoted orders eagerly accepted the task of manning the parish schools, which steadily increased in number and enrollment. A special report in 1903 found 3978 such institutions serving nearly a million pupils in ninety-five communities. A co-operative arrangement with the public authorities, maintained for a time in several Minnesota towns, failed to gain wider application, and by the close of the period at least half the Catholic parishes of the country had built separate schools. Most dioceses, following the example of Cleveland in 1886, organized boards to integrate this work in the principal cities. The Philadelphia diocese established a central Catholic high school in 1890, and again, others followed. The Catholics founded over 300 secondary institutions in this period, most of them parochial or private academies; nearly forty, however, resembled in some respects the public high schools.[7]

Although no other sect undertook the schooling of its children on such a broad scale, at least eight maintained fifty or more academies each in 1900. The majority were in the South, where the public provisions remained inadequate, and many served the elementary grades as well, with pupils of that category outnumbering the academy students. Elsewhere, except for those of the Catholics, private schools in the primary field were disappearing, although, including the Catholic schools, they enrolled a fifth of the urban total at the end of the century.[8] To maintain some of the religious instruction banned from the public schools under constitutional restraints, several sects organized and maintained classes in after-school hours.[9] The Jews especially made many efforts in several communities to support a Talmud Torah where the boys received after-school instruction, but a survey in 1908 revealed that scarcely one in five was enrolled; the girls were left to parental supervision.[10]

Some private schools, founded originally as denominational ventures, developed strong loyalties among supporting families. Most cities had inherited select seminaries for young ladies from earlier decades; a few had similar academies for boys. As the public schools began to overshadow the private ones in size and generally in educational vitality, they eventually displaced most of them. Some, however, survived by removing in the late nineties to the suburbs as country day schools, and a number of the boys' schools, notably some of those in attractive New England villages, secured able educators as headmasters and achieved a reputation for the quality of their social as well as their intellectual training. By the turn of the century several had attained a prestige that assured their boys admittance to and social status at the older colleges and entrance to fashionable society. Yet the increasingly numerous graduates of the public high schools overran the state universities and many old colleges and, indeed, extended the democratic tradition into fields previously reserved for the old family hierarchy.[11]

Even in the South, which had long relied on private or charity schools, a new sense of public responsibility emerged before the turn of the century. The work of the Peabody Fund, created in 1867 to support the development of public education in this war-ravaged region, had its greatest effect in the cities, where a faltering movement for the establishment of public schools for white children first developed in the mid-seventies. By 1890 public school enrollments in a few southern cities had become somewhat comparable to those in the North, although neither the attendance records nor the instruction approached northern or western standards for another decade, and then only for the whites and in a few exceptional schools. The Peabody Fund was exhausted by this time, but the John F. Slater Fund, created in 1882 to promote the education of Negroes, stimulated efforts to meet their neglected needs. By 1910 a few southern cities, notably Atlanta, were reporting more public schools, both primary and secondary, than some northern places of comparable size, though the policy of maintaining a dual system deprived their programs of adequate support.[12] Yet, when viewed against the conditions prevailing in the sixties, the urban schools of the South appeared as a remarkable accomplishment.

If few cities North or South achieved fully adequate educational systems during these decades, the constant pressure for expansion facilitated the adoption of reforms. New buildings were required, and not only did brick and stone displace wood in their construction, but sanitary facilities, heating and lighting improvements, kindergarten rooms, work benches, and—first in the high schools—libraries, laboratories, assembly halls, and, during the nineties, gymnastic and shower rooms, all became standard features. Most of the first high schools were built near the center of town, where their imposing four or five stories gratified civic pride. With the pressure for additional room, new high schools made their appearance in the expanding residential neighborhoods, often on spacious sites. Some of these permitted more conveniently arranged two- or three-story structures, with the windows in each room generally grouped on one side after the eighties; by the late nineties a few school sites included a nearby athletic field.[13]

Of course none of these developments followed easily on the first discovery of a need. Most members of school boards, which increasingly assumed control of the centralized city systems after the war, were men elected with the aldermen from the wards, and many quickly became entangled in politics. Popular schoolmasters vied for appointment as superintendent; those who succeeded sometimes obliged backers by naming their favorites to the teaching staff or by assigning contracts for books, repairs, even new buildings, to their henchmen. Political ethics were often low, as we have noted, and despite the paltry salaries, which averaged between twenty-five and fifty dollars a month during the seventies, many school systems became so burdened by debt and running expenses that even with state aid they could not make the new provisions required by the city's growth.[14]

The recurrent crises and political overturns occasionally brought a leader to the fore who rallied sufficient support to adopt effective measures and push ahead with improvements. Several able men won such renown for their cities that residents elsewhere were stimulated to renewed efforts. The annual conventions of regional teachers' associations afforded opportunities to debate new ideas. Additional groups appeared and issued journals which, together with the annual reports of the U. S. Commissioner of Education after 1870 and those of enlightened state superintendents, helped to promote developments. In some cases the minimal requirements enforced by state supervision effected improvements.[15]

Yet in 1892 when Joseph M. Rice, inspired by two years' study of pedagogy at Jena, made his epochal survey of thirty-six cities, he found their schools appallingly deficient. By interviewing 1200 teachers, he assembled sufficient evidence of "public apathy, political interference, corruption and incompetence" to make his series of nine articles, published in *The Forum*, a topic of nation-wide debate. The occasional bouquet he awarded to promising efforts in Minneapolis, Indianapolis, and a few other cities added force to the indictments he issued against other city systems, where ward bosses and uninterested teachers maintained a fruitless regime.[16]

Despite wide indignation among school men against Rice's "muckraking" exposure, many responsible educators seized the opportunity to renew their demands for independent school boards, professional training for teachers, and more adequate salaries. Good government forces, rallying in many cities, took an active interest in the improvement of their schools. At Baltimore and a few other places these broader movements stemmed from specific complaints against local boards of education. The battles frequently involved a drive to give women a voice on the board, or to reduce its size and assure nonpartisan administration, as well as tenure and higher standing both academically and economically for the teachers. Often, as at Rochester, the campaign for reform focused sufficient attention on the schools to inaugurate a period of vigorous progress.[17]

Another powerful stimulus came from the industrial and commercial character of the emerging city. The desire for technically trained workers, which initiated such private institutions as the Massachusetts Institute of Technology in 1865, the Worcester Free Institute in 1868, and two decades later Pratt Institute in Brooklyn, likewise had its effect on the public-school program. The Worcester school, founded by utilitarians, centered its training on a machine shop; President John D. Runkle of M.I.T., with broader educational objectives, introduced a manual-training course based on an exhibit sent by a Moscow school to the Centennial Exposition at Philadelphia in 1876. The merits of this work in training the hand as well as the head, as set forth in Runkle's reports, stimulated the St. Louis Social Science Association to found a manual-training school on the secondary level under the direction of Calvin M. Woodward. Woodward quickly won the support of business leaders in St. Louis and prompted others in Chicago, Philadelphia, Cleveland, and Toledo to establish similar institutes.[18] Baltimore opened the first public manual-training school in 1883; other cities soon followed.

The first courses in these schools prescribed such rigid techniques that many craftsmen hastened to back the rival Sloyd system introduced from Sweden. Its emphasis on the use and beauty of the articles produced attracted favor in Boston, where a training school was opened in 1885 to prepare teachers for this work in the public elementary schools.[19]

The rapid spread of both manual and technical programs reflected many urban influences. Business leaders quickly saw their value. Although unionists, fearful that labor's control over apprenticeships would be broken, often opposed the courses, such hostility could not stop the private institutions and only slowed the development of specific training classes by the public ones. School men welcomed the new work rooms and benches as a means of arousing the interest of pupils with dull literary talents. Parents felt relieved that some of the hand skills formerly learned at chores about the house were now to be supplied at school. Art teachers lauded the objectives but urged that attention be directed more positively to creative handicraft work and that standards of taste be cultivated. Industrialists, on the other hand, favored more practical instruction in the use of machine tools to help meet their urgent need for skilled workers; after the turn of the century the A. F. of L., ready at last to adjust to machine production, gave its support, too, to factory schools.[20]

The manual-training or industrial-arts movement was in reality a loose association of three or more poorly differentiated educational innovations. An earlier arts-and-crafts movement, which stemmed in part from William Morris in England, came to the Boston schools through the drawing classes introduced by Walter Smith in 1870. Within a few years the movement spread to other towns in Massachusetts and neighboring states and as far west as Milwaukee.[21] Its objectives compared closely with those of the Sloyd process, though the techniques were quite different. The arts-and-crafts program achieved freest expression in private art academies and in the museums; industrial training made its greatest advance in the private institutes that sprang up in a score of large cities before 1900; manual training as a stimulant to slow learners and listless hands found its most fruitful field in upwards of a hundred truant and reformatory schools designed to check juvenile delinquency.[22]

Meanwhile, all three contended for dominance in the public schools, and each won a measure of success. Arts-and-crafts activities became associated with the free kindergarten technique and helped to rejuvenate the primary grades. Manual-training benches found a secure place in urban elementary departments. Public trade or factory schools appeared in thirty-four cities during the early 1900's, while twenty-three technical high schools specialized in vocational training, and many others offered home-economics courses for the girls.[23]

The latter development reflected other urban influences as well. It sprang in part from a charitably inspired Kitchen Garden Association organized at New York in 1880 to back the work of Miss Emily Huntington, a former kindergarten teacher who had organized classes in homemaking for girls in the slums. Kitchen gardens, associated at first with charitable institutions, appeared in several large towns during the next decade, and began in the nineties to stimulate public high schools to organize home-economics classes.[24] Private commercial "colleges," a score or more dating from before the Civil War, multiplied as business groups in practically every city over 50,000 established one or more to train secretaries and accountants. The public authorities began after the turn of the century to offer such courses in the high schools.[25]

These and other urban-centered influences radically transformed the curricula of the public primary and secondary grades and, to a less degree, those in private and parochial schools as well. Although a detailed analysis of the offerings in the high schools of the north-central states failed to detect any sharp distinctions between the courses scheduled in large and small, industrial and commercial cities, and in consolidated rural districts, it revealed several essentially urban trends. The larger schools had increasingly expanded and differentiated their offerings, permitting specialization in broad functional fields, a scheme that reached its culmination at Gary, Indiana, after 1908. The classical languages had lost their hold even in many college-preparatory departments, though modern languages flourished in towns with heavy concentrations of specific immigrant groups. Science courses had multiplied during the nineties and acquired a more theoretical and a less descriptive character as the new emphasis in the universities began to permeate secondary staffs. American history also broke into the curricula of many high schools during the eighties, generally as a first-year subject to be followed by political economy in the last year, as the four-year plan gained acceptance. Grammar and arithmetic were pushed into the lower grades, giving more high-school space for English literature and the "social-life" subjects, which were expanded, under the leadership of John Dewey and his disciples, to include much practical training as well.[26]

Dewey's influence spread from the private Laboratory School he conducted for eight years at Chicago. Inspired by the work he saw in the practice classes previously developed by Parker at the Cook County Normal School, Dewey established his own school early in 1896 to test his pedagogical theories. Believing that learning is one of the by-products of activity, he and his associates developed homelike programs for the subprimary and primary pupils that were designed to explain and enrich the child's natural social experience and to lead him progressively in successive classes into an awareness of Chicago and finally of the larger modern world.[27]

As the schools increasingly recognized the needs of children in cities, an extension of their programs into the summer months occurred. Again the movement began under charitable auspices in metropolitan centers. A start appeared in 1866 at Boston, where the First Church opened a vacation school to take neighborhood children off the streets. Though it was discontinued after a few years, when the number living in the district declined, charitable folk in congested areas elsewhere launched similar ventures. In 1885 the Newark Board of Education opened a public school for a six weeks' summer session. The New York Society for the Improvement of the Conditions of the Poor organized summer classes in the early nineties. More of these soon appeared, sometimes on public-school property, in Chicago, Brooklyn, Boston, and other large cities. When the Gotham authorities accepted full responsibility for ten vacation schools in 1897, the success of the movement was assured, and by 1903, when New York boasted fifty-eight vacation schools, at least two hundred places had similar programs.[28]

The schools in progressive communities served the needs of children in many additional ways. Physical education made its bow with the introduction of Swedish gymnastics in a few city systems in the late seventies, and won a secure place in the schedule of most of them by the nineties, when the provision of school playgrounds and high-school gymnasiums prepared the way for organized athletic teams after the turn of the century. Although public health authorities had visited the schools on numerous occasions to carry out a general vaccination campaign when a smallpox epidemic or other local crisis threatened, the first regular programs for the medical inspection of all pupils appeared at Boston, Chicago, and New York in the middle nineties. Within the next fifteen years at least 410 cities launched similar efforts; many of them engaged full-time school nurses. One result was the recognition of the problem of the handicapped child (first at Providence in 1896). Progressive school systems, notably those of Boston, Chicago, and Rochester, organized special classes for the hard-of-hearing, for stammerers and epileptics, as well as for the mentally backward, and even in a few instances for the gifted. Over 250 towns provided special care for one or more such groups by 1910, when the Cleveland schools also assumed responsibility for a dental-inspection program started a few years earlier by the local dental society on a voluntary basis.[29]

The harmony achieved between theory and practice was illustrated by a host of new extracurricular activities that contributed to the social education propagated by Dewey's followers. An early example, which antedated the formulation of the philosophy, was the school savings bank. J. H. Thiry, a teacher at Long Island City, introduced one of the first in a public school there in 1885, with such success that teachers elsewhere sought his advice in organizing similar ventures. Within five years, over a thousand schools in 158 towns had adopted the system; some liquidated their accounts after a term or two, but a survey in 1910 found many still operating in over a hundred places, with active deposits from 166,525 children.[30] Matching that practical introduction of pupils to a basic aspect of the economy was the student journal, which began to appear in city high schools around 1890. Boys' and girls' clubs and sports contests also multiplied towards the close of the period. With the schools thus offering more exciting experiences to urban youths, the average age of withdrawal mounted, especially in progressive communities.[31]

As the schools developed in stability and in breadth of service, many answered adult needs as well. Evening classes, some dating from before the Civil War, had generally offered only the basic elementary courses to youths forced to work during the day, though occasionally a few adult immigrants sat in to learn English. As the number of adults increased, the character of the work changed. Before 1880 thirty-two cities, following the early lead of Cincinnati in 1856, opened evening high schools. Nearly two hundred more fell into line by the end of the period. The basic courses continued in demand, but a desire for instruction in the new subjects offered by the high schools brought an enrichment of the program.[32]

The importance of this work could scarcely be overstressed in cities whose adults were still largely of rural or foreign origin and limited in formal education to an average of four or five years' schooling.[33] Those

View up Broadway, New York, 1860. *Photograph by Henry T. Anthony, Edward Anthony Stereograph, Courtesy of George Eastman House*

(*Top*) Bird's-eye View of New York and Vicinity, 1858. *Drawn by John Bach-mann, Published by C. Magnus, Courtesy of the New York Public Library*

(*Bottom*) New York Harbor View, 1869. *By A. R. Waud for* Harper's Weekly, *Taken from Plate 126 in Kouwenhoven,* Adventures of America, *Courtesy of Harper & Bros.*

Union Square, New York, *ca.* 1870.
*Kilburn Bros. Stereograph, Courtesy of
George Eastman House*

Old South Church, Boston, with horse cars in foreground, *ca.* 1870. *C. H.
Graves Stereograph, Courtesy of George Eastman House*

Bird's-eye View of St. Louis, *ca.* 1870. *Continent Stereoscopic Co., Courtesy
of George Eastman House*

(*Top*) California Street, San Francisco, *ca.* 1870. *Watkins Stereograph, Courtesy of George Eastman House*

(*Bottom*) River Boats at New Orleans, *ca.* 1870. *Underwood & Underwood Stereograph, Courtesy of George Eastman House*

Calumet Avenue, Chicago, 1874. *Lovejoy & Foster Stereograph, Courtesy of George Eastman House*

Mississippi River Bridge, St. Louis, *ca.* 1874. *Boehl & Koenig Stereograph, Courtesy of George Eastman House*

(*Top*) Machine Hall, Philadelphia Exposition, 1876. *Wilson & Adams Stereograph, Courtesy of George Eastman House*

(*Left*) Detroit Art Museum, Loan Exhibition, 1883. *Earle & Hawley Stereograph, Courtesy of George Eastman House*

(*Right*) Fountain Court, Columbian Exposition, 1893. *B. W. Kilburn Stereograph, Courtesy of George Eastman House*

(Top) Cable Car Traffic on State Street, Chicago, 1885. *J. F. Jarvis Stereograph, Courtesy of George Eastman House*

(Bottom) Elevated in the Bowery, New York, *ca.* 1890. *Keystone View Stereograph, Courtesy of George Eastman House*

New York Skyline, *ca.* 1896; one of the earliest pictorial records of the changing skyline. *By Charles Graham, Courtesy of the New York Public Library*

Panorama of Manhattan Island and Hudson River during Hudson-Fulton Celebration, Sept. 25, 1909. *Phelps Stokes Collection, Courtesy of the New York Public Library*

Ocean Grove and Asbury Park, New Jersey, *ca.* 1900. *Kouwenhoven,* Adventures of America, *Plate 212, Courtesy of Harper & Bros.*

(*Top*) "The Mall," Central Park, New York, *ca.* 1890. *American Stereoscopic Co., Courtesy of George Eastman House*

(*Bottom*) Randolph Street, Chicago, *ca.* 1893. *Jarvis Stereograph, Courtesy of George Eastman House*

Driving on Grand Boulevard, Chicago, *ca.* 1894. *J. F. Jarvis Stereograph, Courtesy of George Eastman House*

Powers Block, Rochester, during the McKinley campaign. *From* Art Work of Rochester (*1896*), *Courtesy of the Rochester Public Library*

Mother and Child at Ellis Island, 1905. *Photograph by Lewis Hine, Courtesy of George Eastman House*

Relaxation at Ellis Island, 1905. *Photograph by Lewis Hine, Courtesy of George Eastman House*

White's Model Tenements, Brooklyn, 1879. *De Forest & Veiller*, The Tenement House Problem, *Courtesy of The Macmillan Co.*

"School Sink," New York's East Side, *ca.* 1896. *R. W. De Forest & L. Veiller*, The Tenement House Problem, *Courtesy of The Macmillan Co.*

(*Right*) Boys Playing on Empty Lot; Stereograph, *ca.* 1900. *Courtesy of George Eastman House*

(*Below top*) Tenement Playground, 1910. *Photograph by Lewis Hine, Courtesy of George Eastman House*

(*Below bottom*) East Side Interior, 1910. *Photograph by Lewis Hine, Courtesy of George Eastman House*

(*Top*) Tenements, Washington, D. C., 1908. *Photograph by Lewis Hine, Courtesy of George Eastman House*

(*Bottom*) Sweatshop in New York, 1910. *Photograph by Lewis Hine, Courtesy of George Eastman House*

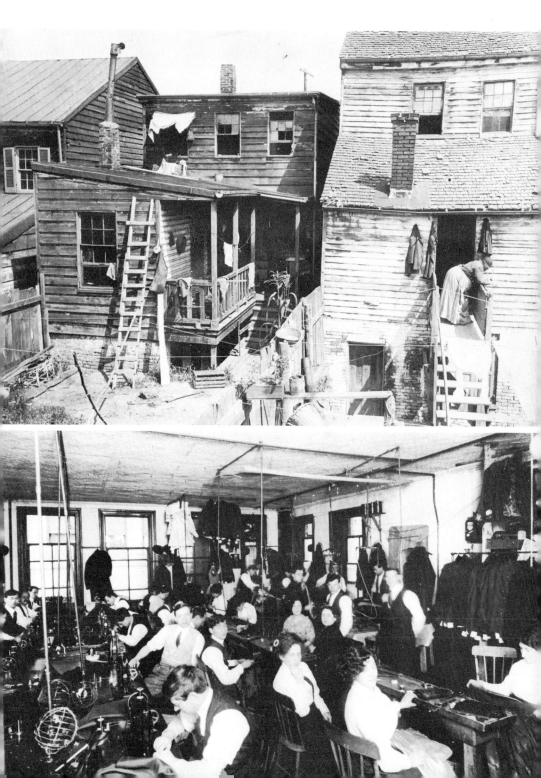

(*Top*) Union Stock Yards, Chicago, *ca. 1905. Griffith & Griffith Stereograph, Courtesy of George Eastman House*

(*Middle*) Night Life in a Pennsylvania Town, *ca. 1908. Photograph by Lewis Hine, Courtesy of George Eastman House*

(*Bottom*) Industrial Pittsburgh, 1909. *Photograph by Lewis Hine, Courtesy of George Eastman House*

with a longer urban background, perhaps with memories of the early high schools and academies or even of college days, were so widely diffused and outnumbered that they permitted the once virile lyceum movement to disintegrate during the seventies.[34] The main functions of the old athenaeums, both their libraries and their lectures, quickly found new sponsors. One of the first, the Chautauqua movement, launched in 1874 as a camp meeting—an outdoor training school for Sunday school teachers—quickly broadened its scope. Attracting the participation of educational and religious leaders, it sent teams of lecturers and entertainers equipped with tents into small communities throughout the country. Its reading courses enjoyed a wide adoption among church groups even in large cities, where they competed with other reading circles, adult study groups, and lecture programs. The athenaeum libraries gave way to more substantial public libraries.[35]

A movement destined to exert wide influence in later decades had its beginning during the nineties in the mothers' clubs developed by the kindergarten teachers of scattered city schools. A National Congress of Mothers drew representatives from some of these groups to Washington in 1897 and three years later effected a permanent organization. The appearance of parents' leagues, mothers' unions, and parent-teacher associations, and the formation of state leagues of these rival groups, prompted an effort in 1908 to merge them all into a united parent-teacher association, though its formation was deferred for seven years.[36]

None of the various adult educational ventures displayed much concern for the mass of urban workers until the success of a "breadwinners' college," started in the New York slums by Thomas Davidson in 1899, proved that immigrant laborers, too, were interested in cultural courses. The death a year later of the eccentric founder of this movement left it in the hands of the students, who made arrangements with the Educational Alliance for a continuation of the classes in the old Hebrew Free School.

Another venture in adult education had commenced some years before when Henry M. Leipziger took over supervision of the night-school courses in six New York City high schools. By stressing practical-science courses, work in civics and other social-life subjects, he created a vital atmosphere. Many prominent citizens accepted invitations to address his assemblies and rejoiced to see the attendance records pass the half-million mark by 1901. Boston, Chicago, and Philadelphia each launched similar experiments in workers' education as the decade advanced.[37]

Perhaps the most dramatic experiment during the last decade of the period was the social-center movement. The night courses in New York

City had brought so many adults into the schools that some of the buildings acquired the character of community centers. An effort to promote that trend was under consideration in the metropolis when the Board of Education in Rochester, where night classes had also developed, ventured in 1908 to establish four social centers at schools in immigrant neighborhoods. Edward J. Ward, the dynamic young director, was full of the social gospel. He quickly organized numerous adult and teen-age clubs in each district and welcomed them to the schoolrooms. They took turns on successive nights in staging lectures, discussions or social events, in a democratic experiment that greatly quickened the life of each neighborhood. Visiting lecturers described the movement with such enthusiasm in national journals that 101 other towns opened 338 school buildings for free community use by 1910. Thirty cities engaged paid supervisors to direct the work of fully organized social centers, and many of them brought reports of a great revival of local civic consciousness to a convention held at Rochester that fall. In the meantime, however, the free discussions in the Rochester social centers had given vent to so much criticism of Boss Aldridge that the modest funds needed to maintain the work were diverted instead to the playgrounds, bringing the pioneer social centers to an end. Ward had already received and accepted a call to organize such a program in the cities of Wisconsin, and Milwaukee soon became the headquarters of this movement for the revitalization of urban neighborhoods.[38]

Thus as the urbanization movement brought increased densities, a greater heterogeneity, and deepening cleavages between various groups, it also spurred efforts to restore friendly human associations within the great impersonal cities of America. The worker who became an employee, losing his handicraft to the machine, sought to better his lot through unionization. The comradeship he developed with his fellows gave him a new sense of belonging; it also had a combative purpose of safeguarding his economic interest that matched the aggressive drives of the capitalist groups. And when, as a result, cities suffered frequent and violent strikes or lockouts, the hardships they produced brought new demands for regulation and speeded the development of agencies to work for industrial harmony.

Even under peaceful conditions, the economy sometimes left great numbers of urban residents destitute, and many public-spirited citizens responded to the challenge of transforming private charity into community welfare. New institutions multiplied as the plight of special groups became apparent; several cities achieved a centralized organization of these programs. Much of the leadership in this work came from the churches, particularly those whose pastors sought to apply religious principles to the everyday problems of urban life. The rise and spread of the social gospel during the last half of the period helped to transform the spirit if not the economy of many cities. It prepared the way for the acceptance of a larger measure of civic responsibility for public health and public welfare. In some instances, notably the spreading blight of the slums, the chief advance was the recognition of a problem. Nevertheless, in each of these major sectors of the urban scene, movements rooted in the city arose and achieved national organization before 1910.

A similar movement had developed a decade or so before the Civil War in regard to the public schools. Many cities now endeavored, and with some success, to fulfill those earlier pledges of a free education for their youth. Some expanded the functions of the public schools to include, in addition to the traditional program, both technical and social training for participation in urban life. A few pioneers in the new field of adult education evolved a conception of neighborhood organization and citizen expression. They sought to bring the residents of urban communities into a more active and understanding relationship with the civic and social affairs of the city.

These varied institutional developments nurtured the growth of professional workers and offered a new social orientation to urban residents. Citizens in the leading metropolitan centers experienced the greatest need and enjoyed the largest variety of opportunities, though the pressure of their numbers rendered all facilities inadequate. Whether the cities large and small could achieve the social reorientation and more abundant life they promised remained to be seen.

IV FORGING AN URBAN CULTURE

[1860–1910]

Urban leadership proved especially effective in cultural fields. A score or more great cities acquired new cultural as well as economic dimensions and progressively extended their influence throughout the country. The wide dispersion of urban centers assured unceasing experimentation in the application of new techniques in recreation, in social intercourse, in both high and low cultural expression. These pluralistic influences were checked, however, as the rapid improvement of the commercial arteries that bound the urban economy together brought countermovements toward standardization.

It would not be difficult to relate most American social and cultural developments during these decades to the urban scene. Certainly the changes, whether of disintegration or of new promise, appeared in greatest profusion in the cities; the history of almost every moderately large town repeated in miniature, often with full detail, the major stages in the country's evolution. Here we are concerned chiefly with those developments in culture (as broadly conceived) that were more directly the product of urban life. Some innovations, as we shall see, responded to new city needs; others sprang from the creative forces gathered there, or received timely support from the energies such communities released. But even as we limit our survey to these more strictly urban influences, we discover emerging under city leadership a new and greatly amplified design for the social and intellectual life of the entire nation.

13. Urban recreation

The plaudits a politician could win, as we have noted above, by extending modest aid to city playgrounds in 1910 contrasted sharply with the prevailing attitude towards recreation a few decades earlier. Not only was the term almost unknown in 1860, but the spirit if not the function and most of its commercial forms had still to be introduced. Although baseball and a few other sports had made an appearance, their character at mid-century recalled the crude and rollicking amusements of frontier days and scarcely attracted the more respectable urban residents. Yet as industrial and commercial affairs increased in momentum and intensity, even the busy owners and managers of stores and factories, as well as their employees, felt the need for relaxation.

Urban groups assumed the lead after the Civil War in the revival of horse racing, the promotion of baseball, and the introduction of new games. It was in the cities that the standardization of basic rules, the partial elimination of gambling, and the development of professional standards occurred. Both the conception of sportsmanship and the appreciation for recreation brought new vitality to urban society.

Baseball demonstrated its value as a release for pent-up energies and a distraction from suppressed feelings at army camps during the war. The popularity the game enjoyed there assured its spread after Appomattox. Intercity contests and regional leagues sprang up, emphasizing the need for standard rules; a hundred local clubs co-operated in 1865 in the organization of the National Association of Baseball Players. As the rivalry between various teams grew in intensity, the problems of integrating and disciplining amateur players prompted Cincinnati to launch the first professional nine in 1869. When the Red Stockings, as they were called, won fifty-six contests on an eastern tour that summer, permitting but one tie, other towns became convinced of the merits of professional players. Soon many places were consolidating their rival local teams into one professional club; those organized at Chicago, St. Louis, Cincinnati, Louisville, Philadelphia, New York, Hartford, and Boston formed a National League in 1876. Strict regulations, designed to assure clean sportsmanship, forbade gambling or book making and the sale of liquor at league games. Improved standards in the layout of the field, in the team's equipment,· which now included gloves, and in news reporting boosted the paid attendance to such a point that the Chicago club opened a new ball park in 1882 and erected the first large grandstand, a model for many to follow.

The independent organization that fall of the American Association reflected the determination of other cities to maintain professional teams and brought the first post-season contest a year later. Although the collapse of that association suspended post-season games in 1891, they were resumed as the World Series in 1903, three years after the reorganization of the American League. Several regional or "bush" leagues were formed on a semiprofessional basis during the eighties; despite fluctuating fortunes, they supplied most northern towns with a busy summer schedule and increased the pressure on stores and factories for the grant of a half-holiday at least once a week. Crowds packed the grandstands and bleachers at the ball parks in a score of cities by the close of the century.[1]

Baseball continued to enjoy precedence on vacant lots and village greens; its more dramatic development as a professional and spectator sport was what chiefly distinguished the game from other participation contests. Cricket, an early rival, received scant attention after the war. Croquet, imported from France and England in 1866, swept the country, attracting youths and adults of both sexes onto the nearest green, and boosted the sales of the newly introduced lawn mowers. The bicycle made a sudden and widespread conquest four years later, but riders soon found the hazards of a fall from the lofty perch over the big front wheel too great to make its use enjoyable on rough roads. Enterprising promoters in large towns built indoor cycling rinks, which served also for roller skating—the new fad of the mid-seventies—and provided shelter for crowds of spectators. Many of the onlookers hastened to acquire one of the new safety bicycles introduced in 1888, and a rash of cycling clubs spread through the cities, prompting the construction of side paths and the paving of streets, and "scorching" along all improved highways in boisterous throngs on Sundays and holidays.[2]

7. Cycling Clubs Parade on Belmont Avenue, Philadelphia, 1879. *Kouwenhoven*, Adventures of America, *Plate 216, Courtesy of Harper & Bros.*

The young men who formed these clubs often felt at a loss during the long winter months unless their group acquired a hall in which they could gather for dancing or other social activities. Indoor baseball received an enthusiastic reception in such clubhouses in 1887; handball and racquets, both from England, found eager players there a decade later, but most of the halls were abandoned as the clubs disintegrated at the end of the century.[3] A few hardy survivals of an earlier group of athletic associations had meanwhile established gymnasiums in each of the larger cities after 1880. There the members practiced the Turner exercises, introduced from Germany some decades earlier, or learned the more recent Swedish calisthenics; some engaged in foot racing, wrestling, boxing, and, towards the close of the period, practiced dives and strokes in the increasingly numerous swimming pools. The gymnasium, which found its way into the Y. M. C. A.'s, the colleges, and some high schools, became an important center of urban recreation. A survey in 1891 found 165 in active use, half of them with trained directors; a much more rapid growth followed the invention of basketball the next year at the Springfield "Y" Training School.[4]

The exercise and excitement these games brought answered many needs of office and store clerks and the young business and professional men who increasingly thronged the central districts of large towns. They often rubbed shoulders with factory workers, too, at the ball parks on a Sunday or holiday, and developed a keener sense of community solidarity than any other experience afforded, as Baltimore, during the heyday of the Orioles in the nineties, and many other cities demonstrated.[5] Both groups turned the bicycle to practical transport use after the close of the century; neither had more than an occasional contact with horse racing and other sporting events that drew some of the old social families and the new rich closer together during these decades.

The ability to own and drive a carriage had become the distinguishing mark of the well-to-do urban family. Possession of a fast trotter often quickened its master's pulse, particularly in the winter months that brought fine sleighing, but only the more dashing sons of the old families and the more venturesome businessmen joined the driving clubs or purchased racing thoroughbreds. Unfortunately, the climax of each driving association's season, the annual week of races at its park or the city fairgrounds, attracted, in addition to its catch of nationally famous horses and huge crowds of spectators, a host of professional gamblers who offended conservative folk and aroused serious opposition to horse racing.[6]

Despite this criticism, race tracks thrived on the outskirts of the major metropolitan centers, and driving parks in the environs of lesser cities. Jerome Park was opened in Westchester in 1866 and Monmouth Park across the Hudson at Long Branch soon after, as well as Washington Park near Chicago; these tracks or their successors outclassed all save Churchill Downs, near Louisville, where the Kentucky Derby was launched in 1875. The driving clubs in Buffalo, Cleveland, Rochester, Springfield, and Hartford joined that year to found a Grand Trotting Circuit, which assured each park an exciting week of sport for many years. Gradually, however, the excesses of the gamblers and the mounting indignation of the public against rigged races provoked such opposition to gambling that several key northeastern states banned it. Some driving parks closed their gates and sold their land for subdivision, but others carried on with local matinee races and horse shows. Exhibitions and sports events helped to sustain a few until the automobile displaced the horse in fashion as well as transportation towards the close of the period.[7]

Several additional sports answered varied urban needs and enjoyed wide favor until the automobile or some other development partially displaced them. Tennis, another British contribution of the mid-seventies, acquired a wide vogue on suburban lawns during a slump in the bicycle craze in the mid-eighties, and it continued to hold a firm place among a young, fashionable set who could afford to maintain courts, pay club dues, and attend frequent tournaments; several cities decided around 1900 to construct courts in the public parks. When prize fighting experienced its spectacular rise with the development of championship bouts after the Civil War, many fans who could not attend the major fights flocked to the beer gardens to witness exhibition matches between some of the principals and their sparring partners or between boxers of local repute. The gamblers and underworld characters who frequented these events gave boxing an unsavory name and prompted legislative action that drove prize fighting underground in many states. Secretive but gory bouts continued to occur in the equally clandestine cock-fighting pits that found a hiding in old barns or cellars on the outskirts of many cities, but the beer gardens turned increasingly to music and dancing.[8]

Excitement over the contests between English and New York yachts for the America's Cup in the late sixties spurred interest in that sport around other great harbors and at towns near inland lakes. In spite of the expense of membership, city yacht clubs increased from fifteen to 125 within the next two decades, and scheduled annual regattas and other events for the numerous classes of boats developed in these years. Interclub and translake as well as transatlantic contests engendered press interest.

Of course the majority of those attracted by water sports had to be content with membership in a rowing club—popular in many places during the seventies—a canoe club, or a camping association. The steadily increasing number of summer cottages that sprang up along rivers, lakes, or seashores within a few miles of many large cities in the eighties and afterward never caught up with the growing desire of their residents to escape from the hot streets during "melting seasons." Mountain hotels in the Catskills, the Adirondacks, and the White Mountains vied for the patronage of eastern urbanites, and the matchless resources of the Rockies began to attract visitors.[9]

Resort towns in the mountains and on the seashore grew into summertime, and in the case of Florida wintertime, cities, where the well-to-do enjoyed an opportunity to bathe, to boat and fish, perhaps to hunt, and in any event to escape urban tensions during vacations of a week or more, which gradually became customary even for the middle classes. Those unable to take such trips flocked to the lakeside parks and sylvan retreats that appeared in the vicinity of most large towns. When, during the depression of the nineties, the promoters of some of these amusement centers faltered, the trolley companies hastily seized control; by 1902 fully a third of the transit companies operated nearby resort parks, which numbered 289 that season and increased to 357 during the next five years.[10] River and lake ports acquired a new diversion in the eighties when, following the decline of the steamboat passenger lines, many captains remodeled their boats for excursion trips. Their moonlight runs with music and dancing became popular on the Great Lakes and especially on the Mississippi, where jazz bands from New Orleans and ragtime players from St. Louis, already in demand at their cabarets and dance halls, added excitement to the showboat rides before the end of the century.[11]

New games generally stimulated the formation of separate clubs, and golf, introduced from Scotland in 1888, was no exception. The country clubs it produced quickly enrolled wealthy members and extended broader services than any of the other urban societies. The need for spacious grounds with an irregular terrain, forced golf-club officials to comb the suburbs for suitable estates, whose mansions often supplied clubhouses that attracted the interest of each member's entire family. Other recreational features were added, as well as dining facilities, and the country clubs, which appeared in the vicinity of all large towns around the turn of the century, acquired an exclusiveness foreign to most sports groups and became the local arbiters of social preference in many cities if not in the great metropolitan centers.[12] Their flexibility enabled them to appropriate the activities of the hunt and polo clubs, which were often mere subsidiaries, and those that the promoters of automobile clubs projected but never accomplished.

Though its organized social functions were truncated, the automobile's rapid introduction after 1900 absorbed much of the energy formerly devoted to other sports clubs. The family car reinforced the cyclist's demand for improved roads, but drove the latter as well as the horse and buggy from the better highways and diverted many backers of the driving and yacht clubs to the purchase and use of this exciting new toy. The staging of road races during the late nineties and the organization of successive "gymkhana" meets on urban fairgrounds kept the early officials of the auto clubs busy. But the members were more appreciative of the opportunity to revive the old custom of family picnics, more responsive to the prospect of a full season's enjoyment of a nearby summer cottage. By the close of the period, when some northeastern cities boasted one car to every twenty families, the automobile clubs had degenerated into service agencies; the popularity of many other adult sports groups was also beginning to wane as a new era of individualized recreation opened.[13]

Nevertheless, before it subsided, the adult-sports movement served as a great integrating force, breaking down many earlier barriers. It also rendered valuable aid to the campaign in behalf of more adequate provisions for children's recreation in the cities. Charitable people in congested Boston made the first advance in this direction in 1885. Most earlier opportunities to play in school yards and on vacant lots had disappeared as urban growth, especially in the metropolitan centers, appropriated such plots for school annexes and other buildings, crowding the children into the streets. The boys, of course, had for years flocked to swimming holes in nearby rivers and streams, or to the docks in port cities, for a refreshing dip in summertime, yet most towns endeavored to stop such activities as dangerous or leading to indecent exposure. Privately operated baths and beach parks advertised their facilities, but since many poor folk, youths as well as adults, lacked the admission fees, New York, Boston, and a few other large places opened public baths primarily for hygienic purposes.[14]

These provisions failed, however, to touch the recreational problems of small children. Fortunately a new incentive for the establishment of playgrounds arrived in the mid-eighties from Germany, where the sand heaps first provided at convenient points in Berlin in 1876 had attracted wide interest and imitation in other cities. Laudatory accounts of Boston's pioneer sandbox of 1886 prompted settlements, churches, and schools to establish ten more within two years. Groups in New York, Chicago, Providence, and Philadelphia quickly took up this work, and the provision of sandboxes spread to Pittsburgh, Baltimore, Milwaukee, and other towns in the early nineties. Sports enthusiasts in metropolitan centers soon joined the settlement-house leaders in advocating play facilities for all boys and girls.[15]

A few cities, notably Chicago in 1886, had previously set aside small areas in their public parks for playing fields, but these concessions, chiefly to young adults, had been grudgingly made, since the parks were regarded as sylvan estates not to be bespoiled by reckless feet. A new attitude began to appear when Boston laid out several playfields in its metropolitan park system in 1893. Philadelphia took similar action that year, yet it was not until Hull-House opened a model playground for children of all ages in 1895 that the pattern, already developed abroad at Dresden and Glasgow, of regularly appointed supervisors in charge of game programs and other activities received a trial in America. Other settlements followed that lead; an Outdoor Recreation League was formed at New York in 1899 to acquire and clear a site and maintain a playground which became known as Seward Park. Its popularity not only inspired similar efforts in many towns but also, in 1903, prompted the New York authorities to condemn for playground purposes several slum sites valued at $2,000,000—a costly move that convinced some other cities of the merits of less tardy action.[16]

Boston opened the first outdoor gymnasium in 1889, on the north bank of the Charles. Featuring a floating tank for swimmers and such apparatus as swings, slides, and horizontal bars, Charlesbank served as a model for bathing piers in New York and elsewhere. It may also have spurred a new development at Louisville, where in 1893 the authorities devised the field house as a retreat for children driven from their playground by bad weather. Again, alert cities fell into line—New York, St. Paul, Denver, and especially Chicago, which equipped its field houses with swimming pools, club rooms, and kitchen facilities. There and at Boston and elsewhere the supervisors introduced arts and crafts, story hours, and other constructive features. Several towns opened rooms in nearby schools as playground shelters; some, as we have seen, carried this development a step further with the creation of social centers.

By 1910, eighty communities were maintaining public playgrounds, and nearly a hundred more had similar facilities under private sponsorship. The Playground Association of America, organized in 1906, had in four years listed 3345 play leaders. Yet Rowland Haynes, its first field secretary, quickly discovered, after an inspection of several progressive centers, that even their model provisions served but a small portion of the children in limited areas, and that the supervision was still quite inadequate.[17]

Most of the early play leaders had to learn their skills on the job. Only a few classes at the Sargent School of Physical Education for Women in Cambridge and others at the Y. M. C. A. training schools in Springfield and Chicago supplied instruction useful to playground directors. To supplement such training, the Playground Association outlined a course of study in 1909, which sixty cities offered in evening school programs the next winter.[18]

Several allied developments revealed that both public and private agencies had become alert to urban recreational needs. Many cities, rapidly extending their park areas after the turn of the century, introduced both active and passive amusements. Chicago had created the pioneer park zoo in 1868; although barely a score appeared before 1900, their number doubled within the next decade.[19] The sports activities in the colleges were not strictly urban manifestations, yet they tended to become such as many of the contests attracted numerous spectators from nearby cities. Meanwhile, the rapid extension of competitive games into the high schools after the turn of the century created new loyalties and aroused a team spirit in many urban neighborhoods.[20] Moreover, the summer camps, which had their experimental beginnings under private auspices during the eighties, developed rapidly in the next decades with the backing of the Y. M. C. A.'s, Y. W.'s, secondary schools, and settlements. Such camps numbered at least twenty-five, all for boys, at the turn of the century, and increased to one hundred and five for boys and forty-one for girls by 1910. The organization at Boston of the Federated Boys' Clubs in 1906 and the launching at New York four years later of the Boy Scout movement (which drew together under English inspiration several earlier boys' clubs, in some instances dating back four decades) gave further assurance that urban youth would increasingly enjoy this "new dimension in American life," as Professor Schlesinger has aptly characterized the recreational awakening.[21]

The urban recreational movement sprang from divergent sources and yielded many rewards for city dwellers. Some games were imported from abroad; others were adopted from earlier pastimes or devised for special purposes. The increased congestion of cities deprived urban Americans of most of the opportunities for relaxation their forebears had enjoyed in a rural or frontier setting and spurred the quest for substitutes. At the same time the closer, yet more impersonal, contacts afforded by urban crowds prompted the development of standardized games and assured popular backing for spectator sports. The general drudgery and monotony of the tasks of both laborers and mechanics and the increased tensions experienced by businessmen tended to crowd both the grandstands and the playing fields of all cities with boisterous enthusiasts. Participants learned a new sense of discipline, called sportsmanship, as well as a team spirit, and the great host on the sidelines enjoyed the excitement generated by the contest. Many acquired a team loyalty, which often helped to breach earlier social barriers and create a new sense of group or community solidarity. Intercity contests abetted this trend and enabled regional rivals to work off their hostilities in a harmless fashion. Meanwhile, the almost universal popularity of baseball and other spectator games spurred the demand for special and regular holidays and for other opportunities to enjoy local events. Thus the sports movement brought the concept of leisure back into the American dream.

These recreational activities followed broad urban trends. The professionalization of many of the athletes, and of the playground leaders, paralleled developments in other fields, as did the commercialization of many sports. The competitive character of most games fostered the growth of leagues and associations that drew neighborhoods and cities into wider relationships. The sports movement not only helped to transform the internal life of growing communities but also contributed to the rapid urbanization of the nation as a whole.

14. *Entertainment and the arts*

An urgent craving for amusement gripped the city's adults as well as its youth. Rapid urban growth had dislocated earlier neighborhood and family pastimes, so that many old residents felt almost as lost in the surging crowds of their city as the uprooted newcomers. Some endeavored to dispel their loneliness with commercial entertainment; others found expression through the popular or the fine arts; still others established their identity by participation in the social clubs with which most cities increasingly abounded.

Several new forms of entertainment appeared, some imported from abroad, some concocted in the boom towns of the West or in the equally turbulent metropolitan centers. Taverns and theaters acquired new functions and experienced a progressive transformation in step with other urban trends. The rapid growth of cities created a rich market for entertainment, and their wide distribution throughout the country provided an opportunity for enterprising promoters to organize great theatrical chains and amusement circuits that rivaled the industrial and utility trusts in extent and influence. Fortunately, these quasi-monopolies never completely stifled local creative and competitive efforts.

The tavern, which continued to serve each new frontier's special needs, gave way to great commercial hotels in the cities, scattering its auxiliary functions to restaurants and saloons, dance halls and theaters. All of these institutions had, of course, appeared before the Civil War, but they now multiplied in number and developed a more specialized character.

Some hotels furnished bed, board, and barber shops for the traveling public; others cared for more permanent residents in much the same fashion. Both types soon acquired additional features—a banquet hall or ballroom, beauty parlors, club rooms, newspaper stands, and clothing shops. The character of the city as well as the status of the hotel was often revealed by the degree to which its lobby evolved from a simple entrance hall into a bustling interior court where news counters and porters' stands flanked the registration desk, while a scattering of chairs and divans accommodated idlers as well as busy men transacting hasty negotiations. Whether the décor was sumptuous, mediocre, or bleak, the activities boisterous, reserved, or furtive, the social atmosphere became increasingly impersonal as the city grew in size.

The patrons of the ever more numerous hotels helped to support new urban facilities for entertainment. Introduced in a few metropolitan centers before the Civil War, the practice of dining out spread to other large cities as the decades advanced. The more cosmopolitan towns afforded a choice of French, Italian, and, by the nineties, Chinese cooking. Few places could rival the gastronomic and atmospheric splendors offered at Delmonico's successive restaurants in New York, but San Francisco quickly won distinction in this field, and many other cities developed dining establishments of special fame. Some were noted for the silver dollars embedded in their marble floors, others for the size of their mirrors, the skill of their chefs or waiters, the eccentricity of their managers, or the entertainment they supplied. These restaurants, along with the pretentious hotels, provided a setting for the social revolution that was sweeping through the cities. It was here that the new rich challenged and in some places overwhelmed the old social hierarchy whose mansions no longer seemed either so elegant or so adequate as in former decades.[1]

Only a limited number of hotels and restaurants performed such functions; the great majority served the restless urban crowds in simpler ways. The dining hour was, in fact, shortened rather than lengthened in most cases, as the introduction of hot dogs, ice-cream cones, and soft drinks popularized the quick-lunch counter. The cafeteria line, devised at Chicago in 1895, began to displace waiters in a few metropolitan restaurants at the close of the century. But in spite of the fact that relatively few people learned to dine out for the sheer pleasure of dining, the development of a new group of luncheon clubs, starting with the Rotarians at Chicago in 1905, brought another significant combination of functions—business and social with dining—that was to change the life patterns of urban businessmen.[2]

In the cow and mining towns of the Great West the taverns persisted and acquired a raw character, attracting gamblers, prostitutes, and other representatives of an uprooted populace. Although law and order eventually triumphed in most places as they achieved urban proportions, the number of single men—miners, cowhands, and lumberjacks—who thronged into the western cities, eager to spend the gold nuggets or silver dollars garnered during lonesome months at bleak camps, exerted a continuing pressure for excitement.

When the tavern no longer sufficed, music and dance halls and other dispensaries of amusement appeared. San Francisco, which became a lively theatrical center in the fifties, sent a troupe of minstrels on an eastern tour a decade later; Virginia City, Denver, and even pious Salt Lake City developed major theaters as well. These and other western towns gave a boisterous welcome to the many dramatic stars, variety shows, and olio dancers who visited there, and even to fledglings making their first bow; the honky-tonk spirit that animated many West Coast troupes made booming Seattle at the turn of the century second only to New York in its burlesque shows.[3]

The western cities exerted a special influence in the entertainment field, and those in the East presented an equally fertile soil for commercial amusements. The beer gardens, introduced by the Germans during the fifties, prospered as their gay sociability spread to most northern towns where these immigrants congregated; whenever the temperance forces triumphed, many convivial patrons retreated behind the closed doors and drawn shades which had converted the still earlier groceries and dram shops into saloons. Most efforts at regulation simply drove such establishments further underground, where their entertainment became more closely linked with professional gambling, prostitution, and new brands of organized crime. "Stall" saloons as well as gambling dens, low music halls, and houses of ill fame reappeared in every city a few months after each raid; moreover, as we have already seen, the corner saloon became the poor man's club by the end of the century, when the lists of such establishments in urban directories exceeded those of ministers and teachers combined.[4]

The low music halls, especially popular in metropolitan centers where strangers sought excitement, brought a resurgence of social dancing in the eighties and nineties. The ragtime players who first gained a hearing in Sedalia, Missouri, in St. Louis and other river towns, the blues singers in these and several southern cities, and the jazz bands of New Orleans—all gave an early taste of a movement that was destined to sweep urban America.[5]

Higher grades of entertainment also thrived and won a more respected position. The cool tolerance with which the better elements had regarded the theater, even as late as the mid-century, gave place to an increasingly enthusiastic acceptance. Soon every community of urban pretensions, which included many with populations under 2500, boasted its "opera house"; cities of 20,000 or more usually had at least two competing theaters as well as other halls ready to welcome a visiting troupe of actors, acrobats, or minstrels.

The theatrical stock companies that struggled for a footing in a dozen places before the Civil War, strengthened occasionally by visiting stars from New York, New Orleans, or Europe, faced a new situation in the late sixties when the improved rail connections encouraged leading actors and producers to set out with an entire company on an extended tour. The wide scattering of cities, all equipped with theaters and spaced short railroad journeys apart, enabled an ambitious manager to book a series of one- or two-night stands across the country, which took many recent metropolitan hits to every alert town. Most of the abler stock players joined the touring companies, and as each troupe required a specialty in the form of a talented star, a versatile repartee for a variety show, a column of shapely legs, or a popular play, the opportunities presented to aspiring thespians and to clever playwrights were unprecedentedly rich.[6]

Although few of the new group of American dramatists made a deliberate effort to interpret the city itself, Augustin Daly's *The Dark City,* Bronson Howard's *Saratoga,* Augustus Thomas's *The Capitol,* David Belasco's *The Charity Ball* and *The City,* and Charles Hoyt's very popular *A Trip to Chinatown,* all portrayed urban situations. Several of the playwrights, as well as a few vaudeville producers, notably Edward Harrigan, also dealt perceptively with metropolitan situations. Many more used the contrast between urban and rural characters and backgrounds to sharpen their action or to amuse audiences whose memories still, in fact, straddled the city line. The increased emphasis on realism was perhaps the response of a youthful urban society to a new social experience not yet sufficiently absorbed to be treated symbolically. And the practice of glorifying the star, which most "vehicles" of the day facilitated, gave expression to the individualism that characterized the American city dweller of this period.[7]

The contributions of a host of talented actors, both native and foreign, added greatly to the joys of city life. It is also pertinent to note that the task of plotting the lengthy tours and holding the troupes together required business rather than dramatic skills. Informal agreements between scattered theaters to book the same plays and stars in succession quickly broke down in practice. Gradually a number of chains developed linking theaters in neighboring places and giving their joint management a more effective bargaining power with stars and producers. The competition for choice performers became so intense that several leading promoters eventually formed a syndicate to control and systematize the tours. Generally one theater in each moderately large town secured exclusive bookings through the trust, thus shutting out local rivals but at the same time limiting its own choices.[8]

The power of the syndicate, headed by Charles Frohman, Marc Klaw, and others, spread widely in the late nineties and continued for more than a decade. That arrangement assured a steady fare to affiliated theaters, as well as regular engagements to the chosen actors and their supporting companies, but the number of independents was so great on each side that rival producers such as David Belasco carried on an effective competition, and rebellious stars such as Mrs. Fiske and Mrs. Carter had little difficulty securing audiences, though they sometimes had to perform in second- or third-rate halls. Since the favorite theater was generally the parade center for local society, which assured a larger and more fashionable crowd, the independents had to strive more earnestly for a hearing. This often led to excesses of emotionalism and other forms of sensationalism, yet Julia Marlowe won her place as an interpreter of Shakespeare by captivating miscellaneous audiences on unsponsored road tours during the late nineties. Other able stars who did not line up with the trust sometimes benefited from the closer association they enjoyed with the rollicking entertainers on the vaudeville stage or in the burlesque troupes, which helped to encourage the fresh outcropping of genuine dramatic talent in America.[9]

New York maintained its dominating influence, and a successful run on Broadway became the goal of every actor and playwright. Luxurious theaters were built in Chicago, Boston, Philadelphia, San Francisco and other cities, many of them larger than the New York standard, but their first nights and regular billings seldom afforded the excitement that similar productions in Gotham engendered. A ring of tryout towns, stretching west from Providence to Rochester and south to Baltimore, enabled cautious managers to gauge their new productions and make last-minute changes before facing the Broadway crowds, which had now become the crucial test.[10]

If, as many critics charged, the commercial organization curbed the creative energies of some playwrights, the profession as a whole received more handsome rewards than any comparable group. The road companies multiplied ten times during the last two decades of the century.

As gas lamps glittering in hundreds of theaters gave place to the more brilliant electric lights, the five thousand thespians of 1880 increased threefold and enjoyed steadier employment.[11] They included not only those who played on the legitimate stage but the members of at least eighteen "Tom companies" in 1900 (when the popularity of *Uncle Tom's Cabin* had already dropped 60 per cent), and also the much more numerous vaudeville, burlesque, and musical comedy troupes. That their combined efforts satisfied an urban need was demonstrated by the popular response. And although the higher services of dramatic art were generally absent, most American towns had at least an annual taste of Shakespeare and occasional treats from contemporary European dramatists as well as the more bounteous domestic output. Moreover, the humor engendered by the comic actors, notably Harrigan and Hart, frequently helped to draw listeners of varied backgrounds closer together, while the gay songs and dances developed a wider zest for music.[12] If the city's underworld was still too inchoate to inspire dramatic presentation, the welcome that places large and small accorded Buffalo Bill's *Wild West Show* and other versions of the vanishing frontier gave new folk heroes to the world of the theater.[13]

Critics in many cities sounded grave warning that the cheaper theaters with their popular shows and vulgar amusements would drive out serious drama. Yet the second- and third-rate houses, where immigrant societies often presented their native productions and where civic groups occasionally staged a morality or historical pageant, served to introduce many newcomers from abroad and from rural America to the delights of the stage. Many of the leading stars graduated from the numerous ranks of the variety troupes, and some skits which first made their appearance on such bills received enough applause to warrant efforts at their refinement. Thus the leg show, which horrified critics of the *Black Crook* performances in the late sixties, nevertheless attracted a great following and won respectability as a feature in some of the light operas that later swept the country. Gilbert and Sullivan's *Pinafore* had popularized that medium in 1878. Still lighter and gayer musical comedies captured urban stages after the success of the *Gayety Girls* in 1894.[14]

The vaudeville theaters, long since purified by Tony Pastor and enlivened by Weber and Fields, among other comedians, multiplied rapidly during the nineties and formed competing circuits or "wheels" of their own. Some managers of metropolitan centers, hoping to check the annual exodus to the beaches, offered roof-garden entertainments

Charles Graham

8. *The School for Scandal* Opening Night in New York Theatre, Jan. 4, 1882. *Kouwenhoven,* Adventures of America, *Plate 209, Courtesy of Harper & Bros.*

during summer months. Their establishments faced a more serious threat from a still newer form of amusement, the cinemas, which spread to every town during the early years of the century.[15]

The invention of the kinetoscope and other ingenious devices for the display of moving pictures in a box had provided an additional curiosity during the nineties at beach resorts and at the entrance to downtown amusement centers. The popularity of the new toy, which delivered a brief and flickering motion picture for a penny, gave rise in many cities to dusky arcades equipped with a dozen or more such machines, each fitted with a different film, sometimes with a phonograph at hand as an additional attraction. As the novelty of a motion picture of a man walking or a railroad engine steaming away wore off, promoters ventured to "shoot" views of popular dances and acrobatic tricks; soon many brief variety skits were shifted from the "boards" to the arcades. When in the late nineties Edison and his rivals developed the vitascope and other machines to throw such pictures on a screen, some theaters hastened to acquire projectors, billing the short films as special features.[16]

These novelties also lost their appeal to sophisticated audiences, but they continued to attract an increasing attendance at the arcades. After the turn of the century, when some of these establishments opened small halls and installed screens, the Nickelodeon was born. As the streams of new patrons lengthened, attracted by the modest price and eager to see a short view of a prize fight, a train robbery or a burlesque dance, such establishments multiplied in the poorer sections of many cities and along the main streets of most towns until they threatened to rival the saloons in number. By 1905 the new entertainment had not only dealt those ancient institutions their first body blow but had also checked the spread of theaters. Within the next five years alert cities and states adopted regulations to assure safety in film projection. As pioneer film producers explored the possibility of projecting news events and more elaborate dramatic scenes, some vaudeville theaters switched wholly to motion pictures; so many new cinemas opened throughout America that one estimate placed their weekly attendance at 10,000,000 by 1910, greatly in excess of all other theaters combined. A spectator amusement able to appeal to the great mass of urban residents had arrived.[17]

If the popularity of the theater and its offspring seemed astonishing, the spread of a taste for music was even more striking. Urban churches assembled full choirs, often paid their organists and leaders handsomely, and developed a rich repertory of religious music; choral societies forged community ties; regimental and city bands took to the road and attracted throngs to indoor and outdoor resorts across the land; orchestral groups struggled for a footing in many cities and helped to focus their awakening civic aspirations on cultural goals. Improved railroad facilities increased the number of touring stars and companies in this as in the theatrical field, but the great activity of local groups and their schools foreshadowed the development of influential regional centers. Only in opera did New York attain undisputed domination in this period.

New York City had by 1860 challenged the earlier primacy of Boston, Philadelphia, and New Orleans in vocal and instrumental music and the opera respectively. It was assisted in each case by the many European stars who landed there and made it their base. After the first visits of Adelina Patti in 1859, Rubinstein in 1872, Fritz Kreisler in 1888, and a host of others, the warm reception they enjoyed, as well as the lucrative returns, brought them back for innumerable tours. New York also became the distribution center for opera companies whose members hailed for the most part from abroad. Its enduring advantages in these fields hastened the successful development of competing opera houses, concert halls, and other facilities for musical entertainment. Visiting stars could count on an early engagement there and a hearty welcome from fellow countrymen. Moreover, a vast continent stretched out before them with its astonishing revelations of the number of earnest listeners who would gather in unexpected places. In Cheyenne, for example, a town of some 5000 in the early eighties, Colonel Mapleson, the London-trained director of a New York opera troupe, found a "refined society" eager to hear opera.[18]

Although it did not take long for the better elements in each new community to proclaim high aspirations and sometimes to erect pretentious opera-house façades in front of modest halls, the hard task of developing appreciative audiences advanced more slowly. The first try at elegance in San Francisco, as well as at Cheyenne and many other places, passed quickly, but the vigor with which some of these towns and many older ones fostered choral groups and other musical societies in the late sixties and seventies gave promise for the future. The Apollo Clubs of Chicago and Cincinnati, the Cecilia Societies of Boston and Philadelphia, the Loring Club of San Francisco, and a few similar groups elsewhere enlisted sufficient support and talent to help establish the regional leadership of their cities in the musical field.[19]

Many influences played a part in these and other towns. The German singing societies in Cincinnati, St. Louis, and Milwaukee, like the older Yankee church choirs in innumerable places, the Handel and Haydn Society at Boston, and the musical conventions sponsored by William Mason there and at Worcester and as far west as Rochester helped to engender a wide taste for singing. Music teachers multiplied in number as well-organized conservatories opened at Boston, Cincinnati, and Chicago in 1867 and at other major centers in later years. Piano manufacturers prospered and sold their products so widely that visiting Europeans were often astonished to find pianos even in humble homes in back-country towns. The invention and improvement of the phonograph and its distribution during the last two decades of this period stimulated an unprecedented rage for popular music, much of it reflecting urban America.[20]

The programs of local choral societies, the winter series of organ recitals, and the subscription concerts of community orchestras often declined after a few years in each city, when able leaders departed or lost their influence. Sometimes the performance of a professional group on tour shattered local confidence, as at Chicago when the first visit by Theodore Thomas and his orchestra in 1869 revealed the limitations of its own Philharmonic Society under the direction of Hans Balatka and postponed serious local efforts for nearly two decades. Generally, however, such a visit served to arouse community aspirations, as it did in Cincinnati, where Thomas, after the first tour, received an invitation in 1873 to help direct a May Festival that became an important event.[21]

Theodore Thomas had first demonstrated the value of competitive effort in New York when, in 1864, he offered an independent series of orchestral concerts that stimulated its older Philharmonic Society to more serious work. A decade later Leopold Damrosch established the Symphony Society, prompting the Philharmonic to call Thomas back as director; their continued rivalry not only raised musical standards in New York to unprecedented heights but also inspired Boston to combine two earlier and poorly supported ventures into its great Symphony Orchestra in 1881. The tours of the Thomas orchestra had challenged music circles in Boston, Philadelphia, and several midwestern cities; the Boston Symphony, backed by Thomas Lee Higginson, undertook similar tours in the eighties, ranging as far west as St. Louis. Both the Thomas orchestra and that of Walter Damrosch, son and successor to Leopold, journeyed as far as San Francisco, awakening musical interests and elevating standards in numerous places. And when Thomas moved to Chicago in 1891, another major orchestra appeared.[22]

The next two decades saw the founding or reorganization of musical societies and orchestras in many cities and the establishment of professional symphonies in at least a dozen rising metropolitan centers. The orchestras launched at Cincinnati in 1895, at Philadelphia in 1900, at Minneapolis in 1903, at St. Louis in 1907, and at San Francisco in 1911, would survive for decades; those at Pittsburgh, Los Angeles, Rochester, St. Paul, Cleveland, New Orleans, and Seattle, if less permanent, helped to prepare the way for more successful ventures in later years.[23] The work of the Peabody Conservatory in Baltimore, the People's Concert Association in Indianapolis, the Musical Society in Milwaukee, and similar bodies elsewhere, fostered many local programs of real merit. Hugo Münsterberg could not help but marvel in 1905 at the wide extent of the movement that had planted musical conservatories and accomplished orchestras in every large city in America.[24]

Although a dozen or more regional centers of musical appreciation thus developed, in each of which at least one newspaper featured a weekly column of criticism, New York retained its leadership in the field of opera. It supported the formation of ten such companies during this period; some of these disbanded after a few years, but the survivors provided rich seasons at the three magnificent opera houses erected in the metropolis, and shared honors with several companies from Europe in supplying the principal inland cities with opera seasons of varying lengths. Chicago also built three sumptuous opera houses; San Francisco, Philadelphia, and Boston each constructed elegant new ones; many other cities maintained pretentious theaters where the annual week of opera provided the climax for the local social season. Near the end of this period, Boston acquired its own opera company and Chicago joined Philadelphia in a co-operative venture in the field.[25]

Other cities achieved their greatest advances in more popular music. Milwaukee and St. Louis as well as Cincinnati and Chicago developed annual festivals; these heavily German cities and a half-dozen more, including New York, Philadelphia, and Baltimore, maintained public park bands; many others hired private bands for special park ceremonies.[26] The numerous opera clubs that appeared from time to time generally devoted their efforts to light or comic opera, and it was chiefly in this realm that American composers made noteworthy contributions, including DeKoven's perennial favorite, *Robin Hood,* and *The Red Mill,* one of Victor Herbert's early works, which dealt with the experiences in Holland of two tourists from the States. Although most composers received their training and much of their inspiration abroad, a few worked with the minstrels and the musical-comedy troupes in cultivating native traditions. Their products, like the popular songs produced in "Tin Pan Alley," reflected major influences from the American city. Charles Hoyt's farce-comedy, *A Trip to Chinatown,* made perhaps the first use in 1890 of urban life and spirit, as George M. Cohan did with much greater skill in the sparkling dialogues and snappy songs of his *Forty-Five Minutes from Broadway* in 1906.[27]

The enthusiastic support of local bands increased with each passing decade and helped to sustain several great commercial bands. The success enjoyed by Patrick S. Gilmore's Band in the seventies and eighties paled before the triumphs of John Philip Sousa during the next quarter-century. Sousa and his rivals attracted eager throngs to armories and

opera halls in winter and to amusement parks, beaches, and vast amphi-
theaters in summertime. The pleasures thus brought not only to the great
cities, where they made regular and lengthy stops, but also to innumerable towns of modest size, visited during frequent cross-country tours,
provided one of the high points of the era. The popular marches written
by Sousa, among others, and the broad repertoire of the leading bands,
as well as the talents of their soloists, raised mass standards of musical
appreciation.[28]

The most original contribution came from a less promising environment—infamous Storyville in New Orleans. There in the late nineties
the Negro street bands, which had over the previous two decades developed their own spirited rendering of popular marches and hymns for
funeral parades, received an opportunity as dance bands in cabarets to
perfect the music later known as classical jazz. Despite, or maybe because of, their lack of academic training, they were able to merge several folk strains—work songs, traces of original West African rhythms,
certainly a strong contribution distilled from old American ballads by
the blues singers, and perhaps something from the minstrels and other
popular songs—into the new and creative forms of jazz. White bands in
New Orleans could not resist the contagious excitement and developed a
somewhat independent brand known as Dixieland jazz; both white and
Negro bands began to reach out for wider audiences, and their impact
increased in the next period.[29]

A major factor in the growth of cities was the lure they held for the
youth of neighboring rural territories and for men and women generally. The bustle and excitement of day-to-day activities comprised
their principal charm to such potential migrants, but the residents themselves, as well as the numerous travelers and other visitors, soon developed special demands for entertainment. Improved lighting facilities
attracted thousands into the streets, encouraging the purveyors of commercial amusements and stimulating the provision of sophisticated forms
of entertainment. Not only did the new convenience for travel and
advancing technology facilitate the parade of troupes and stars from
place to place, but other aspects of the urbanization movement likewise
affected the city's spirit. Thus the impersonality of city crowds was perhaps nowhere more in evidence than at the band concerts and spectacles
so popular around the turn of the century, while the urban theater dramatized man's nostalgia for experiences increasingly missed by city
residents.

Of course urban entertainment, like so many other aspects of the city, presented two or more quite distinct faces. Impersonal but charged with sentimentality before the footlights, behind them it was often harshly realistic and yet rich in personal satisfaction. The cities offered, through their music classes, societies, and concerts, and through theatrical performances, opportunities for creative expression never before equaled in America. Whether or not these advantages were fully realized, the wide selection of leisure time activities proffered by the cities stirred the interest of all groups, from homeless vagrants at the bottom who frequented the penny arcades, to the socialites who hoped to demonstrate their primacy by attendance at the opera. There were rewards for all, including those who sought professional careers, in urban entertainment.

15. The graphic arts and the sciences

The quest for quality evident in some music circles exerted a strong influence, too, on literature and the graphic arts. Active groups in many cities endeavored to establish institutions worthy of comparison with those of Europe and to develop a broad local appreciation for the best cultural traditions. Here the foreign label held a premium unmatched in any other field, chiefly because of the priority European museums and schools enjoyed in the artistic and intellectual world. Many of the ablest American students went abroad for part of their training, and those who returned, together with talented immigrants, frequently assumed leadership in local societies dedicated to the higher arts, the natural sciences, and other cultural endeavors. They enlisted their major support from those business leaders who traveled abroad and acquired there a taste for art or at least an awareness of the distinction that cultural investments could bring them and their communities.

Yet some of the art clubs and institutes, the scientific and literary societies, which fostered high cultural interests in the major cities, dated back to earlier beginnings and resisted new foreign influences. A few of the new groups also acquired a native or regional flavor and endeavored to perfect and defend it from contamination. The controversies between those who sought to cultivate an indigenous culture and those who held that art and literature, like science, must be universal, brought excitement to many intellectual groups and helped to divert America from a folk to an urban cultural course.

The Civil War snuffed out several art groups in the older cities, but at least a dozen persisted and new ones appeared in all large places during the late sixties and seventies. Having survived earlier crises, the two major academies, in Philadelphia and New York, faced a challenge in the seventies when some of their former students who had continued their studies abroad returned with new ideas and techniques. The National Academy of Design in New York had absorbed much of its youth from England and Italy and the Düsseldorf school; most of its aging leaders, however, had since worked too long in America to give immediate or hearty approval to the younger men returning from Munich and Paris. In 1875 some of the latter gathered the more restless students at the academy into an independent Art Students League, where they welcomed new influences, including that of the impressionists a decade later. A few leading independents who deserted the National Academy joined with young men elsewhere to found the Society of American Artists, which brought new vitality to the art schools and societies of scattered cities and thus offset the predominance of New York.[1]

The Centennial Exposition at Philadelphia gave additional impetus to the art movements in many towns. First, of course, it rejuvenated the Pennsylvania Academy of Fine Arts and equipped it with a new gallery. Another group, organized at Philadelphia in 1873, acquired the permanent building that the state erected for fine- and technical-art displays at the Exposition and emerged as the Pennsylvania Museum of Art and Industry. Since most Americans who visited the fair had never seen such a gallery, its extended displays of American as well as foreign paintings proved exhilarating and engendered a new appreciation for art. Artistic implements and handicraft products, exhibited in adjoining rooms, as at the Victoria and Albert Museum in London, awakened an interest in the practical uses of design and gave encouragement to the educational movement launched a few years before at Boston. The school of industrial art, established at the Pennsylvania Museum the next year, became a model for several elsewhere.[2] In Cincinnati, meanwhile, the Women's Centennial Committee, organized to promote the fair, re-formed its ranks in 1877 as the Women's Art Museum Association to work for a local gallery. Similar clubs sprang up in quick succession at Cleveland, Rochester, Columbus, and Worcester as local artists drew together to maintain life classes, stage annual shows, and campaign for public galleries.[3]

Four leading metropolitan centers were already busy establishing art museums. Washington's Corcoran Gallery, which William W. Corcoran gave to the nation in 1869, helped to precipitate action in New York, Boston, and Baltimore. The Peabody Institute, established in Baltimore some years before, opened a permanent gallery in conjunction with its music school. Then Boston, reviving a movement suspended by the war, pressed a drive for funds that netted $260,000 and made possible the erection of a modest building overlooking Copley Square, where in 1876 the Museum of Fine Arts was formally dedicated.[4]

William Cullen Bryant, who headed a similar movement in New York, accepted the chairmanship of a Committee of Fifty organized late in 1869 to launch a campaign for $250,000 to establish a public art museum there. Although many residents bemoaned the fact that the metropolis, third in size among the great cities of the world, lacked a gallery comparable to those of several smaller places, the subscriptions during the first year totaled only $106,000. Yet the committee boldly determined to plan a museum modeled on the best in Europe; it proceeded to collect and exhibit the art of all fields and ages. The selection of a site in Central Park and the construction of the first building, with a lavish expenditure of city funds granted by Boss Tweed, progressed slowly during the seventies but enabled the committee to concentrate its energies on the accumulation of permanent collections. General Louis Palma di Cessola, an American citizen of Italian birth who had spent six years excavating ancient Roman and Greek ruins on Cyprus, was persuaded to sell his priceless antiquities to the museum and accept an appointment as its first full-time director in 1879. The Parks Department appropriated $15,000 for annual maintenance, and the museum, which had operated in rented quarters for nine years, finally dedicated its new building with a gala ceremony on March 30, 1880.[5]

Art groups in several other cities had established galleries in rented quarters, and two had already broken ground for public museums. The Buffalo Fine Arts Academy, chartered in 1862, the San Francisco Institute of Art, which started a decade later, and Washington University at St. Louis, each opened its gallery during the seventies; at least six other colleges maintained art schools and galleries for their students. The Chicago Art Institute, organized in 1879, acquired temporary quarters that fall and soon undertook the construction of its first building on Michigan Avenue, which reached completion in 1882. Meanwhile in Cincinnati the Women's Art Museum Association had successfully united an older art academy and a school of design into a broader Museum Association, which dedicated a public gallery there in 1881.[6]

Although none of these early institutions could boast of extensive collections, their acquisitions increased rapidly. The European grand tour had become fashionable in postwar years, and many wealthy Americans returned from such trips with works of art to embellish their mansions. Several developed important collections for display in private galleries;

a few, such as A. T. Stewart in New York, Mrs. Jack Gardner in Boston, and Daniel W. Powers in Rochester, opened their halls to public visitors at a small fee. When hard times or the death of the chief patron prompted a request for tax exemption, or for direct public support, its refusal in several instances was disillusioning, and most of these collections were eventually sold, permitting alert museums to acquire some choice items. Many art collectors became museum trustees and in time donated their treasures. Thus the tastes of local patrons helped to determine the specialties of each museum.[7] Staff members also exerted an influence, and some developed high standards of selection.

Commercial galleries multiplied in New York; indeed, one or more appeared in every large town, as the market for art works developed. Some of the metropolitan companies became famous for their auctions, among them Chickering Hall on lower Fifth Avenue; another dealer, Roland Knoedler, assembled a collection of canvases which he loaded into a heavily guarded freight car and exhibited in a dozen inland cities on the eve of the Chicago fair. The market's earlier partiality for British and classical art, and for the landscapes that had displaced portraits in favor after the mid-century, became less noticeable by the late eighties, when museum collectors began a search for the great French, Dutch, and Spanish masters and purchased an occasional modern impressionist. Most acquisition programs, however, except at the Corcoran Gallery, avoided contemporary art, with the result that living painters at home and abroad made few museum sales.[8]

Yet the art clubs did enjoy opportunities to stage annual exhibits at the public galleries, and their members made frequent use of museum libraries and sometimes sketched or painted in their halls. Amateur as well as professional or full-time artists multiplied in each town and entered their paintings and other works in an increasing number of shows.

New art institutes sprang up in places as widely scattered as Providence, Kansas City, and New Orleans; Detroit and Milwaukee both opened museums in 1888. Art displays at the annual industrial exhibitions, which started at Milwaukee in 1881, prompted similar programs in Louisville and Minneapolis and helped to strengthen their local groups. A bequest from Frederick Layton, a leading meat packer in Milwaukee, financed the construction of its gallery; Andrew Carnegie included a generous provision for the fine arts in the institute he gave Pittsburgh in 1896. At Indianapolis the ladies took the lead, as in Cincinnati, and maintained a program of annual shows until a bequest of John Herron, a local real estate dealer, established an institute and gallery in 1902. The Exposition at St. Louis, two years later, provided a public Art Palace for that city. Several towns opened galleries in their public libraries—Kansas City in 1898, Syracuse in 1904, Columbus and Seattle in 1907, Newark in 1909—an arrangement which still continued at Hartford, where the Wadsworth Athenaeum had maintained a gallery since 1842.[9] Buffalo and Portland, Oregon, dedicated museum buildings in 1905; local groups at Albany and New Orleans, among other places, acquired temples of art within the next decade, when three-fifths of all cities over 100,000 and many smaller ones could each boast of its gallery.[10]

This rapid development represented a widespread determination on the part of ambitious cities to provide worthy cultural institutions. But the task did not end with the dedication of the buildings. The acquisition of permanent collections and the pressure for the display of special shows created a demand for more exhibit space. New wings were required at the Metropolitan Art Museum in New York, and at Boston, too, where the trustees had to seek a more spacious site a decade later. The Corcoran Gallery in Washington, the School of Design in Providence, and the San Francisco Institute of Art also acquired new buildings during the nineties, and San Francisco rebuilt again after the great fire of 1906. The Art Institute in Chicago took advantage of the enthusiasm for the Columbian Exposition to abandon its congested Michigan Avenue site in 1893 and move to the Lake Front where it was able to fulfill the larger responsibilities of the "Fair City." [11]

Urban visitors to the Columbian Exposition were better prepared for its art displays than their predecessors had been at the Centennial in Philadelphia. Again the Americans held their own against foreign competition; indeed, some critics grumbled that France in particular had sent only works unwanted at home; years later an art historian would describe the entire visual-arts exhibit as "marked by an empty dexterity which knew no national boundaries." But if few of the 9000 paintings aroused excitement, many visitors marveled at the profuse display of outdoor sculpture, most of it plaster of Paris, that decorated the pediments and domes of the buildings whose Roman, Greek, and Renaissance façades were also of plaster painted white. The sense of spacious unity supplied by the lagoon, around which many spectacular structures were built, thrilled millions of Americans and sent them home with new conceptions of civic art and town planning. The organization of the Municipal Art Society at New York had anticipated the fair by a year;

similar associations now sprang up elsewhere as the movement for city beautification gained momentum.[12]

Although the paintings at the fair had failed to create a stir, new controversies were brewing in several art schools and at the annual shows of numerous local clubs, where followers of the French impressionists displayed their new techniques. A few private collectors in Philadelphia, Baltimore, Buffalo, and Columbus, as well as in New York and Chicago, became patrons of the impressionists; several dealers imported such paintings around the turn of the century for traveling exhibits—a service they had increasingly performed for gallery directors after the Metropolitan Museum adopted the policy of displaying occasional loan exhibits in the mid-eighties. Art lovers in the larger cities had increased opportunities to view the great masters of various countries and eras, including the contemporary, both in the museums and at numerous private and commercial galleries.[13]

An early champion of impressionism, the Art Students League received George W. Vanderbilt's support in the erection of a new school and gallery of fine arts at New York in 1892. Its improved facilities helped to boost the enrollment to a thousand by the end of the century, when it was described as the largest and best equipped in the world. The league, like other academies, suffered recurrent crises as the volatile temperaments of some of its teachers clashed and one or another withdrew to found an independent venture. Although the old National Academy merged with the Art Students League in 1906, the number of institutes in New York increased and the students exceeded 9000 at the close of the period, more than the next five cities together could boast.[14]

These figures included the technical as well as the academic schools and covered a wide variety of interests. The ateliers, begun by several young architects on their return from foreign study in earlier years, had spread to a score of cities and enrolled over 3000 students. The arts-and-crafts movement of the seventies had given rise to numerous industrial-art schools, several of them closely associated with the museums; when some tended to stress practical training to the detriment of artistic feeling, a revival of the Pre-Raphaelite doctrine of William Morris prompted the establishment of new Arts and Crafts Societies in a dozen places in the late nineties, which led in turn to the development of several handicraft centers. Their annual displays, promoted by the *Craftsman* at Syracuse, contributed to the city-beautiful movement and to a resurgence of art interest in several centers of adult education, notably Pratt Institute in Brooklyn, Drexel Institute in Philadelphia, as well as the much older Cooper Union in New York, and several elsewhere.[15]

Many of the institutions and museums offered evening classes and, toward the end of the period, summer classes for a broader public, both juvenile and adult. The loan of art exhibits to the city schools for classroom circulation began at St. Louis in 1878, at first under charitable auspices, and took hold at Boston in 1892, when the Public School Art League was organized. Its practice of decorating classrooms spread to other places and aroused an interest among teachers in the facilities at local galleries. A volunteer teacher of public art-appreciation classes, who first conducted tours in the Boston Museum in 1896, also set a pattern soon widely followed; a decade later that museum appointed the first docent to give interpretive talks covering its various collections and displays. Museums in another half-dozen American cities created similar staff posts before 1910, when the first docents appeared in London and on the Continent.[16]

The new conception of a responsibility to interpret art to the public inspired the founding of a museum in Toledo, Ohio. The interest uncovered by a committee that opened a gallery in rented quarters there in 1901 prompted a wealthy collector, Edward D. Libbey, to offer $200,000 for a permanent museum provided other citizens would match it. When the campaign aroused enthusiasm, the directors organized free Saturday and evening classes, weekly criticism sessions for amateur artists, a collectors' league for boys, and other devices that helped to cultivate wide interest; the new museum, when it was opened in 1912, had the largest percentage of citizen participation reported by any in the country.[17] The Brooklyn Institute of Arts, which established its museum in 1889, began to court the public more vigorously after the turn of the century. Even the great Metropolitan Museum, which continued to place major emphasis on building up its collections in all fields of art, discovered new opportunities for service in 1891 when the park authorities demanded that it open its doors on Sunday. The inrush of visitors who often behaved "as though they were in a dime museum" was disconcerting, but the crowds soon became more orderly, and the directors took advantage of the increased attendance to request and secure larger municipal appropriations.[18]

The search for support was a perennial problem everywhere. Though private subscriptions or bequests built most of the public museums, their endowments were usually pledged for the purchase of art, and the membership fees generally proved inadequate for maintenance. A survey of twenty large cities in 1902 revealed that only fourteen granted over $2000 in public funds for museums of art and science; only four gave as much as $50,000. Although the situation improved during the next four years, New York City contributed more than half the $738,000 allotted to museums by the fifteen municipalities reporting at that date, and only eight granted in excess of $10,000 for salaries, equipment, and maintenance. The chief burden still fell on wealthy patrons, and every institution depended in large part on the generosity of its trustees; few were as fortunate as the Metropolitan Museum, which in 1905 secured J. P. Morgan as president of its board.[19]

It is difficult to weigh the influence of the city on the quality of America's artistic expression during this period, but here as in so many other fields the emergence of a broad urban society became evident. The *American Art Annual,* established in 1898, provided a nation-wide coverage of art news and trends. The organization of the American Association of Museums in 1906 brought their directors and staffs closer together on a professional basis. The American Federation of Arts, which appeared three years later, not only assumed publication of the *Annual* but also established the monthly *Art and Progress* and undertook to organize traveling exhibits, twenty-one of which were sent out in 1913. Private dealers, who had previously given much time to that work, generally welcomed the new arrangement and reported the sale of over 5000 paintings at auctions that year for a total of $2,660,000.[20]

Although the galleries thus ranked with the symphony orchestras as objects of civic pride, and art acquired a prestige value similar to that of opera, neither following compared in number with that of the scientific and literary societies, which fostered museums and libraries in many places. Professional musicians, including teachers, numbered 139,000 in 1910—more than either clergymen, lawyers, or technical engineers [21]—yet engineers and the more numerous physicians together numbered almost twice as many as those in music. These two groups, reinforced by some of the still more numerous teachers and miscellaneous individuals in other callings, supplied a host of amateur and professional scientists whose associations comprised another important feature of urban society. Of course science was no more a product of the city than art or music or creative literature, and it was much less locally centered than any of them, but it, too, felt the urban impact and in turn greatly influenced the city's growth.

Scientific and learned societies that antedated the Civil War, though rooted in specific towns, had sought memberships on a state or national basis. Most of them had taken all knowledge as their province; several had installed cabinets of natural history or other displays in rooms adjoining the libraries they maintained, generally in rented quarters. The first widespread effort to develop complete scientific collections occurred at the colleges, whose natural-science departments vied after the mid-century in the accumulation of geological specimens, fossils, skeletons, and other artifacts. Curious individuals could gain admittance to many of these exhibits, but that was not their object; even the twelve state and national museums of 1880 paid little heed to the public, as one of their leaders admitted, noting that the zeal for collecting had obscured the need for meaningful displays.[22]

Yet the revolutionary development of scientific knowledge, stemming in large part from Europe, was already reaching a wide segment of the urban population, and a new group of scientific societies, organized on the community level, began to appear. At least thirty-three such bodies, professing a broad general interest in science, sprang up in cities during the seventies and eighties. These years also saw the formation of more than sixty groups devoted to specialized fields of science. Many of the latter, such as the Microscopical Society fostered by Henry Lomb at Rochester, were quickly absorbed in the more inclusive local academies of science and became one of several specialized sections. Others, like the Geographical Society at Chicago, nurtured by its wide-ranging metropolitan interests, retained their independence or joined with similar groups elsewhere to form national (or on the West Coast, regional) associations to support publications, arrange exhibits, and hold conventions.[23]

The educational work of these societies differed radically from the scientific courses sometimes offered by the athenaeums and lyceums of an earlier day. The new groups scheduled lectures, but their most frequent sessions heard the reports of members on special projects; their annual meetings often featured an elaborate exhibit of the collections or other tangible results of the work of various sections and individuals. Thousands of adults, many with little formal education, eagerly explored the geology, the plant life, or the antiquities of the area, thus helping those with more specialized training to accumulate data that frequently justified the publications they earnestly produced. Other thousands scanned the heavens, probed the secrets of animal and plant tissue, tinkered with mechanical devices, tested chemical reactions, or speculated on the philosophical implications of the scientific theories and discoveries of the day. Although the enthusiasm of many amateurs declined after a time, prompting them to abandon the societies to the professionals, a generation of urban adults acquired a more objective understanding of their environment in the process. And the increasing ranks of the professionals, enlisted from secondary and higher educational institutions, from technical industries, and from the first research laboratories, brought many local societies into closer affiliation with the national scientific associations that had developed from earlier beginnings in metropolitan centers or were organized through the joint effort of several city societies during the eighties or nineties.[24]

Before they lost their popular base, several of the local academies of science took the lead in successful campaigns for a city museum. Societies as widely scattered as those of Portland, Maine, Savannah, Georgia, and San Francisco, as well as several in between, opened halls of natural history or science during the last quarter of the century; similar groups in Davenport, Iowa, Brooklyn, and Milwaukee prodded the public authorities to take such action. The Chicago fair provided a home and a collection of exhibits for the Field Museum, established there in 1894. State and national associations built new museums in the leading metropolitan centers and state capitals. These, with one or two of the older institutions of the national scientific societies and those erected by state authority at Albany and Harrisburg, proved to be the most effective in the field after the close of the century, when the universities were losing interest in their departmental cabinets.[25]

The danger that all museums would lose their appeal was candidly faced by George B. Goode in the late eighties. His discovery that the Smithsonian Institution, of which he became curator in 1887, was so cluttered with displays that its numerous visitors generally departed tired and bewildered, seldom if ever to return, prompted a reconsideration of its purpose. His proposal that exhibits should present a synthesis of an object, placing it in a functional or natural setting, and should provide the curious observer with a suggestive hint as to its significance, charted a path for alert directors, though few as yet had the staffs to undertake such a program.

Several attempts to perform educational functions had already appeared, however, in a few science as well as art museums. The Buffalo Society of Natural Science organized lecture programs for high school classes as early as 1876, and three years later sent out the first exhibits for display and study in schoolrooms—a program later adopted and expanded at Philadelphia and elsewhere. Adult science lectures at the Davenport and Worcester museums in the eighties and field trips sponsored by several institutions a decade later paralleled similar innovations in the art galleries as the educational function gained acceptance.[26]

It was in the city museums, not those of the national academies or at the universities, that the new purpose took hold most rapidly. They set a pattern which the first company museums, established after the turn of the century in Pittsburgh and at four other places, followed from the start. These were in some respects an outgrowth of the technological fairs staged annually by the business groups of scattered towns and thus reflected a promotional spirit. The old Franklin Institute in Philadelphia had organized the first such fair in 1874 as a warm-up for the Centennial, which in turn demonstrated the value of mechanical displays as well as those of science and art.[27]

The Centennial also spurred the formation of numerous historical societies and the publication of many fat volumes on the history of cities and counties. Although most of these local groups disbanded after a few years, others arose and with the state associations and the patriotic societies numbered 153 in 1900. When the historical societies began increasingly to assemble old books and papers and curious articles of the early days from members' attics, their collections overflowed the library rooms or bank lofts initially supplied for storage. Several state and national associations made more adequate provision for such collections in rented halls during the eighties, and in the next decade societies outside the state capitals acquired serviceable headquarters at Worcester, Chicago, and Cleveland. Boston, New York, Philadelphia, Buffalo, and several smaller cities also provided new repositories before the close of the period.[28]

Although these bodies were located in cities and towns, few of them gave close attention to the community's development. Fascinated by the antiquities of the region or the nation, they collected and studied the records of the pioneers and published much concerning the founders and the early village days. Like the genealogical and patriotic societies, which began to appear late in the century, they answered a need, increasingly felt in the unsettled urban society, for family and social roots. Membership conferred the honor of election by respected citizens or the recognition of distinction inherited from one's ancestors.[29]

For the great majority of urban residents who failed to qualify for S. A. R., D. A. R., or Mayflower buttons, their Irish, German, Scottish, Italian, and similar societies also afforded a sense of belonging, and many of these groups experienced a dramatic shift in function during the period. The original benefit and burial societies gave place to building-and-loan associations and young men's clubs, which endeavored to assure their members a wider participation in the city's life. Some of these soon shared their hold on the second and third generation with cultural groups that sought to revive the traditions, especially the plays and music, of their ancestral homelands.[30] New York, San Francisco, and New Orleans had early capitalized on the colorful pageantry provided by the heterogeneity of their populations, and these, with a few others—Cincinnati, St. Louis, Milwaukee, Boston—were already known for the contributions of their immigrant groups.

Of course the ethnic societies did not rival in number or popularity the fraternal bodies (some of them foreign in origin), which multiplied and became more diversified in these decades. Though not exclusively urban, these knights and ladies of a make-believe culture found their greatest joy in erecting imposing temples and staging spectacular parades on busy streets. By an observance of elaborate rituals and ceremonies, millions of urbanites no doubt manifested their desire for a richer and more imaginative life than experience had brought.[31]

Neither the learned societies nor the ethnic and fraternal groups, despite their concentration in cities, were as truly urban as the women's clubs. These organizations, which had their beginnings at New York and Boston in 1868, multiplied in number and spread widely, particularly after 1890. They ranged from religious and ethical societies, through clubs concerned with charitable and cultural endeavors, to purely social groups. Their activities varied accordingly, but many of them included reading and lecture programs; after 1900 they also assumed in several cities an initiative in cultural matters. Some sponsored weekly musicales, others staged plays, conducted handicraft bazaars and historical pageants or championed the cause of art. They epitomized the progress made in these fields by their home towns.[32]

Although the cities nurtured some creative spirits, their most spectacular developments in the natural sciences and the arts were institutional. Earnest groups of amateurs and professionals, drawn together by mutual interests, founded societies, organized cultural activities, and enlisted the support of wealthy patrons. Their exhibits and other programs often stirred local civic pride and served to refute the aspersions of critical visitors. Every place that acquired metropolitan aspirations soon felt the need for a gallery of art and a museum of science; most cities of 200,000 or more achieved one or both of these goals by the close of the period.

This was a new standard of metropolitan distinction. It was imported from Europe, of course, yet the American city radically redesigned the old cultural models. Although these urban museums and galleries were usually erected as memorials to the wives or sons of local magnates and often displayed pretentious respect for cultural styles and achievements that had little indigenous meaning, most of them quickly developed popular educational features undreamed of abroad despite the fact that comparable institutions there were more frequently maintained by public funds. The American metropolis, not content to accept a gallery or a museum as a treasure trove, demanded services of a broader nature before granting municipal assistance.

The museum directors, on their part, were eager to extend their services, for institutional success was more frequently measured in attendance records than in storage inventories. Thus if the art clubs and galleries, as well as the museums and academies of science, were somewhat less closely identified with creative work in American cities than were those of Europe, they nevertheless contributed to the democratic diffusion of cultural sensibilities and played an important role in the urbanization of countless migrants from rural backgrounds on both sides of the Atlantic. Their activities, if not always their content, mirrored the character of their communities; their accomplishments symbolized, if they did not always express, the metropolitan aspirations of the city.

16. *Literature and learning in cities*

Of all mediums of communication and expression, the American cities of the nineteenth century relied chiefly on the printed word. Writing not only retained the primacy won centuries before in the commercial and legal fields, but also strengthened that position in the social and intellectual realms. All cities exerted both public and private efforts to meet the demand. The public libraries on the one hand, the daily press and weekly or monthly magazines on the other, each served an expanding host of readers. It increasingly became apparent that no self-respecting city could shirk its responsibilities in these fields; few were content until they had also provided an institution of higher learning.

Each of these intellectual agencies acquired a pronounced urban character as the half-century progressed. Public libraries, almost non-existent at the start, achieved a recognized place among municipal institutions and greatly improved their services. Local newspapers increasingly recorded the city's daily experience and supplied the only ready medium for the neighborly information that had once held smaller communities together. Magazines sprang up in every important metropolitan center to supplement the daily paper's other functions; local and regional associations joined the colleges in providing opportunities both for higher education and for continued adult participation in intellectual activities.

The women's clubs frequently joined the campaigns for free public libraries in towns not already provided with such institutions by the late nineties. But that movement had made considerable progress in earlier decades. The athenaeums and young men's associations of pre–Civil War years had founded numerous libraries for their members; although most of these disintegrated with the collapse of the lyceum movement, some found new sources of support from generous patrons, others formed the nuclei for public-supported institutions. School-district libraries in several northeastern states also supplied antecedents for public libraries, though most of their collections were later appropriated by the schools themselves. In 1870 the first report of the U. S. Commissioner of Education listed 161 libraries in 105 cities (not including college libraries), most of them open to the public. Seven had as many as 50,000 books, thirty-six exceeded 20,000, and nearly half reported 5000 or more. By 1900 at least 144 libraries had over 50,000 books, and 54 exceeded 300,000, while 1729 now numbered 5000 or more volumes.[1]

This rapid expansion had been achieved with the aid of many generous patrons. The most munificent was Andrew Carnegie, who was so gratified when Allegheny accepted his original gift of a public library, rejected by Pittsburgh in 1881, that he renewed the proposal to Pittsburgh a decade later when it was ready to comply with his terms; he soon extended an offer of similar buildings to other cities willing to provide sites, buy books, and shoulder maintenance costs. By 1907 his gifts to American municipalities, exceeding $32,700,000, had financed the construction of over 1000 central or branch libraries and effectively established the principle of public support.[2] Some towns rejected Carnegie's offer, hoping to receive a fully endowed institution from a local patron, such as Baltimore got from Enoch Pratt in 1882, but most expanding communities soon outgrew these bequests and assumed the major burden of library support.[3]

Again, collaboration among the more progressive leaders greatly increased the effectiveness of this new urban service. A convention of librarians, which met at Philadelphia during the Centennial of 1876, not only organized the American Library Association but also brought such an outpouring of papers that the special report on "Public Libraries in the United States," in which the Bureau of Education reproduced them, became an invaluable manual for trustees and staffs throughout the country. It reviewed the history of early library efforts and described many features of the ten most successful in a rich documentation of experience that served to guide and inspire new ventures. Equally important were the papers dealing with innovations in technique, notably that of Melvil Dewey outlining his classification system, devised and introduced at the Amherst College Library three years before, and that of William F. Poole of the Chicago Public presenting, among other important details, directions for the preparation of a card catalogue. The adoption, with some variations, of these two basic tools made the growing collections of American libraries more accessible to patrons than the books of any in Europe.[4]

The movement had only commenced, and soon the American Library Association was accenting other possible services. One committee prepared a series of sample catalogues to assist small towns in balancing their collections. Another hailed the merits of the branch system evolved at Boston during the early seventies and later adopted in a few other metropolitan centers; its wider application awaited the enthusiasm engendered at the 1898 convention at Chautauqua, where the campaign to take books into residential neighborhoods was launched.[5] An equally significant development, the provision of specialized children's divisions, began during the late seventies in several Massachusetts cities. The Pawtucket Public Library equipped the first separate room with low chairs and tables; Worcester set aside special shelves for children's books; Hartford organized a children's library society. Brooklyn, Milwaukee, and Denver, as well as Boston and Cambridge, opened children's rooms before 1894, when the discussion of such projects at a Lake Placid convention spurred similar efforts in a dozen places. The announcement of a special course for children's librarians at the Pratt Institute Library School in 1896, and the formation in 1900 of the Children's Librarians Section of the American Library Association, revealed the rapid spread of the movement.[6]

Still another campaign, to make libraries active centers of adult education, took hold in Buffalo, Chicago, and St. Louis a year after Herbert B. Adams made such a proposal at the 1887 convention. Soon a dozen public libraries were sponsoring university extension courses, sometimes in collaboration with a nearby college. As the movement spread to other cities, local committees, composed of representatives of science societies, literary clubs, the public schools, and the library, took charge of the program. In many communities hundreds of eager adults enrolled in such courses, generally of ten weeks' duration; they studied English literature, natural science, and American history, to name the most popular three. The courses prospered throughout the nineties, stimulated in some towns, among them Milwaukee and Atlanta, by the opening of fine new library buildings, in others by the mounting clamor of women for admission to nearby colleges and their determination to prove their point by taking advantage of the opportunities at hand.[7]

Interest in these cultural courses flagged in most cities after 1900 as the associated groups branched off in divergent directions. The ladies turned to club activities; the libraries, renewing their campaign for an extension of branches, continued to build up their collections and their circulations; several of the state universities that had joined the movement undertook a re-examination of the field before launching a more strictly academic program of courses a few years later.[8]

Higher education, creative literature, and journalism were no less closely related to urban growth during these decades. Except for the last, they were perhaps more distinctly separate at the start, yet here, too, the city exerted an increasing influence. Both in their subject matter and in their support, academicians and writers experienced a partial reorientation toward the city before 1910.

Many old colleges, generally planted in a village setting, became the nucleus for a new type of community, the college town. When several colleges, responding to the new interest in science and the urban demand for diversified education, transformed themselves during the seventies and after into universities, their towns also acquired fresh vigor. Ithaca, Ann Arbor, and Madison, among others, became university cities, while Cambridge, Evanston, and Berkeley, because of their proximity to great metropolitan centers, became university suburbs. Other colleges, located in or near growing cities, such as Columbia, New York University, the University of Pennsylvania, and Washington University in St. Louis, acquired many characteristics of city universities. Most of the emerging metropolitan communities nurtured old colleges or welcomed the establishment of new ones within their borders. Whereas their philanthropic support increased threefold between 1872 and 1910, public appropriations mounted much more rapidly. State universities and land-grant colleges received generous subsidies; municipal universities made their appearance in Louisville and Cincinnati as well as in New York City, where Hunter joined City College.[9]

Even new institutions established as universities, notably Johns Hopkins in Baltimore, Clark in Worcester, Massachusetts, and the University of Chicago, sprang in large part from the vigorous life of their home cities and reflected local leadership. Although the inspiration derived from German universities was also important, the determination to match and finally to improve on that model achieved a measure of professional eloquence and a degree of academic freedom seldom realized abroad. The cultural interchange between town and gown, so evident at the establishment of Johns Hopkins, became increasingly significant during these decades in such moderately large places as New Haven, Rochester, Columbus, Ohio, and Minneapolis; there and elsewhere literary and scientific stirrings in the city and a more diversified curriculum in the college revealed much mutual stimulation.[10]

Numerous colleges co-operated, as we have seen, with public libraries and citizens groups in the adult-education programs of the eighties and after, and in the late nineties a few of them assumed full responsibility for courses of academic standing. Seven evening colleges established a pattern for many to follow in later decades. An early emphasis on standards enabled them to supply additional training to teachers and other professionals in many urban centers.[11]

Freed from the educational tasks they had assumed in the nineties, some of the literary clubs began to devote more attention to creative work. At least a dozen Shakespeare societies and two Browning clubs achieved sufficient permanence in eastern cities during the eighties to attract notice by the U. S. Commissioner of Education; many sprang up elsewhere before the turn of the century. The women, welcome there, could not join the older men's clubs that had spread inland from the great Atlantic ports before the Civil War, but since most of these, like the Pundit Club at Rochester, were limited in size by the accommodations of a professional man's parlor, additional groups were formed in many towns as cultivated folk, women as well as men, increased in number and met together to read papers and discuss literary and other intellectual matters.[12]

Some of these bodies enrolled professional writers or helped to develop talents latent among their members. Writers' clubs arose in several metropolitan centers, some in the nineties under the name of Ruskin clubs; generally, however, the more creative spirits congregated in less formal gatherings at favorite studios or restaurants described by O. Henry as "literary landmarks." The offices of the *Overland Monthly* and the *Golden Era* had served this purpose successively in San Francisco during the sixties; much better, in fact, than the Bohemian Club organized there in 1872 did thereafter. A group known as the Little Room provided a center at Chicago during the nineties, helping to nurture the *American,* the *Dial,* and the *Chap Book* and to promote an uplift movement in literature. The *Atlantic Monthly* supplied a literary shrine in Boston, especially during the early decades, as none of the rival journals in New York could do, although New York increasingly drew most of the successful magazines, with their editors and contributors, into its metropolitan sphere.[13]

The success of *Harper's Monthly* and *Weekly,* the New York *Ledger,* and a few other early journals prompted the establishment of a host of new magazines during the seventies and in each succeeding decade. Every metropolis had its crop, some aspiring to literary distinction, others promoting social, economic, political, or religious objectives.

Many quickly collapsed, to be replaced in time by similar ventures, but many prospered; at least fifty of the several thousand magazines produced in American cities by 1900 attained a national circulation. Several distributed over 100,000 copies of each issue, which assured their contributors a wide reading public in rural as well as urban settings. The impact of the magazines on civic reform has already been noted, as well as that on the city-beautiful and similar movements. The appearance in any town of a specialized journal devoted to municipal affairs, charity, the schools, sports events, or society revealed the development in each case of active local groups. That was especially true of the birth of literary magazines, notably *The Lark* in San Francisco and *M'lle New York,* both in the nineties, and *Poetry,* founded at Chicago in 1912. Professional writers, however, looked first to the more popular magazines for publication. The mounting circulations of the national journals, especially after the sharp reduction in their prices from 25 to 15 and 10 cents during the mid-nineties, brought a new and rich advertising revenue. Contributors could now demand handsome fees and be assured of a wide audience.[14]

These magazines seldom reached the great mass of working people; directed, as most of them were, to the middle classes, they often seemed deficient for this and other reasons to the more creative writers. Fortunately the daily press, with all its faults, supplied a partial answer to both groups. The rapid growth of cities had transformed the four-page dailies of pre–Civil War years, filled with closely printed notices and advertisements interspersed with political editorials, into lively journals of many pages. Wood and copper engravings, introduced by venturesome magazines in the fifties and sixties, so improved their appearance that the leading dailies soon began to use them in advertisements and a decade later for an occasional political cartoon. When the New York *World* first made political cartoons a daily feature in 1884, other papers quickly imitated it. The employment of special columnists spread widely after their introduction during the sixties; although for a time essayists of established reputations wrote the columns and often achieved a cultivated erudition, as the pace began to quicken, creating jobs for reporters, some of these young men, with fresh literary tastes, introduced a breezier style.[15]

The daily papers, which multiplied in number during the sixties and seventies, soon began, like other commercial and industrial enterprises, to merge and expand in size. The rise of vigorous publishers, such as Charles A. Dana of the *New York Sun* and Joseph Pulitzer of the *World,* intensified competition. They engaged additional reporters and assigned them to special tasks—the police court, the theater, the world of society. Lengthy excerpts from sermons and lectures, erudite commentaries on current magazine articles and books, continued to crowd the now more clearly defined editorial pages; but fulsome on-the-spot reports of sports contests, accidents, fires, crimes, and other sensational events served during the eighties to enliven the other pages. The development of syndicated columns, the emergence of the Associated Press as a monopolistic force, which the United Press finally challenged, and the invention of an improved Hoe press, able to turn out 48,000 twelve-page papers an hour, marked other advances of the eighties.[16]

The next decade saw the introduction of linotype machines, improvements in copper halftones for use on smooth paper supplements, sometimes printed in color, and the evolution of the cartoon into the comic strip. The fierce competition of the late nineties, when Hearst challenged Pulitzer in New York with new sensational techniques, created a "yellow" journalism that reached a score of cities by 1900. Most urban newspapers boosted their circulations and doubled or trebled in size before the close of the period. Even the foreign-language press spread widely across the country; although most of these publications in eighteen languages were printed at and distributed from New York, German dailies, numbering ninety-seven in 1892, flourished in many places. The even more widely scattered Negro papers had by that date increased from ten to 154 since the Civil War; they almost doubled again during the next two decades, helping to carry the newspaper into practically all urban homes by the close of the period.[17]

If techniques of popularization undermined the literary standards of the better papers and of many conscientious magazines, the pressure for human-interest details and for vivid first-hand accounts helped to free young writers from the staid traditions and the formalisms of early post–Civil War decades and encouraged a fresh outburst of literary talent at the turn of the century.

Journalists, reformers, and creative writers alike responded to the challenge of the urban environment; together they produced an increasingly colorful spectrum of city life. Sometimes the distinctions between the three groups disappeared, notably in the case of the muckrakers. These for the most part were journalists whose zeal for reform in the early 1900's produced a new shock technique that found employment as well in some contemporary problem novels, Frank Norris's *The Octopus* in part, and especially Upton Sinclair's *The Jungle*. This writing reflected a period of crisis when the battle for control in many towns was approaching a climax. The spirit of realism that reached vivid expression in these books had developed slowly during previous decades; its advance as well as its literary product supplied a revealing documentation on the city.[18]

A pervasive romanticism among the early post–Civil War writers had forestalled penetrating descriptions of urban life. Many foreign travel journals highlighted the surface details of the larger towns; promotional brochures for each metropolis multiplied, as well as antiquarian volumes, both historical and fictional; essayists and poets wrote disparagingly of urban as contrasted with rural life; but it was not until the eighties that several able writers began to dissect the city. Henry George, who published his provocative *Progress and Poverty* at the opening of the decade, was the first to direct attention to the economics of urban growth. Other writers followed, and nine years later William Dean Howells published *A Hazard of New Fortunes,* with its realistic use of city life as an essential part of the novel's plot.[19]

Many novels of the next two decades had a very special historical relevance. A great number depicted the migration to the metropolis of rural or small-town youths or immigrant peasants. Brander Matthews took an optimistic view in *A Confident Tomorrow;* generally, however, the fictional versions of the trials encountered by such migrants were somber, perhaps none more so than Stephen Crane's *Maggie: A Girl of the Streets,* published in 1893. Few achieved the results wrought by Dreiser a few years later in *Sister Carrie,* a book whose central character was completely transformed by her urban experience. The author's own career had in some respects paralleled that of his heroine, thus providing an abundance of realistic detail. And at the other end of the social ladder, Mrs. Edith Wharton's first-hand knowledge of polite society in New York and Boston greatly assisted her in the graphic portrayal of varied social crises in *The House of Mirth.* In each case the author was not only familiar with the circumstantial details of the setting but also sufficiently understood the basic forces at play, both human and environmental, to bring the action to life.[20]

The fictional accounts of these basic experiences of old and new urbanites were almost as varied as life itself. Howells, who frequently depicted the corroding effects of the city on ambitious newcomers, showed an occasional triumph of character, too, as in the case of Silas Lapham. The crumbling fortunes of the old social elite in numerous towns supplied favorite themes for other writers, and if such groups were not always as completely supplanted, as in New York, Chicago, St. Louis, and other rapidly growing places, the upsurge of the new rich was everywhere apparent. In Boston, Philadelphia, Baltimore, New Orleans, and similar communities, the two groups merged slowly; there the earlier cotillions and assemblies carried on, although their sway was not as absolute as at Richmond and Charleston. The Blue Books and social registers published in a score of cities before the end of the period helped to perpetuate the tradition of a select society, yet they found the qualifications for membership increasingly based on an active participation in charitable and cultural endeavors. Some novelists, taking a cynical view of these activities, made fictional use of them as "social ladders"; others borrowed themes from Veblen's provocative *Theory of the Leisure Class*.[21]

The novels were often revealing in ways that were not intentional. Following the sure lead of Howells and influenced by examples abroad, many writers with rich experience on urban newspapers indorsed the tenets of realism, yet most of them, before the turn of the century, displayed a still greater zeal for gentility. The scorn heaped upon the materialism of their opponents, the "Philistines," gave their own work the character of an uplift movement comparable to that of the civic reformers. Some leading writers frankly accepted this function, notably Ambrose Bierce in San Francisco and Henry Fuller of Chicago, who wrote an article on "The Upward Movement" in which he pinned the city's hopes on its cultivated women. His hero in *The Cliff Dwellers* discovered late, but not too late, the need for more than material success. A host of books championed the efforts of artists, writers, and idealists in many walks of life to bring luster and charm to the city.[22]

The wide reading of such books and magazines might have had a more appreciable effect had not their circulation been confined largely to the genteel protagonists themselves. Some youthful writers, headed by Dreiser, Floyd Dell, and others yet to be heard from, were waging a battle for liberation, if only from their village background, as one critic has put it, yet they managed to "record the depth of confusion" that characterized much human life in the emerging metropolitan centers after the turn of the century.[23]

A basic confusion of standards troubled the life of most urbanites, faced as they were with the increased heterogeneity of growing cities; but the efforts of a new group of social scientists to apply analytical techniques to a study of the community gave promise for the future. Although only six colleges offered courses dealing with urban social conditions in 1890, the number increased fivefold in as many years as the movement gained momentum. The University of Chicago, with a fascinating metropolitan laboratory at its door, listed ten professors of social science or sociology in the mid-nineties, when the term sociology, as descriptive of this field of study, was coming into general use. Most of these courses were oriented toward practical social work at the start, but an increased interest in theoretical analysis appeared by the close of the period.[24]

The impact of the city on the cultural life of America had so disrupted earlier patterns that a distinguished British critic, G. Lowe Dickinson, found it in a state of flux. "In America," he declared in 1909, "there is no culture. There is instruction; there is research; there is technical and professional training; there is specialism in science and in industry; there is every possible application of life to purposes and ends, but there is no life for life's sake." Benjamin I. Gilman, secretary of the Boston Museum of Fine Arts, admitted the truth of the indictment but noted evidences in many places of a new and more broadly shared appreciation for the arts. A series of chamber-music concerts accompanied by explanatory comments at Cambridge, public support for free symphony concerts in Central Park in New York, the efforts of the Drama League in Boston to cultivate an appreciation of good plays, the art leagues formed in several public schools there and in a few elsewhere, the municipal art commissions recently established in many cities, and the activities in all of these fields of the widespread women's clubs—all signalized the new awakening.[25]

Many observers were still less restrained in their optimism in these latter years. Even such a forthright critic as Frederic C. Howe found grounds for hope in the city by 1905. Excited by the richer social and cultural opportunities that concentration in and co-operation within towns afforded, numerous writers saw the promise of America increasingly in urban terms. And if, as Herbert Croly maintained, its traditional promise could be realized only through a new dedication to the democratic purpose of the country's founders, that renewal of spirit was most evident in the urban setting.[26]

The 42,000,000 Americans who in the course of the half-century congregated in cities both suffered and enjoyed experiences that profoundly altered their cultural outlook. As we have seen in earlier chapters, the increased tempo of urban life prompted many residents to seek recreational diversion or to find self-expression in the arts; others turned with eager interest to the printed word for both information and relaxation. Towns large and small established institutions in each of these fields, and the great metropolitan centers acquired a profusion of specialized magazines, libraries, galleries, academies, clubs, and societies of all sorts.

A multitude of new professional workers arose to staff these varied services. And as they developed standards and techniques and founded institutes and intercity federations to promote their causes, a breach often appeared between the amateurs and the professionals, especially in the great cities, similar to that separating politicians from civil servants, philanthropists from social workers. The dilemmas confronting both the lay citizen and the organization man, as he was later to be described, would become sharper and more acute as the urban age gave way to the metropolitan. But already the development of a local version of statesmanship, in cultural as well as in civic and economic fields, was channeling the multiple streams of urban growth toward an early historic confluence.

V THE CULMINATION OF A HALF-CENTURY OF URBANIZATION [1910–1915]

The rise of the city thus connoted much more than the physical transformation of America. It had accompanied and maintained close reciprocation with the commercial and industrial revolutions, the influx of immigrants, and the varied developments of practical science. As a habitat of sticks and stones, mortar and metal, the city was never static; but it was more than a habitat, it was a human society, always changing and developing. And in this capacity it was stimulating man to evolve new civic and social patterns that enabled him to achieve a richer if also a more hectic life. Despite widespread fears that the city was causing a decline in the birth rate, its growth had generated an unprecedented material output and had brought higher standards of health and domestic convenience, as well as a taste of social and cultural fulfillment, within reach of an increasing host of townsmen who already outnumbered the country's entire 1860 population.

Moreover, the cities had served, in addition to their own residents (some of whom, however, could scarcely detect the benefits), the rest of the people of America. The isolation of the frontier and the backwoods had disappeared with the planting of new towns in every area. Steam trains, acting as urban commercial tentacles, had shattered the solitude of almost every valley, drawing the rural inhabitants into rewarding economic and cultural relationships with regional and distant places. Not only did the majority of the nation's leaders spring from or quickly take up residence in the cities, but an increasing number of the issues they faced, as well as the viewpoints they expressed, bore the urban label.[1]

The cities had also paid sacrifices for their surging growth. Expanding commercial districts engulfed many old residential wards, while factories and freight lines segmented established communities and invaded suburban retreats. The inrush of newcomers from abroad had transformed many once-friendly neighborhoods into heterogeneous slums whose densely packed inhabitants often dwelt as indifferent or hostile strangers under the same roof. It was, many felt, a transition period, and the great majority, imbued with a boundless optimism, looked hopefully to the future. Yet the number who rebelled or inadvertently fell out of step was increasing, as the mounting crime ratios disclosed; and recurrent dislocations of the economy left vast hordes destitute.[2]

Alarmed by these miseries, some humanitarian citizens had begun to transform urban charities into welfare agencies; others, blazing with varied degrees of indignation, were demanding political and economic reforms. The sudden upsurge of the progressive movement around 1910 gave cumulative expression in state and national politics to a multitude of grievances dating back several decades in many communities. And since the state legislatures failed to master numerous issues of control, the urban interests, both public and private, turned increasingly to Washington for administrative supervision. Many of the leaders in this movement had served an apprenticeship in local reform campaigns,[3] and their triumphs in the larger arena further revealed the extent to which urban problems had become national issues.

Most cities had lost their former sense of autonomy and much of their provincialism as well. Many had acquired productive specialties that assured a more or less distinctive character but bound the community firmly to the national economy. The great railroad systems, abetted in some respects by the rising industrial empires and dominated after the turn of the century by the financial moguls in New York, had drawn towns large and small into a vast urban galaxy, which hastened the development of new social and cultural as well as political bonds.

As in former decades, each new settlement had to find its place in this larger order. Those of an earlier vintage that now achieved a burst of fresh growth did so by exploiting a useful function of vital importance to the whole. Several expansive commercial hubs, which had already commenced to plant industrial satellites and residential suburbs on their periphery, proceeded to extend an intensified sway by absorbing old and new towns into their metropolitan hinterlands. Some predominantly industrial cities had acquired metropolitan status, too, as the development of their specialties won them nation-wide leadership in restricted fields and encouraged their commercial and banking groups to assert greater independence of rival regional centers and to carve out hinterlands of their own. But as the regrouping of scattered cities and towns into geographic solar systems within the larger urban constellation ushered in a new historic era—one in which the unit of growth was the metropolitan region, virtually a city-state—it also brought many trends of previous decades to their logical fruition.

17. The triumph
of metropolitan regionalism

Although the growth of cities—in number, size and density, as well as economic complexity—was, despite some fluctuations, a continuing process, many of the trends we have followed reached their culmination on the eve of the First World War. The railroads remained the most important interurban arteries, but they now attained their maximum in mileage, for the automobile was already beginning to affect internal city traffic and to stimulate a new and different kind of dispersion. The automobile's major effects would not appear for another decade or so, but its manufacturing centers were already growing rapidly. Indeed, the cities that enjoyed such growth in these prewar years were precisely those that undertook the production of instruments of urban transit or communication—the dynamic ingredients of the greater city or metropolis—and those that fabricated the basic materials for construction.

Technological improvements comprised but one phase of a larger movement toward integration. A reorganization of the banks came in response to numerous demands that had been gaining force in scattered cities over several decades and brought to a head the old contest between New York and its metropolitan rivals. The rise of the regional centers, each with its satellites and subsidiaries, conformed with a pattern that numerous other urban functions were evolving to co-ordinate the activities of the 2405 American municipalities.

The mushrooming urban populations had developed new characteristics that accentuated these trends. The flood of immigrants continued but declined in relative importance as their offspring increased. Greater longevity contributed, in turn, to the permanence of varied economic groups, notably the white-collar workers. The three-layered stratification that had already developed among the residents of most cities found expression in contrasting neighborhoods. A new ecological dualism, with urban and suburban poles, began to supplant the earlier dichotomies between the East and the West, the native and the immigrant, the rural and the urban.

The multiplication of cities, so characteristic of the five decades we have studied, continued with only slight abatement. But the 400 towns that now broke into the census tables (listing all over 2500) arose for the most part, even in the south,⁴ on the outskirts of spreading metropolitan centers. Many old crossroads hamlets suddenly acquired vitality when industrial promoters chose their sites for new factories. In rarer instances, as we have previously noted, an expanding company selected a fresh tract adjacent to one or more transport lines and built a model community, such as the one the American Steel and Wire Company founded at Fairfield, near Birmingham, Alabama, in 1912. More frequently it was an enterprising subdivider, allied in many cases with a builder and perhaps backed by a transit company or some other urban utility, who developed the nucleus for a residential suburb. Whatever the circumstances, the new communities were functional if not always planned offspring of the major urban centers which sent colonies into the open spaces without any intention of releasing control. Thus the statistical growth of cities, once a concentration of rural accretions, had become, instead, a metropolitan sprawl. The indispensable promoters, who in earlier decades had prospered with their communities, gave place to subdividers eager to unload their speculations. These trends gave the emerging metropolis a more impersonal cast.⁵

We have seen in an earlier chapter how the introduction of the trolley saved most cities during the nineties from the densities reached in New York and in crowded centers abroad. Continued urban growth, however, soon concentrated such large throngs in the major towns that improved transit facilities often spread congestion into new areas. The mass of residents in the central wards of the great cities declined as commercial and other functions appropriated the business districts, but the daytime populations rose to new heights, both in number and in the soaring skyscrapers that invaded almost every metropolis by 1915. Yet the emergence of fourteen additional places with 100,000 or more inhabitants during the second decade of the century brought vigorous and formative communities into the metropolitan bracket and prolonged at least statistically the trend toward urban concentration until 1920.⁶

Even some of the old central cities continued to increase their densities, as tenements and apartment houses multiplied, but a counter-movement toward dispersion gained force during the prewar years. Surface extensions of the subways and elevateds inundated many suburbs; the interurbans planted satellites farther out. In the first decade of the century, the population increment of the urbanized areas immediately surrounding the twenty-five major (over 200,000) metropolitan cities already slightly exceeded that of their cores. But it was in the second decade that this shift became marked, especially in such industrial centers as Pittsburgh and Detroit.[7]

A basic aspect of the situation was the dispersion of factories. Rapid industrial growth and advancing technology maintained a constant pressure for more spacious sites. Relocation outside the business district or beyond the city limits often promised an economy in taxes as well as in land costs and permitted solutions of transport and other crucial problems. The development of high-voltage electric cables, first demonstrated between Niagara Falls and Buffalo late in 1896, enabled the power companies of all large places to extend transmission lines into broad hinterlands, where they soon began to absorb small village systems and joined the transit companies in promoting new suburbs and satellites. Not only did such industrial centers as Lowell, Scranton, and Youngstown, as well as Chicago, St. Louis, Pittsburgh, and Detroit, spawn clusters of factories on their outskirts, but many predominantly commercial hubs also developed industrial "parks" on their periphery. Although the migration of old concerns seldom left gaps for long, since other firms quickly appropriated the vacant spaces, most cities now barely maintained, either by annexation or internal growth, their earlier percentages of the national production. It was the metropolitan district, combining the output of urban and suburban factories, that best reflected the cumulative advance of the American economy.[8]

The most striking advance occurred in those metropolitan districts that participated actively in a new phase of the industrial-commercial revolution. Although as a group the great wholesale marts continued their rapid growth, a few industrial centers spurted ahead, in percentages, after 1910. Detroit, the hub of automobile production, Akron, the maker of tires, Cleveland, the oil processor, and Toledo, which also shared in the motor car's rise, all raced with the leaders. The first two outstripped Los Angeles and Seattle, front-runners of the previous decade, and Akron even approached the high proportions of factory workers recorded at New Bedford and Fall River. This concentration of many workers in specialized fields helped, as in the past, to generate technological progress.[9]

Detroit afforded the most pertinent example and supplied the most significant innovations. Indeed, the five years following the christening of the Model-T Ford witnessed the introduction and perfection of assembly-line production. When, despite a rigid standardization of parts for the Model-T in 1908, the new factory on Piquette Street failed to keep pace with the rush of sales, Henry Ford engaged Walter E. Flanders—a disciple of Frederick W. Taylor, the efficiency expert—to lay out a new shop arrangement. By installing line production and effecting a standardization of tasks, Flanders so increased the speed of the assembly process that the factory achieved an output of 10,000 cars within a year. Further mechanization doubled that record in the next season. But the flood of orders continued to mount and prompted Ford to build still another plant at suburban Highland Park. It was there, in 1913, after continued job analysis had reduced many operations to a simple routine, that the output of parts got so far ahead of the assembly force that it inspired two ingenious engineers to apply the overhead trolley system, devised some time before by a Chicago meat packer; their action transformed the assembly line into a moving production chain.[10] The new methods of plant organization not only reduced many mechanics to machine tenders but also challenged other companies to revamp their processes. The new products not only uncovered a vast market but also transformed the street life of all cities and the commercial pattern of the entire nation.[11]

There were other if less spectacular city-building industries in this period. The iron and steel industry, which now contributed heavily to construction as well as to commerce, increased its labor force by half during the second decade and gave additional impetus to Chicago, Milwaukee, and Buffalo among several other cities. As the technological advance accelerated, particularly in the realm of communication, Rochester erected new motion-picture camera and film factories; Schenectady and Cleveland, new plants to meet the demand for electrical appliances; Dayton, new facilities for the production of business machines. It was Dayton, too (where Charles F. Kettering, a young inventor with the Dayton Engineering Laboratories Company—Delco— developed the self-starter in 1911), that pioneered in the manufacture of airplanes, though of course few people suspected its future implications for this and other cities.[12]

Industry still gave more employment than commerce or any other category of work in all the major towns except Kansas City. Other occupations were attracting increased attention, however, even in such factory centers as Pittsburgh and St. Louis, where the percentages in industry now fell slightly below the 42.5 average for all places over

100,000. That drop reflected not only the outward migration noted above but also the diversification characteristic of metropolitan nuclei. The great core cities, whatever their earlier specialties, assumed the character of regional capitals and parceled out some old functions to subsidiary neighbors.[13] A comparative study of the employment ratios of fifty-seven suburbs in 1920 revealed that a majority housed a greater proportion of wage earners than the metropolis they adjoined. Many places, like Homestead and Pullman, supplied manpower for their own factories; others, as dormitory communities, catered to industrial workers in the city, a few even to special ethnic groups; but most suburbs near the cities accommodated a broad assortment of commuters. Generally it was only the more distant satellites (built around factories as at Gary, or a college as at Stanford, or like Scarsdale on a residential scale that automatically screened the inhabitants) that developed specializations in these years just before the First World War.[14]

Important innovations in the building industry foreshadowed the opening of a new era. The invention in 1911 of a machine to make standardized concrete blocks provided a cheap and convenient unit of construction that quickly attracted wide use. The vindication of reinforced concrete in several great fires, notably one at Baltimore in 1904, encouraged promoters to push ahead with large building projects. Improvements in central heating, ventilation, and sanitation raised new standards for apartment houses and office buildings and stimulated the reconstruction of many downtown properties. At the same time the perfection of the septic tank and the wide use of well-drilling machines enabled suburbanites to achieve many urban comforts.[15]

The introduction in 1912 of mechanical refrigerators designed for home kitchens encouraged residents of apartments and individual houses alike to preserve the earlier custom of family dining and slowed the rapid growth of public restaurants, except in a few metropolitan centers. The food-processing industries further contributed to domestic convenience by marketing canned vegetables and juices and preparing other foods for safe shipment and wide distribution. These developments facilitated the split-up of large family aggregates into the smaller primary groups that characterized the large city. Meanwhile, new mortgage practices and other financing devices hastened the construction of housekeeping units of modest size in remodeled and new structures. Although the accumulation of residences never caught up with the demand, and the percentage of home ownership tended to decline, several earnest studies of the housing situation in the light of population trends at least clarified the problem.[16]

:

The cities, particularly in the Northeast, were reaching a turning point in demographic growth. Their populations continued to mount, often at a surprising rate, yet the character was changing. Not only had the areas of recruitment abroad shifted, but the size of the immigrant tide had declined in proportion to the native output, and new channels of internal movement were also developing. Moreover, the urban population was growing older and becoming more evenly balanced between men and women. The chance that it would be split into two sharply distinguished classes was diminishing, for the proliferation of occupations and of consumer products in the spreading metropolitan districts had brought a rapid expansion of the middle classes and blunted the division between wage earner and capitalist.[17]

Most of these trends were slow developments and did not occur simultaneously; they were, nevertheless, interrelated, and the cumulative effect became apparent after 1910. The main source of immigration had shifted over the course of a century from Britain to Ireland to Germany to eastern and southern Europe. The numbers had mounted rapidly in almost every decade, yet the fecundity of earlier arrivals had more than matched that increase; late-comers not only found themselves in a small minority but also discovered the town of their choice, once they could see it in perspective, to be a community of minorities. Even the generation of Americans born of immigrant parents, though it now comprised nearly half the population of many cities and included enough adults to influence their affairs, was such a conglomerate of stocks that it created a cosmopolitan atmosphere and a tolerance for diversity. That spirit was unfortunately often marred in congested districts where, as in the past, newcomers crowded the earlier residents and undercut their job standards. These latent hostilities would become more outspoken in another year or two, when the war forged a new spirit of nationalism.[18]

In some places, notably in the South and on the West Coast, disturbing animosities were already distorting even their progressive movements. The anti-Negro and anti-Japanese sentiments rampant in these respective areas had given rise to white-supremacy doctrines in the early 1900's that drew their sectional leaders together. Their earlier opposition to the English-literacy test for immigrants gave way to strident demands for it and for even more discriminatory restrictions. The influx of many Italians at New Orleans and the spread of other "new" immigrants throughout the rising towns of the South threatened to upset the prevailing White-Negro relationship. Occasional incidents triggered outbursts of race and group hatreds, as in the case of the trial and lynching of Leo Frank, Jewish manager of a pencil factory in Atlanta. *The Menace,* with its insidious anti-Catholicism, and a number of other subversive journals attained large circulations. As Tom Watson, a former progressive, became the spearhead of the movement in the South, Jack London, a socialist, became the spokesman for a similar drive on the West Coast against the "yellow peril" and the "mongrel-bloods" of southern and eastern Europe. The eruption of the Industrial Workers of the World in the lumber camps of the Northwest brought such staunch defenders of nativism as Albert Johnson to Congress.[19]

There, however, the hysteria of the South and the Far West met a check. The progressives of the Northeast were still too confident of their basic democratic ideals and too concerned about positive reforms to give heed to such invidious proposals. Both Democrats and Republicans had long courted naturalized voters and had enrolled prominent leaders of strong ethnic association in their councils; the Bull Moosers, with Frances Kellor and other humanitarians high in their ranks, were ever more staunch in defense of the immigrant. Even Woodrow Wilson, despite his southern background, in 1915 repulsed the renewed efforts of the restrictionists to enact a literacy test with a veto.[20]

Improvements in sanitation and in the medical care of expectant mothers and infants had during the half-century prolonged the life span of the average urbanite by several years, which contributed significantly to the population rise and inevitably to its character. The earlier predominance of males in new or rapidly expanding cities, occasioned in large part by the influx of young men from abroad, disappeared as the longevity of women increased more sharply; among children the sexes were in fairly even balance.[21] This trend would, in its turn, create a new imbalance, but meanwhile it had gone just far enough to strengthen rather than weaken the campaign for woman suffrage, which had long recruited its most vigorous leaders from the expanding middle class. The hopeful optimism of the heterogeneous urban throngs and the democratic good will of the friends of a broader suffrage, both animated the progressive movement.[22]

A further result of the shifting composition of the immigrant stream appeared in the character of many neighborhoods within the larger cities. As newcomers from Germany or Ireland, who held first or second place among immigrant groups in each of the twenty-five principal centers in 1900, gave precedence to Russian Jews, Italians, or Canadians in five of them within a decade, and to these or other new groups in all but St. Louis and Boston by the close of the war, most of the districts they had built or inherited were abandoned to later arrivals. The new occupants changed many street names and shop signs and rechristened the churches; they also brought a new set of customs and furnishings and often recreated a distinctive social atmosphere. After two or three invasions, however, many old neighborhoods lost much of their charm and deteriorated into wretched slums. The elderly migrants from these once-colorful areas often located in such numbers in new wards or suburbs as to give them an ethnic character, but their sons and daughters tended to scatter throughout the city and its environs.[23]

The internal migrations of the native-born were also changing. Excess youths from the farms still responded to the call of the city. Most of them, as in the past, stopped for a season or two in a nearby town, some attending an academy or a college, before moving to a large regional center and finally perhaps to a metropolis. Numerous studies have revealed that the great industrial and commercial cities now drew their recruits from other urban places, often over long distances. The specialization of tasks increasingly required skilled workers or those with the broad experience supplied by travel. Thus many venturesome youths, who impulsively sought their fortunes in the large towns only to become dissatisfied with the common labor and menial jobs most readily available to them there, moved on quickly, and some of them eventually acquired a useful sophistication in the process. Limited evidence indicates that it was the in-migrants from rural or small-town America who moved most frequently, boosting the mobility ratio of most cities far above that of the offspring of local families or even that of immigrants from abroad, who seemed more ready to sink their roots.[24]

A significant new feature in this migratory pattern appeared within the borders of the metropolitan district. Whereas in former decades the rural fringe had lost population to the city, the latter's vitality now reversed the current and sent its surplus into the suburbs. Although growing towns had been spilling over their borders for decades, a significant change now occurred. The succession of overflows and annexations practically came to an end in the early 1900's, particularly in the Northeast, as the outward migrants formed independent communities and resisted the city's advance. The successful development of small sewer and water districts and of the septic tank removed obstacles to this wide dispersal; so did the introduction of trackless trolleys at a few places in 1913, and of jitney buses a year later. The open stretches attracted especially the owners of automobiles, who multiplied fivefold during the early teens and took out 2,445,660 registrations in 1915.[25]

The number of residents classified as suburban mounted from five to seven million during the second decade. They would comprise by

1920 approximately one-fourth of the total inhabitants of twenty-nine metropolitan districts whose central cities topped 200,000. Many among them whose occupation was given as farming were in a special sense urban farmers—truck gardeners, dairymen, and the like, some of whom had themselves fled the crowded towns. Others were gentlemen farmers or retired people of more modest circumstances. Whatever their status, most of them looked to the city for their jobs, their markets, their amusements, and their cultural life. They were glad to escape its congestion and high taxes, its noise and confusion, yet they could not dispense with it, or shake off its heritage. Some of its problems followed them, too, but radical measures lost appeal in their spacious setting; the good will of the progressive seemed for a time more appropriate.[26]

Efforts to co-ordinate varied aspects of the economy and to integrate the productive energies of scattered cities reached at least a partial resolution before the First World War. Abuses arising from excessive competition in some industrial fields had prompted the enactment of legislative curbs and the development of new administrative services. The long struggle to build effective unions achieved a measure of success as the number of workers enrolled reached a new high in 1913. By developing a stable leadership on the national as well as the local level, the A. F. of L. stimulated the growth of a responsible business leadership ready to engage in orderly if not co-operative labor-management dealings. At the same time, the progressive upsurge shunted aside the threat in a few key cities of socialist ascendancy.

Although many industrial giants continued their gargantuan growth, the widespread opposition to monopoly, even within conservative economic circles, stiffened the resistance of the courts and pledged all national parties to some curbs on the trusts. There was no agreement, however, as to the proper measures for their dismemberment or control. The search for a practical approach to this situation and the campaign for a revision of the banking system both reflected metropolitan influences. Urban experience likewise hastened the shift of many progressives from laissez-faire doctrines to the support of positive welfare measures even on the national level.

The shocking exploitation of child labor in many cities, as revealed by innumerable investigations, had prompted twenty-eight states throughout the North and the West to pass laws regulating its use before the turn of the century. Citizen committees in Montgomery, Alabama, and in several textile towns in the South now secured the adoption of similar measures in that region. Provisions for enforcement had increased after 1904, when Florence Kelley and other leaders of the movement in various cities organized the National Child Labor Committee. Under its guidance the reactivation of twenty-five local bodies and the launching of the Child Labor *Bulletin* in 1912 brought striking improvements in several industrial centers. Lax inspection or complete indifference in other places prompted the national committee to draft a federal bill. Although that measure, successfully passed in 1916, was soon held unconstitutional by the Supreme Court, its model provisions inspired the revision and improvement of many state laws. Nevertheless, effective supervision still depended in most places on the determination of citizen committees and the temper of local opinion.[27]

Legal safeguards for working women were also improving. The hostile stand of most judges against early attempts to limit their hours and regulate other working conditions changed after the Supreme Court upheld the state's authority to safeguard the welfare of its women. That notable decision, responding to a pioneer sociological brief by Louis D. Brandeis, hastened the adoption of thirty-nine such laws, blanketing the major industrial regions. The National Consumers League and the Women's Trade Union League helped to extend this protection to women in stores and offices as well as factories; both commenced in 1910 to advocate minimum-wage laws, too. These middle-class groups, strong at Boston and other major commercial hubs, won their first successes in Massachusetts, Oregon, Wisconsin, and California, where the Progressives were eager to attract workmen away from the socialist parties. These reforms, although sincere and substantive, proved strategic as well. The limitation of hours of work for women elicited scorn from radicals, who opposed ameliorative measures, and at the same time threatened a split in Progressive ranks at Los Angeles and elsewhere, yet the defecting malcontents were more than replaced by fresh enlistments from labor, whose leaders began now to endorse such programs.[28]

The number of working women was increasing, especially in the large cities, more rapidly than the sum of the employed or of their sex. This upward trend continued despite a drop in the number of girls under twenty as the child-labor laws took effect. The advance was most rapid in the clerical and sales fields, which were expanding even in towns of moderate size. Although the unions paid little heed to these white-collar trades, they could not overlook the influx of women in certain industries, and women's locals became a feature of the clothing, shoe, and textile unions and a dozen more. Labor's persistent gain in numbers until 1913, when it reached a high of 2,753,400 before the recession of the next year brought a decline, was partly the result of a more concerted drive among women.[29]

Citizens alert for the welfare of women and children in industry discovered a new cause for concern in the mounting accident rates in commerce and industry. A series of investigations around 1910 revealed the inadequacies of the common-law procedures affecting employers' liability. Under the leadership of Seth Low, the National Civic Federation initiated the attack on this problem in 1908. It drafted a workmen's compensation bill for New York and persuaded the A. F. of L. to join in endorsing the reform. Although the courts held that model act of 1910 invalid, a score of similar laws in other industrial states soon provided a convincing demonstration of the advantages of workmen's compensation. A series of decisions by the U. S. Supreme Court sustained this program in 1917.[30]

The gains made by labor and by its friends among the progressives stimulated a new attempt by the heads of various business groups in scattered cities to establish a national association to represent their conservative views. Neither the National Civic Federation, despite its respectable following among industrialists and bankers as well as labor leaders, nor the National Association of Manufacturers with its special concerns, seemed a proper spokesman. The old National Board of Trade also had a limited scope. After some prodding from business leaders in several cities, President Taft's Secretary of Commerce and Labor called a conference in 1912 and invited over 2000 commercial bodies scattered throughout the country to send delegates. Most large and many small cities were represented and participated in the organization of the U. S. Chamber of Commerce. Its leaders undertook to voice the opinions and defend the interest of the business groups of all urban communities. About 300 local organizations and 2000 individuals joined its ranks.[31]

Some chamber leaders, as well as those of the more militant National Association of Manufacturers, hoped to devise more effective curbs for labor and to check meddlesome progressives. Others, animated by a co-operative spirit, sought peaceful and constructive solutions of contemporary problems. The National Civic Federation, with headquarters at New York City and local bodies in many large towns, earnestly explored all possible fields of conciliation.[32]

The most dramatic incident of this sort had a different origin and occurred at Los Angeles. It was in the midst of a crucial contest between progressives and socialists for control of the municipal government that Lincoln Steffens visited the city in 1911. He had come to cover, not the election, but the sensational trial of the McNamara brothers on a charge of dynamiting the Los Angeles *Times*. When he discovered that Clarence Darrow, chief counsel for the defense, seriously doubted the possibility of securing a fair trial because of the tense state of local opinion, Steffens challenged both sides to take a compassionate attitude and recognize that the cause was not to be found in man's evil nature but in the economic system, which had created violent friction between capital and labor. He persuaded the prosecution to accept a plea of guilt and not demand the death penalty. Darrow thus saved the lives of his clients, but their socialist defenders, discredited by the plea, lost the election. Although the united front of conservative and liberal business-men, who thus triumphed, failed to reform the system, as Steffens had hoped, the progressives they placed in office were soon reluctantly bid-ding for labor support as their party endorsed wage-and-hour legislation and workmen's compensation on the state level.[33]

Ida M. Tarbell, another muckraker of the previous decade, was meanwhile compiling evidence for her hopeful book, *New Ideals in Business*. The recreation programs, the sanitary provisions, and the safety devices she found in scattered factories, all impressed her, and impressed other observers, too, as harbingers of the more enlightened industrialism most progressives envisioned.[34]

Not all were as convinced as Miss Tarbell that these measures, gen-erally designed to head off unions, met the full challenge to the system. Among others, Louis Brandeis stood firmly for labor's right to organize. He defended that principle in numerous briefs, holding it of greater value to the worker than a wage increase or a gratuitous bonus. Yet he could not endorse the closed shop. And in a widespread garment strike at New York in 1910 he helped both the Clothing Manufacturers Pro-tective Association and the International Garment Workers Union reach an understanding in the form of a protocol under which each side accepted restraints on its power. Labor took, in place of the closed shop, a preferential or union shop in which the members would enjoy certain advantages and the right of appeal to a grievance board. Union officials won full recognition and equal power with management in the selection of arbitrators. The protocol, which followed a somewhat similar agree-ment reached a decade earlier between newspaper publishers and printers, established a model for other enlightened employers and unions.[35]

The good will that animated many businessmen in the five relatively stable years following 1908 was perhaps best exemplified by the meliorism of the Russell Sage Foundation. When the public announcement of its creation brought a flood of 60,000 letters requesting small loans, the directors sponsored two studies of the problem and established a division of remedial loans in 1910. Many local efforts in this field, some dating from the depression of the mid-seventies and some from that of the mid-nineties, had succumbed, but others, persisting, now organized the National Federation of Remedial Loan Associations. As their combined resources nevertheless fell far short of the demand for small loans, pawnshops and money sharks flourished in most cities. Even in the fifteen states that regulated interest rates, the exaction of an initial fee or other charge enabled these brokers to reap huge profits from their needy customers. Leaders of the national federation and the foundation, undaunted by earlier reverses, corresponded with eighty-five philanthropic lending societies and made textual criticism of numerous bills submitted by conscientious legislators in twenty-four states. Massachusetts passed such a law, sponsored by the Chamber of Commerce and the Legal Aid Society of Boston; seven other commonwealths soon followed, though only that of Oregon proved a success. An anti-loan-shark campaign in Newark, New Jersey, prompted the state legislature in 1914 to adopt the Egan Act based on a model provided by the foundation, which set new standards in the field.[36]

A major source of difficulty lay in the numerous regulations that restrained bankers from engaging in the small-loan business. Co-operative-credit societies, which had long flourished in Canada and abroad, were unknown in the States until 1909, when several were started in Boston and elsewhere. Arthur J. Morris of Virginia introduced similar methods the next year at his Fidelity Savings and Trust Company in Norfolk. His scheme of scheduling repayment in small installments accommodated many borrowers by spreading the burden. Since it also assured profits by charging fines when payments were late, thus circumventing the legal interest rate, the Morris plan soon invaded many communities, and instigated changes in banking laws and practices.[37]

A reform of the banking system had, in fact, become the crucial issue of the prewar period. Abstruse principles of money and banking were involved, but a primary influence on the Federal Reserve System was the decentralized character of America's urban development. Local clearing houses which had taken root in every major metropolis—a few even antedated the national banking act of 1863—supplied a regional pattern for the new system; their loan certificates, so useful during recurrent crises, pointed the way to a more flexible currency. In the end, local experimentation coupled with widespread urban trends proved more significant than either abstract theory or foreign example in fixing the nature of the reform.

The need for a more flexible currency had inspired varied proposals over the years. The paper currency advocated by labor in the late sixties and by other groups in later years, as well as the free silver demands of Bryan and his cohorts, had attracted followers chiefly because of a continuing dissatisfaction with the rigidities of the existing system. Inevitably the heated controversies over bimetallism and other modifications had prejudiced the leading bankers, particularly in New York, against any decentralization of control. Most foreign experience likewise endorsed one strong central reserve bank. Some interior bankers, however, with other students of the problem more alert to the basic sectionalism of America, favored a co-operative arrangement among independent regional banking associations similar to, but more powerful than, the clearinghouse associations set up by the Aldrich-Vreeland Act of 1908.[38]

Some action was necessary in any case. The weaknesses revealed by the great depressions had been attributed to other causes, yet the bankers' responsibility for the brief but sharp crises of 1903 and 1907 could not be disputed. Although the reform moves initiated at Baltimore and Indianapolis had been temporarily sidetracked, even the New York financiers now sensed the urgency of the situation. The National Monetary Commission, formed in May 1908, with Senator Nelson W. Aldrich of the city-state of Rhode Island as chairman, launched a protracted study of the problem. It soon became apparent that the Senator and his principal advisers favored a strong central bank similar to those of several European countries. While the commission was preparing its report and Aldrich was drafting his bill, the National Board of Trade, eager to expedite action, created a Citizen's League for the Promotion of a Sound Banking System. To free it from the odium of New York sponsorship, the board gave leadership in the league to the businessmen of Chicago, with the hope that they could rally support throughout the country. A careful statement of its objectives pledged the director, Professor J. Laurence Laughlin of the University of Chicago, to work for "the co-operation, not dominant centralization, of all banks by an evolution out of our clearing-house experience." [39]

The Citizen's League organized committees of merchants and commercial borrowers in a dozen key cities and endeavored to develop similar backing in smaller places. A shift in the political temper of the country had given the Democrats control of the House of Representatives in 1910 and made Carter Glass of Virginia chairman of its banking committee. Although Senator Aldrich, ready at last with his bill to create a strong central reserve bank, secured the outspoken endorsement of eastern supporters of the Citizen's League, Professor Laughlin and his mid-western associates avoided such a commitment. They rejoiced when Carter Glass invited Henry P. Willis, associate editor of the New York *Journal of Commerce* and a member of the league's resources team, to a conference on the banking situation. Willis found Glass opposed to one central bank but eager to explore the feasibility of a regional system of reserve centers to be co-ordinated by the Comptroller of the Currency. While these discussions were progressing, the Pujo Committee, established by progressives in Congress to investigate the "Money Trust," began to uncover some sensational facts. Its findings alarmed even many conservative businessmen about the dangers inherent in New York's financial predominance, and blasted the last hope of passing the Aldrich bill.[40]

Much was said during the heated campaign of 1912, both by Wilson for the Democrats and by Theodore Roosevelt for the Progressives, against the evils not only of the Money Trust but also of monopolies in general. Roosevelt was against the "bad trusts"; Wilson for a time condemned them all. Taft, who refused to engage in speechmaking, relied on his record of more suits against trusts than Roosevelt could boast. Public antitrust feeling assured a rousing response from the throngs that gathered to hear the contending candidates in cities and towns. But when Wilson and the Democrats won the three-way contest, their internal divisions, as well as the hazards of hasty measures, became apparent. In opposition to Roosevelt's New Nationalism, based on Herbert Croly's book, *The Promise of American Life,* Wilson had proclaimed a New Freedom full of Jeffersonian overtones. The voters had made their choice, but these lofty principles had still to be applied to the practical world in which each city had its warring interests.[41]

In the banking field, as organizations in scattered cities continued to petition for reform, both Glass and Wilson saw an opportunity to strike a blow for economic freedom against the Money Trust in New York by creating a system of regional reserve centers under federal control. Debate raged over the proper number and size of the regions and over the nature and extent of the central control, but practically everybody desired action. Paul M. Warburg, a New York financier with rich foreign experience, advocated the establishment of only three or four reserve centers (if a single banker's bank could not be had). Others, eager to spread the powers and perquisites of such control more widely, proposed as many as twenty districts. When Congress finally compromised on twelve, each with a central bank and one or two branch reserves in other large cities, it brought the banking system into accord with America's dispersed urbanization.[42]

Few if any of the leading bankers of New York or Chicago favored such a wide diffusion of reserves; yet they much preferred the regional system, with its bankers' banks, to one centralized under a governmental authority within the Treasury Department, as Samuel Untermyer, the counsel of the Pujo Committee, proposed. That scheme incorporated Bryan's demand that the federal government issue the currency, which appeared more dangerous to most American bankers than the dispersal of reserves. The Glass-Owen bill as finally drafted made a concession to Bryan by authorizing the federal government to issue the currency in its own name, but at the request and against the reserves of the twelve central banks. After much debate, and only at Wilson's insistence, the bill handed the task of supervision to an independent federal board rather than to the comptroller; following the advice of Brandeis, it placed full responsibility for the appointment of the reserve board in the President's hands, denying banks the power to name even a minority representation. Thus it answered the mounting demands for a flexible credit system in full harmony with the emergent metropolitan regionalism and in the spirit of the progressive protest against monopoly and the Money Trust.[43]

The many compromises fully satisfied no one, yet as the bill took shape attention shifted to the struggle between ambitious cities for selection as reserve centers. A half-dozen choices seemed obvious—New York, Philadelphia, Boston, Chicago, St. Louis, and San Francisco—but the claims of all others were sharply disputed. A canvass of bankers' preferences brought votes for New Orleans, Denver, Seattle, Pittsburgh, Cincinnati, Baltimore, even Washington, though none of these won a place in the Federal Reserve firmament. In their stead the organizational committee chose six other regional favorites: Richmond, Atlanta, and Dallas in the South; Cleveland, Minneapolis, and Kansas City in the Midwest.[44]

Several of the great cities whose aspirations for a central bank were denied found other means for the expansion of their metropolitan influence. Thus the Baltimore Clearing House welcomed the Baltimore branch of the Richmond Federal Reserve Bank to its membership and prolonged its regional sway in the process. During the sharp recession that began late in 1913, the clearinghouse of Baltimore and those of five other nonreserve cities issued loan certificates to relieve the pressure on business groups in their respective districts. Pittsburgh, Cleveland, Detroit, and Los Angeles established stock exchanges; at least in Detroit, where the rising automobile firms relied more on stock sales and the accumulation of their own reserves than on banking credits, the lack of a reserve center was scarcely felt. Indeed, the remarkable vitality enjoyed by several expansive industrial cities not only disclosed wealth-building energies distinct from and independent of the great commercial and banking hubs but also revealed that a new stage of metropolitan diversification had begun.[45]

Washington, which now boasted a third of a million inhabitants, became an increasingly important administrative as well as legislative capital, the center of expanding governmental functions, of press agencies, pressure groups, and a variety of public-relations activities. Eight cities became regional press depots when the introduction in 1914 of automatic typewriters operated by telegraph prompted the Associated Press to reorganize its channels of news distribution. These and additional key places performed similar functions in other fields; the customs districts, for example, numbered forty-nine after 1912, when the ports of entry were reduced to that figure.[46]

If the Democratic antitrust program, as it developed in 1913 and succeeding years, appeared hesitant and indecisive, it mirrored the uncertainties of many urban reformers. Wilson wished to ban several unfair-trade practices, especially the interlocking directorates and joint stockholdings he had battled successfully as governor in New Jersey. But Brandeis, his adviser on monopoly questions, was more interested in regulatory techniques than in absolute bans. His experience as counsel to several large corporations had convinced him that great economic power could be restrained only by competing forces. The task of government, as he saw it, was to safeguard and regulate competition. Winning Wilson's agreement, he helped to draft a measure creating a trade commission to gather the necessary information and perform these services.[47]

The Clayton bill, when finally whipped into shape, embodied most of these objectives, although varied groups inserted qualifications in the course of the debate. The industrial interests secured a modification of the trade-practices clause limiting the ban to those instances that "tend to create a monopoly," while labor and farm representatives procured an insertion declaring that "the labor of human beings is not a commodity or article of commerce," which gave their organizations an implied immunity from prosecution on any charge of restraint of trade. The test, of course, would come in its administration. Meanwhile the personnel of the Federal Trade Commission (which was, like that of the Federal Reserve Board, conservative) revealed that the new experiment would be friendly toward large as well as small business and would fit into the promotional pattern that dominated the American city.[48]

By the eve of the First World War, the history of American cities had reached a new turning point. The diffusion of urban sites had been concluded, and a trend towards consolidation had commenced. Most of the new towns that continued to appear arose on the outskirts of old core cities and represented a different type of urban diffusion. The emergence of the metropolis, a large and imperial city—often a volcanic one—brought a division of the countryside into urban districts or city states. New developments in internal transit and communications abetted these trends and enabled aggressive leaders in the old central towns to enlarge the scope of their influence.

The character of the city's inhabitants was also undergoing a change. Immigrants were losing the preponderant position, even in the work force, as their children grew to maturity; many of the latter joined other urbanites in swelling a new stratum of city life—that of the middle class. The white-collar division of this group gradually outnumbered the old petty-bourgeois faction and provided the mainstay of the progressive movement. It successfully headed off a more radical drive by the socialists for public ownership of many municipal functions and substituted in its stead the more or less moderate regulations of the progressive reformers.

That movement reached a high point when in 1915 it reorganized the national banks under the Federal Reserve System. The distribution and control of bullion and credit had been sharply contested between the cities for decades. New York's metropolitan predominance had increasingly become identified with it. And the struggle of regional centers inland to assert and maintain their independence of the New York money trust had become a major feature of the period. The reserve system quieted that old debate and provided a geographic formula for the division of America into great regional provinces. It could not, however, still the claims of other ambitious centers for larger territories of their own, and in fact many acquired them in some if not all respects as the reorganization of the country into metropolitan areas progressed.

It had required a half-century of rapid urban growth and intercity reorganization to achieve a relatively stable pattern of metropolitan regionalism. Its stability derived chiefly from its capacity for continued extension and subdivision, much as the gridiron street pattern and the steel grills of the skyscrapers facilitated new additions. Each of these urban patterns had a dynamic quality and an open-ended character that were, as John Kouwenhoven has pointed out, characteristically American.[49] Metropolitan regionalism had now acquired that character, too.

18. Civic and social Armageddon

The progressivism of Roosevelt and Wilson reflected an urban imprint in civic and social fields, too. In 1912, T. R.'s shout, "We stand at Armageddon," was stirring chiefly because many of his hearers had participated in local crusades against the corrupt usurpers of municipal authority and the predatory overlords of public utilities. In contrast with the situation a few decades earlier, many citizens were now acutely aware of the enormity of at least some urban maladies. They were eager for leadership. The more excitable took up successive panaceas; others launched surveys and studies in search of causes and cures for community ills. Few denied their gravity, but fewer still suspected their complexity, and that complexity was now compounded as the urban age gave way to the metropolitan age.

Most communities continued as in the past to press a two-pronged attack on their social problems. Private welfare agencies generally assumed the lead, initiating action and then stepping aside to permit the city to broaden the program as soon as it was ready to assume responsibility. The private agencies improved their organizational and fund-raising systems and developed nation-wide associations designed to increase their efficiency in each city and to spur action in the laggard ones. They studied urban problems, proposed solutions, and in some places instigated the appointment of city planning councils to devise long-term applications of these solutions. They also developed new ways of needling the appropriate officials and awakening public opinion on crucial issues.

Many great towns displayed a self-awareness in these prewar years that considerably enlivened their affairs. Candidates unable to produce stirring issues and to wield them dramatically were almost as outmoded as bluestockings bereft of a charity or students without social objectives. Civic groups submitted glamorous plans that elicited wide discussion and some action. Women, campaigning lustily for the vote, also swelled the clamor for temperance and for civic righteousness. Clerics, educators, and journalists, if denied the prestige enjoyed in an earlier village setting,[1] assailed their urban audiences so vigorously that few citizens could remain ignorant of local issues. The national associations and conventions, which assembled delegates from widely scattered communities for mutual edification, promoted co-operative efforts as well as federal and state laws; but such integration seldom caught up with the city's needs and failed to anticipate the changes signalized by the rise of the metropolis.

Although civic reformers had since the mid-nineties derived strength and inspiration from the multiplicity of local experimentation, the profusion of agencies and schemes had often befogged specific issues. Since the first model program of the National Municipal League had failed to solve all dilemmas, its leaders initiated a new attempt in 1913. Again debate raged between the advocates of complete home rule and those who favored state regulation, between the champions of a broad popular decision of all issues and the proponents of government by experts, between the believers in municipal socialism and the defenders of free enterprise. Even the experts differed on some of these issues, and since their struggle for unanimity deferred the adoption of a new municipal program until 1916, it is not surprising that most cities charted a pragmatic course, tacking back and forth as public sentiment shifted.[2]

The advocates of home rule added four states to the eight that had previously granted large charter-making powers to their major towns, but only three of the twelve were predominantly urban, and only in Ohio did the reform achieve a substantive victory for good government. In New York, Massachusetts, Michigan, Wisconsin, and several other states where city growth had reached the metropolitan stage, constitutional provisions for strong state bodies with authority over municipal functions often accompanied those granting the cities a choice between municipal charters drafted in advance by the legislature. In the lexicon of the progressives, however, state-appointed commissions, especially those with authority over utility rates and services, held precedence over unlimited home rule.[3]

Most of the leaders who rose to state and in some cases to national prominence in progressive strongholds had fought valiantly for state administrative safeguards for urban residents. Prominent among the men whose early battles with local utilities had helped to prepare them for larger careers were not only Brandeis, Hughes, and Theodore Roosevelt, as we have seen, but also La Follette in Wisconsin and Hiram Johnson in California. Woodrow Wilson, in 1904 a conservative opposed to state regulatory bodies, learned something of the complexity of municipal government as first president in 1909 of the Short Ballot Association; two years later, as governor of New Jersey, he learned so much more about the corruption of city bosses as well as the greed of urban utilities, and demonstrated such capacity to cope with them, that he emerged as the leading progressive among the Democrats.[4]

Most progressives were as convinced of the merits of a popular referendum in political decision-making as they were of the expert's judgment on complicated and technical matters. They had already discovered by bitter experience, as at Detroit after Mayor Pingree had become governor, that confused issues and a cumbersome ballot could vitiate elections. Each new device to simplify the voting process accordingly received a hearty welcome. The short ballot, advanced by Richard S. Childs of New York in 1909, and the voting machine, perfected at Rochester more than a decade earlier, both spread rapidly in these years. After the National Municipal League first debated the direct primary in 1900, each subsequent session reviewed fresh local experiments in its use; a score of cities adopted the more complicated but speedier approach to a popular choice through the preferential ballot introduced at Grand Junction, Colorado, in 1909.[5]

The initiative, the referendum, and the recall, all basic to the progressives, received frequent application in the urban setting. In fact, the recall of elective officials was first adopted in the Los Angeles charter of 1903. This was more than home rule, it was popular rule, and numerous cities in a score of states, chiefly west of the Mississippi, exercised one or more of the three prerogatives by 1915. Since the grant of decision-making power to the electorate promised to relieve political parties of that responsibility, many reformers, who had become tired of battling the bosses and the vested interests entrenched in all parties, proposed nonpartisan elections for local contests. Rudolph Blankenburg, reform mayor of Philadelphia 1911–1915, even attempted to establish a nonpartisan administration, but it endured only one term. Other equally forthright reformers maintained that the city's hope, like that of the state and the nation, lay in strengthening party responsibility.[6]

The commission form of municipal government, dramatized by Galveston in 1901 and adopted by numerous towns in succeeding years, challenged the favored position of the strong-mayor school. It attracted support from advocates of the short ballot and of nonpartisan elections, although Cleveland demonstrated, in its new charter of 1913, that both of these reforms, as well as the preferential ballot, the initiative, the referendum, and the recall, could be incorporated successfully in a strong-mayor setup. When Dayton, that same year, afflicted by a devastating flood, adopted a charter combining the commission with a city manager and successfully weathered the crisis, this newest plan was widely publicized. Although it stressed expert rather than direct government, its close similarity to the private corporate organization won the backing of businessmen among the progressives; its efficiency also appealed to advocates of economy. Fifty towns, including a few over 50,000 in size, adopted city-manager charters by 1916. The National Municipal League endorsed it as one of several approved forms of municipal government.[7]

Of course neither the commission nor the city-manager form was a panacea, as Memphis, among other towns, discovered. In Memphis in 1909, the triumph of long reform efforts produced a new city charter creating a commission over which Edward H. Crump quickly gained full control. Crump's power mounted as the interest of the reformers flagged, and he soon restored the river-town elements that again made Memphis the "murder capital" of America, where vice and gambling dens abounded and civic spirit withered.[8]

Meanwhile the League of American Municipalities had gradually lost strength as each special category of urban officials founded a separate body. The older body did, however, propagate several active state leagues, while the more dynamic City Managers' Association, established in 1914, provided still another agent for professional co-ordination.[9] Four additional movements at the local level also contributed to the efficiency of city government: fourteen large towns maintained municipal reference libraries by that date; business groups in another half-dozen supported bureaus of municipal research on the pattern improvised at New York in 1906; the investigations of impending urban bills undertaken by the City Club in New York had spurred the emulation of similar bodies in Chicago, Milwaukee, and Cleveland, among other places; and over half the 162 colleges canvassed in 1916 reported courses on municipal administration, with 46 of the largest maintaining government research bureaus or reference libraries.[10]

These agencies, all useful under happy circumstances, were of slight value to communities threatened with strangulation by monopolies. San Francisco, faced with such a predicament, purchased several of its street railways in 1912, a step Seattle followed two years later; more than a hundred towns took over their gas works; and many more produced some electric power. Private companies continued to supply the great volume of citizen needs in these fields, and only in the case of water works did the municipalities bear the major burden. But numerous ports built public docks, and several metropolitan centers displayed public enterprise in ventures that offered general benefits without the prospect of profit, such as bath houses, laundries, and hospitals.

Because of the restraints imposed by the states on their taxing and bonding powers, few cities could advance very far in the direction of municipal socialism. And although the National Municipal League deplored the application of these limits to revenue-producing outlays, it voted down a blanket endorsement of municipal ownership.[11]

Most of these reform efforts dated back a decade or more, and few observers in the lusty years of progressive ascendancy suspected that such advances might be short-lived. The war and the postwar reaction would soon dispel the ebullience of this civic movement. Meanwhile, even some of the reforms were becoming less applicable. Thus the basic principle of home rule lost its universal appeal when its use to defend the rights of small towns within the orbit of an expanding city frustrated broad community efforts to achieve regional integration. A few major centers found a temporary solution by combining city and county governments, as at Los Angeles in 1912; others pressed for large annexations, but the resistance of suburban villages often prevailed. Metropolitan appeals to state legislatures seldom produced the desired result, even from the progressives, which may help to explain the early decline of that movement. The failure of the new urban regions to establish responsible central authorities proved a major handicap to their development.[12]

Since the timetable of reform varied greatly from place to place, the triumphant champion in one locality frequently advanced to state or national prominence in time to aid his fellows in less fortunate communities—sometimes even to assist his faltering successors in the home town. For example, Pingree's leadership as governor of Michigan prepared the way for a new self-government drive in Detroit in 1915. On the other hand, when a reformer had exhausted his usefulness in one town, he sometimes made a new start as an educator or writer in another city—as Frederic C. Howe did when he left Cleveland—still confident that an informed public would correct its most troublesome ills.[13]

Just as many civic reformers achieved effective expression in the progressive movement and through a multiplicity of institutions, both local and national, so in the welfare field the cities developed co-operative agencies and new techniques for the study if not the mastery of their problems. In several cities the charity-organization societies improved their structure; in others they undertook additional services. They acquired a broader influence through the establishment in 1911 of a national association, which promptly launched a campaign for the adoption of its program by laggard towns in the South and West. Assuming leadership in city-wide surveys and other research projects, the Russell Sage Foundation promoted a broad co-ordination of urban efforts, both public and private.[14] Several communities expanded their recreational activities, hoping thereby to check the growth of juvenile delinquency.

Aided by churches and other bodies, the charity-organization societies had wrought a transformation in the public and private welfare agencies of many cities by 1910, yet much remained to be done. The leading publication, *Charities and the Commons*—an amalgam of two earlier journals in New York and Chicago and soon to be renamed *The Survey*—had created a field department five years before to promote extensions of the movement. Numerous towns throughout the country had taken up the work, but at least forty-five over 25,000 in size still lacked such agencies, and many others had lost their leadership. The Russell Sage Foundation also established a charity-organization department, naming Miss Mary E. Richmond as director in 1909; she soon launched a series of annual institutes that supplied valuable assistance to scattered workers in the field. Sixty local bodies joined as charter members of the National Association of Societies for Organizing Charity in 1911, and their number doubled within three years. The professional direction and other standards pledged by its affiliates represented a real advance. Although many towns could not meet the requirement of a paid director or failed to keep adequate individual records, the roster of vigorous societies now included those in such places as Birmingham, Jacksonville, Charlotte, and Memphis in the South, and several cities in the West.[15]

Few of these younger bodies could as yet match the programs of older towns in the East, or those of Minneapolis and St. Paul, which were ably led by Father John A. Ryan.[16] Yet striking advances achieved by both new and old societies marked the opening of a new era in public welfare. Father Ryan brought the Catholic charities into fuller co-operation with their Protestant counterparts in St. Paul. Medical social work, which had its antecedents at Baltimore and Boston in the early 1900's, spread to a score of alert cities and encouraged the establishment of special employment bureaus for the handicapped, special farms for alcoholics, and educational campaigns on the dangers of alcoholism and of sexual irregularities. Collaboration between the leaders of different cities had meanwhile brought a significant change in perspective. Recurrent disasters from fires and floods had forced local organizations to seek new sources of emergency relief; coupled with the ravages of unemployment in 1907 and 1914, they prompted a reassessment of the merits of direct assistance. A few of the societies endorsed widows' pension legislation—a form of outdoor or noninstitutional relief that promised to keep the children in the family. Their support of juvenile courts, probation, and parole likewise reflected a growing disillusionment with institutional treatment and an increased confidence in enlightened public supervision. Together these trends displayed a wide acceptance of the philosophy of public welfare as distinguished from that of private charity.[17]

The happy result in several cities of co-operation between charity organizers and civic reformers prompted further efforts toward integration. Kansas City in 1910 created the first board of public welfare, with full responsibility over all related activities. Other towns quickly followed, and three years later Los Angeles, at the recommendation of its private agencies, appointed a municipal commission with authority over voluntary as well as public relief.[18] Few private agencies were ready to surrender their independence to that extent, yet an increasing number accepted the obligation to open their books and to reveal their methods when the city's charity-organization society or some other local body, such as the chamber of commerce, called for the facts. Some went even further and accepted not only the review but also the direction, at least in planning, of a central agency appointed by the city officials as in Los Angeles, by the chamber as in Denver, or by a delegate assembly as in Pittsburgh. The Pittsburgh plan, initiated in 1908, attracted increasing interest as its professional director successfully overcame several early difficulties. Milwaukee, St. Louis, Cincinnati, and a dozen lesser towns had by 1915 reorganized their charities under councils of social agencies.[19]

This growing recognition of an accountability to the public paralleled moves for greater support. The cost of adequate philanthropy in the increasingly complex urban society was mounting so rapidly that most societies had to seek new sources of income. A joint drive initiated at Denver in 1888 and promoted for several years by its Chamber of Commerce had gradually lost effectiveness, as had the more widely conducted bazaars and donations. A plan used in Elmira, New York, where in 1906 a Federation of Social Service began to collect all charity funds *as needed,* did not seem applicable to larger places. Finally Cleveland, in the midst of a surge of reform in 1913, organized a Federation of Charity and Philanthropy which undertook an annual drive for subscriptions to meet the expenses of all local agencies. Soon Denver, Cincinnati, Baltimore, and a half-dozen other cities established similar fund-raising bodies, which first received the name Community Chest when Rochester in 1918 combined all local and national appeals in one drive.[20]

Although these varied efforts to achieve effective community organization often sprang from a specific crisis and always required earnest local support, the committees and agents of the national association helped to promote more widespread co-operation. When old rivalries between the pet charities of a city's social leaders required outside mediation, the community surveys undertaken at local request by the Russell Sage Foundation were especially useful. The six it initiated in 1913, at Scranton, Atlanta, Topeka, Ithaca, St. Paul, and Springfield, Illinois, had varied local sponsors and objectives. Only the last was comprehensive in scope; it even made an advance over the Pittsburgh Survey of six years earlier by drawing 900 citizens into the investigation as participants. These surveys prompted others at Cleveland, Rochester, and elsewhere under local or outside auspices; many culminated in elaborate exhibits that performed an educational function and stimulated improvements in public health, welfare, and the schools.[21]

The major accomplishments of these prewar years were organizational; they co-ordinated many welfare efforts of previous decades. Especially significant progress occurred in two fields of intensive social work. The settlement houses, after two decades, not only established a national association in 1911, but also began to organize neighborhood councils and to encourage community action as well as free expression of opinion. The somewhat comparable social-center movement, based in Milwaukee, prompted many towns to open the schools for adult use and inspired several philanthropic ladies on Chicago's Gold Coast to organize community councils in nearby slums.[22] These and other efforts to revitalize urban neighborhoods represented a genuine advance.

In some cities the parks and playgrounds absorbed all available funds, but their functions, too, were expanding. Nearly all towns over 30,000 now had playgrounds and employed supervisors to direct games and manage other activities. A survey in 1916 listed 82 zoos, 61 indoor swimming pools, and 149 bathing beaches under public auspices; San Diego boasted the first municipal stadium, opened three years before. Several American towns staged community pageants to vivify their historical traditions. At least thirteen cities appropriated over $10,000 each for band music, and fifty more gave lesser sums. These outlays seemed paltry when compared with the provisions made by comparable places abroad, where both orchestras and theaters received municipal support, but they represented another advance in American municipal responsibility for recreation.

These provisions for the entertainment and amusement of great masses had only a limited value, however, according to Rowland Haynes, secretary of the Playground and Recreation Association of America. The surveys he made at Milwaukee and numerous other places disclosed a great need for more intensive work with small play groups and for an enrichment of the cultural content of the programs. In many of the parks, field houses and bandstands had become vital centers of neighborhood activity, and more were needed. His criticisms brought action in many places. Milwaukee, after its recreational survey, opened dance pavilions in several small parks and playgrounds in an effort to hold the youth as well as the children within their own neighborhoods. Prominent national leaders, such as Wilson and Hughes and William Allen White, joined in praise of that city's playgrounds and in lauding its social-center program; it exemplified, they declared, the best hopes of the day for the regeneration of blighted urban areas.[23]

The significance of both the neighborhood and the metropolis as basic urban units began to dawn on some planners. Surveys, conferences, and test cases helped to establish the authority and to underline the urgency of city planning, zoning, and even housing control. The problems revealed were too large, however, or at least too unfamiliar; aside from a few notable exceptions, little was accomplished.

The city-beautiful movement inspired by its great fair had given a strong impetus to urban planning, and Chicago quite properly reaped an early advantage. Enthusiasm whipped up by a press, lecture, and motion-picture campaign enabled its Planning Commission to start with a practical, if unglamorous, Twelfth Street improvement and to sustain popular interest by following with lake-front reclamation.[24] The visionary schemes proposed elsewhere, in plans sponsored by merchants' clubs, civic leagues, and women's organizations, seldom advanced beyond the paper stage. Few of the thirty-odd cities that created official planning boards before 1914 gave them more than advisory power, and many soon fell into disuse. Nevertheless, those in San Francisco, Philadelphia, and Springfield, Massachusetts, laid out civic centers, designated sites for public buildings, and plotted the routes for new and spacious parkways. Although they were postponed by the war, these plans, like those of Denver, St. Paul, and Cleveland, would ultimately influence each city's development. The grandiose plans for Washington would also require decades for completion, but meanwhile Congress in 1910 created a permanent art commission to supervise improvements throughout the District.[25]

A dozen other major cities acquired vast new park lands, developed neighborhood playgrounds, and made street extensions in accordance with their official plans. Kansas City, with its ambitious parkways almost completed in 1915, at a cost of $15,000,000, stood out as a shining model, which Seattle, Minneapolis, and Detroit, among others, sought to emulate. Boston and New York rejoiced at the opening of great suburban driveways and spacious metropolitan parks and beaches. These projects cost millions, but the decision to purchase land for such public use was often made easy by rapid urban growth.[26]

In contrast, other planning functions, such as the regulation of land uses, had to face court review. Fortunately the old police-power doctrine, that communities could properly exclude nuisances, had found expression in numerous decisions upholding the expulsion of slaughterhouses, laundries, livery stables, even billboards, from urban residential areas. Boston's action limiting the height of buildings had won judicial approval in 1909, but it was not until 1915 that the U. S. Supreme Court sustained a California decision permitting Los Angeles to extend its zoning regulations retroactively over unimproved tracts within its borders. The court, by authorizing the expulsion of an existing brickyard, revealed the planning powers latent in zoning regulations. Although some state judges continued to obstruct the way, and most planning and zoning boards hesitated to press the matter, the adoption of a comprehensive zoning ordinance by New York City in 1916 opened a new era of urban self-control.[27]

The National Planning Association, which considered these matters at length and exhibited the paper plans of aspiring cities at its annual conclaves, was reluctant to tackle the more acute problems of urban housing. Accordingly, several of the men who had called the first planning conference in 1909 met separately the next year to establish the National Housing Association. The division between the two movements proved unfortunate for both. While the former enlisted enthusiastic official as well as popular support, the latter had a richer background of experience in urban studies and a firmer grip on the conscience of many forthright citizens.[28]

Surveys of the housing situation in New York, Boston, and a few other great cities dated back several decades, as we have seen, and organizations had arisen to cope with the evils thus uncovered. Other surveys followed, and additional towns—San Francisco, Richmond, Providence, even salubrious Minneapolis and Columbus—joined the ranks of those ready to recognize such problems. Housing committees of local civic leagues, chambers of commerce, or women's clubs got official housing commissions created in St. Louis, Philadelphia, and the Commonwealth of Massachusetts. The welfare departments of Kansas City and Chicago and officials in New York City began to clear a few scattered slum areas for playgrounds; a congressionally appointed board assumed the task of eradicating, or requiring the improvement of, the unsanitary dwellings that had clustered along the capital's alleys. Pittsburgh adopted an ordinance against the smoke nuisance in 1912 and endeavored to enforce restrictions tried out a few months before in Cleveland and Chicago. Nine urban states granted their towns larger control over local construction. At least eighty-two cities drafted building codes and undertook some responsibility for the regulation of new housing before 1914.[29]

Unfortunately, the extent and urgency of the problem seemed to grow with each survey. Earlier attempts by a few humanitarians to build model tenements had failed to elicit the expected response. Alfred T. White's three projects had long since demonstrated their merits; the City and Suburban Homes Company continued to expand its properties until it served 11,000 tenants by 1915, but these produced scarcely a ripple in New York's vast pool of slums. The Charlesbank Homes in Boston, the Schmidlapp Houses in Cincinnati, and the remodeling operations of the Octavia Hill Association at Philadelphia and elsewhere appeared equally insignificant when contrasted with the existing expanse of wietched dwellings and the volume of new but unco-ordinated construction.[30]

Yet private builders were achieving great advances in the standards of safety and convenience embodied in their construction, which also increased in volume. Perhaps the most efficient structures of these years were the great skyscraper office buildings—notably the fifty-one-story Woolworth Tower, designed in a free Gothic style by Cass Gilbert and completed as the crowning point of Manhattan's skyline in 1913. No residential project, not even the garden apartments equipped with kitchenettes, devised by Andrew J. Thomas and introduced at Jackson Heights, Long Island, in 1910, could match the efficiency or the convenience of the mammoth commercial towers.[31]

A significant new experiment was taking shape in Forest Hills Gardens on Long Island. Erected by the Russell Sage Foundation in

1912, it was a group of apartment houses built around a railroad station and designed as a model suburban community. But Clarence A. Perry, one of its residents, whose first job with the foundation had been to study the social-center movement at Rochester and Milwaukee, soon discovered that the social life possible in blighted areas was sadly lacking in Forest Hills. Certain structural arrangements and the absence of a common school and playground joined with other features to obstruct the development of a true neighborhood. The lessons Perry learned there would help, years later, to redirect housing reformers and city planners toward the restoration of community units.[32]

While Perry was reflecting on the relationships between architecture and social life in urban neighborhoods, student residents at numerous settlement houses were uncovering similar links between the character and frequency of crime on the one hand and the conditions of the local environment on the other. An upsurge of juvenile delinquency prompted earnest surveys of the problems in a half-dozen cities within as many years. In addition to these, which included New Haven and Los Angeles, eight other cities launched studies of child welfare, and two of truancy. The discovery that juveniles as well as adults formed more or less permanent clubs or gangs, and sometimes used them for criminal ends, cast a new light on the problem. To many thoughtful social workers, juvenile delinquency, even adult vice and crime, began to appear more as a reflection of community disintegration than as individual sins. The concentration of many criminal incidents in depressed neighborhoods made remedial action there seem still more urgent.[33]

Additional study was needed before a comprehensive program could be devised; meanwhile, Mrs. Louise de Koven Bowen, Chicago socialite and friend of Jane Addams, organized a Juvenile Protective Association to help keep children out of court. The association sponsored numerous boys' clubs and campaigned for the opening of city schools for community use during evening hours. Like the older Juvenile Court, the Chicago Court of Domestic Relations, established in 1911, preferred probation over incarceration, but the future of their charges, when sent back into the old neighborhoods, began to disturb some judges.[34] The wider use of both probation and parole for adult criminals stirred public concern, too, over the hazards to the localities where they congregated.

Similar problems troubled other cities. In San Francisco the nefarious activities in the Barbary Coast area finally provoked the authorities to close its dance halls in 1913. After several months of strict enforcement, the old dives disappeared, but a new breed of "taxi-dance halls" sprang up in other parts of town. Generally the new establishments banned liquor and endeavored to require good deportment both on the part of the girls they hired and among the seamen they accommodated along with other lonely men. The pattern quickly spread to the great metropolitan centers in the East. This commercialization of the dancing-partner relationship shocked many communities, but in Chicago Mrs. Bowen defended those managers who maintained "dry" and otherwise decent places. She greatly preferred neighborhood dance halls to the downtown marathon, where couples were more apt to resort after the dance to a nearby hotel room.[35]

Mrs. Bowen and the Chicago Women's Club she founded, as well as similar groups there and elsewhere, gave increased attention in these prewar years to the problems of young women in cities. The Chicago Vice Commission, appointed as a result of the joint crusade of Gypsy Smith and the Federation of Churches, issued a revealing report in 1910 which aroused sufficient indignation to force the authorities to close the red light district. The movement spread quickly to many large towns. All but six major metropolitan centers appointed such commissions, and a score of them reported within the next few years; a dozen other bodies studying related aspects of the problem also issued reports. The attack on the social evil extended from Portland, Maine, to Portland, Oregon, from Minneapolis in the North to Atlanta in the South. Authorities in most places quickly closed the vice districts and banned streetwalkers. Although the surveys failed to substantiate all the lurid charges made in the press concerning the kidnaping of young girls and the drugging of those whose usefulness was exhausted, they disclosed sufficient evidence of a widespread white-slave trade to justify the Mann Act, which Congress adopted in 1910. One federal agent soon discovered an operator who controlled houses in eight cities and shipped his girls back and forth as the moral climate in each town dictated.[36]

The campaign proved widely effective, at least for a time, but many communities soon discovered that the trade had been decentralized, not abolished. Road houses and cabarets sprang up in nearby resorts or on formerly quiet lanes beyond the limits. Streetwalkers of a more sophisticated appearance invaded even respectable neighborhoods, and so many young girls practiced the trade on an individual basis that alert observers began to recognize them as the female contingent of the growing numbers of juvenile delinquents.[37]

The popular fear that the rising tide of crime would engulf all cities helped prohibitionists and other social reformers as they worked for enactment of their favorite measures. Later statistical studies have plotted crime graphs that soared to unprecedented heights during the "dry" jazz age that followed—but whether or not the outcome vindicated the prohibitionists, the issue they presented commanded increased attention in many cities during these prewar years.[38]

Though led by city men and women and carried forward by institutions they founded, the prohibition movement attracted votes most readily in the predominantly agrarian states and in rural districts elsewhere. Indeed the Anti-Saloon League reflected in some respects an anti-urban bias. Whereas many towns had enacted Sunday-closing ordinances and other moderate temperance measures, the effect had usually been to drive the worst establishments to the outskirts, where the old rural communities often proved unable, in face of the invading commercial resorts, to maintain even moderate restraints. Only state-wide prohibition promised relief, and rural voters pressed successfully for such action in a dozen states before the close of this period. Of them, however, only Washington and Colorado had large cities, and there the pluralities for prohibition fell precariously low. Leaders of the Anti-Saloon League saw that their best hope for wider triumphs lay in a national amendment, which might enable the agrarian states to rally sufficient votes in the rural areas of their industrial neighbors to carry the day. Although their strategy worked, later events disclosed that they had miscalculated the resistance of reluctant cities. The denouement would add still another factor to those marking the close of an era of progressive urban adjustment and ushering in a new age of metropolitan complexity.[39]

Many urban civic movements reached full circle during the progressive era. The old demand for home rule became less insistent as the adoption of state and federal regulations in many fields narrowed the scope of local sovereignty. Moreover, the stubborn exclusiveness of both old and new suburban towns in the vicinity of expansive metropolitan centers often obstructed the great cities' efforts to achieve civic integration. Meanwhile, an increased reliance by the states on the superior technical knowledge and judicial wisdom of appointive administrative boards reversed the trend toward responsible self-government; the new urban regions lacked not simply a mayor and a council but any central civic authority.

Yet if the cities were thus forced to rely on some old and once discredited instruments of government, the circumstances contrasted sharply with those of former decades. The new boards and commissions operated under the scrutiny of jealous administrators and a vigilant press. Vigorous men were achieving professional status in certain municipal fields, and their devoted nonpartisanship differed greatly from the preceding generation's lack of interest. Research bureaus and expert surveys uncovered obscure facts for the guidance of leaders and citizens.

There was a broader recognition of the community's responsibility for the welfare of its residents. Under the direction of a new body of professional workers, many of whom shared the dedication of the social gospel divines, the private welfare agencies attained an efficiency never before equaled. Some of the leaders of these bodies, and some officials, too, broadened their conception of community responsibility to encompass the juvenile if not always the adult criminal, and also the wretched slum area. City planning councils generally lacked sufficient power to develop effective programs, but a few seminal ideas, which now made their appearance, would receive greater attention as the metropolitan age advanced.

19. Cultural fulfillment and disenchantment

If only briefly, in the years just before the First World War, many residents of American cities enjoyed a sense of cultural fulfillment. Their churches had achieved a warm spirit of brotherly co-operation among differing faiths and displayed compassion for the shortcomings of transgressors as well as the sufferings of the needy. Their schools, placing increased emphasis on the individual child, also promised rich opportunities to all elements of the community, as educators encouraged higher education and adult participation. Their most learned men were confidently elaborating a harmonious pattern of thought and custom based on a pragmatic interpretation of experience, which appeared unchallengeable. Many of their artists were enjoying exhilarating applause as entertainers or as interpreters of the contemporary scene. Only a few in each field, scornful of shams and hypocrisies, the first to detect the conformities and superficialities of the "organization man," seemed perversely out of step. Fewer still suspected that the rapidly flowing stream of American life would soon plunge them again into a welter of confusion on metropolitan as well as international levels.

The co-operation effected by the major Protestant sects through the establishment of the Federal Council of Churches in 1908 was, as we have seen, a response to the turmoil of the city. Advocates of the social gospel, eager to enlist all men in the crusade for a better society, had labored earnestly for a united council. On its formation they moved promptly for the appointment of a Commission on the Church and Social Service to study the problems created by the city. They endeavored not only to work in harmony with men of dissimilar creeds but also to achieve an enlightened reasonableness. Such lofty views failed to appeal to all urbanites, of course; metropolitan throngs often welcomed the old-fashioned plea for the salvation of repentant sinners.

Charles Stelzle, the first chairman of the new commission, was a product himself of an earlier religious awakening in the city. A "son of the Bowery," he knew the East Side slums as a child and as a young mechanic before his call to the ministry. After training at Moody's Bible Institute in Chicago, he had filled working-class parishes in Minneapolis and St. Louis as well as New York; later, as a Presbyterian field worker, he had visited hundreds of towns urging pastors and laymen to develop more effective services for the working people in their neighborhoods. He had stimulated ministerial unions in 125 places to name official delegates to central trades' councils and had attended many labor conventions himself. In his new post he worked successfully, at the Federal Council's 1912 session in Chicago, for the adoption of a strongly worded social creed.[1]

The next two years saw the ratification of that creed by the national assemblies of several leading denominations. Earnest men from many urban parishes supported an endorsement, not only of its indictment of child labor and social injustice, but also of its defense of the worker's right to organize and bargain collectively for shorter hours, higher wages, and a host of other benefits. Enthusiasm for the new social ideals proved so strong that when some of the more traditional members proposed the launching of a co-operative religious revival, designed especially to reach unchurched men and boys in urban centers, the Commission on the Church and Social Service took on the task and made the Men and Religion Forward Movement, as it was called, an effective instrument of the social gospel.[2]

As the first part of his assignment, Stelzle in 1911 conducted a survey of seventy cities to determine the nature of the problem. His report, based on numerous quick visits and on replies to a questionnaire, revealed that saloons still outnumbered churches three to one, that socialists had increased fivefold during the previous decade, that poolrooms comprised 62.2 per cent of all places of amusement, that contrary to the general impression over half the boys arrested during the previous year had American, not foreign, parents. The investigation also disclosed that men and boys supplied barely a third of the attendance at church services. To correct that situation, the movement carried an intensively organized campaign of evangelism into downtown churches and theaters throughout the land. It also labored behind the scenes to promote the adoption, by the officials of innumerable neighborhood parishes, of a hundred specific recommendations designed to help them develop warm relationships with youth and with working people.[3]

Although most clergymen, like the great majority of their communicants, feared socialism, its doctrines and especially its humanitarian objectives presented a sharp challenge to many churchmen. The Christian-socialist fellowships within several Protestant denominations had lost much of their influence after the rise, around the turn of the century, of a materialistic and actively political socialism. Yet many of the clergy retained strong sympathies for its ideals; a few even resigned their charges to help carry the movement to its all-time peak in 1912.[4]

The threat to the major parties appeared more genuine as Socialists captured varied posts in three hundred towns and assumed control in eight of them that fall. Yet the movement, which had profited from the wide attack on the status quo, dwindled rapidly as the tasks of administration entailed uninspiring compromises on the part of their elected officials and as the progressive forces in general began to subside. The outbreak of war brought socialists and Christian pacifists closer together; their joint opposition to militarism sprang, however, from different beliefs, and each group waged its fight independently. Thus the frail link between liberal Christianity and socialism gradually disintegrated.[5]

The more moderate champions of the social gospel, such as Stelzle and Walter Rauschenbusch, prevailed over the Christian socialists and won official endorsement from the leading denominations, but they did not fully capture the great bulk of church members nor effectively reach the urban masses. Many workmen were Catholics whose clergy had so far taken little part in this movement. Moreover, of the vast number unidentified with any church, only a small portion responded, and fewer still joined the traditional Protestant bodies. Most of the labor temples and other city missions conducted by leading churchmen in several of the larger towns expired after a few years. Nevertheless, these men changed the official viewpoints of their denominations and infused a more truly democratic spirit into many urban congregations. They also established more cordial relations with some labor leaders and with the civic and political forces as well.[6]

Yet somehow their idealism and their social compassion failed to stir the excitement engendered by the Anti-Saloon League or to attract the crowds that followed Billy Sunday. That dynamic ex-ballplayer, also a street-mission convert, conducted extended campaigns of a month or more each in twenty-nine cities during these prewar years. Unlike Stelzle, he was obsessed with a fear of personal, not social, damnation, and his sensational techniques, though widely effective for a time, repelled liberal theologians and conservative citizens alike. Yet gospel missions that sprang up in his wake, or independently, flourished in the industrial and lower-middle-class sections of many towns as emotional speakers shouted weekly, sometimes nightly, appeals to sinners to repent. Loose federations of Elim Tabernacles and other fundamentalist groups spread from place to place, threatening a new division in urban religious outlooks at the very time that a broad and tolerant co-ordination of the older sects seemed assured.[7] Their persistence demonstrated that the redemption of the city and especially of the great metropolis was still unfinished.

John Dewey, whose concept of the public school as a social center had provided the name and the philosophy for that significant community program, had captured the imagination of city school men as truly as the social gospel had enlivened urban churches. His treatise, *The School and Society* (1899), reached its eleventh printing by 1915; its impact, together with that of his experimental school for the training of elementary teachers at the University of Chicago, had shaken many old traditions and formulated new techniques of instruction centered on the child. The older grade pattern, based on a set quantity of knowledge, persisted in most schools, but it had acquired a more flexible curriculum. A new spirit was evident; and in 1913 the National Educational Association appointed a Commission on the Reorganization of Secondary Education, which five years later produced a report of far-reaching influence.[8]

Of course the philosophy of pragmatism and the technique of experimentation were rationalizations, in a broad sense, of American urban experience. Growing cities had required growing schools, creating many opportunities for new beginnings. Some older schools, sensing their stagnation, readily accepted a reinterpretation of their objectives; others, exploring new fields of instruction in response to urgent community needs, welcomed a statement that promised to encompass and integrate their efforts. Many citizens responded with enthusiasm as the educators perfected a program and an ideology that enabled the schools to assume a more creative role both in the life of the city and in the nation's growth.[9]

Although Dewey merited great acclaim for his service in this and other respects, most of the experimentation came, as in the past, from courageous innovators in scattered cities. Frank Parsons, whose contributions had fructified many fields,[10] opened the first vocational bureau at Boston in 1908. This pioneer guidance clinic, supported by the Civic Service House, soon stimulated the launching of similar public or private bureaus at Cincinnati, Grand Rapids, and Des Moines, and in 1912 prompted the University of Chicago to offer a course for guidance counselors.[11]

The earlier movement for vocational education had produced a wide variety of elementary and secondary institutions and created a need for larger support. A fear among educators that local industrial interests would divert the program into a carefully controlled regimen for the training of complacent workers, prompted an appeal to the progressives for state and federal aid and supervision. In 1914, Congress moved to establish a National Commission on Vocational Education; disagreement over its control delayed action for three years, but the bill, when passed, assured federal support for such training in urban as well as agrarian fields.[12]

Although public and private vocational schools thus arose in most cities, their number and enrollment never rivaled those of the more traditional schools, many of which were acquiring a new character. The junior high school, introduced at Columbus in 1908, spread to 167 towns in the North and West; this intermediate school supplied an additional break in the educational process—a new turning point at which pupils might conveniently choose their proper course.[13]

The emphasis on preparation for college had already slackened in many city systems. Some high schools specialized in commercial or industrial subjects; some in a rounded education for responsible citizenship. Nevertheless, the demand for academic instruction continued and produced an increasing number of aspirants for higher learning. Neither the state universities nor the private colleges, though they now exceeded five hundred, could accommodate all the applicants. Many cities began to admit postgraduates to special classes in their high schools. California, hard pressed to keep up with its mounting population and far distant from the concentration of colleges in the East, granted its cities the power to add two years of advanced study to the high-school program. By 1914 a half-dozen of its largest towns had created the prototype of the public junior college. Philanthropic groups in fifty cities across the land transformed old academies and seminaries into junior or senior colleges. Almost every self-respecting community now required a temple of higher learning, and where private philanthropy failed to meet the need, demands for public action increased. Toledo and Akron joined the four metropolitan centers that maintained four-year colleges at public expense.[14]

The evening-school programs, launched several decades earlier, had meanwhile taken a new turn. Most of the academic work was abandoned to college extension classes, now available in many cities, which accommodated working students, teachers, and other adults unable to meet the full-time schedule. Night courses at the public schools specialized instead in industrial or applied arts, in English and the basic aspects of civics, and in other subjects designed to help adult immigrants and indeed all newcomers adjust to the urban environment. Thus a vast new educational program, later called Americanization, began to take shape in a few cities before the outbreak of war transformed its character and spread it across the land.[15]

The justification often given for the constant expansion of the educational program was its social usefulness, yet that argument invited a challenge, and school men were constantly in search of convincing proof. Several boards had ordered elaborate surveys of their school facilities after the turn of the century; it was not until 1910, however, that a few began to see the merits of engaging an outside investigator, free from local political or personality ties, to evaluate their educational programs. Some of the early investigators, whose reports disclosed unexpected deficiencies, inevitably encountered harsh criticism. Several developed elaborate techniques of analysis in order to assure objectivity. Joseph M. Rice of New York, after a careful study of the teaching practices of thirty-six cities, devised a method of measuring results that seemed fairly reliable and brought the superintendents of twenty-four progressive towns together to found the Society for Educational Research. Before the independent investigator had become firmly established, however, Baltimore determined in 1911 to establish a permanent research bureau in conjunction with its public school system. Soon other cities, too, added professional supervisors to their regular staffs.[16]

The presence of inspectors and of other adults was becoming a familiar experience to pupils as well as officials. Over five hundred school systems reported regular programs for the medical examination of the eyes, ears, and teeth of all students by 1915. This tenfold advance in five years was accomplished as 268 cities engaged school nurses and 130 established permanent dental clinics, many with large support from private sources. School visitors also included state inspectors watchful for the welfare of handicapped pupils, women's club representatives eager to hang paintings or to brighten the classroom in other ways, and parents galvanized to action by Mothers' and Parent-Teacher Associations.[17]

The wide adoption in these years of movable desks, invented at Rochester in 1905, facilitated the use of classrooms as adult social and educational centers in the evening and permitted a more flexible student program during the day. Springfield, Massachusetts, installed a motion-picture screen and projector in one high-school auditorium for both day and evening use. Many school libraries became branches or stations of the city system in order to serve the whole community.[18]

The public-library movement had now spread to all cities over 50,000 and to many smaller ones. Neighborhood branch systems extended the services, as in Brooklyn, where there were twenty-eight branches, not counting the school substations. The Cincinnati library opened a teachers' room; Los Angeles inaugurated the first series of story hours. Several fine new buildings completed in these prewar years supplied meeting rooms for clubs, as well as a special children's room and other anticipations of the divisional system with which Cleveland's main library was already experimenting in temporary quarters in 1914. The traveling library, first introduced on the outskirts of Washington nearly a decade before, was becoming more popular; as motor trucks replaced horses, a few metropolitan counties undertook to extend book services to their outlying residents.[19]

The museums, which had also acquired an established role, especially in the metropolis, were developing their own techniques for the enrichment of community life. Another half-dozen large cities accepted public responsibility for the maintenance of such institutions, dedicated to science and industry, sometimes to local history as well. Wealthy patrons erected elegant new buildings for them in a few places, notably at Los Angeles in 1914; San Diego, as several towns had done before, got one in 1915 as the state's contribution to its Panama-California Exposition. The Park Museum in Providence, Rhode Island, devised a science puzzle to hold and direct the attention of youngsters visiting its halls. In Charleston, South Carolina, America's oldest museum brought its program into line with those of a dozen progressive institutions by preparing traveling exhibits for circulation throughout the schools of the area. Old Independence Hall at Philadelphia began in 1914 to provide docent service for scheduled tours by children's classes. Some museum directors, recognizing their broader educational responsibilities, employed art as well as science in perfecting their displays. At Albany, Arthur C. Parker completed his Indian habitat groups which first placed life-size manikins with appropriate artifacts in natural human (or community) settings.[20]

The graphic and audio-visual arts still depended largely on philanthropic, associational, or commercial support. A few cities had granted some municipal aid to their art galleries, and many hired musicians for park bands in summer and even winter series, but such subsidies did not often reach creative artists. In the theater, too, the large rewards went to the popular entertainers. Most of the wealthy patrons of music and art gave their commissions and grants to those with the greatest following or with established names abroad. Yet new currents were stirring in all art realms, and little groups of earnest and imaginative young men and women in several great metropolitan centers provided a foretaste of the controversies that would mark the next era of urban growth.

Although the art galleries, lacking the utilitarian rationale of the museums of science and industry, found the municipal authorities reluctant to grant full maintenance support, several additional places now acquired sumptuous buildings. Hartford, Toledo, Los Angeles, Rochester, Minneapolis, and Cleveland, all dedicated imposing classical or Renaissance structures, the gifts of wealthy residents. The Cleveland gallery's opening in 1916 marked a turning point in museum history, for the carefully designed Colonial rooms and other features, including provision for organ recitals, represented a broadening of the program and spurred innovations elsewhere. The galleries vied with the science museums in serving schoolchildren; some organized classes for adults as well. Brooklyn opened the first children's museum in 1913, and Boston the second soon after. An increased number of cities granted some public assistance in return for these benefits; finally, in 1914, St. Louis took over the art building inherited a decade earlier from its fair, as the first city art museum.[21]

Yet neither these impressive quasi-public institutions nor the proliferating institutes and schools of art satisfied all related interests. The photographers, whose early "picture emporiums" had given wall space to painters in many towns before the art clubs acquired galleries, had been scornfully excluded from most of the latter until a few won acclaim in Europe for the artistic quality of their portraiture. Art galleries in Philadelphia, Buffalo, and elsewhere experimented cautiously, around the turn of the century, with photographic exhibits. But Alfred Stieglitz, who had become editor of *American Amateur Photographer* shortly after his return to America in 1890, was determined to achieve genuine artistic standards and full recognition. He wanted a salon and a magazine devoted exclusively to art photography. In 1902 he staged a demonstration exhibit at the National Arts Club in New York and at its close organized a group known as the Photo-Secession. He launched a handsome quarterly, *Camera Work,* and opened a Little Gallery on Fifth Avenue in 1905. Emphasizing their distinction from traditional members of the craft by taking the name sometimes used to describe modern artists on the Continent, the photo-secessionists soon found that their objectives and those of the European artists were surprisingly complementary. The Little Gallery began to display some of Edward J. Steichen's photographs of Auguste Rodin and his sculptures; it gradually included a few of Rodin's drawings, and water colors by Cézanne, whom Steichen had met in Paris, as well as abstractions by Picasso and other modernists. By 1910 the Little Gallery had become the center of a coterie of venturesome artists, talented photographers, and curious patrons.[22]

Interest in contemporary art appeared in other cities, notably Baltimore and Buffalo; a group of eager "secessionists" gathered at New York in 1912 to form a National Association of American Painters and Sculptors. The great Armory Show it staged a year later assembled representative paintings and sculptures by most of the leading post-impressionists abroad and by several of their American disciples. The exhibit shocked many established artists and critics, and their widely published comments attracted an unending flow of visitors from all classes in New York, as well as art critics and patrons from distant cities. A sufficient number of appreciative defenders arose to project all over the country a lively debate on the function and purpose of art, stimulating a new concern for standards in schools and galleries.[23]

The division between sophisticated and traditional tastes was not unique to the graphic arts, although its appearance there was more sudden and startling than in most other arts. American cities had absorbed much of the best Europe had to offer in several cultural fields, and creative local groups were busily generating contributions of their own. A new spirit of native independence was asserting itself in music; a new medium was emerging for drama. While the great city orchestras and theaters were still trying to assimilate the successive waves of Western culture and to incorporate them into the maturing national tradition, local contributions, full of crude native vitality, began to command attention.[24]

Musical trends afforded perhaps the most striking example. The performances of the nine major symphony orchestras of 1911 stimulated renewed efforts to establish professional bodies of high quality at Cleveland and Los Angeles, though the war delayed their inauguration for a year or two. A few directors, notably Walter Damrosch at New York and Stokowski at Philadelphia, maintained exacting musical standards in their programs, and Boston resumed its search for fresh inspiration, even by Americans. In some places the directors were accused of sweetening their offerings with popular favorites in order to draw the crowds, but despite such measures, struggling orchestras in several large cities faced budgetary problems. Those of Pittsburgh and Indianapolis, hard-pressed by the competition of dramatically successful bands, suspended operation.[25]

The brass bands, which drew more extensively on American composi-tions, enjoyed an undiminished popularity in these prewar years. They carried their stirring marches into small as well as large towns and on triumphant tours abroad. More and more places engaged park bands for lengthy summer seasons. Apparently they gratified a widespread craving for community solidarity similar to that which inspired an increasing number of community festivals. Among the latter were the Festivals of Song and Light staged by Claude Bragdon in the public parks at Roches-ter, Syracuse, Buffalo, and New York in the last years of peace.[26]

The real burst of musical vitality, however, was occurring in the less pretentious setting of urban cabarets and dance halls. Ragtime and the blues had already won their place on innumerable vaudeville stages, and the jazz bands, which had begun to drift up the Mississippi from New Orleans around the turn of the century, now found permanent lodgment in Chicago and New York. Together they contributed a new zest to life in the congested quarters of the great metropolitan centers. Songs like the "St. Louis Blues" (1914) spread quickly throughout the towns; the rebukes pronounced by some academic musicians against the jazz bands scarcely diminished the commotion they created. It would require sev-eral years to prove their contributions to American music, but mean-while they were transforming the social patterns of vast portions of the city's youth.[27]

The situation in the theater was somewhat analogous, but with impor-tant differences. There the theatrical syndicate, which had established its sway over a nation-wide circuit, continued to serve a rich fare of enter-tainment. If commercial considerations prompted undue concessions to the popular taste for farces, such as *Twin Beds* by Margaret Mayor, or extravaganzas like *Kismet* by Edward Knoblock, and encouraged fre-quent use of name actors in hackneyed vehicles, and too subservient a dependence for their quality offerings on the audience appeal of foreign stars and plays—still, millions of theatergoers enjoyed exhilarating sea-sons. New and luxurious houses arose in several cities, some dedicated to legitimate drama, some to the rampaging vaudeville skits, yet the total number held fairly steady in contrast to the expansion of the motion-picture chains, which now took over many theaters. After 1910 the booking offices in New York tightened their grip on the regional circuits even in the vaudeville field, while the invasion of ticket scalpers in the metropolis and elsewhere further removed control from the interested public.[28]

The standardization of the commercial theater had, however, provoked several efforts either to correct its evils or to compensate for them. The Drama League of America, founded at Evanston, Illinois, in 1910, organized active branches in numerous cities. Its charter pledged support for good plays; although "uplifters" with little knowledge of drama sometimes responded in embarrassing numbers, the study groups the league sponsored in many neighborhoods fostered an appreciation for the more intellectual offerings and helped to launch a number of community playhouses. The little-theater movement had its foreign antecedents, too, as well as important roots in urban settlement houses and in a few universities. Jane Addams's Hull-House theater of 1900, the famous workshop established by Professor George P. Baker at Harvard for the experimental production of new plays, and the efforts of scattered towns to stage local anniversary pageants with dramatic effect—all contributed to the rapid spread of these vital little groups. Boston, Chicago, and New York each produced thriving troupes of talented players.

The little theaters also provided a catalyst for the development of zestful neighborhood dramatic associations in various sections of these vast metropolitan conglomerates. The movement spread quickly to a dozen other large cities. Although none rivaled the success achieved by the Neighborhood Playhouse on Grand Street in New York, the fifty established before 1917 contributed a new spirit to the American theater at a crucial moment. The courses offered at Harvard and elsewhere by Baker and other professors of drama shared this fresh approach and contrasted sharply with the academic traditionalism in most cultural fields. Many of their students would later acquire positions of influence on the legitimate stage, in motion pictures, or as playwrights or critics; some who shifted to other fields remembered their early connections with the community theater as sufficiently rewarding.[29]

Few as yet foresaw the full extent of the cinema's challenge to the theater and to other forms of amusement. The rapid multiplication of nickelodeons and dime theaters had opened a new market in every town, but had scarcely invaded the province of drama. Already, however, improvements in technology and innovations in subject matter gave promise of more serious competition. The rise of favorite stars, such as Mary Pickford and Charlie Chaplin, created popular idols unprecedented in human history. With the production of *Birth of a Nation* in 1915, urban and rural America acquired a new medium of common experience that outranked all but the newspapers in coverage.[30]

Forces characteristic of other aspects of the nation's urban development had their influence in each of these cultural fields. As we have previously noted, the great variety of immigrant traditions quickened the reception of foreign contributions. The trend toward monopoly control, represented by the theatrical syndicate and the booking office in the theater, reached motion pictures with the rise by 1915 of great production companies and regional chains. These trends also provoked repeated efforts at widespread organization among the performers. Although their first protective association of 1896 failed, the actors rallied in 1913 to found a national Equity Association, which endeavored to establish wage and hour minimums and other standards on the job. The musicians had achieved a similar organization with the formation of the American Federation of Musicians in 1896 which now steadily expanded its membership. The American Society of Composers, Authors, and Publishers, founded in 1914, and the American Federation of Arts, which started five years earlier, endeavored to prescribe standards and establish safeguards for these creative workers. New regional and national journals appeared in each field, among them *The Drama* at Chicago in 1911 and *The Musical Quarterly* four years later at New York; *Art and Progress* changed its name again at the close of the period to the *American Magazine of Arts*.[31]

The universities, several of them by 1910 great centers of research, contributed in significant ways to each of these cultural fields and to that of literature as well. Their music schools and art departments, most of which eagerly served their communities, long antedated the drama courses; though all stressed the academic tradition, they sometimes sheltered and often produced experimental spirits. The total work of these great institutions and of the more numerous colleges was of course much broader. For decades they had served as the principal intermediaries between American youth and the intellectual heritage of the Western world. Although in their origin and purpose most of them were little related to the urban scene, the city had drawn them increasingly into its sphere of influence. Not only were many shedding earlier denominational ties and turning to the city for new sources of energy and larger growth; some were also finding, in the urban laboratory at their door, fascinating subjects for research.[32]

By 1910 well over half the cities of at least moderate size had acquired an academic grove, if only, in some cases, a bleak city square surrounding a converted mansion. Several metropolises had two or more of the nation's 500 colleges, whose total enrollment now exceeded 300,000 and whose faculty numbered 30,000. Although not many places could properly be described as college or university towns,[33] faculty members elsewhere often played active roles in the affairs of even major cities. Their extension programs reached thousands of adults; their numerous public lectures also contributed to the intellectual life of the community. Academic specialists frequently responded to requests for expert advice on public-health questions or other municipal problems. Many participated in local betterment campaigns and in social functions. Their very presence contributed a sense of adequacy and self-respect to many cities.[34]

Some universities did much more than temper the pervasive materialism of urban America. The graduate programs undertaken at Johns Hopkins and a few other places in the seventies and afterward had directed research workers into political science, economics, and other social studies, as well as into engineering and several natural sciences that inevitably involved the city. As the decades advanced, scholars at Harvard, Columbia, Pennsylvania, Michigan, Chicago, and Wisconsin increasingly used the local community as a laboratory. Some went further, especially at Madison, where they developed so many expert services for both urban and rural residents that the "Wisconsin Idea" inspired emulation elsewhere.[35]

Many of these activities involved controversial questions and aroused criticism from political and other vested interests adversely affected. Repeated efforts to discipline or discharge offending professors focused public attention on the question of academic freedom. Controversies erupted in several places as a few socialists and similarly outspoken critics of monopolies and other power groups lost their jobs—notably Edward W. Bemis, Frank Parsons, and Edwin A. Ross, who were all active in urban reform. Many citizens began to ponder the threat of subversion on the one hand and on the other the danger of thought control. If, as Professor Hofstadter has recently argued, the circumstances did not often justify the ready charge of conspiracy, a widespread suspicion of "tainted wealth" brought heavily endowed colleges under closer scrutiny. Many of the faculty, increasingly uncertain of their tenure, joined the American Association of University Professors, organized at Baltimore in 1913; many more welcomed the strong statement it issued two years later on academic freedom.[36]

The charge that political leaders in Wisconsin were seeking to create a university state, rather than a state university, disappeared with the final defeat of the Progressives in 1914. The meliorism that at first characterized most collegiate social research declined steadily as further knowledge disclosed more difficulties and complexities. The early teens saw the firm establishment of a battery of fairly distinct social sciences and at least a tentative systemization of their techniques. Each essayed an inductive study of the environment from a particular focus—economic, political, social, cultural, psychological, or historical.[37]

The first three specializations gave immediate attention to the city, and their pioneers, as our footnotes have indicated, contributed to a broad assault on its problems. Richard T. Ely and John R. Commons at Wisconsin led in the study of conflicts between capital and labor; John W. Burgess at Columbia analyzed civic and political functions; Charles R. Henderson at Chicago surveyed social maladjustments. These and other social scientists sought earnestly for practical solutions of the problems confronting the cities and besetting mankind in general. With most intellectuals of the period, they accepted the pragmatic philosophies of William James and John Dewey and soberly regarded themselves, in the latter's terminology, as social engineers. Yet that same pragmatism, which subjected all theory to the acid test of practice, prompted a quick discard of many hopeful hypotheses and justified such a broad indictment of contemporary social, economic, and political systems, that even a courageous scholar like Richard T. Ely began to stress the primary need to accumulate more knowledge before taking precipitate action. Wesley C. Mitchell, sensing the future demands of a metropolitan economy, endeavored to perfect new techniques for measurement; Charles H. Cooley, shunning the imponderable complexities, took up the study of internal group relationships; and in 1915 Robert E. Parks at Chicago published a significant paper, "The City, Suggestions for the Study of Human Behavior in the City Environment." [38]

If urban slums provided the cradle, as some have put it, for the social sciences, they also rocked American literature out of its complacency. Groups of talented writers in several major cities had already developed a keen interest in the urban environment. Their books had described many aspects of its life with what has been called critical realism. Their indignation over the corruption and cruelty that surrounded them was as sharp as that of the humanitarians and the reformers, and their readiness to indict false aesthetic, as well as ethical, standards had prompted the establishment of several "little" magazines.[39] Yet, as in the field of music, it was not the learned editors or the university faculty members but a number of sensitive writers experiencing the metropolis at first hand who produced the insights that probed the emotions of many of the city's victims.

Theodore Dreiser's powerful novels, four of which erupted in these prewar years, captured the bafflement and defeat experienced by many eager youths who migrated to the cities. It was the great city, the metropolis, that had confronted and almost overwhelmed Dreiser. Chicago in the nineties, even St. Louis, Cleveland, Pittsburgh, and certainly New York had, before his arrival, grown beyond the urban stage in which the social structure assured a friendly welcome to restless newcomers. A lonely, brooding writer, Dreiser quickly saw the sham, the brutality, the irrationality that frustrated many rootless folk, but he failed to understand as a participant any of the earnest movements endeavoring to correct the situation. Scornful of the hypocrisy of some philanthropic efforts, he cut loose from his Catholic heritage and employed morals chiefly as a base for his scathing indictment of urban society.[40]

The shock his alienation produced helped to direct other writers toward an uninhibited approach to urban life. By 1910 a number were discovering that the frustration and disintegration characteristic of metropolitan society had spread to some outlying communities. *Spoon River Anthology,* by Edgar Lee Masters, was a product of this realization, and its reception in 1914 disclosed the presence of a small coterie of "liberated" intellectuals within the vast expanse of Chicago. Harriet Monroe's *Poetry* provided a new champion for young writers there in 1912, joining the *Friday Literary Review* in this service. The appearance of Margaret Anderson's *Little Review* two years later enlarged and strengthened the circle.[41]

When Dreiser moved to New York he supplied one of several links between the Chicago group and the larger one developing in Greenwich Village. The socialistic *Masses* (1911), the *New Republic* (1914), and the *Seven Arts* (1916) rallied youthful critics and writers there to a clamorous assault on established traditions in art and literature as well as on the materialism of the social system. As at Chicago, they welcomed new voices abroad—Havelock Ellis, Gertrude Stein, Sigmund Freud, Ezra Pound—and the new symbolism in graphic art, thus performing an important function of the great metropolis. Through the vitality of their own fellowship they also demonstrated, though quite unconsciously, the creative values congenial neighborhoods and societies possessed. Mabel Dodge's famous salon on Fifth Avenue supplied a refreshing oasis at which representatives of dissident factions gathered to revel in their disenchantment.[42]

But in the fervor of their liberation they lost perspective. By tilting

against a "grotesque effigy of gentility" and repudiating all former standards, they provoked not only the hostility of incensed leaders in academic circles but also that of the broader community they hoped to
reach. Fascinated by the city, rather than, like some of their intellectual
predecessors, repelled by it, they nevertheless missed the "rhythm" of the
great city, which in 1907 had impressed even the nature-loving William
James as "magnificent." Instead they expressed the dissidence created
by the rise of a new type of urbanism—metropolitanism—which called
for a new period of adjustment and integration.[43]

Of course the emerging metropolitan environment was only one of
many factors that stimulated and conditioned the literary and artistic
stirrings of the prewar years. Many, indeed most writers living in great
cities or small sensed some urban compulsions, but there was no hidden
determinism controlling intellectual responses nor, for that matter,
directing the course of man's economic, civic, and social evolution. Yet
it is perhaps instructive to note how interrelated man's responses frequently are. That at least has been a major thesis in this study of America's urbanization.

We have seen how policies and techniques of settlement, of production, and of distribution contributed to the growth and decay of cities;
how these in turn created civic and social problems that required new
adjustments: and how men and women of all ranks and places, organizing to work for the goals they sought, achieved through strife and compromise sufficient economic integration to enable the urban population,
which mounted in these decades to half the nation's total, to attain an
unprecedented state of material well-being.

More specifically we have seen how the nation's vast expanse encouraged innumerable urban settlements whose growth provided commercial
and organizational focuses for amorphous hinterlands and progressively
supplied the market for an increasing agricultural output. We have seen
how the rise of cities released dynamic energies and nurtured technological advances which together produced such lavish rewards that few
citizens gave serious consideration to socialistic or co-operative proposals. Private enterprise, producing real as well as speculative bounties, acquired a firm hold on the urban-industrial economy, even within
the ranks of organized labor. It fostered the development of powerful
corporations and of countervailing forces, such as craft and trade unions
and employers' associations; their incessant struggles brought new and
greater vitality to the urban marketplace; they also gave rise to insistent
demands for some form of community control.

We have seen how, on the one hand, the rapid growth of cities created urgent needs for community services and safeguards, and how, on the other hand, civic pride ripened to meet them. The long years of municipal corruption, highlighted by the rise of city bosses, though explained in part by the absorbing opportunities the city's growth presented to private enterprise, eventually challenged the public conscience in both the civic and the moral field. It produced a resurgence of community spirit that brought reform to municipal functions, and gave rise to new conceptions of social welfare and town planning.

We have also seen how impermanent—better still, dynamic—each new accomplishment proved to be, as the multiple chain reactions of urbanization created ever more complex human relationships within each city and throughout the broader urban firmament until, in the last decade or so before the First World War, these varied trends had transformed the pattern of American urban life from one of widely dispersed cities, loosely dominated by New York, into a society tenuously organized under national authority—a matrix of poorly co-ordinated metropolitan regions.

Furthermore, we have seen how citizens in many communities became increasingly aware of the social implication of their political decisions; how some of them developed techniques for the formulation and perfection of their policies, surveying local conditions or opinions and using outside or even foreign ideas when the circumstances warranted; how their increased self-consciousness not only enabled them to achieve higher civic and social standards but also prompted many to seek new cultural levels of expression; and how, despite almost revolutionary changes in every aspect of society, they had risen to a crescendo of reform during the progressive movement and formulated a new pattern of urban integrality.

Finally, as we break this historical account off at the point where the emergence of unexpected metropolitan complexities marked the opening of a new era, it has been interesting to note that the younger men in the great cities were already fumbling with new symbols of expression in the arts, seeking new standards of measurement in the sciences, experimenting with new techniques of production and control in the economic and civic realms. They were also demonstrating, through the fellowship enjoyed in their intimate coteries of artists, dramatists, writers, and scientists, some of the traditional values of community life. The innumerable associations, local and national, of technicians, humanitarians, workers, and businessmen, not forgetting the women's clubs, had often yielded similar values, compensating at least in part for the decline of neighborliness that accompanied the city's growth in size and heterogeneity. Although the extent and character of their accomplishments proved unsatisfying to some, urbanites were the first to proclaim it, and many were busy devising new techniques and seeking new standards for the future.

Thus the cities of America had served, throughout the half-century under review, as creative laboratories. They were laboratories in an even more fundamental sense than that grasped by a few emerging social scientists in key universities, for their work was both theoretical and practical. It was in these busy laboratories that a democratic society had formulated, tested, and applied the principles and fabricated the instruments of an urban civilization. By 1915, however, the process of America's urbanization had reached a turning point. The increased size and complexity of the cities and the mounting significance of their interrelationships had transformed many into metropolitan centers effecting important structural changes in their organization and calling for increased functional specialization. New and perplexing problems and difficult adjustments loomed ahead for all urbanites.

Notes

Preface

1. See the discussion of some of these studies in Otis D. Duncan and Albert J. Reiss, Jr., *Social Characteristics of Urban and Rural Communities, 1950* (New York, 1956), pp. 19–28.
2. Louis Wirth supplied useful definitions in the 1930's; see his collected papers in *Community Life and Social Policy*, A. J. Reiss, Jr., ed. (Chicago, 1956), pp. 110–176. Renewed interest in this problem developed after the publication of Hope Tisdale's article on "The Process of Urbanization" in *Social Forces*, XX: 311–316. The narrowed meaning he proposed has stirred varied responses; see A. J. Reiss, Jr.,'s chapter in *The Metropolis in Modern Life*, R. M. Fisher, ed. (New York, 1955), and Eric Lampard's article on "The Study of Urbanization" in the *American Historical Review* (Oct., 1961), pp. 49–61.
3. Lampard, *loc. cit.*
4. For a convenient bibliographical review of the early books, see Blake McKelvey, "American Urban History Today," *American Historical Review*, LVII (July, 1952), pp. 919–929. Lampard, *loc. cit.*, lists some of the more recent books.

Introduction

1. Eric E. Lampard, "The History of Cities in the Economically Advanced Areas," *Economic Development and Cultural Change* (The Univ. of Chicago Research Center in Economic Development and Cultural Change, 1955), III: 102–119, supplies a comprehensive review of this development.
2. Bureau of the Census, *Current Population Reports, Population Characteristics*, Series P-23, No. 1 (Aug. 5, 1949). The census of 1860 did not list these places separately, but a later *Supplementary Analysis* (1906), after working over the manuscript data of earlier censuses, produced a statistical recapitulation of "urban places" from 1790 forward.
3. Anthony Trollope, *North America* (New York, 1951 ed.), pp. 191–196; Bayrd Still, *Mirror for Gotham* (New York, 1956), pp. 167–204; U. S. *Census* (1910), Pop., I: 80; Ralph Weld, *Brooklyn Village, 1816–1834* (New York, 1938); Jean Gottmann, *Megalopolis* (New York, 1961), pp. 102–138.
4. Robert G. Albion, *The Rise of New York Port: 1815–1860* (New York, 1939); Trollope, *op. cit.*, p. 195.
5. Blake McKelvey, "The Erie Canal: Mother of Cities," New-York Historical Society *Quarterly*, Jan., 1951, pp. 55–80; Blake McKelvey, *Rochester: The Water-Power City: 1812–1854* (Cambridge, 1945) [cited below as *Rochester, I*], pp. 205–241; John T. Horton, *Old Erie—The Growth of an American Community* [Buffalo] (New York, 1947), I: 22–172.
6. Albion, *op. cit.*, pp. 84–94, 411, *passim;* Eric E. Lampard in Harvey S. Perloff and associates, *Regions, Resources, and Economic Growth* (Baltimore, 1960), pp. 109–112.
7. Carl Bridenbaugh, *Cities in the Wilderness* (New York, 1938), and *Cities in Revolt* (New York, 1955).

8. Constance M. Green, *American Cities in the Growth of the Nation* (New York, 1957), pp. 26–38; Edward C. Kirkland, *Men, Cities, and Transportation: 1820–1900* (Cambridge, 1948), I: 92–266, 320, 334; Albion, *op. cit.*, pp. 34–37, 74, 374–376, 390–393, 402; Trollope, *op. cit.*, pp. 219–255; Rollin G. Osterweis, *Three Centuries of New Haven: 1638–1938* (New Haven, 1953), pp. 191–309; Oscar Handlin, *Boston's Immigrants, 1790–1865* (Cambridge, 1941), p. 226; C. F. Ware, *The Early New England Cotton Manufacture* (Boston, 1931); Robert K. Lamb, "The Entrepreneur and the Community," in William Miller, ed., *Men in Business* (Cambridge, 1952), pp. 91–119.

9. Trollope, *op cit.*, pp. 290–305, 462–464; David Macrae, *The Americans at Home* (New York, 1952), pp. 91–95, 462–499; George B. Tatum, *Penn's Great Town* (Philadelphia, 1961), pp. 80–100, Plate 108.

10. U. S. *Census* (1860), III: 522–527, 537; Albion, *op. cit.*, pp. 390–393; J. W. Livingood, *Philadelphia-Baltimore Trade Rivalry: 1780–1860* (Harrisburg, 1947), pp. 2–12; Trollope, *op. cit.*, pp. 368–372.

11. Green, *op. cit.*, pp. 9–18; Livingood, *op. cit., passim;* Albion, *op. cit.*, pp. 379–384, 390–393, 417; Catherine E. Reiser, *Pittsburgh's Commercial Development: 1800–1850* (Harrisburg, 1951), pp. 85–112, 153–155; Trollope, *op. cit.*, pp. 295–303, 452–454; George A. Sala, *America Revisited* (London, 1883), pp. 120–129.

12. Richard C. Wade, *The Urban Frontier* (Cambridge, 1959). This scholarly study provides an illuminating documentation for the next several pages. See also Perloff, *op. cit.*, pp. 113–121.

13. Wade, *op. cit.*, pp. 39–59; Green, *op. cit.*, pp. 41–56, 73–74; U. S. *Census* (1860), III: 453–456, 483. Essex County in Massachusetts exceeded Hamilton County in Ohio in number of workers, wages, and value added. Trollope, *op. cit.*, pp. 369–375.

14. Albion, *op. cit.*, pp. 104–118, 389–393; Green, *op. cit.*, pp. 72–73; U. S. *Census* (1910), Pop., I: 54, 74, 80.

15. Albion, *op. cit.*, p. 405, note; Wyatt W. Belcher, *The Economic Rivalry Between St. Louis and Chicago: 1850–1880* (New York, 1947), pp. 26–31, 41–54; Green, *op. cit.*, pp. 61–66; J. D. Andrews, *Report of . . . on the Trade and Commerce of . . . the Great Lakes and Rivers* (Washington, 1954), pp. 613–812; U. S. *Census* (1860), I: xxxi–xxxii.

16. Bayrd Still, "Patterns of Mid-Nineteenth Century Urbanization in the Middle West," *Mississippi Valley Historical Review*, XXVIII (Sept., 1941), pp. 187–206; Bessie L. Pierce, *A History of Chicago* (New York, 1940), II: 40–61; Green, *op. cit.*, 100–110; Albion, *op. cit.*, pp. 93–94, 118–121; George R. Taylor and Irene Neu, *The American Railway Network: 1861–1890* (Cambridge, 1956), see maps; Belcher, *op. cit.*, pp. 31–38, 55–71.

17. Belcher, *op. cit.*, pp. 92–138; Pierce, *Chicago*, II: 62–149; Green, *op. cit.*, pp. 49–65, 100–110; Trollope, *op. cit.*, pp. 122–126; Albion, *op. cit.*, pp. 384–386.

18. Franklin Walker, *San Francisco's Literary Frontier* (New York, 1939).

19. Samuel L. Clemens, *Mark Twain's Travels with Mr. Brown* (New York, 1940), pp. 31, 259–262.

20. See also Morton White's account of the reaction of Henry Adams to New York in 1868, Lloyd Rodwin, ed., *The Future Metropolis* (New York, 1961), p. 220.

21. Clemens, *op. cit.*, pp. 122–145, 154–157.

22. Charles N. Glaab, "Visions of Metropolis: William Gilpin and Theories of City Growth in the American West," *Wisconsin Magazine of History* (Autumn, 1961), pp. 21–31.

23. Christopher Tunnard and Henry Hope Reed, *American Skyline* (Boston, 1955), pp. 39–42, 59–63; Anthony N. B. Garvan, *Architecture and Town Planning in Colonial Connecticut* (New Haven, 1957); National Resources Committee, *Urban Planning and Land Policies* (Washington, 1939), II: 15–17; Turpin C. Bannister, "Early Town Planning in New York State," *New York History*, XXIV (1943), pp. 185–195.

24. U. S. *Census* (1880), XVIII and XIX, *Social Statistics of Cities*, Parts I and II, includes the street maps of some 300 cities.

25. Wade, *op. cit.*, pp. 27–35; Still, "Patterns of Urbanization," *loc. cit.*

26. Walter Muir Whitehill, *Boston, A Topographical History* (Harvard, 1959), pp. 95–118; see a reminiscent account of Columbus in 1860 by William Dean Howells, *Literary Friends and Acquaintances* (New York, 1902), pp. 2–3; B. J. Lossing, "Growth of Cities in the U. S.," *Harper's New Monthly Magazine* (1853), VII: 171–175; Handlin, *op. cit.,* pp. 106–117.
27. Vera Shlakman, *Economic History of a Factory Town* (Smith College Studies in History, XX, 1935), pp. 11–150; Robert Ernst, *Immigrant Life in New York City: 1825–1865* (New York, 1949); Emory R. Johnson and others, *History of Domestic and Foreign Commerce of the U. S.* (Washington, 1915), I: 224–253.
28. *Hunt's Merchant's Magazine,* XIII: 245–259, 417–426; XIX: 383–386; XXIV: 263–301; Andrews, *op. cit.,* pp. 613–812.
29. David M. Ellis, "Albany and Troy—Commercial Rivals," *New York History:* XLI (1943), pp. 484–511; McKelvey, *Rochester,* II: 109; Kenneth Sturges, *American Chambers of Commerce* (New York, 1915), pp. 1–20; Sidney Fine, *Laissez Faire and the General Welfare State* (Ann Arbor, 1956), pp. 10–23.
30. Nelson M. Blake, *Water for the Cities* (Syracuse, 1956); Edgar W. Martin, *The Standard of Living in 1860* (Chicago, 1942), pp. 38–42, 284–287; Still, "Patterns of Urbanization," *loc. cit.*
31. Martin, *op. cit.,* pp. 239–243, 267–269, 282–284; Pierce, *Chicago,* II: 330–338; Still, *op. cit.,* pp. 190–198, 200–202.
32. Frank Presbrey, *The History and Development of Advertising* (New York, 1929), pp. 236–244; Martin, *op. cit.,* pp. 313–318; Still, *op. cit.,* pp. 197–200, 202.
33. Martin, *op. cit.,* pp. 44–47, 89–112.
34. Martin, *op. cit.,* pp. 170–174; McKelvey, *Rochester,* I: 340–342; Pierce, *Chicago,* II: 461–465; James Ford and others, *Slums and Housing* (Cambridge, 1936), pp. 72–149.
35. Martin, *op. cit.,* pp. 106–112, 149–160, 167–180, 261–265; Chauncey M. Depew, ed., *One Hundred Years of American Commerce* (New York, 1895), I: 141–142.
36. Martin, *op. cit.,* pp. 94–97, 113–114.
37. Martin, *op. cit.,* pp. 114–116, 120–128, 140–143.
38. Carl Bode, *The American Lyceum* (New York, 1956); Still, *op. cit.,* pp. 202–206; U. S. Bureau of Education, *Public Libraries in the U. S., Special Report,* I (1876), pp. 384–385, 837–1007.
39. Martin, *op. cit.,* pp. 305–333, 358–363; Laurence V. Coleman, *The Museum in America* (Washington, 1939), I: 6–15; Oliver W. Larkin, *Art and Life in America* (New York, 1949), pp. 102–120; Foster R. Dulles, *America Learns to Play* (New York, 1940), pp. 20–118; Glenn Hughes, *A History of the American Theatre* (New York, 1951), pp. 150–195; Ralph S. Rusk, *The Literature of the Middle Western Frontier* (New York, 1926), pp. 27–78.
40. F. Garvin Davenport, *Cultural Life in Nashville on the Eve of the Civil War* (Chapel Hill, 1941); McKelvey, *Rochester,* I: 343–365; Constance M. Green, *Washington, Village and Capital, 1880–1878* (Princeton, 1962), pp. 200–229.
41. Dixon Wecter, *The Saga of American Society* (New York, 1937), pp. 6, 134–156; John Coolidge, *Mill and Mansion* (New York, 1942), pp. 128–140; Pierce, *Chicago,* I: 189, 265, 274; McKelvey, *Rochester,* I: 286–287, 349.

Part I

1. See the maps showing "Old," "Medium Aged," and "New Cities" in the National Resources Committee, *Our Cities* (Washington, 1937), Figs. 17, 18, 19.
2. *Ibid., Population Statistics,* III (Washington, 1937), p. 8. See also Tables 26–29 in Perloff, *op. cit.,* pp. 126–128.

CHAPTER 1: *The Diffusion of Urban Sites*

1. Edward C. Kirkland, *Industry Comes of Age: 1860–1897* [*The Economic History of the U. S.*, Vol. V] (New York, 1961), pp. 2, 13–24, 163–164; Thomas C. Cochran, "Did the Civil War Retard Industrialization?" *Mississippi Valley Historical Review*, Sept., 1961, pp. 197–210. Although Professor Cochran, after examining the statistics of industrial output and the percentages of increase for successive decades, answers his question in the affirmative, he recognizes "the possibility that northern victory had enhanced the capitalists' spirit." His analysis, however, does not question the increased absorption of industrial production by the cities, nor does it consider the impact of that concentration on urban growth.
2. Green, *Washington*, pp. 230–271; Green, *American Cities*, pp. 222–228; Margaret Leech, *Reveille in Washington: 1860–1865* (New York, 1941).
3. Emerson D. Fite, *Social and Industrial Conditions in the North During the Civil War* (New York, 1910), pp. 14–15, 42–77, 93–95.
4. Pierce, *Chicago*, II: 92–114; William T. Hutchinson, *Cyrus Hall McCormick* (New York, 1935), II: 87–99.
5. Fite, *op. cit.*, pp. 78–104; Osterweis, *op. cit.*, pp. 351–354; Kirkland, *op. cit.*, p. 163.
6. Kirkland, *op. cit.*, pp. 43–51; Harlan W. Gilmore, *Transportation and the Growth of Cities* (Glencoe, 1953), pp. 50–67.
7. Slason Thompson, *A Short History of American Railways* (New York, 1925), and Stewart H. Holbrook, *The Story of American Railroads* (New York, 1947) are convenient general summaries. See also Ida M. Tarbell, *The Nationalizing of Business: 1878–1898* [*A History of American Life*, Vol. IX] (New York, 1936), pp. 91–112; George R. Taylor and Irene D. Neu, *The American Railroad Network: 1861–1890* (Cambridge, 1956); Samuel P. Hays, *The Response to Industrialism: 1885–1914* (Chicago, 1957), pp. 4–17.
8. Kirkland, *op. cit.*, pp. 55–57, 69–74.
9. John Moody, *The Railroad Builders* (New Haven, 1919), pp. 33–40.
10. Moody, *op. cit.*, pp. 49–63, 100–115; Kirkland, *op. cit.*, pp. 75–88.
11. See the maps in Taylor and Neu, *op. cit.*, and in Moody, *op. cit.*; Edward C. Kirkland, *Men, Cities and Transportation: A Study of New England History: 1820–1900* (Cambridge, 1948), pp. 112 ff.
12. Harry H. Pierce, *Railroads of New York: A Study of Government Aid: 1826–1875* (Cambridge, 1953), pp. 187–193 and *passim*.
13. Raymond W. Albright, *Two Centuries of Reading, Pa., 1748–1948* (Reading, 1948); William Z. Ripley, *Railroads and Railroad Rates* (New York, 1912 [1923]), pp. 37–43; *Cost of Living in American Towns: Report of an Inquiry by the Board of Trade of London* . . . (U. S. Senate Document No. 22, 62nd Congress, 1911), p. xi; Thomas C. Cochran and William Miller, *The Age of Enterprise* (New York, 1942), pp. 30–135.
14. Paul W. Gates, *The Illinois Central Railroad and Its Colonizing Works* (Cambridge, 1934), pp. 138–141, 147–148; Belcher, *op. cit.*, pp. 158–206; Pierce, *Chicago*, II: 40–64; III: 65–70.
15. Randolph C. Downes, *Lake Port* (Toledo, 1951), pp. 74–77; Bayrd Still, *Milwaukee: The History of a City* (Madison, 1948), pp. 175, 352; Mildred Hartsough, *The Twin Cities as a Metropolitan Market* (Minneapolis, 1925), pp. 72–87.
16. N. S. B. Gras and H. M. Larson, *Casebook in American Business History* (New York, 1939), pp. 373–385; John F. Stover, *The Railroads of the South, 1865–1900* (Chapel Hill, 1955), pp. 34–35, 210–232.
17. Louis M. Hacker and B. B. Kendrick, *The United States Since 1865* (New York, 1949 ed.), p. 161, estimate the total public contributions to railroads at three fifths of the construction costs before 1870; Stover, *op. cit.*, pp. 186–196; Hays, *op. cit.*, pp. 17–19.

18. Moody, *op. cit.*, pp. 121–137; Glenn C. Quiett, *They Built the West: An Epic of Rails and Cities* (New York, 1934), pp. 3–81, 143–540; Tarbell, *op. cit.*, pp. 17–23; Carl C. Rister, *The Southwestern Frontier: 1865–1881* (Cleveland, 1928), pp. 295–301; James C. Illson, *J. Sterling Morton* (Lincoln, Neb., 1942), pp. 167–213; Richard C. Overton, *Gulf to Rockies* (Austin, 1953); James P. Shannon, *Catholic Colonization on the Western Frontier* (New Haven, 1957), pp. 1–13.

19. Henry C. Haskell, Jr., and R. B. Fowler, *City of the Future* (Kansas City, 1950), pp. 38–58; William Miller, *History of Kansas City* (Kansas City, 1881); A. Theodore Brown, *A History of Kansas City to 1870* (MS of forthcoming vol.), pp. 270–290.

20. Quiett, *op. cit.*, pp. 82–142; Ray B. West, *Rocky Mountain Cities* (New York, 1949); Ralph H. Brown, *Historical Geography of the U. S.* (New York, 1948), pp. 349–350, 455–461; James B. Hedges, *Henry Villard and the Railways of the Northwest* (New Haven, 1930), pp. 112–133; Marshall Sprague, *Newport in the Rockies* (Denver, 1961), pp. 15–79.

21. Sprague, *op. cit.*, pp. 47–249; Green, *American Cities*, pp. 129–146; Clyde L. King, *The History of the Government of Denver . . .* (Denver, 1911), pp. 93–101, 160–170; Quiett, *op. cit.*, pp. 129–148.

22. Quiett, *op. cit.*, pp. 182–255; Brown, *op. cit.*, pp. 423–492; Mrs. Fremont Olds, *San Francisco* (San Francisco, 1961).

23. Richard Bigger and J. D. Kitchen, *How the Cities Grew* (Los Angeles, 1952), pp. 1–33; Glenn S. Dumke, *The Boom of the Eighties in Southern California* (San Marino, 1944); Remi A. Nadeau, *City Makers* (New York, 1948); Grace H. Stimson, *Rise of the Labor Movement in Los Angeles* (Berkeley, 1955), pp. 68–80; Carey McWilliams, *Southern California Country* (New York, 1936); Quiett, *op. cit.*, pp. 217–338; Oscar O. Winters, "The Rise of Metropolitan Los Angeles: 1870–1910," The Huntington Library *Quarterly*, X (Aug., 1947), 391–398.

24. Quiett, *op. cit.*, pp. 339–498; George S. Perry, *Cities of America* (New York, 1947), *passim;* Hedges, *op. cit.;* Moody, *op. cit.*, pp. 138–178.

25. Quiett, *op. cit.*, pp. 439–495; Green, *op. cit.*, pp. 167–180; Remi Nadeau, *Los Angeles: From Mission to Modern City* (New York, 1960), pp. 94–98. Among the West Coast cities, San Francisco, the oldest, still held the lead with 416,912 residents in 1910. Los Angeles, with 319,198 was rapidly catching up, and Seattle, with 237,194, had overtopped Portland's 207,214 and Tacoma's 83,743.

26. T. Lynn Smith, "The Emergence of Cities," in R. B. Vance and N. J. Demerath, *The Urban South* (Chapel Hill, 1954), pp. 24–45.

27. E. Merton Coulter, *The South During Reconstruction: 1865–1877 [A History of the South, VIII]* (Baton Rouge, 1947), pp. 234–274; C. Vann Woodward, *Origins of the New South: 1877–1913* (Louisiana University, 1951), pp. 107–139; Gerald M. Capers, *The Biography of a River Town: Memphis, Its Heroic Age* (Chapel Hill, 1939), pp. 186–234; Emory R. Johnson, ed., *History of Domestic and Foreign Commerce of the U. S.* (Washington, 1915), II: 82–83, 94; Thomas J. Wertenbaker, *Norfolk, Historic Southern Port* (Durham, 1931); Edgar Watkins, "Geography, Railroads, and Men Made Atlanta," *The Atlanta Historical Bulletin* (Oct., 1948), VIII: 71–88; John W. Rogers, *The Lusty Texans of Dallas* (New York, 1951), pp. 190–204; *Cost of Living in American Towns:* (U. S. Senate Doc. 22, 1911), pp. 48–98, 219–230, 243–256, 288–298; Overton, *op. cit., passim;* Hays, *op. cit.*, pp. 121–129. An account of a modest development in the South at High Point, N. C., is contained in Rupert B. Vance, *All These People* (Chapel Hill, 1945), pp. 294–302; see also Anthony M. Tang, *Economic Development in the Southern Piedmont: 1860–1950* (Chapel Hill, 1958), pp. 22–95.

28. Edgar B. Wesley, *Owatonna, The Social Development of a Minnesota Community* (Minneapolis, 1938); Hugh Morrison, *Louis Sullivan* (New York, 1935), pp. 207–211, 372–374. See Merle Curti, *The Making of An American Community* (Stanford, Cal., 1959) for a probing study of an agrarian county that developed several small trading hamlets. See also Lewis Atherton, *Main Street*

on the Middle Border (Bloomington, 1954), pp. 330–348, 360–362, for an illuminating account of the economic dreams of small town residents.

29. John L. McCarty, *Maverick Town: The Story of Old Tascosa* (Norman, Okla., 1946); Dumke, *op. cit.*, pp. 90–92, 244–275; Dick King, *Ghost Towns of Texas* (San Antonio, 1953); Green, *op. cit.*, pp. 149–156; George D. Lyman, *The Saga of the Comstock Lode* (New York, 1934). Although this is a fictionalized account, its documentation, 359–399, is revealing. See also the discussion of increased specialization in Eric E. Lampard, "The History of Cities in the Economically Advanced Areas," *Economic Development and Cultural Change,* Jan., 1955, pp. 86–90 ff.; Shannon, *op. cit.*, pp. 125–186.

30. Angie Debo, *Prairie City: The Story of an American Community* (New York, 1944), p. 92; George E. Mowry, *The California Progressives* (Berkeley, 1951), p. 9 and *passim;* E. G. Campbell, *The Reorganization of the American Railroad System, 1893–1900* (New York, 1938); B. H. Meyer, *Railroad Legislation in the U. S.* (New York, 1909), pp. 189–195; see, however, Thomas C. Cochran, *Railroad Leaders: 1845–1890* (Cambridge, 1953), pp. 202–217.

31. Pierce, *Chicago,* II: 81–88, III: 74–78; Allan Nevins, *The Emergence of Modern America* [A History of American Life VIII] (New York, 1927), pp. 168–169; Kirkland, *op. cit.* (1961), pp. 108–126.

32. Lee Benson, *Merchants, Farmers and Railroads: Railroad Regulations and New York Politics: 1850–1887* (Cambridge, 1955), pp. 9–28; George H. Miller, "The Granger Laws: A Study of the Origin of State Railway Control in the Upper Mississippi Valley" (Ph.D. Thesis, University of Michigan, 1951); Isaiah L. Sharfman, *The Interstate Commerce Commission* (New York, 1931), I: 11–35; Hays, *op. cit.*, pp. 48–58.

33. Kirkland, *op. cit.* (1961), pp. 126–130; Sidney Fine, *Laissez Faire and the General Welfare State* (Ann Arbor, 1956), pp.303–304.

34. Benson, *op. cit.*, pp. 29–79; Campbell, *op. cit.*, pp. 19–29; Arthur M. Johnson, *The Development of American Petroleum Pipelines* (Ithaca, 1956), pp. 26–48; Kirkland, *op. cit.* (1961), pp. 118, 126–128.

35. Thomas C. Cochran, *Railroad Leaders: 1845–1890* (Cambridge, 1953), pp. 184–201; Benson, *op. cit.*, pp. 80–246; Tarbell, *op. cit.*, pp. 96–106; W. Z. Ripley, *Railroads, Rates and Regulation* (New York, 1923), pp. 441–486; Kirkland, *op. cit.* (1961), pp. 126–136.

36. National Resources Committee, *Urban Government,* Supplement I: 27, 53; *ibid., Population Statistics, Urban Data,* p. 8; U. S. *Census* (1910), Pop., I: 67.

CHAPTER 2: *The Emergence of Industrial Cities*

1. Edgar M. Hoover, *The Location of Economic Activity* (New York, 1948). See Edward Ullman, "A Theory of Location for Cities," *American Journal of Sociology,* Vol. 46 (May, 1941), pp. 853–863, for a review of several theories concerning the location of cities.

2. Numerous books recognize this contribution, but few have treated it adequately. See Kirkland, *op. cit.*, pp. 237–261; Harold U. Faulkner, *The Decline of Laissez Faire: 1897–1917* (New York, 1951), pp. 92–114; Hays, *op. cit.*, pp. 48–58. For an early study of urban contributions, see Arthur Shadwell, *Industrial Efficiency* (London, 1909). For an able geographical study of urban economy, see Gunnar Alexandersson, *The Industrial Structure of American Cities* (Lincoln, Nebraska, 1956).

3. Charlotte Erickson, *American Industry and the European Immigrant: 1860–1885* (Cambridge, 1957); Eric E. Lampard in Harvey S. Perloff and associates, *Regions, Resources and Economic Growth* (Baltimore, 1960), pp. 122–221.

4. Kirkland, *op. cit.* (1961), pp. 133–142; Edmund E. Day, "An Index of the Physical Volume of Production," *Review of Economic Statistics,* II (Oct., 1920), p. 294; Ray B. West, Jr., *Rocky Mountain Cities* (New York, 1949), pp. 230–255;

Paul H. Landis, *Three Iron Mining Towns* (Ann Arbor, 1938); Alexandersson, *op. cit.*, pp. 27–34. See the bibliography in Caroline Bancroft's fictionalized history of Central City, Colorado, *Gulch of Gold* (Denver, 1958), pp. 365–376.

5. T. A. Rickard, *A History of American Mining* (New York, 1932), pp. 91 and *passim;* U. S. *Census* (1900), Occupations, p. 728; Peter Roberts, *Anthracite Coal Communities* (New York, 1904); Chauncy D. Harris, "A Functional Classification of Cities in the United States." *Geographic Review*, Vol. 33 (Jan., 1930), pp. 86–96. See also Kirkland, *op. cit.* (1961), pp. 137–162.

6. Muriel E. Sheppard, *Cloud by Day* (Chapel Hill, 1947); *Cost of Living in American Towns* (Senate Doc. 22, 1911), pp. 337–339, 344–348. See also Henry L. Hunker, *Industrial Evolution of Columbus, Ohio* (Columbus, 1958), pp. 39–55, for an account of how Columbus absorbed the energies of nearby mining districts.

7. Herman F. Otte, *Industrial Opportunity in the Tennessee Valley of Northwestern Alabama* (New York, 1940), pp. 20–26; Vance and Demerath, *op. cit.*, pp. 10–12; Woodward, *op. cit.*, pp. 314–316.

8. Johnson, *op. cit., passim;* Thomas Greenwood, *A Tour of the States and Canada* (London, 1883), pp. 94–100; Tarbell, *op. cit.*, pp. 74–79; Cochran and Miller, *op. cit.*, pp. 135–146. See also, John P. Herrick, *Empire Oil* (New York, 1949).

9. Chester M. Destler, *American Radicalism: 1856–1901* (New London, 1946), Chapter VII.

10. Randolph C. Downes, *Lake Port* [Lucas County History Series III] (Toledo, 1951), pp. 59–93; U. S. *Census* (1900), Occupations, p. 742; (1910), IX: 996–997.

11. Henrietta Larson, *The Wheat Market and the Farmer in Minnesota, 1858–1900* (New York, 1926); Mildred Hartsough, *The Twin Cities* (Minneapolis, 1925), pp. 36–46; Henry C. Haskell, Jr., and R. B. Fowler, *City of the Future: A Narrative History of Kansas City, 1850–1950* (Kansas City, 1950); Gerald M. Capers, *River Town, Memphis* (Chapel Hill, 1939), pp. 220–228; Alice Lantherman, "Kansas City as a Grain and Milling Center," *Missouri Historical Review*, XLII (1947), pp. 132–155; *Cost of Living in American Towns* (Senate Doc. 22, 1911), pp. 243–283; Alexandersson, *op. cit.*, pp. 34–35, 86–88.

12. Erickson, *op. cit.*, pp. 65–105; Mary R. Coolidge, *Chinese Immigration* (New York, 1909), pp. 357–401. Boston's sudden emergence as an industrial city in the fifties has been attributed to cheap immigrant labor—see Oscar Handlin, *Boston's Immigrants: 1790–1865* (Cambridge, 1951), pp. 79–87.

13. George W. Chase, *History of Haverhill* (Haverhill, 1921), pp. 532–536; Edgar M. Hoover, *Location Theory and the Shoe and Leather Industries* (Cambridge, 1937), pp. 219–228.

14. *Ibid.*, pp. 229–255; Horace B. Davis, *Shoes, The Workers and the Industry* (New York, 1940), p. 17 and *passim;* Blake McKelvey, "A History of the Rochester Shoe Industry," *Rochester History*, Apr., 1953, pp. 6–20; U. S. Industrial Commission, *Reports,* VII: 176–180, 369–370; Alexandersson, *op. cit.*, pp. 80–82.

15. Thomas R. Smith, *The Cotton Textile Industry of Fall River, Mass.; A Study of Industrial Localization* (New York, 1944), pp. 40–99; Marcus L. Hansen, *The Immigrant in American History* (Cambridge, 1940), pp. 154–174; Arthur W. Calhoun, *A Social History of the American Family* (Cleveland, 1919), III: 67; *Cost of Living in American Towns* (Senate Doc. 22, 1911), pp. 197–203, 208–214, 231–238; Shadwell, *op. cit.*, pp. 208–230.

16. Vera Shlakman, *Economic History of a Factory Town: A Study of Chicopee, Mass.* [Smith College Studies in History, XX] (Northampton, 1935), pp. 151–225; Margaret T. Parker, *Lowell: A Study of Industrial Development* (New York, 1940), pp. 85, 118–147; Constance M. Green, *Holyoke, Mass.* (New Haven, 1939), pp. 137–251; U. S. Industrial Commission, *Report,* VII (1900), pp. 68–84, 90, 219–226, 343–348; Hansen, *op. cit.*, pp. 160–174, 188–190; Alexandersson, *op. cit.*, pp. 63–70; Faulkner, *op. cit.*, pp. 142–144.

17. Anthony M. Tang, *Economic Development in the Southern Piedmont* (Chapel Hill, 1958), pp. 22–65 ff.; Smith, *op. cit.*, pp. 80–121; Herbert Lahne, *The Cotton Mill Worker* (New York, 1944), pp. 70–84, 175–195; Melvin T. Copeland, *The*

Cotton Manufacturing Industry of the United States (Cambridge, 1923), pp. 27–133; F. B. Garver, F. M. Boddy and A. J. Nixon, *The Location of Manufactures in the United States: 1899–1929* (Minneapolis, 1933), pp. 65–75; Broadus Mitchell and George S. Mitchell, *The Industrial Revolution in the South* (Baltimore, 1930), pp. 126–140; William H. Simpson, *Life in Mill Communities* (Clinton, S. C., 1943), pp. 14–25.

18. Smith, *op. cit.*, pp. 119–121; Parker, *op. cit.*, p. 210 ff. But see also Victor S. Clark, *History of Manufactures in the United States* (New York, 1929), II: 181–198; Shlakman, *op. cit.*, pp. 196–198; Green, *American Cities*, pp. 82–90.

19. Erickson, *op. cit.*, pp. 139–147; Bayrd Still, *Milwaukee, The History of a City* (Madison, 1948), pp. 329–332 and *passim;* Pierce, *Chicago*, II: 89; Blake McKelvey, *Rochester, The Flower City: 1854–1890* (Cambridge, 1949) [cited below as *Rochester*, II], pp. 106–107, 238–240; Thomas C. Cochran, *Pabst Brewing Company: The History of an American Business* (New York, 1949); *Cost of Living in American Towns* (Senate Doc. 22, 1911), pp. 152–157, 257–265, 373–376.

20. McKelvey, *Rochester*, II: 227, 243, 322, 380; U. S. Industrial Commission *Report*, XV (1901), *passim;* Carl Wittke, *We Who Built America* (New York, 1940), pp. 392–401. See Erickson, *op. cit., passim.*

21. Jesse E. Pope, *The Clothing Industry in New York* [University of Missouri Studies, Vol. I] (St. Louis, 1905), pp. 45 ff.; U. S. Industrial Commission *Report* (1901), pp. xxiv–xxxii, xlviii, 316–384, 449–490; *Cost of Living in American Towns* (U. S. Senate Doc. 22, 1911), pp. 20–21, 23, 137–138; Edward E. Pratt, *Industrial Causes of Congestion of Population in New York City* (New York, 1911), pp. 79–86. See also Moses Rischin, *The Promised City: New York's Jews, 1870–1914* (Cambridge, 1962), pp. 51–68.

22. Mabel A. Magee, *Trends in Location of the Women's Clothing Industry* (Chicago, 1930), pp. 9–11, 133–134; Leonard A. Drake and Carrie Glasser, *Trends in the New York Clothing Industry* (New York, 1942), pp. 39–47; Louis Levine, *The Women's Garment Workers* (New York, 1924), pp. 1–195; Calhoun, *op. cit.*, III: 74–75; *Cost of Living in American Towns* (Senate Doc. 22, 1911), pp. 18–24, 75–78, 105–108, 137–141, 154–156, 162–166, 177–179, 323–324; Charles Hirschfeld, *Baltimore: 1870–1900* [Johns Hopkins Studies in History and Political Science, Series 59, No. 2] (Baltimore, 1941), pp. 41–42, 57–63.

23. *World Almanac* (1889), p. 91; U. S. *Census* (1880), Compendium, p. 8; Cochran and Miller, *op. cit.*, pp. 135–153; Margaret G. Myers, *The New York Money Market* (New York, 1931), I: 213–233; Pierce, *Chicago*, III: 192–233; Douglas North, "Capital Accumulation in Life Insurance Between the Civil War and 1905," in William Miller, *Men of Business* (Cambridge, 1952), pp. 238–253. See also Kirkland, *op. cit.* (1961), pp. 216–236.

24. McKelvey, *Rochester*, II: 98–126, 200–256.

25. Roger Burlingame, *Engines of Democracy* (New York, 1940), pp. 95–125, *passim;* Herbert N. Casson, *The History of the Telephone* (Chicago, 1910); Hays, *op. cit.*, pp. 48–58; Kirkland, *op. cit.* (1961), pp. 163–182.

26. Harold C. Passer, *The Electrical Manufacturers, 1875–1900* (Cambridge, 1953); Blake McKelvey, *Rochester, The Quest for Quality* (Cambridge, 1956) [cited below as *Rochester*, III], pp. 256–272; Faulkner, *op. cit.*, pp. 115–134; Alexandersson, *op. cit.*, pp. 48–49, 62–63.

27. Felix Frankfurter, *The Public and Its Government* (New Haven, 1930), pp. 9–10; *Recent Social Trends in the United States* (New York, 1934), pp. 125–127; Edward W. Byrn, *The Progress of Invention in the Nineteenth Century* (New York, 1900).

28. U. S. *Census* (1900), VII: 503–509; Hirschfeld, *op. cit.*, pp. 44–46, 76–82; Kirkland, *op. cit.* (1961), pp. 196–214; Fine, *op. cit.*, pp. 146–151.

29. John Moody, *The Truth About the Trusts* (New York, 1904), pp. 453–476; William Miller, "American History and the Business Elite," *Journal of Economic History*, IX (1949), 184–208; Cochran and Miller, *op. cit.*, pp. 135–153, 181–191; Faulkner, *op. cit.*, pp. 153–164.

30. Abbott P. Usher, *A History of Mechanical Inventions* (Cambridge, 1954), pp. 401–406; Paul W. Keating, *Lamps for a Brighter America* (New York, 1954),

pp. 21 ff.; Joel H. Monroe, *Schenectady, Ancient and Modern* (Schenectady, 1914), pp. 277–280; Passer, *op. cit.*, pp. 52–57, 100–104, 321–330; Kirkland, *op. cit.* (1961), pp. 195–215.

31. *MacRae's Blue Book* (New York, 1910); Byrn, *op. cit.*, pp. 76–87, 171–182, 459–460; Clark, *op. cit.*, II: 377–387; III: 165–170; Bruce Bliven, *The Wonderful Writing Machine* (New York, 1954); Lee, *op. cit.*, pp. 97–104.

32. Arthur S. Dwing, *Corporate Promotions and Reorganizations* (Cambridge, 1914), pp. 249–268; Lloyd Morris, *Not So Long Ago* (New York, 1949), pp. 229–265; Shlakman, *op. cit.*, pp. 200–205; Merrill Denison, *The Power to Go* (New York, 1956), pp. 92–180; *Cost of Living in American Towns* (Senate Doc. 22, 1911), pp. 172–175; H. H. McCarty, *Industrial Migration in the United States, 1914–1927* (Iowa City, Iowa, 1930), p. 10; Ralph C. Epstein, *The Automobile Industry* (New York, 1928), pp. 123, 209, 257–260, 296; Green, *op. cit.*, pp. 199–203; Alexandersson, *op. cit.*, pp. 49–54.

33. Henry R. Seager and C. A. Gulick, Jr., *Trust and Corporation Problems* (New York, 1929), pp. 48–60, 367–398; Destler, *op. cit.*, pp. 105–134; R. H. Bremner, "The Civic Revival in Ohio," *American Journal of Economics and Sociology* (1951), X: 417–429; Fine, *op. cit.*, pp. 126–164; Faulkner, *op. cit.*, pp. 175–186, 202–210.

34. U. S. *Census* (1900), VII: ccxix–ccxxiv; (1910), X: 901–975; Glenn E. McLaughlin, *Growth of American Manufacturing Areas* (Pittsburgh, 1938), pp. 127–132, 186–188.

35. Kenneth Sturges, *American Chambers of Commerce* (New York, 1915), pp. 11–43; Still, *op. cit.*, pp. 345–348.

36. Still, *op. cit.*, pp. 345–348; see also Lloyd Graham and Frank H. Severance, *The First Hundred Years of the Buffalo Chamber of Commerce* (Buffalo, 1945), p. 142 ff.; U. S. Industrial Commission *Report*, VII (1900), pp. 16–17, 990–999; XIV: 439–460; see also Hirschfeld, *op. cit.*, pp. 36–38; Pierce, *Chicago*, III: 80, 93, 475.

37. Sturges, *op. cit.*, pp. 117–166, 231–240; William G. Rose, *Cleveland, The Making of a City* (Cleveland, 1950), pp. 537, 542; George W. Doonan, "Commercial Organizations in Southern and Western Cities," U. S. Bureau of Foreign and Domestic Commerce, *Special Agents Series*, No. 79, 1914; Hunker, *op. cit.*, pp. 53–55.

38. Sturges, *op. cit.*, *passim*; Howard L. Childs, *Labor and Capital in National Politics* (Columbus, 1930); Paul Studenski, "Chambers of Commerce," *Encyclopedia of the Social Sciences*, III: 325–329; Fine, *op. cit.*, pp. 96–125.

39. U. S. Bureau of the Census, *Historical Statistics of the United States: Colonial Times to 1957* (Washington, 1957), pp. 139–140, 283–284; Kirkland, *op. cit.* (1961), pp. 278–305, 399–409.

40. *Historical Statistics of the United States to 1957*, pp. 544–546; Faulkner, *op. cit.*, pp. 52–63.

CHAPTER 3: *The Transformation of the Metropolis*

1. Wyatt W. Belcher, *The Economic Rivalry Between St. Louis and Chicago: 1850–1880* (New York, 1947); N. S. B. Gras and H. M. Larson, *Casebook in American Business History* (New York, 1939), pp. 373–402.

2. Edward E. Pratt, *Industrial Causes of Congestion of Population in New York City* [Columbia University Studies in History, etc., Vol. 43, No. 1] (New York, 1911), pp. 68–90; Moses Rischin, *The Promised City: New York's Jews, 1870–1914* (Cambridge, 1962), pp. 51–70.

3. Pierce, *Chicago*, III: 64–163; U. S. *Census* (1910), VIII: 87–91, 275; McLaughlin, *op. cit.*, pp. 98–99, 125–126, 158–159, 181–182.

4. U. S. *Census* (1900), *Occupations*, Tables 42 and 43; (1910), IV, Table III. See the illuminating discussion of these cities in *Cost of Living in American Towns*

(U. S. Senate Doc. No. 22, 1911); Hirschfeld, *op. cit.*, pp. 32–42; Pratt, *op. cit.*, pp. 26–44; Arthur Shadwell, *Industrial Efficiency* (London, 1909), pp. 202–208, 238–272.

5. U. S. *Census* (1910), VIII: 84, 91; U. S. Industrial Commission *Report* XV: 316–388; see Ralph Weld, *Brooklyn Is America* (New York, 1950); Pratt, *op. cit.*, pp. 90–115.

6. McLaughlin, *op. cit.*, pp. 193–251; McKelvey, *Rochester,* III: 332; Constance M. Green, *History of Naugatuck, Conn.* (New Haven, 1948), pp. 127–147, 193–195.

7. N. S. B. Gras, *An Introduction to Economic History* (New York, 1922), pp. 268–292. Professor Gras, writing in 1922, was considering these developments after another decade of growth when the list of cities had shifted considerably, but I have tried to apply his principles to the 1910 list; U. S. *Census* (1900), *Occupations,* Table 43.

8. McLaughlin, *op. cit.*, pp. 108, 168, 252–276, 289–340; Ida M. Tarbell, *The Nationalization of Business* (New York, 1936), pp. 7–9, 81–85, 213–214, 222–225; Oscar Handlin, *This Was America* (Cambridge, 1949), pp. 423–431; *Cost of Living in American Towns* (Senate Doc. 22, 1911), pp. 337–348.

9. McKelvey, *Rochester,* III: 254–255; McKelvey, "Rochester's Metropolitan Prospects in Historical Perspective," *Rochester History,* July, 1957.

10. Eric Brunger, "Dairying and Urban Development in New York State: 1850–1900," *Agricultural History,* Vol. 29, pp. 169–174; Amos H. Hawley, *Human Ecology* (New York, 1950), p. 377; Hayes, *op. cit.*, pp. 110–115; U. S. Department of Agriculture *Year Book* (1940), pp. 111–170; Lampard, *op. cit.*, pp. 151–169.

11. National Resources Committee, *Population Statistics,* No. 3, *Urban* (Washington, 1937), pp. 32–33.

12. U. S. *Census* (1910), I: 74–77; X: 901–975.

13. Graham R. Taylor, *Satellite Cities* (New York, 1915); Harold C. Syrett, *The City of Brooklyn, 1865–1898* (New York, 1944); Harry Hansen, *Scarsdale: From Colonial Manor to Modern Community* (New York, 1954); Harlan P. Douglass, *The Suburban Trend* (New York, 1925); Howard B. Woolston, *A Study of the Population of Manhattanville* [Columbia University Studies in History, Economics and Public Law, Vol. 35, No. 2, 1909], pp. 26–31 ff.; Richard Bigger and James D. Kitchen, *How the Cities Grew* (Los Angeles, 1952), pp. 138–152; Edwin A. Cottrell and Helen L. Jones, *Characteristics of the Metropolis* (Los Angeles, 1952), pp. 7–46; Leo F. Schnore, "The Timing of Metropolitan Decentralization," *Journal of the American Institute of Planning,* Vol. 25 (Nov., 1959), No. 4: 200–206.

14. Ida M. Tarbell, *New Ideas in Business* (New York, 1916), pp. 145–155; Christopher Tunnard and Henry H. Reed, *American Skyline: The Growth and Form of Our Cities and Towns* (Boston, 1955), pp. 165–169; Taylor, *op. cit.*, pp. 28–67, 91–126.

15. Margaret F. Byington, *Homestead: The Households of a Mill Town* (New York, 1910); Taylor, *op. cit.*, pp. 68–90; Tunnard and Reed, *op. cit.*, pp. 162–165; U. S. *Census* (1910), X: 901–975; Pierce, *Chicago,* III: 53, 159, 270.

16. Morris S. Daniels, *The Story of Ocean Grove: 1869–1919* (New York, 1919); Millard C. Faught, *Falmouth, Mass.: Problems of a Resort Community* (New York, 1945); Isidor Cohen, *Historical Sketches and Sidelights of Miami, Florida* (Miami, 1925), pp. 3–133; Chauncy D. Harris, "A Functional Classification of Cities in the United States," *Geographical Review* (1943), pp. 86–99; Earl Pomeroy, *In Search of the Golden West* (New York, 1957); Edo McCullough, *Good Old Coney Island* (New York, 1957).

17. Edward C. Kirkland, *Dream and Thought in the Business Community: 1860–1900* (Ithaca, 1956), pp. 83–113.

18. Benson, *op. cit.*, pp. 29–54; Gras, *op. cit.*, pp. 281–292.

19. Roy S. MacElwee, *Port Development* (New York, 1926), pp. 206–241, 273–287; *Proceedings of the Third National Conference on City Planning* (Philadelphia, 1911).

20. Emory R. Johnson, *History of Domestic and Foreign Commerce of the United*

States (Washington, 1915), II: 81–83, 94–95; Frank C. Bowen, *A Century of Atlantic Travel, 1830–1930* (Boston, 1930), pp. 111, 122, 125–127, 130–151, 170–173, 176, 183–191, 206, 211–212, 216–217, 228, 236, 241, 250; Kirkland, *op. cit.* (1961), pp. 296–301.

21. Jean Gottmann, *Megalopolis* (New York, 1961), pp. 102–135.

22. Laurence F. Schmeckebier, *The Customs Service: Its History, Activities and Organization* (Baltimore, 1924), pp. 19, 26.

23. John Ferry, *A History of the Department Store* (New York, 1960), pp. 35–69, 101–181; John Tebbel, *The Marshall Fields* (New York, 1947), pp. 21–45; Frank Presbrey, *The History and Development of Advertising* (New York, 1929), pp. 306–377; Robert W. Twyman, *History of Marshall Field and Company, 1852–1906* (Philadelphia, 1954); Frank M. Mayfield, *The Department Store Story* (New York, 1949), pp. 27–45; H. Pasdermadjian, *The Department Store* (New York, 1954), pp. 1–35; Ralph M. Hower, *History of Macy's of New York: 1858–1919* (Cambridge, 1943); Pierce, *Chicago*, III: 172–182.

24. James A. Barnes, *Wealth and the American People* (New York, 1949), pp. 526–527; Presbrey, *op. cit.*, pp. 284–288; Pierce, *Chicago*, III, pp. 182–191; Kirkland, *op. cit.* (1961), pp. 264–274.

25. Gras and Larson, *op. cit.*, pp. 479–492; Gras, *Introduction to Economic History*, pp. 292–314; Hartsough, *op. cit.*, pp. 60–193; Handlin, *This Was America*, pp. 349–352; U. S. Industrial Commission *Report* (1900), VII: 450–468, 990–999; Ralph M. Hower, *History of . . . Ayer & Son* (Cambridge, 1949).

26. Presbrey, *op. cit.*, pp. 274–278, 338–365; James P. Wood, *Magazines in the United States* (New York, 2nd ed., 1956), pp. 270–279, 288; David M. Potter, *People of Plenty* (Chicago, 1954), pp. 166–169.

27. Douglas North, in William Miller, ed., *Men in Business* (Cambridge, 1952), pp. 241–253.

28. Richard Hofstadter, *The Age of Reform: From Bryan to F. D. R.* (New York, 1955), pp. 219–230; Louis Brandeis, *Other People's Money* (New York, 1914), pp. 12–13.

29. Louis N. Robinson and Rolf Nugent, *Regulation of the Small Loan Business* (New York, 1935), pp. 38–95.

30. U. S. Industrial Commission *Report* (1900), VII: 16–27, 990–999; Oscar E. Anderson, *Refrigeration in America* (Princeton, 1953), pp. 37–107; S. S. Huebner, "Scope and Function of the Stock Market," *Annals*, Vol. 35 (1910), pp. 483–489; Pierce, *Chicago*, III, 93, 105–106, 134–135. Chicago had a Lumbermen's Exchange, a Livestock Exchange, a Corn Exchange, a Stock Exchange, and numerous similar groups.

31. Gras and Larson, *op. cit.*, pp. 333–343; Margaret G. Myers, *The New York Money Market* (New York, 1931), I: 295–298.

32. Twentieth Century Fund, *The Security Market* (New York, 1935), pp. 257, 748–754; "Report of Committee on Speculation in Securities," New York *Senate Documents* (1910), No. 2; George W. Edwards, *The Evolution of Finance Capitalism* (New York, 1938), pp. 145, 167, 194, 199–201; Myers, *op. cit.*, I: 298–314; Sidney M. Robbins and Nestor E. Terlockyj, *Money Metropolis* (Cambridge, 1960), pp. 3–13, 38–40, 96–98, 148–154.

33. Charles A. Conant, *History of Modern Banks of Issue* (New York, 1927), pp. 407–418; Davis R. Dewey, *Financial History of the United States* (New York, 1931), pp. 383–391; Robbins and Terlockyj, *op. cit., passim.*

34. Conant, *op. cit.*, pp. 430–437, 707; Dewey, *op. cit.*, pp. 479–481; Myers, *op. cit.*, I: 248; Pierce, *Chicago*, III: 192–206.

35. Raymond W. Goldsmith, *A Study of Saving in the United States* (Princeton, 1955), I: 83–87; Myers, *op. cit.*, pp. 234–287; Edwards, *op. cit.*, pp. 183–190; O. M. W. Sprague, *History of Crises Under the National Banking System* [National Monetary Commission] (Washington, 1910), pp. 216–320; Faulkner, *op. cit.*, pp. 22–51.

36. Myers, *op. cit.*, pp. 242, 392–408; Henry R. Seager and Charles Gulick, Jr., *Trust and Corporation Problems* (New York, 1929), pp. 49–337; Edward T. B. Perine, *The Story of the Trust Companies* (New York, 1916), pp. 122–307.

37. Edwards, *op. cit.*, pp. 190–200; Walter E. Spahr, *The Clearing and Collection of Checks* (New York, 1926), pp. 144–160; Charles A. Hales, *The Baltimore Clearing House* (Baltimore, 1940), pp. 108–111; Perine, *op. cit.*, pp. 291–296; G. W. Woodworth, *The Detroit Money Market* (Ann Arbor, 1932), pp. 32–38; J. L. Laughlin, *The Federal Reserve Act: Its Origin and Problems* (New York, 1933), pp. 3–14; *Statistical Abstract* (1891, 1911); Sprague, *op. cit.*, pp. 45–50, 90–104, 252–256; Faulkner, *op. cit.*, pp. 45–51, 198–219.
38. Thomas C. Cochran and William Miller, *The Age of Enterprise* (New York, 1942), pp. 182–202; E. G. Campbell, *The Reorganization of the American Rail-Road System, 1893–1900* (New York, 1938).
39. Robert H. Wiebe, "The House of Morgan and the Executive, 1905–1913," *American Historical Review*, Oct., 1959, pp. 49–60; Kirkland, *op. cit.* (1961), pp. 306–324; Faulkner, *op. cit.*, pp. 35–51.
40. U. S. *Census* (1910), *Population*, I: 54, 74, 80, 86. The percentages for 1910 are based on the 1860 definition of an urban total comprising the sum of places of 8000 or more residents.
41. See, however, Gottmann, *op. cit.*, pp. 102–135. Although Gottmann's contention that "Megalopolis," the East Coast supercity, was already emerging in the early 1900's seems farfetched, his tables reveal that New York, without adding Philadelphia, was no longer the overwhelming metropolis it once had seemed.
42. Kirkland, *op. cit.* (1956), pp. 1–49, 145–167; Miller, *op. cit.*, pp. 286–304; Faulkner, *op. cit.*, pp. 170–182.

CHAPTER 4: *The Lure of the City*

1. Arthur M. Schlesinger, *The Rise of the City* [A History of American Life, X] (New York, 1933), pp. 67–70; U. S. *Census* (1910), I: 67–68, 72; Samuel L. Loomis, *Modern Cities and Their Religious Problems* (New York, 1887), pp. 14–54; *Recent Social Trends in the United States* (New York, 1934), pp. 282–304.
2. Warren S. Thompson and P. K. Whelpton, *Population Trends in the United States* (New York, 1933), pp. 18–29, 53–56; Bureau of the Census, *A Century of Population Growth* (1909), p. 72, see the map showing areas of population decline; C. Warren Thornthwaite, *Internal Migration in the United States* (Philadelphia, 1934), pp. 10–12, Plates I, II, IV.
3. Hamlin Garland, *A Son of the Middle Border* (New York, 1923 ed.), p. 271.
4. Anselm Strauss, *Images of the American City* (Glencoe, 1961), pp. 182–198.
5. Bureau of the Census, *Historical Statistics of the United States: Colonial Times to 1957* (1957), pp. 14, 283–284. Although rural population growth appeared to exceed that of the cities in the 1870's, the many new towns established in that decade that did not reach 2500 until later would, if tabulated as urban or separated from the rural total, have given the city the lead there, too.
6. Among the business leaders who achieved success in New York and Chicago were many who made their start in lesser towns. Of 300 New York financiers named in a master list by A. D. H. Smith in *Men Who Run America* (New York, 1936), pp. 331–339, one-third were born there, another third in rural or small-town America, one-fourth in other cities and one-twelfth abroad. From a random sample of 360 of the 3045 millionaires of 1892 listed in Sidney Ratner's *New Light on the History of Great American Fortunes* (New York, 1953), I checked 50 in New York and Cincinnati who had made the *National Cyclopedia of American Biography*. Of these, 60 per cent moved there from other cities and towns.
7. U. S. *Census* (1910), I: 184.
8. U. S. *Census* (1910) *Abstract*, pp. 55, 80, 92, 210–214; Everett S. and Anne S. Lee, "Internal Migration Statistics for the United States," *Journal of the American Statistical Association*, Vol. 55 (Dec., 1960), pp. 664–697.

9. Bureau of the Census, *Immigrants and Their Children*, 1920 [Census Monograph VII] (Washington, 1927), p. 45; Rowland T. Berthoff, *British Immigrants in Industrial America* (Cambridge, 1953); U. S. Industrial Commission *Reports*, XV, *passim; Cost of Living in American Towns* (U. S. Senate Doc. 22, 1911), pp. xii–xiv; Thompson and Whelpton, *op. cit.*, pp. 65–68, 70–74.

10. *Immigrants and Their Children*, pp. 26, 27, 29; U. S. *Census* (1890), *Population,* I: xcii; Carl Wittke, *We Who Built America: The Saga of the Immigrants* (New York, 1940), pp. 331–338, 405–471.

11. Erickson, *op. cit.*, pp. 8–87.

12. Wittke, *op. cit.*, pp. 105–120, 126–128 ff.; James P. Shannon, *Catholic Colonization of the Western Frontier* (New Haven, 1957); Erickson, *op. cit.*, pp. 88–106, 192; Joseph A. Wytrwal, *America's Polish Heritage* (Detroit, 1961), pp. 148–160, 168–180, 191–196; Rischin, *op. cit.*, pp. 54, 98–100.

13. See the urban nationality data in *U. S. Census of Occupations* (1910); *Recent Social Trends* (New York, 1934), pp. 680–683, shows that the percentages of those over 15 who married increased from 55.3 in 1890 to 57.3 in 1910; Thompson and Whelpton, *op. cit.*, pp. 83–105.

14. U. S. *Census* (1880), XII: 180–184; (1900), III: 286–555. The total urban surplus for some 350 registration cities in 1900 was 126,883, or slightly over .066 per cent of the population of these cities and approximately one-fourth of the annual urban increment for the decade; Thompson and Whelpton, *op. cit.*, pp. 208, 214–227.

15. Mazyck P. Ravenel, ed., *A Half Century of Public Health* (New York, 1921), pp. 14–30 ff.; U. S. *Census* (1900), III: lvi–lxii; Thompson and Whelpton, *op. cit.*, pp. 241–242, 253–257, 278–288.

16. U. S. *Census* (1900), I: 172, 432 ff.; *Immigrants and Their Children*, pp. 25–27; Loomis, *op. cit.*, pp. 67–79; Thompson and Whelpton, *op. cit.*, pp. 155–160, 301–311.

17. See, however, the excellent study by Thompson and Whelpton cited above.

18. *Immigrants and Their Children*, pp. 385–388.

19. *Ibid.*, pp. 385–396; Theodore C. Bleger, *Norwegian Migrations to America* (Northfield, Minn., 1940), pp. 482, 498–499.

20. William Q. Thomas and F. Znaniecki, *The Polish Peasant in Europe and America* (New York, 1927), II: 1511–1644; see also Wittke, *op. cit.*, pp. 405–471; Wytrwal, *op. cit.*, pp. 64, 77–81.

21. Kate H. Claghorn, "The Foreign Immigrant in New York City," U. S. Industrial Commission *Report* (1901), XV: 449–492; Oscar Handlin, *The Uprooted* (Boston, 1951), p. 144 ff.; *Immigrants and Their Children*, pp. 78–81, 385–388; George A. Sala, *America Revisited* (London, 1883), pp. 37–54; Marcus L. Hansen, *The Immigrant in American History* (Cambridge, 1940), pp. 167–174, 188–190; *Cost of Living in American Towns*, pp. x–xiv, and see page references under Immigration in index.

22. Thompson and Whelpton, *op. cit.*, pp. 23–53.

23. U. S. *Census* (1910), I: 434–436; Mary R. Coolidge, *Chinese Immigration* (New York, 1909), pp. 401–459; Wittke, *op. cit.*, pp. 458–467.

24. John Higham, *Strangers in the Land: Patterns of American Nativism: 1860–1925* (New Brunswick, 1955), pp. 39–44; Richard Mayo-Smith, *Emigration and Immigration* (New York, 1890); Erickson, *op. cit.*, pp. 12–31, 95–102, 202.

25. Higham, *op. cit.*, pp. 46–87; Wittke, *op. cit.*, pp. 332–338; Erickson, *op. cit.*, pp. 148–166.

26. Higham, *op. cit.*, pp. 70–87; Isaac A. Hourwich, *Immigration and Labor* (New York, 1922), pp. 82–147; Wittke, *op. cit.*, pp. 500–518; Robert E. Park and Herbert A. Miller, *Old World Traits Transplanted* (New York, 1921).

27. Wittke, *op. cit.*, pp. 458–468; Higham, *op. cit.*, pp. 165–175.

28. U. S. *Census* (1910), I: 178, 185–186; T. J. Woofter, Jr., *Negro Problems in Cities* (New York, 1928), pp. 1–30; Gunnar Myrdal, *An American Dilemma* (New York, 1944); *Cost of Living in American Towns*, p. xiii, and see reference under Negroes in index. For a study of early integration efforts in Washington,

1865–1878, see Constance M. Green, *Washington, Village and Capital, 1800–1878* (Princeton, 1962), pp. 272–286, 297–309, 321–326, 333–338.

29. Higham, *op. cit.*, pp. 102–112; Barbara M. Solomon, *Ancestors and Immigrants: A Changing New England Tradition* (Harvard, 1956), pp. 102–136.

30. U. S. *Census* (1860), I: xxxi–xxxii. This table shows that the foreign born in the large cities of the North ranged from 14.8 per cent in Portland, Maine, to 59.7 in St. Louis.

31. Frances W. Gregory and Irene D. Neu, "The American Industrial Elite in the 1870's" in William Miller, ed., *Men in Business* (Cambridge, 1952), pp. 193–211. These scholars find only 10 per cent of the "Industrial Elite" of the period to be foreign-born, but the 187 men in their sample were chosen from three fields—textiles, steel, and railroads—scarcely fields in which new immigrant enterprise would flourish. Of the American-born, 25 per cent were from the farms, and another 25 per cent from small towns.

32. U. S. *Census of Occupations* (1900), pp. clxxxiii–ix; (1910), see urban nationality tables. See also Bemis, *op. cit.*, pp. 67–107; *Cost of Living in American Towns*, pp. xiii, lxxxi–xci; Wittke, *op. cit.*, pp. 392–401; Rischin, *op. cit.*, pp. 95–103, 258–265.

33. Numerous scholars have wrestled with this problem. For a review of the periodical literature, see Raymond Mack, Linton Freeman, and Seymour Yellin, *Social Mobility: Thirty Years of Research and Theory* (Syracuse, 1957). Sidney Rather, *op. cit.*, not only republishes two long-forgotten contemporary lists of American millionaires, of 1892 and 1902, but discusses many of the books that have dealt with the question. The most recent book by Seymour M. Lipset and Reinhard Bendix, *Social Mobility in Industrial Society* (Berkeley, 1959), deals only indirectly with this period—see pages 30–38, 43–45, 103–104, 114–143—but cites an unpublished manuscript by Susanne Keller, "The Social Origins and Career Lines of Three Generations of American Business Leaders" [Ph.D. Thesis, Columbia, 1953] that is most pertinent.

34. Louis Adamic, *A Nation of Nations* (New York, 1945); Mabel Newcomer, *The Big Business Executive* (New York, 1955), pp. 42–45; W. Lloyd Warner, *Big Business Leaders in America* (New York, 1955), pp. 24–27, 190–195; C. Wright Mills, "The American Business Elite: A Collective Portrait," *Journal of Economic History* (1945), V: Supplement, pp. 20–44; William Miller, "American Historians and Business Elite," *Journal of Economic History* (1949), IX: 184–208; Oscar Handlin, ed., *The Positive Contribution by Immigrants* (Unesco, 1955); Hofstadter, *The Age of Reform*, pp. 136–138, 385–386; C. Wright Mills, *The Power Elite* (New York, 1956), pp. 94–117, 127–138, 385–386; William Miller, ed., *Men in Business* (Cambridge, 1952), pp. 193–211, 286–306. See also the materials cited in note 33 above, especially the reference to Miss Keller, who found that the percentage of Anglo-Saxons in the leadership ranks in her sample dropped from 87 to 77 between 1870 and 1900 and continued to decline to 65 per cent by 1950.

35. McKelvey, *Rochester*, II: 129; McKelvey, *Rochester*, III: 161; U. S. *Census* (1890) *Population*, I, Pt. I: 580–603. See also the excellent discussion of statistical sources on internal migration by E. S. and A. S. Lee, *loc. cit.*, cited in note 8, above.

36. E. Digby Baltzell, *Philadelphia Gentlemen: The Making of a National Upper Class* (Glencoe, Ill., 1958).

37. Baltzell, *op. cit.*; Solomon, *op. cit.*, pp. 47–49; John P. Bocock, "The Irish Conquest of Our Cities," *Forum*, XVII (April, 1894), pp. 186–195. At a session of the American Historical Association Convention in Washington, Dec. 29, 1961, on "Stratification and Mobility in American Society," Professor E. Digby Baltzell of the University of Pennsylvania commented extemporaneously on his study of the national or intercity patrician class that emerged around 1900.

38. U. S. *Census of Occupations* (1910), see urban nationality tables. See also Bemis, *op. cit.*, pp. 67–107; *Cost of Living in American Towns*, pp. xiii, lxxi–xci; Isaac A. Hourwich, *Immigration and Labor* (New York, 1922, 2nd ed.), pp. 50–220. See also Chapter IX, below.

CHAPTER 5: *From Horse Cars to Rapid Transit*

1. Emerson P. Schmidt, *Industrial Relations in Urban Transportation* (Minneapolis, 1937), pp. 3–9; U. S. *Census, Social Statistics of Cities* (1886), 2 vols., *passim;* Pierce, *Chicago,* II: 324–329; Faulkner, *op. cit.,* pp. 220–225.
2. Christopher Tunnard and Henry H. Reed, *American Skyline* (Boston, 1955), pp. 127–130; Siegfried Giedion, *Space, Time and Architecture* (Cambridge, 1954), pp. 193–201.
3. Robert W. DeForest and Lawrence Veiller, eds., *The Tenement House Problem* (New York, 1903), I: 57–65, 129–170; J. T. Holdsworth, *Economic Survey of Pittsburgh* (Pittsburgh, 1912), pp. 77–129; Homer Hoyt, *One Hundred Years of Land Values in Chicago* (Chicago, 1933), pp. 86–95; *Cost of Living in American Towns* (U. S. Senate Doc. 22, 1911), pp. xxi–xxiv; Joseph Lee, *Constructive and Preventive Philanthropy* (New York, 1902), pp. 31–33; Kirkland, *op. cit.* (1961), pp. 255–261; U. S. Industrial Commission, *Report,* XIV (1901), pp. 595–603.
4. Tunnard and Reed, *op. cit.,* pp. 124–138; Henry Wright, *Rehousing Urban America* (New York, 1935), pp. 16–23.
5. McKelvey, *Rochester,* II: 82–83, 118, 137–138, 210.
6. Walter Muir Whitehill, *Boston, A Topographical History* (Cambridge, 1959), pp. 119–173; Robert A. Woods, ed., *The City Wilderness* (New York, 1898); *idem, Americans in Process* (Boston, 1902). See the map of Boston's horse-car routes of 1880, *Social Statistics of Cities* (1886), I: 110. And see also Sam B. Warner, Jr., *Streetcar Suburbs: The Process of Growth in Boston, 1870–1900* (Cambridge, 1962). This detailed analysis, which appeared too late for use in my study, richly amplifies the Boston story.
7. A. M. Schlesinger, *The Rise of the City* (New York, 1933), pp. 82–85; Schmidt, *op. cit.,* pp. 3–7; J. R. Commons, "Immigration and Its Economic Effects," U. S. Industrial Commission, *Report* (1901), pp. 316–492; Helen Campbell, *Darkness and Daylight* (Hartford, 1897), pp. 411–419; *Cost of Living in American Towns,* pp. 24–31; James Ford, with collaborators, *Slums and Housing* (Cambridge, 1936), I: 120–149.
8. Max West, "Franchises in New York," in Edward W. Bemis, ed., *Municipal Monopolies* (Boston, 1899), pp. 391–397; James B. Walker, *Fifty Years of Rapid Transit* (New York, 1918), pp. 2–126. For a description of New York's seventeen horse-car lines and four elevateds of 1880, see *Social Statistics of Cities* (1886), I: 564–566.
9. Walker, *op. cit.;* Cleveland Rodgers and Rebecca B. Rankin, *New York, The World's Capital City* (New York, 1948), pp. 197–199; West, *op. cit.,* pp. 392–404.
10. Tunnard and Reed, *op. cit.,* pp. 124–125; Edith E. Wood, *The Housing of the Unskilled Wage Earner* (New York, 1919), pp. 35–38; Claghorn, *op. cit.,* pp. 482–483; *Cost of Living,* pp. 24–31; Ford, *op. cit.,* I: 149–226, II: 869–902; De Forest and Veiller, *op. cit.,* I: 3–5, 81–107.
11. West, *op. cit.,* pp. 405–409; Harold C. Syrett, *The City of Brooklyn, 1865–1898* (New York, 1944), pp. 144–154; Alexander Klein, *The Empire City* (New York, 1955), pp. 148–166.
12. H. G. Tyrell, *History of Bridge Engineering* (Chicago, 1911), pp. 237–239, *passim;* John A. Fairlie, *Municipal Administration* (New York, 1922 ed.), pp. 243–244; Bureau of the Census, *Statistics of Cities* (1909), pp. 176–181.
13. Herbert H. Vreeland, "The Street Railways of America," in C. M. Depew, ed., *One Hundred Years of American Commerce* (New York, 1895), pp. 141–148; Harold C. Passer, *The Electrical Manufacturers, 1875–1900* (Cambridge, 1953), pp. 218–221, 237–249.
14. Bureau of the Census Special Reports, *Street and Electric Railways* (1907), p. 23; Federal Housing Administration, *The Structure and Growth of Residential Neighborhoods in American Cities* (Washington, 1939), pp. 96–104.

15. *Statistics of Cities* (1890), pp. 9–12, 50.
16. *Ibid.*, pp. 9–12; Hoyt, *op. cit.*, pp. 96–99, 201–203; Edith Abbott, *The Tenements of Chicago* (Chicago, 1936), pp. 8–56.
17. Amos H. Hawley, *Human Ecology* (New York, 1950), pp. 382–395, see the maps of Detroit and Chicago depicting shifts in land use from period to period.
18. Pierce, *Chicago*, III: 42–44, 50–56; Fine, *op. cit.*, p. 361.
19. Wood, *op. cit.*, pp. 39–41; Carroll D. Wright, *The Slums of Baltimore, Chicago, New York and Philadelphia* (Commissioner of Labor, *Special Report*, No. 7, 1894); Adna F. Weber, "Rapid Transit and the Housing Problem," *Municipal Affairs* (1903), VI: 409–417; *Statistics of Cities* (1902–03), pp. 108–119, 132–133; Wilcox, *op. cit.*, pp. 236, 353; U. S. Industrial Commission, *Report* (1901), XIV: 595–603; *Statistics of Cities* (1909), p. 78; *Cost of Living in American Towns*, pp. 130–132, 143–148.
20. Giedion, *op. cit.*, p. 208.
21. John H. Jallings, *Elevators* (Chicago, 1919), pp. 69, 84, 163; Ronald Grierson, *Electric Elevator Equipment for Modern Buildings* (New York, 1924), p. 2; McKelvey, *Rochester*, II: 118; Tunnard and Reed, *op. cit.*, pp. 156–161.
22. Hugh Morrison, *Louis Sullivan: Prophet of Modern Architecture* (New York, 1935), pp. 54–63, 140–156, 354; Carl W. Condit, *The Rise of the Skyscraper* (Chicago, 1952), pp. 17–49, 112–139; Giedion, *op. cit.*, pp. 193–209, 366, 385; Pierce, *Chicago*, III: 499–500; James M. Fitch, *American Building: The Forces That Shape It* (Boston, 1948), pp. 109–122; John Burchard and Albert Bush-Brown, *The Architecture of America, A Social and Cultural History* (Boston, 1961), pp. 246–262, *passim*.
23. Bureau of the Census, *Telephones and Telegraphs* (Special Report of 1902, Washington, D. C., 1906), pp. 5–67; McKelvey, *Rochester*, II: 253–254.
24. Syrett, *op. cit.*, pp. 208–215; Clifford W. Patton, *The Battle for Municipal Reform . . . 1875–1900* (Washington, 1940), pp. 9–10, 20–21 ff.; Frank Parsons, *The City for the People* (Philadelphia, 1901 ed.), pp. 45–56.
25. Kirkland, *op. cit.* (1961), pp. 206, 209–210; Faulkner, *op. cit.*, pp. 227–228.
26. Delos F. Wilcox, *Great Cities in America* (New York, 1910), pp. 263–269; Bemis, *op. cit.*, pp. 509–537; Schmidt, *op. cit.*, pp. 34–36; *Street and Electric Railways* (1907), p. 99; E. H. Higgins, "Municipal and Private Management of Street Railways . . . ," *Municipal Affairs* (Sept., 1897), pp. 477–480; Pierce, *Chicago*, III: 216–221.
27. Pierce, *Chicago*, III: 216–222; Lincoln Steffens, *The Shame of the Cities* (New York, 1904), pp. 250–253; Ray Ginger, *Altgeld's America* (New York, 1958), pp. 107–109, 173–174, 179–183, 253–256.
28. West, *op. cit.*, pp. 394; Robert E. Cushman, *The Independent Regulatory Commission* (New York, 1941), pp. 24–27; Schmidt, *op. cit.*, pp. 52–59.
29. Walker, *op. cit.*, pp. 2–224; Wilcox, *op. cit.*, II: 488–504, 509–518, 542–544; *Statistics of Cities* (1909), p. 80.
30. *Street and Electric Railways* (1907), p. 265, see the map showing the extent of these lines in the Middle West; William F. Gephart, *Transportation and Industrial Development in the Middle West* (New York, 1909), pp. 232–241.
31. McKelvey, *Rochester*, III: 248; Ernest S. Griffith, *Modern Development of City Government* (London, 1927), pp. 261–262.

CHAPTER 6: *The Shame of the Cities*

1. Fred A. Shannon, *The Organization and Administration of the Union Army* (Cleveland, 1928), II: 25, 94, *passim*; Emerson D. Fite, *Social and Industrial Conditions in the North During the Civil War* (New York, 1910), pp. 220–227, 286–290.

2. Thomas C. Delvin, *Municipal Reform in the United States* (New York, 1896), pp. 3–5 ff.; Fairlie, *op. cit.,* pp. 90–94; Oscar Handlin, ed., *This Was America* (Cambridge, 1949), pp. 324–326.

3. Cited in Griffith, *op. cit.,* p. 71 n.; McKelvey, *Rochester* II: 134–136; Still, *op. cit.,* pp. 248–250; Frederick R. Clow, *Comparative Study of City Finances* (American Economic Association Publication, 3rd Series), II (1901); 11–13.

4. Griffith, *op. cit.,* pp. 62–69, 79; Patton, *op. cit.,* pp. 10–17; Fred K. Vigman, *Crisis of the Cities* (Washington, 1955), pp. 7–10.

5. James H. Malone, "Municipal Conditions in Memphis, Tennessee," National Conference of Good City Government, *Proceedings* (1896), pp. 111–113; Griffith, *op. cit.,* pp. 66–70; Patton, *op. cit.,* pp. 52–54; Vigman, *op. cit.,* pp. 8–14.

6. James Bryce, *The American Commonwealth* (New York, 1927 ed.), II: 111–135; McKelvey, *Rochester,* II: 258–265; Syrett, *op. cit.,* pp. 25–54; Wilcox, *op. cit.,* pp. 27–29. See also Constance M. Green, *Washington, Village and Capital, 1800–1878* (Princeton, 1962), pp. 339–362, for an account of how Washington lost self-government to Congress.

7. Fairlie, *op. cit.,* pp. 231–233; Bureau of the Census, *Statistics of Cities* (1905), pp. 348 ff.; *ibid.* (1909), pp. 65–75.

8. Arthur S. Dewing, *Corporate Promotions and Reorganizations* (Cambridge, 1914), pp. 412–425; *Statistics of Cities* (1909), pp. 61–75.

9. Seba Eldridge, *Development of Collective Enterprise* (University of Kansas, 1943), pp. 82–89; Fairlie, *op. cit.,* pp. 273–278; Nelson M. Blake, *Water for the Cities* (Syracuse, 1956), pp. 265 ff.; McKelvey, *Rochester,* II: 136–137, 261–263.

10. Richard H. Shryock, *The Development of Modern Medicine* (New York, 1947 ed.), pp. 239–284; Fairlie, *op. cit.,* pp. 165–166; William I. Maxwell, *Lincoln's Fifth Wheel* (New York, 1956).

11. Stephen Smith, *The City That Was* (New York, 1911); Mazyck P. Ravenel, ed., *A Half Century of Public Health* (New York, 1921), pp. 3–13, 141–143; J. Lee, *op. cit.,* pp. 37–51.

12. Henry I. Bowditch, *Public Hygiene in America* (Boston, 1877), pp. 29, 72, 99–105.

13. Blake, *op. cit.,* pp. 260–286; Ravenel, *op. cit.,* pp. 14–43, 163–166; Shryock, *op. cit.,* pp. 293–295.

14. Ravenel, *op. cit.,* pp. 94–101; Edgar Sydenstricker, "The Vitality of the American People," *Recent Social Trends* (New York, 1934), pp. 605 ff.

15. George W. Rafter and M. N. Baker, *Sewage Disposal in the United States* (New York, 1894), pp. 169–186; Pierce, *Chicago,* II: 330, 334; Blake, *op. cit.,* pp. 263–266; Lloyd Lewis and H. J. Smith, *Chicago, The History of Its Reputation* (New York, 1929), pp. 267–273.

16. Eldridge, *op. cit.,* pp. 87–92; Fairlie, *op. cit.,* pp. 250–253; Rafter and Baker, *op. cit.,* pp. 6–22, 187–202; Bowditch, *op. cit.,* pp. 35–72; *Statistics of Cities* (1909), pp. 18–35, 88–119.

17. Charles V. Chapin, *Municipal Sanitation in the United States* (Providence, 1901), pp. 160–260; *Statistics of Cities* (1909), pp. 120–147; E. E. Wood, *The Housing of the Unskilled Wage Earner* (New York, 1919), p. 53; Cyrenus Wheeler, Jr., "Sewers Ancient and Modern with an Appendix (on the Auburn, N. Y., sewers)," *Cayuga County (N. Y.) Historical Society Collections,* V (1887), pp. 15–108.

18. T. R. Pirtle, *History of the Dairy Industry* (Chicago, 1926), pp. 128–131 ff.; Chapin, *op. cit.,* pp. 260–422; Ravenel, *op. cit.,* pp. 148–149; Eric Brunger, "Dairying and Urban Development in New York State, 1850–1900," *Agricultural History,* XXIX: 169–174.

19. Ward Harrison, *et al., Street Lighting Practice* (New York, 1930); Henry Schroeder, "History of Electric Light," *Smithsonian Miscellaneous Collection,* Vol. 76, No. 2, 1923; Fairlie, *op. cit.,* pp. 281–289; Chester M. Destler, *American Radicalism, 1865–1901* (New London, 1946), pp. 105–134, 245–247; McKelvey, *Rochester,* III: 36–37; Pierce, *Chicago,* III: 328–330; *Statistics of Cities* (1909), pp. 80–81, 186–189.

20. Loomis, *op. cit.*, pp. 102–103; Henry M. Boies, *Prisoners and Paupers* (New York, 1893), pp. 88–137; Frederic M. Thrasher, *The Gang* (Chicago, 1936 ed.), pp. 17–39; Herbert Asbury, *The Gangs of New York* (New York, 1937), pp. 79–85; Vergil W. Peterson, *Barbarians in Our Midst* (New York, 1952), pp. 26–96; Nevins, *op. cit.*, pp. 201, 330–331; Campbell, *op. cit.*, pp. 352–380.

21. Fairlie, *op. cit.*, pp. 133–137, 142–144; Raymond B. Fosdick, *American Police Systems* (New York, 1920), pp. 79–137.

22. Cesare Lombroso, "Why Homicide Has Increased in the United States," *North American Review*, No. 165 (1897), pp. 641–648; No. 166 (1898), pp. 1–9; Asbury, *op. cit.*, pp. 278–324; National Resources Committee, *Urban Government*, I (1939), pp. 250–260; Schlesinger, *op. cit.*, pp. 21, 111–115; *Recent Social Trends*, pp. 288, 291, 1139–1145; Campbell, *op. cit.*, pp. 398–410; Charles A. Ellwood, "Has Crime Increased in the United States Since 1880?" American Institute of Criminal Law *Journal*, I (1910), pp. 378–385.

23. Charles H. Parkhurst, *Our Fight With Tammany* (New York, 1895); Theodore Roosevelt, *An Autobiography* (New York, 1913), pp. 207–222; William McAdoo, *Guarding a Great City* (New York, 1906); McKelvey, *Rochester*, III: 86–87.

24. Roscoe Pound, *Criminal Justice in the American City* [Criminal Justice in Cleveland, VI] (Cleveland, 1922), pp. 62–69; Fosdick, *op. cit.*, pp. 27–57, 326–354.

25. Blake McKelvey, *American Prisons* (Chicago, 1936), pp. 135–136, 217–218; Samuel H. Popper, *Individualized Justice: Fifty Years of Juvenile Court and Probation Services in Ramsey County, Minnesota* (St. Paul, 1956), pp. 1–4, 19–21.

26. U. S. *Census* (1880), XXI: 566–574; James Buel, *Mysteries and Miseries of America's Great Cities* (San Francisco, 1883); McAdoo, *op. cit.*, pp. 49–69; McKelvey, *Rochester*, III: 134–135; Parkhurst, *op. cit.*, pp. 170–176.

27. Rudi Blesh, *Shining Trumpets, A History of Jazz* (New York, 1946), pp. 198–203; Herbert Asbury, *The French Quarter* (New York, 1936), pp. 424–450; Schlesinger, *op. cit.*, pp. 156–159; Harold U. Faulkner, *The Quest for Social Justice: 1898–1914* [A History of American Life, XI] (New York, 1937), pp. 159–160; Chapin, *op. cit.*, p. 526.

28. Walter C. Reckless, *Vice in Chicago* (Chicago, 1933), pp. 1–54.

29. John G. Woolley and William E. Johnson, *Temperance Progress in the Century* (Philadelphia, 1903), pp. 142–194.

30. Lincoln Steffens, *The Autobiography of* . . . (New York, 1931), pp. 235–238, 416–421; Frederic C. Howe, *The Confessions of a Reformer* (New York, 1925), pp. 51–55; Patton, *op. cit.*, pp. 8–17; Delvin, *op. cit.*, pp. 10–25.

31. Harold Zink, *City Bosses in the United States* (Durham, 1930), pp. 3–50; Bryce, *op. cit.*, II: 118–125.

32. M. R. Werner, *Tammany Hall* (New York, 1928), pp. 204–302; Bryce, *op. cit.*, II: 379–405; Klein, *op. cit.*, pp. 207–216.

33. Patton, *op. cit.*, pp. 18–24; Bryce, *op. cit.*, II: 406–448; Faulkner, *op. cit.*, pp. 91–99.

34. Donald W. Disbrow, "The Progressive Movement in Philadelphia, 1910–1916," Ph.D. Thesis, University of Rochester, 1956, Typescript, pp. 1–27.

35. Lincoln Steffens, *The Shame of the Cities* (New York, 1904), *passim*; Walton Bean, *Boss Ruef's San Francisco* (Berkeley, 1952); George M. Reynolds, *Machine Politics in New Orleans: 1897–1926* (New York, 1936); George E. Mowry, *The California Progressives* (Berkeley, 1951), pp. 25–30.

36. Bryce, *op. cit.*, I: 642.

37. Bryce, *op. cit.*, II: 379–405; Crosswell Bowen, *The Elegant Oakey* (New York, 1956), pp. 249–263. Bryce apparently deleted most of the specific charges against Hall from his later editions.

38. See the reports on brothels in U. S. *Census* (1880), XXI: 566–574; (1890), XXIII: 1024–1030; Faulkner, *op. cit.*, pp. 159–162.

CHAPTER 7: *Civic Renaissance*

1. Patton, *op. cit., pp.* 25–33; Griffith, *op. cit.,* p. 144; George Vickers, *The Fall of Bossism* (Philadelphia, 1883); Pierce, *Chicago,* III: 345–359; Russell B. Nye, *Midwestern Progressive Politics: 1870–1958* (Michigan State University, 1959), pp. 174–180.
2. Howard L. McBain, *The Law and Practice of Municipal Home Rule* (New York, 1916), pp. 68–117; Griffith, *op. cit.,* pp. 72–74, 147–148; Patton, *op. cit.,* pp. 69–71.
3. The *American Journal of Politics,* I–V (1892–1894), became the *American Magazine of Civics,* VI–IX (1894–1896), and was absorbed by the *Arena* in 1897; see *Arena,* XVIII (1897), pp. 108–112.
4. Frank M. Stewart, *A Half Century of Municipal Reform* (Berkeley, 1950), pp. 3–4, 11–12.
5. *Ibid.,* pp. 12–16; Patton, *op. cit.,* pp. 27–34; Griffith, *op. cit.,* pp. 143–144, 150; Vickers, *loc. cit.;* Syrett, *op. cit.,* pp. 55 ff.
6. *Proceedings of the Conferences for Good City Government* (1894–1900), I–IV; Stewart, *op. cit.,* pp. 15–27, 174–177; Patton, *op. cit.,* pp. 34–37; William H. Tolman, *Municipal Reform Movements in the United States* (New York, 1895), pp. 1–96; Lloyd Lewis and H. J. Smith, *Chicago: The History of Its Reputation* (New York, 1929), pp. 235–237, 243–251; Lincoln Steffens, *The Shame of the Cities* (New York, 1904), pp. 240–249; Vigman, *op. cit.,* pp. 32–40.
7. Stewart, *op. cit.,* p. 26; *American Journal of Politics,* V (1894): 67–72.
8. Stewart, *op. cit.,* pp. 18, 26, 147; *Municipal Affairs,* March, 1897; *ibid.,* June, 1897, pp. 301–316; McKelvey, *Rochester,* III: 75–82.
9. Stewart, *op. cit.,* pp. 22–28; *Proceedings of the Annual Conference for Good City Government,* 1895–1897, *passim.*
10. Stewart, *op. cit.,* pp. 28–44; National Municipal League, *A Municipal Program* (New York, 1900).
11. Stewart, *op. cit.,* pp. 44–49; John G. Thompson, *Urbanization: Its Effect on Government and Society* (New York, 1927), pp. 226–231, 297–300.
12. Griffith, *op. cit.,* pp. 88–98, 115–120; Patton, *op. cit.,* pp. 67–69; Brand Whitlock, *Forty Years of It* (New York, 1914), pp. 112–150; Fairlie, *op. cit.,* pp. 92–102; Syrett, *op. cit.,* pp. 91–94, 107–137; Alfred B. Conklin, *City Government in the United States* (New York, 1894), pp. 1–37; Destler, *op. cit.,* pp. 246–247.
13. Griffith, *op. cit.,* pp. 156–157; Patton, *op. cit.,* pp. 48–51; "Hazen S. Pingree," *Dictionary of American Biography,* XIV: 621–622; William P. Lovett, *Detroit Rules Itself* (Boston, 1930), pp. 31–39; Nye, *op. cit.,* pp. 170–181. See also Ari Hoogenboom, *Outlawing the Spoils: A History of the Civil Service Reform Movement, 1865–1883* (Urbana, 1961), pp. 187–197, 360, 364.
14. Steffens, *op. cit., passim;* C. C. Regier, *The Era of the Muckrakers* (Chapel Hill, 1932), pp. 59–82; Stewart, *op. cit.,* pp. 48–49; Wilcox, *op. cit.,* pp. 249–269; Mowry, *op. cit.,* pp. 23–38; McBain, *op. cit.,* pp. 113–118 ff.
15. Whitlock, *op. cit.,* pp. 112–155; McKelvey, *Rochester,* III: 82–92; Bryce, *op. cit.,* I: 677–679; James P. Wood, *Magazines in the United States* (2nd ed., New York, 1956), pp. 131–146; Louis Filler, *Crusaders for American Liberalism* (New York, 1939), pp. 80–188.
16. *Statistics of Cities* (1906), pp. 36–41; National Resources Committee, *Urban Government,* I (1939): 181–183; Frederick R. Clow, *Comparative Study of City Finances* [Pub. of Amer. Ed. Assoc., 3rd Series, Vol. II] (1901), pp. 106–126; Stewart, *op. cit.,* pp. 126–128.
17. National Resources Committee, *Urban Government,* I: 186–187; New York Senate *Document* (1891), No. 80.
18. Edward R. Hardy, *The Making of the Fire Insurance Rate* (New York, 1927), pp. 175–178; F. C. Oviatt, "Historical Study of Fire Insurance in the United States," *Annals* (1906), XXVI: 352–375.

19. Fairlie, *op. cit.*, pp. 152–156; John V. Morris, *Fires and Firefighters* (Boston, 1955), pp. 259–273, 338–340, *passim;* B. Holly's *System of Water Supply and Fire Protection* (Lockport, 1872); Pierce, *Chicago,* III: 307–308; McKelvey, *Rochester,* II: 136–138, 202.
20. George E. Waring, Jr., *Street Cleaning* (New York, 1898), pp. 1–128; William F. Morse, *The Collection and Disposal of Municipal Waste in the United States* (New York, 1908), pp. 665–728; *Statistics of Cities . . . for 1902 and 1903,* pp. 120–131; *ibid.,* 1909, pp. 36–53.
21. Chapin, *op. cit.*, pp. 742–758; Fairlie, *op. cit.*, pp. 258–260; *General Statistics of Cities* (1909), pp. 34, 36, 62, 120–147.
22. McKelvey, *Rochester,* III: 82, 93, 104; Griffith, *op. cit.*, pp. 162–163.
23. Reiger, *op. cit.*, pp. 67–68; Green, *Holyoke,* pp. 268–276; Syrett, *op. cit.*, pp. 70–73, 194–200.
24. Whitlock, *op. cit.*, pp. 136–150.
25. Alpheus T. Mason, *Brandeis: A Free Man's Life* (New York, 1947), pp. 106–140; Steffens, *op. cit.*, pp. 114–120; Stewart, *op. cit.*, pp. 132–133; Frederic C. Howe, *The Modern City and Its Problems* (New York, 1915); pp. 59–60, 149–164; Alfred Lief, *Brandeis* (New York, 1936), pp. 45–93; Syrett, *op. cit.*, pp. 170–174; Pierce, *Chicago,* III: 327–333.
26. Frederic C. Howe, *The Confessions of a Reformer* (New York, 1925), pp. 85–166; Tom L. Johnson, *My Story* (New York, 1913); Robert H. Bremner, "The Civic Revival in Ohio," *American Journal of Economics and Sociology,* X: 301–302, XI: 99–110.
27. Bureau of Census, *Telephones and Telegraphs* [Special Reports, 1902] (Washington, 1906); Frank Parsons, "The Telephone," Edward W. Bemis, ed., *Municipal Monopolies* (New York, 1899), pp. 326–361; McKelvey, *Rochester,* III: 250–252; Herbert N. Casson, *The History of the Telephone* (Chicago, 1910), pp. 32–117, 145–156, 160–161, 186–193.
28. Casson, *op. cit.*, pp. 128–134; E. B. Meyer, *Underground Transmission and Distribution for Electric Light and Power* (New York, 1916), pp. 1–18.
29. *General Statistics of Cities* (1909), pp. 80–81, 184–189; Henry F. Bryant, "Underground Tunnels for Wires," *Cosmopolitan,* Vol. 26 (1899), pp. 439–446; McKelvey, *Rochester,* III: 38–39.
30. Rev. C. H. Parkhurst, *My Forty Years in New York* (New York, 1923), pp. 106–145; Tolman, *op. cit.*, pp. 185–219; Klein, *op. cit.*, pp. 229–231.
31. Norman N. Gill, *Municipal Research Bureaus* (Washington, 1944), pp. 12–18; Lorin Peterson, *The Day of the Mugwump* (New York, 1961), pp. 47–54.
32. See the able contributions by John R. Commons, Frank Parsons, M. N. Baker, and Bemis, in Bemis, *op. cit.;* Commission on Public Ownership and Operation, *Municipal and Private Operation of Public Utilities* (National Civic Federation, 1907); Constance M. Green, *Holyoke, Mass.* (New Haven, 1939), pp. 268–277; Carl D. Thompson, *Public Ownership* (New York, 1925), pp. 252 ff.; Griffith, *op. cit.*, pp. 262–264; Wilcox, *op. cit.*, pp. 227–237; Mann, *op cit.*, pp. 137–139.
33. Fairlie, *op. cit.*, pp. 302–309; *General Statistics of Cities* (1909), p. 81.
34. Howe, *Confessions of a Reformer,* pp. 150–175; Johnson, *op. cit.*, pp. 156–250; Mowry, *op. cit.*, pp. 1–135.
35. Ben B. Lindsey and Rube Borough, *The Dangerous Life* (New York, 1931); *Dictionary of American Biography,* VI: 489–491.
36. Mason, *op. cit.*, pp. 109–117, 126–140.
37. Clyde L. King, *The History of the Government in Denver . . .* (Denver, 1911), pp. 160–294; Regier, *op. cit.*, pp. 83–107; Lincoln Steffens, *The Struggle for Self-Government* (New York, 1906); Merlo J. Pusey, *Charles Evans Hughes* (New York, 1951), I: 132–217; Lief, *op. cit.*, pp. 45–94; Destler, *op. cit.*, pp. 1–31, 162–211, 239–254; Richard Hofstadter, *The Age of Reform* (New York, 1955), pp. 164–246; David A. Shannon, *The Socialist Party of America, A History* (New York, 1955), pp. 1–42; Still, *op. cit.*, pp. 279–300; Mann, *op. cit.*, pp. 195–198; Mowry, *op. cit.*, pp. 86–103. See also J. Joseph Huthmacher, "Urban Liberalism and the Age of Reform," *The Mississippi Valley Hist. Rev.,*

Sept. 1962, pp. 231–241, in which he urges a larger recognition of labor's contribution to the reform movement. Much of his evidence, however, applies to the years after 1910.

38. Griffith, *op. cit.*, pp. 265–270; *General Statistics of Cities* (1909), pp. 78–89; M. N. Baker, *Municipal Engineering and Sanitation* (New York, 1906), pp. 30–34.

39. National Municipal League, Committee on Metropolitan Government, *The Government of Metropolitan Areas in the United States* (1930), pp. 157–217; National Resources Committee, *Urban Government*, I (1939): 31–32; Richard Bigger and J. D. Kitchen, *How the Cities Grew* (Los Angeles, 1952); Pierce, *Chicago*, III: 331–339.

40. *Urban Government*, I: 35, 63, 65.

41. Arthur S. Dewing, *Corporate Promotions and Reorganizations* (Cambridge, 1914), pp. 413–457; Henry R. Seager and Charles A. Gulick, Jr., *Trust and Corporation Problems* (New York, 1929), pp. 67, 92–95, 402–412.

42. William Allen White, *The Old Order Changeth* (New York, 1910), pp. 33–39, 47–53; Griffith, *op. cit.*, pp. 277–280; Stewart, *op. cit.*, pp. 102, 107, 109; Peterson, *op. cit.*, pp. 12–46.

43. *Urban Government*, I: 234–238; Stewart, *op. cit.*, pp. 147–150.

44. Griffith, *op. cit.*, pp. 297–303.

45. Griffith, *op. cit.*, pp. 273–277, 286–291; Stewart, *op. cit.*, pp. 50–56; Bryce, *op. cit.*, I: 666–676.

46. National Resources Committee, *Urban Government*, II (1939): 21.

47. Bryce, *op. cit.*, I: 642–650; Arthur N. Holcombe, *State Government in the United States* (New York, 1931), pp. 164, 288–290; J. M. Mathews, "Municipal Representation in State Legislatures," *National Municipal Review* (1923), XII: 135–141.

CHAPTER 8: *Planning the City Beautiful*

1. Walter G. Marshall, *Through America* (London, 1882); Willard Glazier, *Peculiarities of American Cities* (Philadelphia, 1886); William Archer, *America Today* (New York, 1899). See also the recent study by Sam B. Warner, Jr., *Streetcar Suburbs* (Cambridge, 1962).

2. Christopher Tunnard, *The City of Man* (New York, 1953), pp. 187–191; Frederick L. Olmsted, Jr., and Theodora Kimball, eds., *Frederick Law Olmsted, Landscape Architect, 1822–1903* (New York, 1922), I: 123–130, II: 34–43; Frederick Law Olmsted, "The Town-Planning Movement in America," *Annals*, Vol. 51 (January, 1914), pp. 172–181.

3. Olmsted and Kimball, *op. cit.*, I: 23; Christopher Tunnard and Henry H. Reed, *American Skyline* (Cambridge, 1955), pp. 135–138; Wilcox, *op. cit.*, pp. 360–361; Fairlie, *op. cit.*, pp. 264–266; *The Architectural Record* (1916), Vol. 40: 499–504; Sigfried Giedion, *Space, Time and Architecture* (Cambridge, 1954), pp. 647–660; Pierce, *Chicago*, III: 314–320.

4. Tunnard and Reed, *op. cit.*, pp. 137–138; Fairlie, *op. cit.*, p. 266; Glazier, *op. cit.*, pp. 57, 85, 140, 264, *passim*.

5. Walter M. Whitehill, *Boston: A Topographical History* (Cambridge, 1959), pp. 158–165.

6. Tunnard, *op. cit.*, pp. 138–186, 192–207; Olmsted and Kimball, *op. cit.*, I: 14–23; U. S. National Resources Committee, *Urban Planning and Land Policies* (Washington, 1939), II: 82–85, 89–92.

7. Ida M. Tarbell, *New Ideas in Business* (New York, 1916), pp. 135–160; Edith E. Wood, *The Housing of the Unskilled Wage Earner* (New York, 1919), pp. 115–128; Leifur Magnusson, *Housing by Employers in the United States* [U. S. Bureau of Labor Statistics *Bulletin*, No. 263, Oct., 1920], pp. 8–109; R. T. Ely,

"Pullman," *Harper's Magazine,* Vol. 70 (1885), pp. 453–465; Tunnard and Reed, *op. cit.,* pp. 162–169; U. S. National Resources Committee, *Urban Planning and Land Policies* (Washington, 1939), II: 47–50; Pierce, *Chicago,* III: 52–53.

8. Tunnard and Reed, *op. cit.,* pp. 156–161; Marcus T. Reynolds, *Housing of the Poor in Cities* [Amer. Ec. Assoc. Pub., VIII: 135–262] (Baltimore, 1893), pp. 210–238; Pierce, *Chicago,* III: 56–62; Ford, *op. cit.,* II: 879–890 and Plate II, D.

9. E. E. Wood, *op. cit.,* pp. 91–100; R. W. DeForest and L. Veiller, eds., *The Tenement House Problem* (New York, 1903), I: 97–99, 107–116; Jacob A. Riis, *How the Other Half Lives* (New York, 1919), pp. 289–294; *Cost of Living in American Towns* (1911), pp. xx–xxviii, 5–15, 24–41; Pierce, *Chicago,* III: 52–56.

10. James Ford with collaborators, *Slums and Housing* (Cambridge, 1936), I: 142–204; Robert W. De Forest, "A Brief History of the Housing Movement in America," *Annals of the Academy of Political and Social Science* (January, 1914), Vol. 51: 8–12; Riis, *op. cit.,* pp. 2–155; Wood, *op. cit.,* pp. 35–44; Watson, *op. cit.,* pp. 287–290; Louise Ware, *Jacob A. Riis* (New York, 1938), pp. 39–162; Lee, *op. cit.,* pp. 47–63; *Cost of Living in American Towns* (Senate Doc. 22, 1911), pp. 11–15, 24–41.

11. Wood, *op. cit.,* pp. 49–51; Robert A. Woods, *Americans in Process* (Boston, 1902), pp. 38–39, 82–89; De Forest and Veiller, *op. cit.,* I: xxix, 57–65; *Cost of Living in American Towns,* pp. 108–114; Handlin, *op. cit.,* pp. 106–117. See also Warner, *op. cit.,* pp. 91–106.

12. Edith Abbott, *The Tenements of Chicago: 1908–1935* (Chicago, 1936), pp. 8–56; Harvey W. Zorbaugh, *Gold Coast and Slum* (Chicago, 1929), pp. 3–39; Edith E. Wood, *Slums and Blighted Areas in the United States* (F. E. A. Housing Division, *Bul.,* I (Washington, 1935), pp. 36–40; *Cost of Living in American Towns,* pp. 143–148; Pierce, *Chicago,* III: 51–63, 322–323.

13. Wood, *Housing the Unskilled,* pp. 39–41; Abbott, *op. cit.,* p. 53; Carroll D. Wright, *The Slums of Baltimore, Chicago, New York and Philadelphia* (U. S. Commissioner of Labor, Special Report, No. 7, Washington, 1894).

14. Wood, *Slums and Blighted Areas,* pp. 41–68; *ibid., Housing the Unskilled,* pp. 45–90; De Forest and Veiller, *op. cit.,* pp. 109–170.

15. Robert Hunter, "Housing Problems in the United States," *Municipal Affairs* (1902), VI: 333–346; Watson, *op. cit.,* pp. 291–293; Riis, *op. cit.;* A. Weber, "Improved Tenement Homes for American Cities," *Municipal Affairs,* I (1897): 747–750; Lee, *op. cit.,* pp. 64–83; Ford, *op. cit.,* II: 870–874, 880–890, 899–903; Horatio M. Pollock and W. S. Morgan, *Modern Cities* (New York, 1913), pp. 55–59.

16. Wayne Andrews, *Architecture, Ambition and Americans* (New York, 1955); Tunnard and Reed, *op. cit.,* pp. 179–187; Oliver W. Larkin, *Art and Life in America* (New York, 1949), pp. 284–294, 310–317; Giedion, *op. cit.,* pp. 358–360, 370.

17. Tunnard and Reed, *op. cit.,* pp. 187–190; Morrison, *op. cit.,* pp. 80–110, 178–191; Edward A. Roberts, "Civic Art in Cleveland," *Craftsman* (1906), IX: 45–51; Anderson, *op. cit.,* pp. 220–224; Tunnard, *op. cit.,* pp. 303–309; Charles Moore, *Daniel H. Burnham, Architect, Planner of Cities* (Boston, 1921), I: 29–68; Giedion, *op. cit.,* pp. 391–393; Pierce, *Chicago,* III: 501–508, 511–512.

18. *Municipal Affairs* (1899), III: 582–601, 706–714, *passim.*

19. Robert A. Walker, *The Planning Function in Urban Government* (Chicago, 1941), pp. 5–15; Charles M. Robinson, *The Improvement of Towns and Cities* (New York, 1901), and *Modern Civic Art, or the City Made Beautiful* (New York, 1903); Tunnard and Reed, *op. cit.,* pp. 190–192.

20. Sidney Fiske Kimball, *American Architecture* (New York, 1928), pp. 171–187; Laurence Vail Coleman, *Museum Buildings* (Washington, 1950), pp. 54–56; Moore, *op. cit.,* I: 136–229.

21. John DeW. Warner, "Civic Centers," *Municipal Affairs* (March, 1902), pp. 1–23; Richard M. Hurd, "The Structure of Cities," *ibid.,* pp. 24–43; Current Notes

on Public Art, *ibid.,* pp. 275–282; Joseph Danneberg, "The Advance of Civic Art in Baltimore," *Craftsman* (1906), IX: 202–231; Herbert E. Law, "The San Francisco of the Future," *ibid.,* pp. 511–521; Flavel Shurtleff, "Progress of City Planning," National Conference of City Planning, *Proceedings* (1913), pp. 18–22, 134–136.

22. Lee, *op. cit.,* pp. 87–97; McKelvey, *Rochester,* III: 109–110.
23. Condit, *op. cit.,* pp. 147–248; Morrison, *op. cit.,* pp. 191–212; Giedion, *op. cit.,* pp. 375–378, 386–390.
24. *World Almanac* (1910), p. 726; John C. Van Dyke, *The New New York* (New York, 1909), pp. 93–112; Hoyt, *op. cit.,* pp. 329–330.
25. Walker, *op. cit.,* pp. 48–64; Edward M. Bassett, *Zoning* (New York, 1936), pp. 14, 22–23; Charles Zueblin, *American Municipal Progress* (New York, 1916), pp. 332–334; Hoyt, *op. cit.,* p. 211; Fine, *op. cit.,* p. 361.
26. Olmsted, "The Town Planning Movement in America," *Annals* (January, 1914), p. 181.
27. Walker, *op. cit.,* pp. 223–274; Hoyt, *op. cit.,* pp. 200–224; Walter D. Moody, *Wacker's Manual of the Plan of Chicago* (Chicago, 1924 ed.); *Cost of Living in American Towns,* pp. 143–149.
28. Walker, *op. cit.,* pp. 10–12; "Proceedings of the First National Conference on City Planning" (Washington, 1909), *Senate Documents,* No. 422, 61st Congress, 2nd Session; Second National Conference on City Planning, Rochester, *Proceedings* (Boston, 1910).

CHAPTER 9: *The Workers and Their Unions*

1. Samuel L. Loomis, *Modern Cities and Their Religious Problems* (New York, 1887), pp. 54–107.
2. U. S. *Census* (1890), VII: xlvii–liii; (1910), VIII: 31, 33, 57; U. S. *Census, Special Report on Occupations* (1904), pp. li–liii. The average number of wage earners per establishment mounted very slowly before 1900 when a new definition of establishment distinguished between the factories and the hand and neighborhood industries; *ibid., Census Monograph,* III: 21–34; Thomas Woody, *A History of Women's Education in the United States* (New York, 1929), II:9; Amos H. Hawley, *Human Ecology* (New York, 1950), p. 376. For a discussion of the statistical problems of distinguishing wage earners from others in the occupational tables, see Leo Wolman, *The Growth of American Trade Unions, 1880–1923* (New York, 1924), pp. 75–81.
3. Gerald N. Grob, *Workers and Utopia* (Chicago, 1961), pp. 3–10; Thomas C. Cochran and William Miller, *The Age of Enterprise* (New York, 1942), pp. 230–232; *Census Monograph,* III: 35–45; Norman J. Ware, *The Labor Movement in the United States, 1860–1895* (New York, 1929), pp. 1–6.
4. John R. Commons, ed., *A Documentary History of the American Industrial Society* (Cleveland, 1910), IX: 23–24, 67–70, 118–125; McKelvey, *Rochester,* II: 73–76; Frederick L. Ryan, *Industrial Relations in the San Francisco Building Trades* (Norman, Calif., 1936), pp. 7–14; N. Y. *Census* (1865), pp. 512–518. See the tables on wages and prices in Edgar W. Martin, *The Standard of Living in 1860* (Chicago, 1942), pp. 407–431; Grob, *op. cit.,* pp. 8–9.
5. John R. Commons and associates, *History of Labour in the United States* (New York, 1918), I: 14–25, 39–41; Emerson D. Fite, *Social and Industrial Conditions in the North During the Civil War* (New York, 1910), pp. 105–110, 183–212.
6. George E. O'Neill, ed., *The Labor Movement: The Problem of Today* (Boston, 1887), pp. 345–348; Martin, *op. cit.,* pp. 432–433.
7. Commons, *Documentary History,* pp. 89–102; Commons, *History of Labour,* II: 26–37.

8. Commons, *History of Labour,* II: 86–87, 96–120; Ware, *op. cit.,* pp. 5–11; Thomas ϑI. Greer, *American Social Reform Movements . . . Since 1865* (New York, 1949), pp. 9–37; Grob, *op. cit.,* pp. 11–12.

9. Commons, *Documents,* IX: 126–168; Chester McA. Destler, *American Radicalism, 1865–1901* (New London, 1946), pp. 50–57; Sidney Fine, *Laissez Faire and the General Welfare State* (Ann Arbor, 1956), pp. 305–307, 316–320; Grob, *op. cit.,* pp. 12–26.

10. Commons, *History of Labour,* II: 5–11, 53–55. Jonathan Grossman, "Co-operative Foundries," *New York History,* XXIV (April, 1943); 196–210; Jonathan Grossman, *William Sylvis, Pioneer of American Labor* (New York, 1945), pp. 189–210; Grob, *op. cit.,* pp. 14–15, 19–21.

11. O'Neill, *op. cit.,* pp. 196–203; Nicholas P. Gilman, *Profit Sharing Between Employer and Employee* (Boston, 1889), pp. 317, 359; Commons, *History of Labour,* II: 76–79, 111.

12. *Ibid.,* pp. 86–87, 92–93, 120–127; Commons, *Documents,* IX: 42–51, 168–215; O'Neill, *op. cit.,* pp. 133–148; Arthur Mann, *Yankee Reformers in the Urban Age* (Cambridge, 1954), pp. 175–184; Ware, *op. cit.,* pp. 18–21; Grob, *op. cit.,* pp. 22–52.

13. Commons, *History of Labour,* II: 123–143; O'Neill, *op. cit.,* pp. 137–140.

14. Commons, *History of Labour,* II: 157–166, 207–222; O'Neill, *op. cit.,* pp. 148–157; McKelvey, *Rochester,* II: 118–123.

15. Edward W. Bemis, "Cooperatives in New England," and "Cooperatives in the Middle States," *Johns Hopkins University Studies,* VI (1888): 37–329; N. S. B. Gras and Henrietta M. Larson, *Casebook in American Business History* (New York, 1939), pp. 723–724; Otto C. Lightner, *The History of Business Depressions* (New York, 1922), pp. 160–180; L. H. Feder, *Unemployment Relief in Periods of Depression* (New York, 1936), pp. 41–43, 67–70.

16. Commons, *History of Labour,* II: 235–239; Ira Kipnis, *The American Socialist Movement: 1897–1912* (New York, 1952), pp. 7–10.

17. Commons, *History of Labour,* II: 185–285; O'Neill, *op. cit.,* pp. 220–224.

18. O'Neill, *op. cit.,* pp. 157–162.

19. Commons, *History of Labour,* II: 185–285; Henry George, *Progress and Poverty* (New York [1879], 1942, 15th ed.); Donald D. Egbert and Stow Persons, eds., *Socialism in American Life* (Princeton, 1952), I: 233–242; Pierce, *Chicago,* III: 352–353; Fine, *op. cit.,* pp. 289–295; Grob, *op. cit.,* pp. 81–84.

20. Ryan, *op. cit.,* pp. 14–15; Grace H. Stimson, *Rise of the Labor Movement in Los Angeles* (Berkeley, 1955), pp. 60–67; George E. Mowry, *The California Progressives* (Berkeley, 1951), pp. 9–17; Grob, *op. cit.,* pp. 84–85.

21. Charlotte Erickson, *American Industry and the European Immigrant: 1860–1885* (Cambridge, 1957), pp. 139–166; Commons, *Documents,* IX: 74–88; Carl Wittke, *We Who Built America* (New York, 1940), pp. 513–515; Isaac A. Hourwich, *Immigration and Labor* (New York, 2nd ed., 1922), pp. 1, 99 ff.; Commons, *History,* III: 1821; O'Neill, *op. cit.,* pp. 220–232; U. S. Industrial Commission, *Report* (1901), XV: 449–492.

22. Joseph A. Hill, *Women in Gainful Occupations, 1870–1920* [Census Monograph, IX] (Washington, 1929), pp. 30–58; *Recent Social Trends,* I: 711–718; Cecile T. LaFollette, *A Study of the Problems of 652 Gainfully Employed Married Women Homemakers* (New York, 1934), pp. 3–7; Woody, *op. cit.,* II: 2–37; Wolman, *op. cit.,* pp. 97–108; Harold U. Faulkner, *The Decline of Laissez Faire: 1897–1917* (New York, 1951), pp. 250–260.

23. Robert A. Christie, *Empire in Wood: A History of the Carpenters' Union* (Ithaca, 1956), pp. 61–78.

24. Leo Wolman, "The Boycott in American Trade Unions," *Johns Hopkins University Studies in History,* XXXIV (1916), No. 1; Ernest R. Spedden, "The Trade Union Label," *Johns Hopkins University Studies,* XXVIII (1910), No. 2; Commons, *History of Labour,* II: 308–315; Ryan, *op. cit.,* pp. 18–20.

25. Commons, *History of Labour,* II: 310–429; Emerson P. Schmidt, *Industrial Relations in Urban Transportation* (Minneapolis, 1937), pp. 106–114; T. V. Powderly, *The Path I Trod* (New York, 1940), pp. 47–160; Samuel Rezneck,

"Patterns of Thought and Action in an American Depression, 1882–1886," *American Historical Review* (January, 1956), pp. 284–307; O'Neill, *op. cit.*, pp. 397–428; Pierce, *Chicago*, III: 276–280; Grob, *op. cit.*, pp. 60–78.

26. Schmidt, *op. cit.*, pp. 121–127; McKelvey, *Rochester*, III: 46–51; Marion C. Cahill, *Shorter Hours* (New York, 1932); Ware, *op. cit.*, pp. 65–242; Grob, *op. cit.*, pp. 99–118.

27. Lewis L. Lorwin, *The American Federation of Labor* (Washington, 1933), pp. 13–31; Mann, *op. cit.*, pp. 180–184; Grob, *op. cit.*, pp. 119–162.

28. Commons, *History*, II: 400–429, 442–466, 503–509; *U. S. Industrial Commission*, VII: 112–120 ff.; Clarence E. Bennett, *Employers Associations in the United States* (New York, 1922), pp. 21–22 ff.; Lorwin, *op. cit.*, pp. 27–29; McKelvey, *Rochester*, III; 51–52; Pierce, *Chicago*, III: 290–293, 353–354.

29. Commons, *History*, II: 495–504, 520–536; III: 116–126; IV: 20–50; Donald L. McMurry, *Coxey's Army* (Boston, 1929); Ware, *op. cit.*, pp. 28 ff. Only in coal mining did industrial unionism revive in the late nineties, and John Mitchell's United Mine Workers exerted little influence on the labor movements in the more urbanized centers.

30. Commons, *History*, III: 403–468; U. S. *Industrial Commission*, VII: 121–136.

31. Josephine Goldmark, *Impatient Crusader: Florence Kelley's Life Story* (Urbana, Ill., 1953), pp. 51–64 ff.; Faulkner, *op. cit.*, pp. 256–261.

32. Henry R. Seager and C. A. Gulick, *Trusts and Corporation Problems* (New York, 1929), pp. 339–412; Ida M. Tarbell, *Nationalizing of Business*, pp. 203–219; U. S. *Industrial Commission*, VII: 68–87; XIV: xlii–xliv; U. S. Census Bureau, *Monograph*, III: 91–98; See also Edith Abbott, "The Wages of Unskilled Labor in the United States, 1850–1900," *Journal of Political Economy*, XIII (1905), pp. 321–367; Alvin H. Hansen, "Factors Affecting the Trend of Real Wages," *American Economic Review*, XV (1925), pp. 27–42; Wesley C. Mitchell, *History of the Greenbacks* (Chicago, 1903).

33. *Cost of Living in American Towns* (U. S. Senate Doc. 22, 1911), pp. v, xxxvii–lxxvi. See also Arthur Shadwell, *Industrial Efficiency* (London, 2nd ed., 1909), pp. 377–384.

34. Ida M. Tarbell, *New Ideals in Business* (New York, 1916), pp. 172–176, 231–233 ff.; idem., *Nationalizing of Business*, pp. 168–186; Gilman, *op. cit.*, pp. 296–330, 386–388; U. S. *Industrial Commission*, XIV: 358–410; Commons, *History*, III: 318–337, 359–376; Jackson M. Anderson, *Industrial Recreation* (New York, 1955), pp. 42–54; Joseph Lee, *Constructive and Preventive Philanthropy* (New York, 1902), pp. 97–104; McKelvey, *Rochester*, III: 259–262; Faulkner, *op. cit.*, pp. 269–273.

35. Jesse E. Pope, *The Clothing Industry in New York* [University of Missouri Studies in Social Science], 1905, I: 45–212; *Industrial Commission*, VII: 181–190; XIV and XVII, *passim; Cost of Living in American Towns* (Senate Doc. 22, 1911), pp. 5–8, 16–19; Wittke, *op. cit.*, pp. 335, 439; Moses Rischin, *The Promised City: New York's Jews: 1870–1914* (Cambridge, 1962), pp. 61–68, 171–183. But see also Hourwich, *op. cit.*, pp. 362–374.

36. Commons, *History of Labour*, IV: 289–317; Louis Levine, *The Women's Garment Workers* (New York, 1924), pp. 8–195; Rischin, *op. cit.*, pp. 184–194.

37. Christie, *op. cit.*, pp. 79–136, 155–163; Faulkner, *op. cit.*, pp. 280–289; Grob, *op. cit.*, pp. 186–195.

38. Commons, *History*, II: 521–537; IV: 13–19, 82–143; Frank T. Stockton, "The Closed Shop in American Trade Unions," *Johns Hopkins University Studies*, XXIX, No. 3 (1911); Stimson, *op. cit.*, pp. 132–133; Cochran and Miller, *op. cit.*, pp. 232–248; Irving Bernstein, "The Growth of American Unions," *American Economic Review*, June, 1954, pp. 301–318; Wolman, *op. cit.*, pp. 33, 85 and *passim.*

39. Bonnett, *op. cit.*, pp. 291–437; Commons, *History*, IV: 48–50, 129–137; Harwood L. Childs, *Labor and Capital in National Politics* (Columbus, 1930); Lorwin, *op. cit.*, pp. 76–92; Ryan, *op. cit.*, pp. 114–122; Marguerite Green, *The National Civic Federation and the American Labor Movement, 1900–1925* (Washington, 1956), pp. 1–106.

40. Seba Eldridge, *Development of Collective Enterprise* (Lawrence, Kansas, 1943), pp. 338–347; Charles R. Henderson, *Industrial Insurance in the United States* (Chicago, 1911); I. M. Rubinow, *Social Insurance* (New York, 1916), pp. 169–174, 284–295; M. Green, *op. cit.*, pp. 107–132; Faulkner, *op. cit.*, pp. 275–279.
41. Destler, *American Radicalism*, pp. 162–209; Commons, *History of Labour*, II: 449–455, 509–520; Mann, *op. cit.*, pp. 185–198; M. Green, *op. cit.*, pp. 133–189.
42. Kipnis, *op. cit.*, pp. 25–106, 189–369; Daniel Bell, "The Background and Development of Marxian Socialism in America," in Egbert and Person, *op. cit.*, I: 242–302; Bayrd Still, *Milwaukee* (Madison, 1948), pp. 310–318; Fine, *op. cit.*, pp. 338–346.
43. Commons, *History*, IV: 230–240; Constance M. Green, *American Cities* (London, 1957), pp. 183–184.
44. Commons, *History*, III: 303–315, 337–358, 550–572; Clarence B. Thompson, *Scientific Management* (Cambridge, 1914), pp. 3–40.
45. Commons, *History*, III: 55–63; Tarbell, *Nationalizing of Business*, pp. 178–182, 262, 275–277; Jonathan T. Lincoln, *The City of the Dinner Pail* (Boston, 1909); James Dombrowsky, *The Early Days of Christian Socialism in America* (New York, 1936), pp. 124–125, 132–170; Milton J. Nadworny, *Scientific Management and the Unions* (Cambridge, 1955), pp. 1–33; Goldmark, *op. cit.*, pp. 78–130; Rischin, *op. cit.*, pp. 195–198.

CHAPTER 10: *From Charity to Community Welfare*

1. U. S. Bureau of Census, Special Report, *Benevolent Institutions* (1910), pp. 86–257; John O'Grady, *Catholic Charities in the United States* (Washington, 1930), pp. 72–76 ff.
2. Emerson D. Fite, *Social and Industrial Conditions in the North During the Civil War* (New York, 1910), pp. 275–310; C. Howard Hopkins, *History of the Y. M. C. A. in North America* (New York, 1951), pp. 84–103; E. Merton Coulter, *The Confederate States of America, 1861–65* (St. Louis University, 1950), pp. 417, 424–439; Marjorie B. Greenbie, *Lincoln's Daughters of Mercy* (New York, 1944), pp. 37–208; William Q. Maxwell, *Lincoln's Fifth Wheel* (New York, 1956); Ernest R. Graves, *The American Woman* (New York, 1944), pp. 212–215, 232–336.
3. Henry I. Bowditch, *Public Hygiene in America* (Boston, 1877), pp. 99–102; Rischin, *op. cit.*, pp. 103–106.
4. U. S. Commissioner of Education, *Report* (1877), pp. cxcii–ccii; *Benevolent Institutions* (1910), *passim*.
5. David M. Schneider and Albert Deutsch, *The History of Public Welfare in New York State: 1867–1940* (Chicago, 1941), pp. 35–49; William R. Stewart, *The Philanthropic Work of Josephine Shaw Lowell* (New York, 1911), pp. 72–77; Allan Pinkerton, *Strikes, Communists, Tramps and Detectives* (New York, 1878), pp. 25–66; Carlos C. Closson, Jr., "The Unemployed in American Cities," *Quarterly Journal of Economics* (1894), pp. 168–217, 195–196; McKelvey, *Rochester*, II: 147–148; Pierce, *Chicago*, III: 241–242; L. H. Feder, *Unemployment Relief in Periods of Depression* (New York, 1936), pp. 37–70.
6. Schneider and Deutsch, *op. cit.*, pp. 37–49; Robert W. Kelso, *The Science of Public Welfare* (New York, 1928), pp. 125–134; John T. Horton, *Old Erie—The Growth of an American Community* (New York, 1947), I: 251–253; Feder, *op. cit.*, pp. 59–62.
7. Frank D. Watson, *The Charity Organization Movement in the United States* (New York, 1922), pp. 175–216; Stewart, *op. cit.*, pp. 122–196; O. C. McCulloch, "History of Charity Organizations," National Conference of Charities, *Proceedings* (1880), pp. 123–126; (1881), pp. 192–195; Robert H. Bremner, *From the Depths: The Discovery of Poverty in the United States* (New York, 1956), pp. 50–57.

8. Watson, *op. cit.*, pp. 181–186, 199–201, 214–221.
9. Sidney H. Coleman, *Humane Society Leaders in America* (Albany, 1924); Roswell C. McCrea, *The Humane Movement* (New York, 1910).
10. Watson, *op. cit.*, pp. 222–245, 545; *Benevolent Institutions* (1904); Bremner, *op. cit.*, pp. 46–52.
11. Hopkins, *op. cit.*, pp. 101–173; Blake McKelvey, "The Y. M. C. A.'s First Century in Rochester," *Rochester History*, January, 1954, pp. 1–19; Pierce, *Chicago*, III: 443–444.
12. Mary S. Sims, *The Natural History of a Social Institution—the Y. W. C. A.* (New York, 1936), pp. 1–49; Anna V. Rice, *A History of the World's Y. W. C. A.* (New York, 1947), pp. 36–47.
13. Mrs. J. C. Croly, *The History of the Women's Club Movement in America* (New York, 1898), pp. 620–621; Mrs. F. J. Shepard, "The Women's Educational and Industrial Union," Buffalo Historical Society, *Publication*, XXII: 147–187; McKelvey, *Rochester*, III: 11–12, 83.
14. Watson, *op. cit.*, pp. 248–265; Closson, *op. cit.*, pp. 453–477, 499–502; McKelvey, *Rochester*, III: 58–59; Feder, *op. cit.*, pp. 72–85, 126–129.
15. Charles Hirschfeld, *Baltimore, 1870–1900* (Baltimore, 1941), pp. 144–154; Watson, *op. cit.*, pp. 266–286; Commons, *History of Labour*, III: 166, 218–219; Feder, *op. cit.*, pp. 85–91, 98–158, 171–217.
16. Vida D. Scudder, *On Journey* (New York, 1937), pp. 83–84, 109–111, 135–141; Mann, *op. cit.*, pp. 217–226; Rischin, *op. cit.*, pp. 205–208.
17. Robert A. Woods and A. J. Kennedy, *The Settlement Horizon* (New York, 1922), pp. 1–51; O'Grady, *op. cit.*, pp. 288–294.
18. Jane Addams, *Twenty Years at Hull-House* (New York, 1910); James L. Linn, *Jane Addams, A Biography* (New York, 1935), pp. 90–178.
19. Howard E. Wilson, *Mary McDowell: Neighbor* (Chicago, 1928), pp. 15–60; R. L. Duffus, *Lillian Wald* (New York, 1938), pp. 31–57; Minnie Goodnow, *Nursing History* (Philadelphia, 9th ed., 1953), pp. 197–198.
20. Louise Wade, "Graham Taylor, Social Pioneer: 1851–1938," Ph.D. Thesis, University of Rochester, 1954.
21. Linn, *op. cit.*, pp. 190–208; Robert A. Woods, ed., *The City Wilderness* (Boston, 1898); U. S. Commissioner of Education, *Report (1909)*, II: 2318–2325; *Hull-House, Maps and Papers* (Chicago, 1895); Mann, *op. cit.*, pp. 114–123; Bremner, *op. cit.*, pp. 60–66; see also Lawrence A. Cremin, *The Transformation of the School* (New York, 1961), pp. 58–65.
22. Linn, *op. cit.*, pp. 170–178; Lorence M. Pacey, ed., *Readings in the Development of Settlement Work* (New York, 1950), pp. 222–225; Herbert H. Lou, *Juvenile Courts in the United States* (Chapel Hill, 1927), pp. 19–24; Bremner, *op. cit.*, pp. 218–225; Samuel H. Popper, *Individualized Justice: Fifty Years of Juvenile Court and Probation Services in Ramsey County, Minn.* (St. Paul, 1956), pp. 1–10; Josephine Goldmark, *Impatient Crusader, Florence Kelley's Life Story* (Urbana, 1953), pp. 66–120.
23. Alfred Cohen, *Statistical Analysis of American Divorce* (New York, 1932), pp. 58–137; Arthur W. Calhoun, *A Social History of the American Family* (Cleveland, 1919), III: 67–70, 85–176, 261–276; *Recent Social Trends*, pp. 680–704; *Statistics of Cities* (1902–03), pp. 134–135.
24. *Benevolent Institutions* (1904), p. 11; Watson, *op. cit.*, pp. 281–307; O'Grady, *op. cit.*, pp. 417–420; Boris D. Bogen, *Jewish Philanthropy* (New York, 1917), pp. 44–48; Barbara M. Solomon, *Pioneers in Service: The History of the Jewish Philanthropies of Boston* (Boston, 1956), pp. 1–69; Rischin, *op. cit.*, pp. 98–110.
25. Mazyck P. Ravenel, *A Half Century of Public Health* (New York, 1921), pp. 236–281; Wilbur C. Phillips, *Adventuring for Democracy* (New York, 1940), pp. 18–35.
26. Ravenel, *op. cit.*, pp. 150–151, 277–281, 306–310; Phillips, *op. cit.*, pp. 18–60; McKelvey, *Rochester*, III: 82, 163.
27. Ravenel, *op. cit.*, pp. 299–320; Joseph Lee, *Constructive and Preventive Philan-*

thropy (New York, 1902), pp. 109–158; *Benevolent Institutions* (1910), pp. 60–72, 86 ff.

28. Charles V. Chapin, *Municipal Sanitation in the United States* (Providence, 1901), pp. 528–556, 602–620; Richard H. Shryock, *The Development of Modern Medicine* (New York, 1947), pp. 346–348; Eldridge, *op. cit.*, pp. 360–364; *Recent Social Trends*, pp. 656–657; *Benevolent Institutions, 1910*, pp. 19–21, 68, 81–84.
29. Helen Clapesattle, *The Doctors Mayo* (Minneapolis, 1954 ed.), pp. 1–319.
30. Fairlie, *op. cit.*, pp. 166–170; Ravenel, *op. cit.*, pp. 147–148.
31. Chapin, *op. cit.*, pp. 791–796; *Municipal Affairs* (June, 1897), I: 367–368; Lee, *op. cit.*, pp. 148–158.
32. John L. Thomas, "Workingmen's Hotels," *Municipal Affairs* (1899), III: 73–94; Albert B. Wolfe, *The Lodging House Problem in Boston* (Cambridge, 1913), pp. 6–38; Paul Kennaday, "New York's Hundred Lodging Houses," *Charities*, Feb. 18, 1905.
33. Emery A. Brownell, *Legal Aid in the United States* (Rochester, 1951), pp. 7–8, 170–172; Watson, *op. cit.*, pp. 299–300; McKelvey, *Rochester*, III: 140; Pierce, *Chicago*, III: 435.
34. Watson, *op. cit.*, pp. 287–309; Hirschfeld, *op. cit.*, pp. 146–148; Fairlie, *Municipal Activities*, pp. 189–192; Joseph Lee, *Constructive and Preventive Philanthropy* (New York, 1902); Ernest V. Hollis and A. L. Taylor, *Social Work Education in the United States* (New York, 1951), pp. 9–11; U. S. Commissioner of Education *Report* (1915), I: 345–359; Mary E. Richmond, *The Long View* (New York, 1930), pp. 36–38, 86–104, 183–185.
35. U. S. Commissioner of Education *Report* (1915), I: 345–359; *The Craftsman*, IX (1906), pp. 620–633; Bremner, *op. cit.*, pp. 67–85, 145–159.

CHAPTER 11: *The Emergence of the Social Gospel*

1. George A. Sala, *America Revisited* (London, 1883), I: 120–126; James Bryce, *American Commonwealth* (New York, 1924 ed.), II: 781–783; Arthur M. Schlesinger, *The Rise of the City: 1878–1898* (New York, 1933), pp. 330–332.
2. Aaron I. Abell, "The Catholic Factor in Urban Welfare: The Early Period, 1850–1888," *The Review of Politics*, July, 1952, p. 290 ff.
3. Abell, *op. cit.*, pp. 289–324; John O'Grady, *Catholic Charities in the United States* (Washington, 1930), pp. 46–171; Helen Campbell, *Darkness and Daylight* (Hartford, 1898), pp. 49–88, 185–207, 224–254, 381–396; Arthur Mann, *Yankee Reformers in the Urban Age* (Cambridge, 1954), pp. 24–51; Timothy L. Smith, *Revivalism and Social Reform* (New York, 1957), pp. 170–174.
4. Barbara M. Solomon, *Pioneers in Service* (Boston, 1956), pp. 4–20; Selig Adler and T. E. Connolly, *From Ararat to Suburbia* (Philadelphia, 1960), pp. 114–138; Pierce, *Chicago* II: 23–24, 356, 368; III: 38–42; McKelvey, *Rochester*, II: 169–179; Rischin, *op. cit.*, pp. 94–107.
5. Solomon, *op. cit.*, pp. 21–69; Pierce, *Chicago*, III: 447–449; Adler and Connolly, *op. cit.*, pp. 138–159; McKelvey, *Rochester*, II: 306–308, 381–383; III: 35, 58; Rischin, *op. cit.*, pp. 103–111.
6. Boris D. Bogen, *Jewish Philanthropy* (New York, 1917), pp. 27–36, 93, 96, 113–122, 133, 233–250; Samuel Joseph, *History of the Baron de Hirsch Fund* (New York, 1935); Carl Wittke, *We Who Built America* (New York, 1940), pp. 333–335; Rischin, *op. cit.*, pp. 54, 99–100.
7. U. S. Commissioner of Education *Report* (1914), I: 450–451; Solomon, *op. cit.*, pp. 28–29, 44; Isaac B. Berkson, *Theories of Americanization* (New York, 1920), pp. 56–59; William I. Thomas and F. Znaniecki, *The Polish Peasant in Europe and America* (New York, 2nd ed., 1927), II: 1522–1654.
8. Rischin, *op. cit.*, pp. 117, 124–127, 157–160, 174–184, 201–202, 212, 242.

9. Aaron I. Abell, *The Urban Impact on American Protestantism, 1865–1900* (Cambridge, 1934), pp. 6–8, 11–15, 26–27, 55–56, 90–94; Charles H. Hopkins, *The Rise of the Social Gospel in American Protestantism: 1865–1915* (New Haven, 1940), pp. 39, 113–115; Josiah Strong, *Our Country: Its Possible Future and Its Present Crisis* (New York, 1885), pp. 17–106; Pierce, *Chicago,* II: 368, III: 41.

10. Richard Hofstadter, *Social Darwinism* (Philadelphia, 1944), pp. 68–85; Schlesinger, *op. cit.,* pp. 322–329; Hopkins, *op. cit.,* pp. 56, 123–134; Blake McKelvey, "When Science Was on Trial in Rochester: 1850–1890," *Rochester History,* October, 1946; Mann, *op. cit.,* pp. 73–101; Pierce, *Chicago,* III: 429–437; Russel B. Nye, *Midwestern Progressive Politics* (Lansing, 1959), pp. 152–154.

11. Rev. W. H. Daniels, ed., *The Temperance Reform* (New York, 1878), pp. 251–510; McKelvey, *Rochester,* II: 140–141, 147–148, 279–280; Pierce, *Chicago,* III: 421–427.

12. John M. Barker, *The Saloon Problem and Social Reforms* (Boston, 1905), pp. 179–195; McKelvey, *Rochester,* III: 95–106; Clarence A. Perry, *Wider Use of the School Plant* (New York, 1913), pp. 249–290; Raymond Calkins, *Substitutes for the Saloon* (Boston, 1901); Robert H. Bremner, *From the Depths: The Discovery of Poverty in the United States* (New York, 1956), pp. 80–81. See also Andrew Sinclair, *Prohibition, the Era of Excess* (Boston, 1962), pp. 91–105.

13. Abell, *op. cit.,* pp. 21–26; Hopkins, *op. cit.,* pp. 42–49; Mann, *op. cit.,* pp. 86–97.

14. Abell, *op. cit.,* pp. 35–42, 137–143; Henry M. Boies, *Prisoners and Paupers* (New York, 1893), pp. 88–137; Rowland T. Berthoff, *British Immigrants In Industrial America* (Cambridge, 1953); Pierce, *Chicago,* III: 438–443; Nye, *op. cit.,* pp. 155–157.

15. Washington Gladden, *Recollections* (New York, 1909), pp. 241–352; Henry F. May, *Protestant Churches and Industrial America* (New York, 1949), pp. 171–175.

16. Abell, *op. cit.,* pp. 48, 50, 59–74, 112; May, *op. cit.,* pp. 183–187; Bremner, *op. cit.,* pp. 57–60.

17. May, *op. cit.,* pp. 188–192; Hopkins, *op. cit.,* pp. 131–134, 217–218; Abell, *op. cit.,* pp. 114–115; Blake McKelvey, "Walter Rauschenbusch's Rochester," *Rochester History,* October, 1952.

18. Louise C. Wade, "Graham Taylor, Social Pioneer: 1851–1938," Ph.D. Thesis, University of Rochester, pp. 50–123; Bremner, *op. cit.,* pp. 57–71.

19. Abell, *op. cit.,* pp. 147–153; May, *op. cit.,* pp. 185–186; Hopkins, *op. cit.,* pp. 154–155; McKelvey, *Rochester,* III: 123–126; Schlesinger, *op. cit.,* pp. 339–343.

20. Abell, *op. cit.,* pp. 75–88; Wade, *op. cit.,* pp. 124–584; James Dombrowsky, *Early Days of Christian Socialism in America* (New York, 1936), pp. 96–106; Hopkins, *op. cit.,* pp. 173–183.

21. McKelvey, *Rochester,* III: 131–136.

22. *Ibid.,* pp. 136, 140, 143; Hopkins, *op. cit.,* pp. 215–232.

23. McKelvey, *Rochester,* III: 138–144; Walter Rauschenbusch, *Christianizing the Social Order* (New York, 1912), pp. 440–442; Vernon P. Bodein, *The Social Gospel of Walter Rauschenbusch . . .* (New Haven, 1944); Rochester Theological Seminary *Bulletin,* No. 69.

24. Abell, *op. cit.,* pp. 166–193; Harold U. Faulkner, *The Quest for Social Justice, 1898–1914* (New York, 1931), pp. 218–224.

25. Arthur C. Calhoun, *A Social History of the American Family* (Cleveland, 1919), III: 85–105.

26. Robert A. Woods, ed., *The City Wilderness* (Boston, 1898), pp. 176–286; Albert B. Wolfe, *The Lodging House Problem in Boston* (Cambridge, 1913), pp. 6–7; Jacob A. Riis, *How the Other Half Lives* (New York, 1919 ed.), pp. 193–198; Charles H. Hopkins, *History of the Y. M. C. A. in North America* (New York, 1951), pp. 239–240.

27. Abell, *op. cit.,* pp. 118–136; Herbert A. Wisbey, Jr., *Soldiers Without Swords* (New York, 1955), pp. 1–149.

28. Carl Wittke, *We Who Built America* (New York, 1940), pp. 500–505; H. J. Desmond, *A. P. A. Movement* (Washington, 1912); W. H. J. Traynor, "Policy and Power of the A. P. A.," *North American Review*, 162 (1896), pp. 658–666; Theodore Maynard, *The Story of American Catholicism* (New York, 1941), pp. 496–497; John Higham, *Strangers in the Land* (New Brunswick, N. J., 1955), pp. 61–62, 80–87.

29. Herbert Asbury, *The Great Illusion* (New York, 1950), pp. 95–100; Maynard, *op. cit.*, pp. 433–469; O'Grady, *op. cit.*, pp. 275–429; Bogen, *op. cit.*, pp. 83–274; Aaron I. Abell, *American Catholicism and Social Action: A Search for Social Justice, 1865–1950* (Garden City, N. Y., 1960), pp. 54–188; Mann, *op. cit.*, pp. 47–49; John A. Ryan, *Social Doctrine in Action: A Personal History* (New York, 1941), pp. 50–120; Robert D. Cross, *The Emergence of Liberal Catholicism in America* (Cambridge, 1958), pp. 26–119; Sinclair, *loc. cit.*

30. Abell, *Urban Impact*, pp. 90–110; Hopkins, *op. cit.*, pp. 113–115; Dombrowsky, *op. cit.*, pp. 98–99; Higham, *op. cit.*, p. 39.

31. Hopkins, *op. cit.*, pp. 302–315.

32. John M. Glenn, etc., *Russell Sage Foundation: 1907–1946* (New York, 1947), pp. 1–30; Paul U. Kellogg, ed., *The Pittsburgh Survey*, 6 vols. (New York, 1911–1914); Bremner, *op. cit.*, pp. 154–157.

CHAPTER 12: *The Pervasive Vitality of City Schools*

1. Ellwood P. Cubberley, *Public Education in the United States* (Boston, 1934 ed.), pp. 385–392; Mary S. Barnes, ed., *Autobiography of Edward Austin Sheldon* (New York, 1911); Andrew P. Hollis, *The Contribution of the Oswego Normal School* (Boston, 1898), pp. 5–38; Lawrence A. Cremin, *The Transformation of the School* (New York, 1961), pp. 11, 93, 134.

2. Cubberley, *op. cit.*, pp. 392–393, 457, 472–475, 740; Merle Curti, *The Social Ideas of American Educators* (New York, 1935), pp. 310–348, 379–395, 499–521; Charles F. Adams, Jr., *The New Departure in the Schools of Quincy* (pamphlet, Boston, 1879), pp. 31–51; Cremin, *op. cit.*, pp. 14–20, 128–132; James B. Conant, *Slums and Suburbs* (New York, 1961), pp. 138–140.

3. Charles F. Thwing, *A History of Education in the United States Since the Civil War* (New York, 1910), p. 99; U. S. Commissioner of Education *Reports* (1889–90), II: 617–693, 868–873, 1030; Cubberley, *op. cit.*, pp. 385–400; Hollis, *op. cit.*, pp. 26–75; Vernon L. Mangun, *The American Normal School: Its Rise and Development in Massachusetts* (Baltimore, 1928), pp. 139–161.

4. Cubberley, *op. cit.*, pp. 429, 563–576; U. S. Commissioner of Education *Reports* (1880), lxvi–lxxxvi; (1889–90), II: 604–606; (1889–1900), I: 85–116; III: 1794–1851, 2646; *A Cyclopedia of Education* (1928 ed.), I: 285–295; Curti, *op. cit.*, pp. 234–239; D. S. Sneeden, "The Public Schools and Juvenile Delinquency," *Education Review* (April, 1907), 33: 374–385.

5. U. S. Commissioner of Education *Reports* (1886–87), II: 496–506; (1899–1900), II: 2119–2122, 2140–2141, 2563–2568; (1903), I: 563–566; Schlesinger, *op. cit.*, pp. 166–171.

6. U. S. Commissioner of Education *Reports* (1873), pp. 846–849; (1880), pp. 492–520; (1889–1900), II: 2563–2568; (1905), I: 529–535; Cubberley, *op. cit.*, pp. 456–461; Albert B. Faust, *The German Element in the United States* (New York, 1927), II: 237.

7. J. A. Burns and B. J. Kohlbrenner, *A History of Catholic Education in the United States* (New York, 1937), pp. 121–123, 141–145, 184–187, 246–249; Morgan M. Sheedy, "The Catholic Parochial Schools of the United States," U. S. Commissioner of Education *Report* (1903), I: 1079–1101; Edwin E. Slosson, *The American Spirit in Education* (New Haven, 1921), pp. 199–206; Cubberley, *op. cit.*, pp. 233–240; Theodore Maynard, *The Story of American*

Catholicism (New York, 1941), pp. 466–478; Robert D. Cross, *The Emergence of Liberal Catholicism in America* (Cambridge, 1958), pp. 180–205.

8. U. S. Commissioner of Education *Reports* (1899–1900), pp. 1794–1797, 2158–2159.

9. A. P. Stokes, *Church and State in the United States* (New York, 1950), II: 525–532, 553–572.

10. Israel Friedlaender, "Jewish Education in America," U. S. Commissioner of Education *Report* (1913), I: 365–391.

11. Robert D. Cole, *Private Secondary Education for Boys in the United States* (Philadelphia, 1928), pp. 1–37, 78–122; C. Wright Mills, *The Power Elite* (New York, 1956), pp. 63–68, 106–107.

12. U. S. Commissioner of Education *Report* (1889–90), II: 609–614; 1073–1102; (1898–1900), pp. 613–615; (1910), II: 701–842; Cubberley, *op. cit.*, pp. 663–676; Edgar W. Knight, *Public Education in the South* (Boston, 1922), pp. 337–432; Schlesinger, *op. cit.*, pp. 163–166.

13. Fletcher B. Dresslar, *American Schoolhouses* [U. S. Bureau of Education Bulletin 444 (1910)]; Cubberley, *op. cit.*, pp. 604–606; Warren R. Briggs, *Modern American School Buildings* (New York, 1909), pp. 195–399.

14. U. S. Commissioner of Education *Reports* (1880), p. xv; (1889–90), II: 617–693; Barnes, *op. cit.*, pp. 165–166.

15. Cubberley, *op. cit.*, pp. 707–711; U. S. Bureau of Education, *Biennial Survey: 1920–22*, I: 461–474.

16. Cremin, *op. cit.*, pp. 3–8; *The Forum*, Oct., 1892-June, 1893.

17. McKelvey, *Rochester*, III: 73, 81–85; Bayrd Still, *Milwaukee* (Madison, 1948), pp. 415–416; Charles Hirschfeld, *Baltimore, 1870–1900* [Johns Hopkins Studies, LIX, No. 2], pp. 84–132; Cremin, *op. cit.*, pp. 20–22, 86–87.

18. Charles A. Bennett, *History of Manual and Industrial Education Up to 1870* (Peoria, Ill., 1926), pp. 361–370; Charles A. Bennett, *History of Manual and Industrial Education, 1870–1917* (Peoria, 1937), pp. 310–389; Hartley Grattan, *In Quest of Knowledge* (New York, 1955), pp. 211–212; Cremin, *op. cit.*, pp. 23–34.

19. Lewis F. Anderson, *History of Manual and Industrial School Education* (New York, 1926), pp. 157–162, 180–190; U. S. Bureau of Education, *Art and Industry* [Special Reports] (1892), II: 355–447; (1898), IV: 13–202, 741–810; Bennett, *op. cit.* (1937), pp. 471–476.

20. Isaac E. Clarke, *Industrial and High Art Education in the United States* (Washington, 1885); Curti, *op. cit.*, pp. 236–239; Cremin, *op. cit.*, pp. 34–41.

21. Clarke, *op. cit.*, pp. 45–79, 295–303, 386–404; Bennett, *op. cit.* (1937), pp. 295–300 ff.

22. U. S. Bureau of Education, *Art and Industry* (1897), III: 448–728, 907–931; (1910), II: 1205–1247, 1277–1295.

23. "Industrial Education in the United States," U. S. Commissioner of Education *Report* (1910), I: 223–253; Layton S. Hawkins, C. A. Prosser, J. C. Wright, *Development of Vocational Education* (Chicago, 1951); Grattan, *op. cit.*, pp. 212–218; Bennett, *op. cit.* (1937), pp. 389–463.

24. U. S. Bureau of Education, *Art and Industry* (1892), II: 255–298, 327–333; Anderson, *op. cit.*, pp. 170–179; Thomas Woody, *A History of Women's Education in the United States* (New York, 1929), II: 57–64.

25. U. S. Commissioner of Education *Reports* (1880), pp. 480–491; (1889–1890), II: 2182–2199; John E. Stout, *The Development of High School Curricula in the North Central States from 1860 to 1918* (Chicago, 1921), pp. 74, 193, 288.

26. Stout, *op. cit.*, pp. 72–73, 179–180, 284, 287; Cubberley, *op. cit.*, pp. 506–528, 530–544, 549–555.

27. Cremin, *op. cit.*, pp. 135–142.

28. Henry S. Curtis, "Vacation Schools, Playgrounds and Settlements," U. S. Commissioner of Education *Report* (1903), I: 1–12; (1887–88), pp. 213–214; (1899–1900), I: 334–336; Cubberley, *op. cit.*, pp. 611–613.

29. U. S. Commissioner of Education *Reports* (1907), I: 432–437; (1910), I: 140–141; (1913), I: 435–449; Cubberley, *op. cit.*, pp 524–527, 555, 570, 577–587,

606–609; Still, *op. cit.*, p. 414; McKelvey, *Rochester,* III: 103–104, 111, 385; National Resources Committee, *Urban Government,* I: 10–11.
30. U. S. Commissioner of Education *Reports* (1888–89), I: 655–668; (1910), I: 137–138; (1911–12), I: 172–173.
31. U. S. Commissioner of Education *Reports* (1894–95), II: 1161–1170; (1899–1900).
32. Cubberley, *op. cit.*, pp. 428, 587–589; U. S. Commissioner of Education *Reports* (1880), pp. ccxxxix–ccxlii; (1910), II: 696, 770–778.
33. Schlesinger, *op. cit.*, pp. 171–172.
34. David Mead, *Yankee Eloquence in the Middle West: The Ohio Lyceum, 1850–1870* (East Lansing, 1951), pp. 201–238.
35. Schlesinger, *op. cit.*, pp. 172–174; J. H. Vincent, *The Chautauqua Movement* (Boston, 1886), pp. 1–92; U. S. Commissioner of Education *Reports* (1891–92), I: 937–945; (1894–95), 977–1077; (1899–1900), I: 300–302; Nicholas M. Butler, ed., *Education in the United States* (New York, 1910 ed.), pp. 824–864; Charles F. Horner, *The Life of James Redpath and the Development of the Modern Lyceum* (New York, 1926), pp. 119–250.
36. U. S. Bureau of Education, *Biennial Survey* (1924), I: 679–682.
37. Grattan, *op. cit.*, pp. 219–222; Thomas Davidson, *The Education of the Wage Earners* (Boston, 1904), pp. 96–220; Curti, *op. cit.*, pp. 240–242; Clarence A. Perry, *Wider Use of the School Plant* (New York, 1913), pp. 203–206; Cremin, *op. cit.*, pp. 70–75; Rischin, *op. cit.*, pp. 212–213, 216.
38. U. S. Commissioner of Education *Reports* (1911–12), I: 170–172; (1915), I: 44; McKelvey, *Rochester,* III: 95, 102, 106–107; Clarence E. Rainwater, *The Play Movement in the United States* (Chicago, 1922), pp. 92–116; [Edward J. Ward] *Rochester Social Centers and Civic Clubs* (Rochester, 1909); Perry, *op. cit.*, pp. 249–290.

CHAPTER 13: *Urban Recreation*

1. John A. Krout, *The Annals of American Sport* (New Haven, 1929), pp. 121–143; Jesse F. Steiner, *Americans at Play* (New York, 1933), pp. 6–8; Allan Nevins, *The Emergence of Modern America, 1865–1878* (New York, 1932), pp. 219–221; Schlesinger, *op. cit.*, pp. 311–312; Harold U. Faulkner, *The Quest for Social Justice, 1898–1914* (New York, 1937), pp. 285–286; Foster R. Dulles, *America Learns to Play* (New York, 1940), pp. 185–191.
2. Krout, *op. cit.*, pp. 172–181; Steiner, *op. cit.*, pp. 6–7; Nevins, *op. cit.*, pp. 223–224; Schlesinger, *op. cit.*, pp. 312–314; Dulles, *op. cit.*, pp. 191–196.
3. Krout, *op. cit.*, pp. 219–221; McKelvey, *Rochester,* III: 179–182.
4. Krout, *op. cit.*, pp. 185–213; 266–270; Schlesinger, *op. cit.*, pp. 316–317; U. S. Commissioner of Education *Reports* (1891–92), I: 494–589; (1896–97), I: 552–560.
5. Krout, *op. cit.*, pp. 122–140; McKelvey, *Rochester,* III: 175–182.
6. McKelvey, *Rochester,* II: 346, 349–350; III: 178; Dulles, *op. cit.*, pp. 230 ff.
7. Krout, *op. cit.*, pp. 36–56; Nevins, *op. cit.*, p. 219; Schlesinger, *op. cit.*, p. 309; Faulkner, *op. cit.*, pp. 288–289; Frank G. Menke, *The Encyclopedia of Sports* (New York, 1953), I: 576–579; Dulles, *op. cit.*, pp. 226, 239–243.
8. Krout, *op. cit.*, pp. 150–152, 229–231; Bayrd Still, *Milwaukee* (Madison, 1948), pp. 404–405; Schlesinger, *op. cit.*, pp. 309–310, 314–315; Faulkner, *op. cit.*, p. 290.
9. Krout, *op. cit.*, pp. 298–308; Faulkner, *op. cit.*, pp. 287, 293; Dulles, *op. cit.*, pp. 239–240; Earl Pomeroy, *In Search of the Golden West: The Tourist in Western America* (New York, 1957), pp. 6–72, *passim.*
10. Faulkner, *op. cit.*, pp. 282–284; U. S. Census Bureau, *Special Report on Street and Electric Railways* (1907), p. 93; Morris S. Daniels, *The Story of Ocean*

Grove: 1869–1919 (New York, 1919); Millard C. Faught, *Falmouth, Massachusetts, Problems of a Resort Community* (New York, 1945).

11. Rudi Blesh, *Shining Trumpets, A History of Jazz* (New York, 1946), pp. 217–219; Barry Ulanov, *A History of Jazz in America* (New York, 1954), pp. 79–81, 91–93; McKelvey, "The Port of Rochester," *Rochester History*, Oct., 1954, pp. 13–15.

12. Krout, *op. cit.*, pp. 282–285; Frank G. Menke, *Encyclopedia of Sports* (Chicago, 1939), p. 173.

13. Lloyd Morris, *Not So Long Ago* (New York, 1949), pp. 221–284; Dulles, *op. cit.*, pp. 308–312; McKelvey, *Rochester*, III: 183–186.

14. Joseph Lee, *Constructive and Preventive Philanthropy* (New York, 1902), pp. 148–153.

15. Clarence E. Rainwater, *The Play Movement in the United States* (Chicago, 1922), pp. 23, 50, 54; Lee, *op. cit.*, pp. 123–129.

16. Rainwater, *op. cit.*, pp. 55–63; Faulkner, *op. cit.*, p. 180; U. S. Commissioner of Education *Report* (1903), I: 9–21; Elizabeth Halsey, *The Development of Public Recreation in Metropolitan Chicago* (Chicago, 1940), pp. 20–28.

17. Halsey, *op. cit.*, pp. 24–47, and *passim;* McKelvey, *Rochester*, III: 175; Rainwater, *op. cit.*, pp. 17–22, 68–117; Steiner, *op. cit.*, pp. 15–21; Rowland Haynes, "Recreation Survey," Milwaukee Bureau of Economy and Research, *Bulletin*, No. 17, 1912.

18. Walter L. Stone, *The Development of Boys' Work in the United States* (Nashville, 1935), pp. 90–95; Rainwater, *op. cit.*, pp. 242–248; Charles E. Doell and Gerald B. Fitzgerald, *A Brief History of Parks and Recreation in the United States* (Chicago, 1954), pp. 57–59.

19. Alfred R. Conklin, *City Government in the United States* (New York, 1894), pp. 52–63; U. S. Census, *Statistics of Cities* (1905), p. 359.

20. Krout, *op. cit.*, pp. 259, 265; Faulkner, *op. cit.*, pp. 283–294; McKelvey, *Rochester*, III: 179–180.

21. P. Sargent, *Handbook of Summer Camps* (Boston, 1926 ed.), pp. 17–24; Stone, *op. cit.*, pp. 35–63; W. Oursler, *The Boy Scout Story* (New York, 1955), pp. 13–14, 34–35; R. K. Atkinson, *The Boys' Club* (New York, 1939), pp. 22–31; Schlesinger, *op. cit.*, p. 318

CHAPTER 14: *Entertainment and the Arts*

1. Robert Shaplin, "That Was New York: Delmonico," *The New Yorker*, Nov. 17, 1956, pp. 99–131; Bayrd Still, *Mirror for Gotham* (New York, 1956), pp. 176–177, 222–223, 235–236; Earl Pomeroy, *In Search of the Golden West* (New York, 1957); George A. Sala, *America Revisited* (London, 1885), pp. 187–273; William Archer, *America Today* (New York, 1899), pp. 98–107.

2. Dixon Wecter, *The Saga of American Society* (New York, 1937), pp. 286–288; Joseph N. Kane, *Famous First Facts* (New York, 1950), pp. 103, 390.

3. Glenn Hughes, *A History of the American Theatre: 1700–1950* (New York, 1951), pp. 215–227, 306–310; Montrose J. Moses, *The American Dramatist* (Boston, 1925), pp. 231–236; Oral S. Coad and Edwin Mims, Jr., *The American Stage* [Pageant of America Series, XIV] (New Haven, 1929), pp. 181–183; Lloyd Morris, *Curtain Time* (New York, 1953), pp. 155–175.

4. M. M. Davis, *Exploitation of Pleasure* (New York, 1911), pp. 14–17 (quoted in Scott E. W. Bedford, ed., *Readings in Urban Sociology* (New York, 1927), pp. 657–659; Foster R. Dulles, *America Learns to Play* (New York, 1940), pp. 220–223; Bayrd Still, *Milwaukee* (Madison, 1947), pp. 259–426; William G. Rose, *Cleveland, the Making of a City* (Cleveland, 1950), pp. 256, 496, 498.

5. Marshall Stearns, *The Story of Jazz* (New York, 1956), pp. 99–123, 140–164.

6. Arthur Hornblow, *A History of the Theatre in America* (Philadelphia, 1919), II: 238–317; Mary C. Crawford, *The Romance of the American Theatre* (Bos-

ton, 1925), pp. 204–205, 290–309, 219–354; Harlowe R. Hoyt, *Town Hall Tonight* (Englewood Cliffs, N. J., 1955), pp. 1–24 *passim,* see his numerous views of early city theaters; Morris, *op. cit.,* pp. 216–229, 240–271; Coad and Mims, *op. cit.,* pp. 252–264.

7. Arthur H. Quinn, *A History of the American Drama: From the Civil War to the Present Day* (2nd ed., New York, 1937), I: 212–296; Arthur M. Schlesinger, *The Rise of the City* (New York, 1933), pp. 290–296; Moses, *op. cit.,* pp. 277–291.

8. McKelvey, *Rochester,* III: 216–218; Morris, *op. cit.,* p. 265; Crawford, *op. cit.,* pp. 384–392.

9. Coad and Mims, *op. cit.,* pp. 264, 308–309; Hornblow, *op. cit.,* pp. 298–333; Moses, *op. cit.,* pp. 241–244, 351–359; Norman Hapgood, *The Stage in America: 1897–1900* (New York, 1901), pp. 6–38.

10. Hornblow, *op. cit.,* pp. 334–351; Alan S. Downes, *Fifty Years of American Drama, 1900–1950* (Chicago, 1951), pp. 1–10.

11. Schlesinger, *op. cit.,* pp. 291–292; U. S. *Census* (1880), I: 744; (1900), II: cxliv.

12. Coad and Mims, *op. cit.,* pp. 196–197; Moses, *op. cit.,* pp. 277–291; Dulles, *op. cit.,* pp. 217–219, 236–239; McKelvey, *Rochester,* III: 219–222.

13. Schlesinger, *op. cit.,* pp. 298–299; Dulles, *op. cit.,* pp. 216–217.

14. Cecil Smith, *Musical Comedy in America* (New York, 1950), pp. 3–152; Schlesinger, *op. cit.,* pp. 299–301; Dulles, *op. cit.,* p. 237; Stearns, *op. cit.,* pp. 109–122; Douglas Gilbert, *American Vaudeville: Its Life and Times* (New York, 1940), pp. 61–207; David Ewen, *The Story of America's Musical Theater* (Philadelphia, 1961), pp. 13–49, 58–76.

15. Gilbert, *op. cit.,* pp. 3–326; Hughes, *op. cit.,* Ch. XI; Harold U. Faulkner, *The Quest for Social Justice: 1898–1914* (New York, 1937), pp. 297–300; Ewen, *op. cit.,* pp. 46–57.

16. Morris, *op. cit.,* pp. 1–26; Faulkner, *op. cit.,* pp. 295–297; McKelvey, *Rochester,* III: 222–224.

17. Morris, *op. cit.,* pp. 27–64; Dulles, *op. cit.,* pp. 287–295.

18. Henry C. Lahee, *Annals of Music in America* (Boston, 1922), pp. 36–94.

19. Louis C. Elson, *The History of American Music* (2nd ed., New York, 1925), pp. 82–86; Lahee, *op. cit.,* pp. 56, 65.

20. Frank L. Dyer and T. C. Martin, *Edison, His Life and Inventions* (New York, 1910), II: 693–694; Elson, *op. cit.,* pp. 82–86; Schlesinger, *op. cit.,* pp. 302–305; U. S. Commissioner of Education *Reports* (1899–1900), I: 349–352; U. S. *Census* (1910), VIII: 494. The piano manufacturers more than doubled in number and increased the number of their employees and the value of their products tenfold. The Edison companies sold over 1,310,000 phonographs and 97,845,000 records before 1910.

21. John H. Mueller, *The American Symphony Orchestra* (Bloomington, 1951), pp. 101, 113; Pierce, *Chicago,* II: 426; III: 492–494; John T. Howard, *Our American Music* (New York, 1954), pp. 270–274.

22. Elson, *op. cit.,* pp. 55–60; Mueller, *op. cit.,* pp. 44–46, 55–56; 70–71, 79–83, 101–105, 123–125, 144–146; Schlesinger, *op. cit.,* pp. 306–307; Pierce, *Chicago,* III: 493–494.

23. Mueller, *op. cit.,* pp. 113–116, 122–125, 136–140, 144–148, 150–156, 161, 165, 174; Lahee, *op. cit.,* pp. 95–98, 117–119; Elson, *op. cit.,* pp. 68–79; Faulkner, *op. cit.,* pp. 267–270; McKelvey, *Rochester,* III: 198, 200–202.

24. Mueller, *op. cit.,* pp. 176, 187; Lahee, *op. cit.,* pp. 283, 297–298; Hugo Munsterberg, *The Americans* (London, 1905), pp. 476–478; Still, *Milwaukee,* pp. 406–408.

25. Lahee, *op. cit.,* pp. 294–295; Faulkner, *op. cit.,* pp. 268–270.

26. Elson, *op. cit.,* pp. 88–94; U. S. Commissioner of Education *Report* (1899–1900), I: 354–357.

27. J. W. McSpadden, *Opera and Musical Comedies* (New York, 1954), pp. 367, 523–525; Cecil Smith, *Musical Comedy in America* (New York, 1950), pp. 30–162; Isaac Goldberg, *Tin Pan Alley* (New York, 1930), pp. 60–233; Ewen, *op. cit.,* pp. 65–76.

28. H. W. Schwartz, *Bands in America* (Garden City, N. Y., 1957).
29. Rudi Blesh, *Shining Trumpets, A History of Jazz* (New York, 1946), pp. 108–112, 154–221; Stearns, *op. cit.*, pp. 1–164.

CHAPTER 15: *The Graphic Arts and the Sciences*

1. Samuel Isham, *The History of American Painting* (New York, 1927), pp. 363–396; Marchal E. Landgren, *Years of Art: The Story of the Art Students League* (New York, 1940), pp. 17–44; Oliver Larkin, *Art and Life in America* (New York, 1949), p. 265; David H. Dickason, *The Daring Young Men* (New York, 1953), pp. 141–143; U. S. Commissioner of Education *Report* (1914), I: 375–399; Eliot Clark, *History of the National Academy of Design, 1825–1953* (New York, 1954).
2. H. W. Henderson, *The Pennsylvania Academy of Fine Arts* (Boston, 1911), pp. 218–221; Isaac E. Clarke, *Education in the Industrial and Fine Arts in the United States* (U. S. Bureau of Education, Washington, 1885), pp. clv–clxxii, 45–77.
3. Edna M. Clark, *Ohio Art and Artists* (Richmond, 1932), pp. 125–130, 211–218; *American Art Annual* (1914), XI: 159–160; McKelvey, *Rochester*, II: 333–334.
4. Julia de Wolf Addison, *The Boston Museum of Fine Arts* (Boston, 1924); Corcoran Gallery, *Handbook* (1933), pp. 15–17; *Dictionary of American Biography*, IV: 440.
5. Winifred E. Howe, *A History of the Metropolitan Museum of Art* (New York, 1913), pp. vii–viii, 105–192; Aline B. Saarinen, *The Proud Possessors* (New York, 1958), pp. 72–74.
6. *American Art Annual* (1914), XI: 52–56, 87–91, 183–184, 283–285; Clark, *Ohio Art and Artists*, pp. 211–216; *Blue Book of the Buffalo Fine Arts Academy, 1931–1943* (Buffalo, 1943), pp. 20–24.
7. Sadakichi Hartmann, *A History of American Art* (New York, 1934 ed.), pp. 284–285; Hugo Münsterberg, *The Americans* (London, 1905), p. 491; Charles H. Caffin, *The Story of American Painting* (New York, 1907), pp. 160–164; Walter Pach, *The Art Museum in America* (New York, 1948), pp. 60–69, 88; U. S. Bureau of Education, *Art and Industry* [Special Report, IV] (1898), pp. xxiv–xlvi, lll; U. S. Commissioner of Education *Report* (1873), pp. xcvii, 802–808; Saarinen, *op. cit., passim.*
8. McKelvey, *Rochester*, III: 18–19, 206–208; Pach, *op. cit.*, pp. 80, 98–100, 118–120, 132–136.
9. *American Art Annual* (1914), XI: 165–166, 323–326, 332–334, 349; *ibid.* (1915), XII: 87; "Fields of Art in the United States," *Scribner's Magazine* (1896), XX: 649–652; Still, *op. cit.*, pp. 411–412; U. S. Commissioner of Education *Report* (1905), pp. 168–169.
10. *American Art Annual* (1914), XI: 12, 270, 283–285, 299–300; *ibid.* (1915), XII: 93–97; Carrie W. Whitney, *Kansas City, Mo.* (Chicago, 1908), pp. 596–598, 600–602; Portland Art Association, *50th Anniversary Exhibition* (Portland, Ore., 1942).
11. Howe, *op. cit.*, pp. 231, 256; Addison, *op. cit.*, pp. xvii–xx; *Dictionary of American Biography*, IV: 440; *American Art Annual* (1914), XI: 52, 87–91, 142–144, 332–334; Saarinen, *op. cit.*, pp. 82–87.
12. Larkin, *op. cit.*, pp. 311–317; *American Art Annual* (1914), XI: 235; U. S. Commissioner of Education *Report* (1899–1900), p. 340; Saarinen, *op. cit.*, pp. 12–16.
13. Pach, *op. cit.*, pp. 120, 169–176; *Buffalo Blue Book* (1943); Isham, *op. cit.*, pp. 390–396; Howe, *op. cit.*, pp. 215–216; Saarinen, *op. cit.*, pp. 15, 19, 97–99, 158–162.
14. Landgren, *op. cit.*, pp. 35–44, 59–85; *American Art Annual* (1914), XI: 12–14.

15. A. D. F. Hamlin, "Twenty-Five Years of American Architecture," *The Architectural Record* (July, 1916), 40: 1–14; Dickason, *op. cit.*, pp. 164–181; U. S. Bureau of Education, *Art and Industry* [Special Report, III] (Washington, 1897), pp. 448–610, 907–931; U. S. Commissioner of Education *Report* (1914), I: 399.

16. U. S. Commissioner of Education *Report* (1895–96), II: 1363–1366; (1905), pp. 161–169; (1913), I: 292–295.

17. Clark, *Ohio Art and Artists,* pp. 219–221; U. S. Commissioner of Education *Report* (1914), I: 502–503.

18. *American Art Annual* (1914), XI: 12–14, 230; U. S. Commissioner of Education *Report* (1905), p. 164; (1914), p. 508; Howe, *op. cit.*, pp. 244–247.

19. *U. S. Statistics of Cities* (1902 and 1903), pp. 241–243; (1906), pp. 161–165, 297–301; Howe, *op. cit.*, pp. 250–256; Saarinen, *op. cit.*, pp. 72–77, 82–84, 86–87.

20. *American Art Annual* (1914), pp. 12–18.

21. U. S. Bureau of Education, *Biennial Survey* (1924), I: 452.

22. U. S. Commissioner of Education *Report* (1893–94), pp. 1511–1534; Laurence V. Coleman, *Museum Buildings* (Washington, 1950), pp. 255–257.

23. E. G. Dexter, *A History of Education in the United States* (New York, 1904), p. 552; U. S. Commissioner of Education *Report* (1893–94), II: 1511–1551; Ralph S. Bates, *Scientific Societies in the United States* (New York, 1945), pp. 97–122; McKelvey, *Rochester,* II: 322, 357.

24. "Engineers Club of St. Louis," Association of Engineering Societies, *Journal* (1900), XXIV: 158–174; Frederick Starr, "The Davenport Academy of Natural Sciences," *Popular Science Monthly* (1897), LI: 83–98; Bates, *op. cit.*, pp. 96–121; McKelvey, *Rochester,* III: 20, 230–231.

25. Coleman, *op. cit.*, pp. 255–263; U. S. Commissioner of Education *Report* (1893–94), II: 1511–1562; (1913), I: 299–311; Alma S. Wittlin, *The Museum, Its History and Its Tasks in Education* (London, 1949), pp. 143–145; Münsterberg, *op. cit.*, pp. 433–435.

26. Grace F. Ramsey, *Educational Work in Museums of the United States* (New York, 1938), pp. 4–23, 69–82, 153–166; U. S. Commissioner of Education *Report* (1913), I: 302–306; (1915), I: 540–545; George B. Goode, "The Museum of the Future," Smithsonian Institution, *Annual Report* (1897), II: 259.

27. Laurence V. Coleman, *Company Museums* (Washington, 1943), pp. 105, 112, 151, 152; *American Art Annual* (1914), XI: 28; U. S. Bureau of Education, *Art and Industry* [Special Report, III] (1897), pp. 35–42.

28. Dexter, *op. cit.*, pp. 552; U. S. Commissioner of Education *Report* (1893–94), II: 1570–1615; Historical Societies in the United States, *A Handbook* (Washington, 1944).

29. The American Association for State and Local History, *Historical Societies in the United States and Canada, A Handbook* (Washington, 1944); *American Art Annual* (1914), XI: 28; Coleman, *Museum Buildings,* pp. 255–263; Richard Hofstadter, *The Age of Reform* (New York, 1955), pp. 138–140.

30. Albert B. Faust, *The German Element in the United States* (New York, 1927), II: 271–277, 390, 667–671; Emil Lengyel, *Americans from Hungary* (New York, 1948), pp. 156–205; Isaac B. Berkson, *Theories of Americanization* (New York, 1920), pp. 112–142; Peter Wiernik, *History of the Jews in America* (New York, 1912), pp. 247–249, 284–305; McKelvey, *Rochester,* III: 146–161; Thomas and Znaniecki, *op. cit.*, II: 1520–1644; Rowland T. Berthoff, *British Immigrants in Industrial America* (Cambridge, 1953), pp. 175–212; Joseph A. Wytrwal, *Americans of Polish Heritage* (Detroit, 1961), pp. 148–235.

31. Charles W. Ferguson, *Fifty Million Brothers* (New York, 1937); Noel P. Gist, *Secret Societies: A Cultural Study of Fraternalism in the United States* [University of Missouri Studies, 1940], pp. 9–12, 42–43, 129–131.

32. Mrs. J. C. Croly, *The History of the Woman's Club Movement in America* (New York, 1898), pp. 15–62, 85–88; M. I. Wood, *The History of the General Federation of Women's Clubs* (New York, 1912); McKelvey, *Rochester,* III: 194–197.

CHAPTER 16: *Literature and Learning in Cities*

1. U. S. Commissioner of Education *Reports* (1870), pp. 541–542; (1895–96), I: 340–521; (1899–1900), I: 923–1165.
2. Theodore W. Koch, *A Book of Carnegie Libraries* (New York, 1917); Burton J. Hendrick, *The Life of Andrew Carnegie* (New York, 1932), II: 200–207, 253–257.
3. Sidney Ditzon, *Arsenals of a Democratic Culture* (Chicago, 1947), pp. 97–164; Richard H. Hart, *Enoch Pratt, the Story of a Plain Man* (Baltimore, 1935), pp. 50–67.
4. U. S. Bureau of Education, *Public Libraries in the United States* [Special Report, I] (Washington, 1876).
5. Arthur E. Bostwick, *The American Public Library* (New York, 1929), pp. 15–16, 190–196, 213–231; Ditzon, *op. cit.,* pp. 175–176.
6. Effie L. Power, *Library Service for Children* (Chicago, 1930), pp. 3–7; Gwendolen Rees, *Libraries for Children: A History and a Bibliography* (London, 1924), pp. 86–134; Arthur Goldberg, *The Buffalo Public Library* (Buffalo, 1937), pp. 90, 115.
7. U. S. Commissioner of Education *Reports* (1899–1900), I: 304–312; (1913), I: 337–342; Ditzon, *op. cit.,* pp. 80–96; C. Hartley Grattan, *In Quest of Knowledge, A Historical Perspective on Adult Education* (New York, 1955), pp. 185–189.
8. John R. Morton, *University Extension in the United States* (Birmingham, Ala., 1953), pp. 9–20; McKelvey, *Rochester,* III: 20–21, 235.
9. Jesse B. Sears, "Philanthropy in the History of American Higher Education," *U. S. Bureau of Education Bulletin,* 1922, No. 26, pp. 53–80; R. H. Eckelberry, "History of the Municipal University in the United States," *U. S. Bureau of Education Bulletin,* 1932, No. 2, pp. 7–126; Charles F. Thwing, *A History of Higher Education in America* (New York, 1906), pp. 418–445.
10. W. Carson Ryan, "Studies in Early Graduate Education," Carnegie Foundation for the Advancement of Teaching, *Bulletin,* No. 30, 1939; B. McKelvey, "Professors Make Good Citizens," University of Rochester Library *Bulletin,* Spring, 1950; Richard Hofstadter and W. P. Metzger, *The Development of Academic Freedom in the United States* (New York, 1955), pp. 413–467.
11. John Dyer, *Ivory Towers in the Market Place* (Indianapolis, 1956), pp. 38–39.
12. U. S. Commissioner of Education *Report* (1893–94), II: 1563–1570; *The Literary Club of Cincinnati: 1849–1949* (Cincinnati, 1949); McKelvey, *Rochester,* III: 15–16, 225–230; Dixon Wecter, *The Saga of American Society* (New York, 1937), pp. 252–285; Joseph Hatton, *Henry Irving's Impressions of America* (London, 1884), pp. 261–263.
13. Franklin Walker, *San Francisco's Literary Frontier* (New York, 1939), pp. 116–283; Bernard Duffey, *The Chicago Renaissance in American Letters* (Michigan State College Press, 1954), pp. 51–67, 128–134; William Dean Howells, *Literary Friends and Acquaintances* (New York, 1902), pp. 113–288; James P. Wood, *Magazines in the United States* (2nd ed., New York, 1956), pp. 36, 80–104; Anna A. Chapin, *Greenwich Village* (New York, 1917), pp. 209–240.
14. Wood, *op. cit.,* pp. 105–164; Van Wyck Brooks, *The Confident Years, 1885–1915* (New York, 1952), pp. 1–20, 168; Frederick J. Hoffman, Charles Allen, C. F. Ulrich, *The Little Magazine, A History and a Bibliography* (Princeton, N. J., 1946), p. 7; Louis Filler, *Crusaders for American Liberalism* (New York, 1939), pp. 5–65 and *passim;* Frank L. Mott, *A History of American Magazines, 1885–1905* (Cambridge, 1947).
15. Wood, *op. cit.,* pp. 84–90; James M. Lee, *History of American Journalism* (revised ed., Boston, 1923), pp. 349–387.
16. H. W. Baehr, Jr., *The New York Tribune Since the Civil War* (New York, 1936), pp. 225–235; Mott, *op. cit.,* pp. 421–442.
17. F. L. Mott, *American Journalism* (New York, 1941), pp. 442–600; Lee, *op. cit.,*

pp. 317–404; Frederick G. Detweiler, *The Negro Press in the United States* (Chicago, 1922), pp. 24–62. See also Moses Rischin, *The Promised City: New York's Jews, 1870–1914* (Cambridge, 1962), pp. 115–143.
18. Grant C. Knight, *The Strenuous Age in American Literature: 1900–1910* (Chapel Hill, 1954); Louis Filler, *Crusaders for American Liberalism* (New York, 1939).
19. George A. Dunlap, *The City in the American Novel, 1789–1900* (Philadelphia, 1934); Louis Wann, *The Rise of Realism: 1860–1900* (New York, 1949); Robert H. Walker, "The Poet and the Rise of the City," *Mississippi Valley Historical Review,* June, 1962, pp. 85–99.
20. Blanche H. Gelfant, *The American City Novel* (Norman, 1954), pp. 42–97, 107–119; Dunlap, *op. cit.,* pp. 11–44; William V. O'Connor, *An Age of Criticism: 1900–1950* (Chicago, 1952); Marcus Cunliffe, "Stephen Crane and the American Background for Maggie," *American Quarterly* (Spring, 1955), pp. 31–44.
21. Wecter, *op. cit.,* pp. 134–237; Dunlap, *op. cit.,* pp. 100–127; Knight, *loc. cit.;* Mrs. John K. Van Rensselaer, *The Social Ladder* (New York, 1924); Hofstadter, *The Age of Reform,* pp. 131–172; C. Wright Mills, *The Power Elite* (New York, 1956), pp. 33–34, 39–55.
22. Duffey, *op. cit.,* pp. 27–74; Brooks, *op. cit.,* pp. 163–215; Dunlap, *op. cit.,* pp. 128–168.
23. Duffey, *op. cit.,* pp. 127–194.
24. U. S. Commissioner of Education *Report* (1894–95), II: 1124–1221; A. W. Small, "Fifty Years of Sociology in the United States (1865–1915)," *American Journal of Sociology* (1916), XXI: 734–768; William Diamond, "On the Dangers of an Urban Interpretation of History," pp. 69–78, in E. F. Goldman, ed., *Historiography and Urbanization* (Baltimore, 1941).
25. U. S. Commissioner of Education *Report* (1913), I: 292–294; Scott E. W. Bedford, ed., *Readings in Urban Sociology* (New York, 1927), pp. 620–622, 627, 636–641.
26. Frederic C. Howe, *The City: The Hope of Democracy* (New York, 1905), pp. 6–26; Samuel L. Loomis, *Modern Cities and Their Religious Problems* (New York, 1887), pp. 17–106; F. J. Kingsbury, "The Tendency of Men to Live in Cities," *Journal of Social Science,* Nov., 1895, pp. 1–17; Herbert Croly, *The Promise of American Life* (New York, 1914), pp. 7–26.

CHAPTER 17: *Metropolitan Regionalism*

1. A. M. Schlesinger, *The Rise of the City* (New York, 1933), pp. 80–81; Paul H. Johnstone, "Old Ideals versus New Ideas" in *Farmers in a Changing World* [U. S. Department of Agriculture *Year Book*] (Washington, 1940), pp. 111–170 (especially 159–167), 159–167.
2. Frederic C. Howe, *The Modern City and Its Problems* (New York, 1915), pp. 34–65.
3. Richard Hofstadter, *The Age of Reform* (New York, 1955), pp. 144–145.
4. Rupert B. Vance and N. J. Demerath, eds., *The Urban South* (Chapel Hill, 1954), pp. 28–37.
5. U. S. *Census* (1920), I: 50, 53, 64–75, lists 474 urban centers of 2500 or more not included in the 1910 tables; Graham R. Taylor, *Satellite Cities* (New York, 1915), pp. 237–259; Ida M. Tarbell, *New Ideals in Business* (New York, 1916), pp. 23–45; Herbert B. Doran and A. G. Hinman, *Urban Land Economics* (New York, 1928), pp. 94–95; Marion Clawson, R. B. Held, and C. H. Stoddard, *Land for the Future* (Baltimore, 1960).
6. Leo F. Schnore, "The Timing of Metropolitan Decentralization," *Journal of the American Institute of Planning,* XXV, Nov., 1959, pp. 200–206; Doran and

Hinman, *op. cit.*, pp. 99–101; Carl W. Condit, *The Rise of the Skyscraper* (Chicago, 1952), pp. 245–247; W. C. Clark and J. S. Kingston, *The Skyscraper* (New York, 1930), p. 6, reports a survey which found 185 skyscrapers in 40 cities in 1920. See also Christopher Tunnard and H. H. Reed, *American Skyline* (New York, 1955), pp. 206–209.

7. Schnore, *loc. cit.;* Warren S. Thompson, *Population, The Growth of Metropolitan Districts in the United States, 1900–1940* (Washington, 1948), pp. 5–7, 27–50; H. Paul Douglass, *The Suburban Trend* (New York, 1925), pp. 38–73; Amos H. Hawley, *The Changing Shape of Metropolitan America: Deconcentration Since 1920* (Glencoe, 1956), pp. 12–23.

8. H. H. McCarty, *Industrial Migration in the United States: 1914–1927* (Iowa City, 1930), pp. 65–76; Douglass, *op. cit.*, pp. 86–92; Doran and Hinman, *op. cit.*, pp. 102–111; Taylor, *op. cit.*, pp. 1–27 ff.; Hawley, *op. cit.*, pp. 130–139, 165–170; John G. Glover and William B. Cornell, *The Development of American Industries* (New York, 1951 ed.), p. 617.

9. U. S. *Census* (1920), I: 63–64, 76; III: 131; Glover and Cornell, *op. cit.*, pp. 203–219, 557–559, 808–818.

10. Lloyd Morris, *Not So Long Ago* (New York, 1949), pp. 296–297, 331–338.

11. Merrill Denison, *The Power to Go* (New York, 1956), pp. 92–180, 291; Ralph C. Epstein, *The Automobile Industry* (New York, 1928), pp. 14–101.

12. U. S. *Census* (1920), III: 128–239; Doran and Hinman, *op. cit.*, pp. 102–103; John W. Oliver, *History of American Technology* (New York, 1956), pp. 470–508; Harold U. Faulkner, *The Quest for Social Justice* [A History of American Life, XI] (New York, 1937), pp. 130–139; Morris, *op. cit.*, p. 321.

13. Doran and Hinman, *op. cit.*, pp. 102–103; William L. Bailey, "The Twentieth Century City," *American City*, XXXI (Aug., 1924), pp. 142–143; Thompson, *op. cit.*, pp. 1–12; Glenn E. McLaughlin, *The Growth of American Manufacturing Areas* (Pittsburgh, 1938), pp. 81–89, 98–99.

14. Douglass, *op. cit.*, pp. 87–92 ff.; Taylor, *op. cit.*, pp. 1–214; Harry Hansen, *Scarsdale* (New York, 1954).

15. Oliver, *op. cit.*, pp. 467–471; Faulkner, *op. cit.*, pp. 155–156.

16. Leo Grebler, David M. Blank, and Louis Winnick, *Capital Formation in Residential Real Estate* (Princeton, 1956), pp. 23, 38–40, 45–47, 82, 100, 114–122, 162–171; Oliver, *op. cit.*, pp. 465–471; Conference on Research in Income and Wealth, *Problems of Capital Formation* (Princeton, 1957), pp. 18–22, 40; U. S. National Resources Committee, *Urban Planning and Land Policies* (Washington, 1939), pp. 165–167 ff.

17. Hofstadter, *op. cit.*, pp. 215–217; Warren S. Thompson and P. K. Whelpton, *Population Trends in the United States* (New York, 1933), *passim*.

18. Niles Carpenter, *Immigrants and Their Children* (U. S. Census, *Monograph* VII, 1927), pp. 385–388, 395–397, 407–408; Thompson and Whelpton, *op. cit.*, pp. 293–311; Hofstadter, *op. cit.*, p. 177; John Higham, *Strangers in the Land* (New Brunswick, 1955), pp. 158–165.

19. Higham, *op. cit.*, pp. 165–186; Samuel P. Hayes, *The Response to Industrialism: 1885–1914* (Chicago, 1957), pp. 125–129; George Mowry, *The California Progressives* (Berkeley, 1951).

20. Higham, *op. cit.*, pp. 186–193, 239–240; Carl Wittke, *We Who Built America* (New York, 1940), pp. 498–507.

21. Carpenter, *op. cit.*, pp. 158–168, 205, 409; National Resources Committee, *Population Statistics,* III, *Urban* (Washington, 1937), pp. 8, 15 ff.; U. S. *Census* (1920), III: 148 ff.; Thompson and Whelpton, *op. cit.*, Tables 34 and 52.

22. Louis Filler, *Crusaders for American Liberalism* (New York, 1939), pp. 268–273; National American Woman Suffrage Association, *Victory, How Women Won It* (New York, 1940), pp. 76–94, 107–139.

23. Carpenter, *op. cit.*, p. 389 ff. The Germans still led in St. Louis, the Irish in Boston. See also Faulkner, *op. cit.*, pp. 12–17.

24. Niles Carpenter, "Migration Between City and Country in the Buffalo Metropolitan Area," in N. E. Himes, eds., *Economics, Sociology, and the Modern World* (Cambridge, 1935), pp. 269–291; C. Warren Thornthwait, *Internal Mi-*

gration in the United States (Washington, 1934), pp. 24–31; Sidney Goldstein, "Repeated Migration as a Factor in High Mobility Rates," *American Sociological Review* (Oct., 1915), XIX: 536–541; Dorothy S. Thomas, *Research Memorandum on Migration Differentials* [Social Science Research Bulletin 43] (New York, 1938), pp. 175–268.

25. Douglass, *op. cit.,* pp. 1–73; Thompson and Whelpton, *op. cit.,* pp. 29–32; R. C. Epstein, *The Automobile Industry* (Chicago, 1928), pp. 14–18, 317; E. P. Schmidt, *Industrial Relations in Urban Transportation* (Minneapolis, 1937), pp. 23–25.

26. Douglass, *op. cit.,* pp. 74–270; U. S. *Census* (1920), I: 63–72. We need more evidence concerning political trends in the suburbs.

27. Elizabeth S. Johnson, "Child Labor Legislation," in Commons, *History of Labour,* III: 406–450; McKelvey, *Rochester,* III: 133, 289; Faulkner, *op. cit.,* pp. 184–188; Lorene M. Pacey, *Readings in the Development of Settlement Work* (New York, 1950), pp. 222–225; Josephine Goldmark, *Impatient Crusader: Florence Kelley's Life Story* (Urbana, Ill., 1953), pp. 78–100.

28. Elizabeth Brandeis, "Labor Legislation," in Commons, *History of Labour,* III: 466–514; Mowry, *The California Progressives,* pp. 144–145; Hofstadter, *op. cit.,* p. 240; Alice Henry, *The Trade Union Woman* (New York, 1915), pp. 61–88; Alpheus T. Mason, *Brandeis: A Free Man's Life* (New York, 1946), pp. 248–254; Goldmark, *op. cit.,* pp. 143–191.

29. *Recent Social Trends,* I: 711–721; Joseph A. Hill, *Women in Gainful Occupations: 1870–1920* [Census *Monograph,* IX] (Washington, 1929); Leo Wolman, *The Growth of American Trade Unions, 1880–1923* (New York, 1924), pp. 33, 91–108 ff.; Henry, *op. cit.,* p. 145 ff.

30. Harry Weiss, "Employers' Liability and Workmen's Compensation," in Commons, *History of Labour,* III: 564–577; Marguerite Green, *The National Civic Federation and the American Labor Movement: 1900–1925* (Washington, 1956), pp. 245–265; I. M. Rubinow, *Social Insurance* (New York, 1916 ed.), pp. 169–184.

31. Harwood L. Childs, *Labor and Capital in National Politics* (Columbus, O., 1930), pp. 9–14, 65–69, 110–114.

32. Robert H. Wiebe, "Business Disunity and the Progressive Movement, 1901–1914," *Mississippi Valley Historical Review,* March, 1958, pp. 664–685.

33. Mowry, *op. cit.,* pp. 38–56, 143–147; Grace H. Stimson, *The Rise of the Labor Movement in Los Angeles* (Berkeley, 1955), pp. 366–406.

34. Tarbell, *op. cit.;* M. Green, *op. cit.,* pp. 37–89; Faulkner, *op. cit.,* pp. 60–61. See also Rischin, *op. cit.,* pp. 243–252.

35. Mason, *op. cit.,* pp. 290–306; Jean T. McKelvey, ed., *Profession of Labor Arbitration* (Washington, 1957), p. 5.

36. Louis N. Robinson and Rolf Nugent, *Regulation of Small Loan Business* (New York, 1935), pp. 48–104; John M. Glenn, L. Brandt and F. E. Andrews, *Russell Sage Foundation: 1907–1946* (New York, 1947), pp. 136–151.

37. Robinson and Nugent, *op. cit.,* pp. 89–94; Wesley C. Mitchell, *Business Cycles* (New York, 1927), p. 369; Raymond J. Saulnier, *Industrial Banking Companies and Their Credit Practices* (New York, 1940), pp. 1, 15–17.

38. Laurence Laughlin, *The Federal Reserve Act, Its Origin and Problems* (New York, 1933), pp. 3–14; Paul M. Warburg, *The Federal Reserve System: Its Origin and Growth* (New York, 1930), I: 11–33; Henry P. Willis, *The Federal Reserve System* (New York, 1923), pp. 1–23.

39. Laughlin, *op. cit.,* pp. 15–58; Warburg, *op. cit.,* I: 582–586; Charles A. Hales, *The Baltimore Clearing House* (Baltimore, 1940), pp. 104–111; Willis, *op. cit.,* pp. 33–84; Arthur S. Link, *Wilson: The New Freedom* (Princeton, 1956), pp. 199–201.

40. Laughlin, *op. cit.,* pp. 56–137; Warburg, *op. cit.,* I: 34–177; Willis, *op. cit.,* pp. 84–135.

41. George E. Mowry, *Theodore Roosevelt and the Progressive Movement* (Madison, 1946), pp. 274–283; Henry F. Pringle, *Theodore Roosevelt* (New York, 1931), pp. 201–215; Arthur S. Link, *Wilson: The Road to the White House*

(Princeton, 1947), pp. 467–528; William Diamond, *The Economic Thought of Woodrow Wilson* (Baltimore, 1943), pp. 87–98; Herbert Croly, *The Promise of American Life* (New York, 1909); Goldman, *op. cit.*, pp. 188–217; John W. Davidson, ed., *A Crossroads of Freedom: The 1912 Campaign Speeches of Woodrow Wilson* (New Haven, 1956). See G. Warren Nutter, *The Extent of Enterprise Monopoly in the United States, 1899–1939* (Chicago, 1951) for a statistical study of the relative size of monopoly-controlled industry at various dates from 1899 to 1939.

42. Warburg, *op. cit.*, II: 231–302; Laughlin, *op. cit.*, pp. 100–208; Carter Glass, *An Adventure in Constructive Finance* (New York, 1927), pp. 1–254; Willis, *op. cit.*, pp. 116–167; Arthur S. Link, *Woodrow Wilson and the Progressive Era: 1910–1917* (New York, 1954), pp. 43–47.

43. Glass, *op. cit.*, pp. 93–132; Willis, *op. cit.*, pp. 168–260; Link, *Wilson, The Progressive Era*, pp. 47–53; *idem.*, *Wilson: The New Freedom*, pp. 202–240; Mason, *op. cit.*, pp. 397–399.

44. *The Location of Reserve Districts in the United States* [U. S. Senate Document, 63rd Congress, 2nd Session, Vol. 16] (Washington, 1914); Willis, *op. cit.*, pp. 561–597.

45. Hale, *op. cit.*, pp. 21, 120–128; W. E. Spahr, *The Clearing and Collection of Checks* (New York, 1926), p. 161; G. W. Woodworth, *The Detroit Money Market* (Ann Arbor, 1932), pp. 18–20, 40–45; Twentieth Century Fund, *The Security Markets* (New York, 1935), pp. 748–754.

46. Alfred M. Lee, *The Daily Newspapers in America* (New York, 1937), pp. 527–528; *World Almanac* (1916), p. 469.

47. Mason, *op. cit.*, pp. 400–408; Link, *Wilson, The New Freedom*, pp. 417–444; *idem.*, *Wilson and the Progressive Era*, pp. 66–73; Richard L. Watson, Jr., "Woodrow Wilson and His Interpreters: 1947–1957," *Mississippi Valley Historical Review*, Sept. 1957, pp. 212–219.

48. Link, *Wilson and the Progressive Era*, pp, 67–80; Hofstadter, *op. cit.*, pp. 230–232, 242–252; Mason, *op. cit.*, pp. 400–408; Diamond, *op. cit.*, pp. 98–112.

49. John Kouwenhoven, *The Beer Can by the Highway* (New York, 1961), pp. 39–73.

CHAPTER 18: *Civic and Social Armageddon*

1. Richard Hofstadter, *The Age of Reform* (New York, 1955), pp. 148–163, 185–196.

2. Frank M. Stewart, *A Half Century of Municipal Reform* (Berkeley, 1950), pp. 50–65, 164–165.

3. Walter T. Arndt, *The Emancipation of the American City* (New York, 1917), pp. 35, 89, 261–285; Frederic C. Howe, *The City, the Hope of Democracy* (New York, 1909 ed.), pp. 76–81, 149–164; Robert H. Bremner, "The Civic Revival in Ohio," *American Journal of Economics and Sociology*, XI, pp. 99–110; E. P. Schmidt, *Industrial Relations in Urban Transportation* (Minneapolis, 1937), pp. 56–67.

4. George E. Mowry, *The California Progressives* (Berkeley, 1951), pp. 11–114; Alpheus T. Mason, *Brandeis: A Free Man's Life* (New York, 1946), pp. 88–241; Arthur S. Link, *Wilson: The Road to the White House* (Princeton, 1947), pp. 122–132, 245–269.

5. Arndt, *op. cit.*, pp. 73–78, 134–135; Stewart, *op. cit.*, pp. 94–95, 98–102; William P. Lovett, *Detroit Rules Itself* (Boston, 1930), pp. 34–69; McKelvey, *Rochester*, III: 69–70, 264; Richard S. Childs, *Civic Victories* (New York, 1952).

6. Frederic C. Howe, *The Modern City* (New York, 1915), pp. 99–104; Harold U. Faulkner, *The Quest for Social Justice, 1898–1914* (New York, 1937), pp. 85–

86; Stewart, *op. cit.*, pp. 95–96; Donald W. Disbrow, "The Progressive Movement in Philadelphia: 1910–1916," Ph.D. Thesis, University of Rochester, 1956, pp. 47–97.

7. Howe, *The Modern City*, pp. 99–116; Arndt, *op. cit.*, pp. 78–87; Stewart, *op. cit.*, pp. 73–76; Chester E. Rightor, *City Manager in Dayton* (New York, 1919); Harold A. Stone, D. K. Price, and K. H. Stone, *City Manager Government in the United States* (Chicago, 1940), pp. 6–32.

8. William D. Miller, *Memphis: During the Progressive Era: 1900–1917* (Memphis, 1957), pp. 64–180.

9. Stewart, *op. cit.*, p. 75; National Resources Committee, *Urban Government*, I: 185–186.

10. Stewart, *op. cit.*, pp. 89–90, 102–104, 140–141; Norman N. Gill, *Municipal Research Bureaus* (Washington, 1944), pp. 17–19, 27–28; Lorin Peterson, *The Day of the Mugwump* (New York, 1961), pp. 46–58, 144, and *passim*.

11. Carl D. Thompson, *Public Ownership* (New York, 1925), pp. 222–230, 252–260, 269, 307–320; Howe, *The Modern City*, pp. 170–171; Stewart, *op. cit.*, pp. 36, 59; Faulkner, *op. cit.*, pp. 120–128.

12. National Municipal League, *The Government of Metropolitan Areas in the United States* (New York, 1930), pp. 62–68, 120–134, 203–224, 252–271; National Resources Committee, *Urban Government*, I: 31–33; Arthur N. Holcombe, *State Government in the United States* (New York, 1931), pp. 288–290; Stewart, *op. cit.*, p. 76.

13. Lovett, *op. cit.*, pp. 34–36; Frederic C. Howe, *The Confessions of a Reformer* (New York, 1925), p. 240 ff.

14. John M. Glenn, Lillian Brandt, and F. E. Andrews, *Russell Sage Foundation, 1907–1946* (New York, 1947).

15. Frank D. Watson, *The Charity Organization Movement in the United States* (New York, 1922), pp. 337–365; Glenn, Brandt, and Andrews, *op. cit.*, pp. 125–135; Vance and Demerath, *op. cit.*, pp. 254–257.

16. Watson, *op. cit.*, p. 359; John A. Ryan, *Social Doctrine in Action: A Personal History* (New York, 1941), pp. 121–127.

17. Watson, *op. cit.*, pp. 366–399; 411–413; Glenn, etc., *op. cit.*, pp. 85–96, 102–114.

18. Watson, *op. cit.*, pp. 399–406.

19. Watson, *op. cit.*, pp. 407–410, 419–428; Ernest V. Hollis and A. L. Taylor, *Social Work Education in the United States* (New York, 1951), pp. 12–17.

20. Watson, *op. cit.*, pp. 240–243, 401–402, 428–436; Rupert B. Vance and N. J. Demerath, eds., *The Urban South* (Chapel Hill, 1954), pp. 254–256; McKelvey, *Rochester*, III: 319.

21. Glenn, etc., *op. cit.*, pp. 177–190; McKelvey, *Rochester*, III: 111; Shelby M. Harrison, *Social Conditions in an American City* [Springfield Survey] (New York, 1920); Francis H. McLean, *The Charities of Springfield, Ill.* (New York, 1915); Allen Eaton, ed., *A Bibliography of Social Surveys* (Russell Sage, N. Y., 1930), pp. xvi–xxiii, 1–450.

22. R. A. Woods and A. J. Kennedy, *The Settlement Horizon* (New York, 1922), pp. 351–361, 397–400; H. W. Zorbaugh, *Gold Coast and Slum* (Chicago, 1929), pp. 201–210; Wilbur C. Phillips, *Adventuring for Democracy* (New York, 1940), pp. 140–149; Clarence E. Rainwater, *The Play Movement* (Chicago, 1922), pp. 91–117.

23. *General Statistics of Cities* (1916), pp. 71–87; Rainwater, *op. cit.*, pp. 91–168; Scott E. W. Bedford, ed., *Readings in Urban Sociology* (New York, 1927), pp. 620–641; Rowland Haynes, *Recreation Survey* [Milwaukee Bureau of Economy and Efficiency, *Bulletin,* 17] (Milwaukee, 1912).

24. Robert A. Walker, *The Planning Function of Urban Government* (Chicago, 1941), pp. 231–239; Lloyd Lewis and Henry J. Smith, *Chicago, The History of Its Reputation* (New York, 1929), pp. 312–322.

25. F. L. Olmstead, "The Town Planning Movement in America," *Annals* (Jan. 1914), LI: 172–181; Walker, *op. cit.*, pp. 12–20, 133–140; Christopher Tunnard and H. H. Reed, *American Skyline* (Boston, 1955), pp. 191–193, 212–213.

26. Faulkner, *op. cit.*, pp. 282–284; George B. Ford, "The Park System of Kansas City, Mo.," *Architectural Record* (Dec., 1916), XL: 499–504; Roland Cotterill, "The Parks, Playgrounds and Boulevards of Seattle," *American City* (1912), VII: 204–207; *General Statistics of Cities*, 1916, pp. 12–15, 22.
27. Walker, *op. cit.*, pp. 50–67; Lewis and Smith, *op. cit.*, I: 259–260; James Ford and collaborators, *Slums and Housing* (Cambridge, 1936), I: 227–233.
28. Walker, *op. cit.*, pp. 10–12; Ford, etc., *op. cit.*, I: 122–225.
29. Edith E. Wood, *The Housing of the Unskilled Wage Earner* (New York, 1919), pp. 45–58, 80–90; E. E. Wood, *Slums and Blighted Areas in the United States* [Housing Division *Bulletin* I] (Washington, 1935), pp. 35–68; Robert W. De Forest, "A Brief History of the Housing Movement in America," *Annals,* Jan., 1914, LI: 8–16; J. T. Holdsworth, *Report of the Economic Survey of Pittsburgh* (Pittsburgh, 1912), pp. 31–45.
30. Wood, *Housing the Unskilled*, pp. 91–114; R. W. De Forest and L. Veiller, *The Tenement House Problem* (New York, 1903), I: 97–116.
31. Tunnard and Reed, *op. cit.*, pp. 206–208, 220–223; Talbot F. Hamlin, *The American Spirit in Architecture* [Pageant of America, XIII] (New Haven, 1926), p. 286.
32. Clarence A. Perry, *Housing for the Machine Age* (New York, 1939), pp. 205–211; Lewis and Smith, *op. cit.*, pp. 6–15.
33. Eaton, *op. cit.*, pp. 38–46, 85–88, 312–315; Frederic M. Thrasher, *The Gang* (Chicago, 1936 ed.), pp. 17, 38–39, 510–518; Herbert Asbury, *The Gangs of New York* (New York, 1937), p. 296 ff.
34. Louise de Koven Bowen, *Growing Up with a City* (New York, 1926), pp. 104–140; William N. Gemmill, "Chicago Court of Domestic Relations," *Annals* (Jan., 1914), LI: 115–123.
35. Paul G. Cressey, *The Taxi-Dance Hall* (Chicago, 1932), pp. 177–195; Bowen, *op. cit.*, pp. 121–125.
36. Walter C. Reckless, *Vice in Chicago* (Chicago, 1933), pp. 1–77; Bowen, *op. cit.*, pp. 128–130; Eaton, *op. cit.*, pp. 302–303, 325–327.
37. Reckless, *op. cit.*, pp. 99–266.
38. E. H. Sutherland and E. C. Ghelke, "Crime and Punishment," *Recent Social Trends* (New York, 1933), II: 1125–1127; National Resources Committee, *Urban Government* (1939), I: 250–270.
39. Herbert Asbury, *The Great Illusion* (New York, 1950), pp. 120–126; Charles Merz, *The Dry Decade* (New York, 1931), pp. 1–20; Paul A. Carter, *The Decline and Revival of the Social Gospel: Social and Political Liberalism in American Protestant Churches, 1920–1940* (Ithaca, 1956), pp. 31–37.

CHAPTER 19: *Cultural Fulfillment and Disenchantment*

1. Charles H. Hopkins, *The Rise of the Social Gospel in American Protestantism: 1865–1915* (New Haven, 1940), pp. 281–283, 312–317; Charles Stelzle, *A Son of the Bowery* (New York, 1926), pp. 1–166.
2. Hopkins, *op. cit.*, pp. 288–298, 316–317; Harold U. Faulkner, *The Quest for Social Justice: 1898–1914* (New York, 1937), pp. 209–213, 219–221.
3. Charles Stelzle, *American Social and Religious Conditions* (New York, 1912), pp. 234–240; Stelzle, *Son of the Bowery*, pp. 154–155.
4. Henry F. May, *Protestant Churches and Industrial America* (New York, 1949), pp. 235–262; Hopkins, *op. cit.*, pp. 233–244; Paul A. Carter, *The Decline and Revival of the Social Gospel* (Ithaca, 1956), pp. 11–14.
5. Faulkner, *op. cit.*, pp. 67, 108; Frederick E. Haynes, *Social Politics in the United States* (New York, 1924), pp. 213–215; Henry F. May, *The End of American Innocence* (New York, 1959), pp. 12–14.
6. Hopkins, *op. cit.*, pp. 280–301; Francis Downing, "American Catholicism and

the Socio-Economic Revolution in the United States," in J. N. Moody, ed., *Church and Society* (New York, 1953), pp. 858–876; McKelvey, *Rochester,* III: 138–139, 143–144; Carter, *op. cit.,* pp. 14–15; Aaron I. Abell, *American Catholicism and Social Action* (Garden City, N. Y., 1960).

7. Herbert W. Schneider, *Religion in Twentieth Century America* (Cambridge, 1952), pp. 1–20; William T. Ellis, *Billy Sunday, The Man and His Message* (Philadelphia, 1936), pp. 485–517. See also Paul A. Carter, *The Decline and Revival of the Social Gospel: Social and Political Liberalism in American Protestant Churches, 1920–1940* (Ithaca, 1954); May, *op. cit.,* pp. 126–127.

8. Faulkner, *op. cit.,* pp. 189–196; William E. Drake, *The American School in Transition* (New York, 1955), pp. 456–460.

9. Merle Curti, *The Social Ideas of American Educators* (New York, 1935), pp. 242–245.

10. Arthur Mann, *Yankee Reformers in the Urban Age* (Cambridge, 1954), pp. 126–144.

11. Charles A. Bennett, *History of Manual and Industrial Education, 1870–1917* (Peoria, Ill., 1937), pp. 517–542; H. G. Good, *A History of American Education* (New York, 1956), pp. 446–447.

12. Bennett, *op. cit.,* pp. 528–537, 542–550; Layton S. Hawkins, C. A. Prosser, and J. C. Wright, *Development of Vocational Education* (Chicago, 1951), pp. 1–122.

13. U. S. Commissioner of Education *Report* (1914), I: 44–52, 147–157; Drake, *op. cit.,* p. 461; *Recent Social Trends,* I: 337–338.

14. Faulkner, *op. cit.,* pp. 194–196; R. H. Eckelberry, *The History of the Municipal University in the United States* [U. S. Bureau of Education *Bulletin* (1932), No. 2], pp. 5–7, 31–33, 57–60, 70–79, 109–160, 165–189; John Dyer, *Ivory Tower in the Market Place* (Indianapolis, 1956), pp. 35–37, 188–189.

15. C. H. Grattan, *In Quest of Knowledge: An Historical Perspective on Adult Education* (New York, 1955), pp. 185–193, 212–222; Isaac B. Berkson, *Theories of Americanization: A Critical Study* (New York, 1920), pp. 55–107.

16. Drake, *op. cit.,* p. 425; Good, *op. cit.,* pp. 397–405; U. S. Commissioner of Education *Report* (1914), I: 37–60, 531–536.

17. U. S. Commissioner of Education *Report* (1907), pp. 432–437; (1915), I: 409–431; *Recent Social Trends,* I: 378–379.

18. U. S. Commissioner of Education *Report* (1913), I: 435–449; (1920–22), I: 679–682.

19. U. S. Commissioner of Education *Report* (1913), I: 326–341; *Library Journal,* July 1914, pp. 521–522; Nov. 1914, pp. 823–830; *Annals,* Nov. 1924, pp. 66–68, 116.

20. Laurence V. Coleman, *Museum Buildings* (Washington, 1950), pp. 3, 263–265; U. S. Commissioner of Education *Report* (1914), I: 498–508; (1915), I: 540–557; B. McKelvey, "The Historic Origins of Rochester's Museums," *Rochester History,* October, 1956, pp. 13–15.

21. Coleman, *op. cit.,* pp. 3, 28, 111, 150, 171, 265; *The Architectural Record,* September, 1916; Ralph Purcell, *Government and Art* (Washington, 1956), pp. 36–38; U. S. Commission of Education *Report* (1915), I: 546–550.

22. Beaumont Newhall, *The History of Photography* (New York, 1949), pp. 119–139; Oliver W. Larkin, *Art and Life in America* (New York, 1949), pp. 325–327, 354–360; Aline B. Saarinen, *The Proud Possessors* (New York, 1958), p. 198.

23. Larkin, *op. cit.,* pp. 360–367; *Art and Progress* (April, 1913), pp. 925–932, 940; May, *op. cit.,* pp. 244–246.

24. See Henry F. May, "The Rebellion of the Intellectuals, 1912–1917," *American Quarterly* (Summer, 1956), pp. 114–126.

25. John H. Mueller, *The American Symphony Orchestra* (Bloomington, Ind., 1951), pp. 48–181; Louis C. Elson, *The History of American Music* (New York, 1925), pp. 67–87.

26. H. W. Schwartz, *Bands of America* (Garden City, N. Y., 1957), pp. 237–260;

McKelvey, *Rochester,* III: 204–205; Claude Bragdon, *More Lives Than One* (New York, 1938), pp. 71–77.

27. Gilbert Chase, *American Music from the Pilgrims to the Present* (New York, 1955), pp. 433–484; Rudi Blesh, *Shining Trumpets: A History of Jazz* (New York, 1946), pp. 218–225; Marshall W. Stearns, *The Story of Jazz* (New York, 1956), pp. 67–108.

28. Glenn Hughes, *A History of the American Theater* (New York, 1951), pp. 355–359; Douglas Gilbert, *American Vaudeville: Its Life and Times* (New York, 1940), pp. 228–394.

29. Hughes, *op. cit.,* pp. 362–373; Constance D. Mackay, *The Little Theater in the United States* (New York, 1917), pp. 14–23 ff.; Bernard Duffey, *The Chicago Renaissance in American Letters* (Michigan State College, 1954), pp. 239–246; May, *End of American Innocence,* pp. 253, 288–290; Rischin, *op. cit.,* pp. 133–137, 218.

30. Hughes, *op. cit.,* pp. 378–379; Lloyd Morris, *Not So Long Ago* (New York, 1949), pp. 42–127; McKelvey, *Rochester,* III: 222–224.

31. Hughes, *op. cit.,* pp. 367, 376–377; John T. Howard, *Our American Music* (New York, 3rd ed., 1954), p. 742.

32. May, *op. cit.,* pp. 56–64, 298–301; McKelvey, *Rochester,* III: 234–240.

33. C. D. Harris, "A Functional Classification of Cities in the United States," *Geographic Review* (1943), XXXIII: 86–99; for a sociological analysis of a university city, see Kimball Young, J. L. Gillin, and C. L. Dedrick, *The Madison Community* [University of Wisconsin Studies in Social Science and History, No. 21] (Madison, 1934).

34. John C. French, *A History of the University Founded by Johns Hopkins* (Baltimore, 1946), pp. 88–118, 166–179; McKelvey, "Professors Make Good Citizens," University of Rochester Library *Bulletin,* Spring, 1950.

35. Richard Hofstadter and C. DeWitt Hardy, *The Development and Scope of Higher Education in the United States* (New York, 1952), pp. 46–47, 57–67; Merle Curti, ed., *American Scholarship in the Twentieth Century* (Cambridge, 1953), pp. 18, 38–41; Merle Curti and Vernon Carstensen, *The University of Wisconsin* (Madison, 1949), II: 3, 24, 71–72, 100, 109, 549.

36. Richard Hofstadter and W. P. Metzger, *The Development of Academic Freedom in the United States* (New York, 1955), pp. 413–477; Curti, ed., *American Scholarship,* pp. 19–23.

37. Curti and Carstensen, *op. cit.,* II: 187–196; Curti, ed., *American Scholarship,* pp. 38–46.

38. Curti, ed., *American Scholarship,* pp. 48–59, 171–186; T. V. Smith and L. D. White, eds., *Chicago, An Experiment in Social Science Research* (Chicago, 1929), pp. 4–13; George A. Lundberg, Read Bain and Nels Anderson, eds., *Trends in American Sociology* (New York, 1929), pp. 261–296; A. B. Hollingshead, "Community Research," *American Sociology Review,* April, 1948, pp. 136–140; May, *op. cit.,* pp. 153–165.

39. Duffey, *op. cit.,* pp. 3–193; Frederick J. Hoffman, C. Allen, and C. F. Ulrick, *The Little Magazine* (Princeton, 1946), pp. 1–17; Alfred Kazin, *On Native Grounds* (New York, 1942), pp. 169–173; May, *op. cit., passim;* Rischin, *op. cit.,* pp. 121–133.

40. Blanche H. Gelfant, *The American City Novel* (Norman, Okla., 1954), pp. 42–94; V. F. Calverton, *The Liberation of American Literature* (New York, 1932), pp. 406–413; Alfred Kazin and Charles Shapiro, *The Stature of Theodore Dreiser* (New York, 1955); see also Theodore Dreiser, *The Color of a Great City* (New York, 1923).

41. Duffey, *op. cit.,* pp. 132–138, 143–167, 172–193; Calverton, *op. cit.,* pp. 413–417; Ludwig Lewisohn, *Expression in America* (New York, 1932), pp. 367–392; Lewis Atherton, *Main Street on the Middle Border* (Bloomington, Ind., 1954), pp. 285–329; May, *op. cit.,* pp. 251–271.

42. Kazin, *op. cit.,* pp. 165–173; Duffey, *op. cit.,* pp. 135–136, 157; Goldman, *op. cit.,* pp. 220–232; May, "The Rebellion of the Intellectuals," *loc. cit.*

43. William Van O'Connor, *An Age of Criticism* (Chicago, 1952), pp. 3–93;

Curti, ed., *American Scholarship*, pp. 11–126; May, *End of American Inno-cence*, pp. 271–285; William James is quoted by Morton White in Lloyd Rodwin, ed., *The Future Metropolis* (New York, 1961), p. 223. See also Morton and Lucia White, *The Intellectual Versus the City: From Thomas Jefferson to Frank Lloyd Wright* (Cambridge, 1962).

Bibliography

Abbott, Edith, *The Tenements of Chicago, 1908–1935*. Chicago, 1936.

Abbott, Edith, "The Wages of Unskilled Labor in the United States, 1850–1900," *Journal of Political Economy*, XIII, pp. 321–367, 1905.

Abell, Aaron I., "American Catholic Reaction to Industrial Conflicts: The Arbitral Process, 1885–1900," *Catholic Historical Review*, XLI. January, 1956.

Abell, Aaron I., *American Catholicism and Social Action: A Search for Social Justice, 1865–1950*. Garden City, N. Y., 1960.

Abell, Aaron I., "The Catholic Factor in Urban Welfare: The Early Period, 1850–1880," *The Review of Politics*, XIV. July, 1952.

Abell, Aaron I., *The Urban Impact on American Protestantism, 1865–1900*. Cambridge, 1943.

Adamic, Louis, *A Nation of Nations*. New York, 1945.

Addams, Jane, *Twenty Years at Hull-House*. New York, 1939.

Addison, Julia de Wolf, *The Boston Museum of Fine Arts*. Boston, 1924.

Adler, Selig, and T. E. Connolly, *From Ararat to Suburbia*. Philadelphia, 1960.

Albion, Robert G., *The Rise of New York Port: 1815–1860*. New York, 1939.

Albright, Raymond W., *Two Centuries of Reading, Pa., 1748–1948*. Reading, 1948.

Alexandersson, Gunnar, *The Industrial Structure of American Cities*. Lincoln, Neb., 1956.

Allen, Hugh, *Rubber's Home Town, The Real-Life Story of Akron*. New York, 1949.

Allison, Edward M., and Boies Penrose, *Philadelphia: 1681–1887, A History of Municipal Development*. Baltimore, 1887.

American Journal of Sociology. March, 1955.

Anderson, Elin L., *We Americans: A Study of Cleavage in an American City* [Bloomington]. Cambridge, 1937.

Anderson, Jackson M., *Industrial Recreation, A Guide to Its Organization and Administration*. New York, 1955.

Anderson, Lewis F., *History of Manual and Industrial School Education*. New York, 1926.

Anderson, Nels. *The Hobo*. Chicago, 1923.

Anderson, Nels, *Men on the Move*. Chicago, 1940.

Anderson, Nels, and Eduard C. Lindeman, *Urban Sociology*. New York, 1928.

Anderson, Oscar E., *Refrigeration in America*. Princeton, 1953.

Anderson, Wilbert L., *The Country Town, A Study of Rural Evolution*. New York, 1906.

Anderson, William, *American City Government*. New York, 1925.

Andrews, J. D., *Report of . . . on the Trade and Commerce of . . . the Great Lakes and Rivers*. Washington, 1954.

Andrews, Wayne, *Architecture, Ambition and Americans*. New York, 1955.
Andrews, Wayne, *Battle for Chicago*. New York, 1946.
Annals of the American Academy of Political and Social Science, Volume 242, November, 1945.
Archer, William, *America To-Day*. New York, 1899.
Arndt, Walter T., *The Emancipation of the American City*. New York, 1917.
Arps, Louisa Ward, *Denver in Slices*. Denver, 1959.
Asbury, Herbert, *The French Quarter*. New York, 1936.
Asbury, Herbert, *The Gangs of New York*. New York, 1937.
Asbury, Herbert, *The Great Illusion: An Informal History of Prohibition*. New York, 1950.
Atherton, Lewis, *Main Street on the Middle Border*. Bloomington, Ind., 1954.
Atkinson, R. K., *The Boys' Club*. New York, 1939.
Aveling, Edward, and Eleanor Marx Aveling, *The Working-Class Movement in America*. London, 1891.
Baehr, Harry W., Jr., *The New York Tribune Since the Civil War*. New York, 1936.
Bailey, William L., "The Twentieth Century City," *American City*, XXXI: 142–143. August, 1924.
Baker, Gordon E., *Rural Versus Urban Political Power*. Garden City, N. Y., 1955.
Baker, M. N., *Municipal Engineering and Sanitation*. New York, 1906.
Baltimore: A Picture History, 1858–1958. Commentary by Francis F. Beirse. New York, 1957.
Baltzell, E. Bigby, *Philadelphia Gentlemen, The Making of a National Upper Class*. Glencoe, Ill., 1958.
Bancroft, Caroline, *Gulch of Gold, A History of Central City, Colorado*. Denver, 1958.
Bannister, Turpin C., "Early Town Planning in New York State," *New York History*, XXIV, 1943.
Barker, John M., *The Saloon Problem and Social Reform*. Boston, 1905.
Barnes, James A., *Wealth of the American People, A History of Their Economic Life*. New York, 1949.
Barnes, Mary S., ed., *Autobiography of Edward Austin Sheldon*. New York, 1911.
Bassett, Edward M., *Zoning; The Laws, Administration, and Court Decisions During the First Twenty Years*. Russell Sage Foundation. New York, 1940.
Bates, E. Catherine, *A Year in the Great Republic*. 2 volumes. New York, 1887.
Bates, Ralph S., *Scientific Societies in the United States*. New York, 1945.
Bean, Walton, *Boss Ruef's San Francisco*. Berkeley, 1952.
Beasley, Norman, and George W. Stark, *Made in Detroit*. New York, 1957.
Bedford, Scott E. W., ed., *Readings in Urban Sociology*. New York, 1927.
Belcher, Wyatt W., *The Economic Rivalry Between St. Louis and Chicago, 1850–1880*. New York, 1947.
Bemis, Edward W., ed., *Municipal Monopolies*. New York, 1899.
Benjamin, S. G. W., "American Art Since the Centennial," *The New Princeton Review*, IV: 14–30. July, 1887.
Bennett, Charles A., *History of Manual and Industrial Education Up to 1870*. Peoria, 1926.
Bennett, Charles A., *History of Manual and Industrial Education, 1870 to 1917*. Peoria, 1937.
Benson, Lee, *Merchants, Farmers and Railroads: Railroad Regulation and New York Politics, 1850–1887*. Cambridge, 1955.
Bergel, Egon E., *Urban Sociology*. New York, 1955.
Berkson, Isaac B., *Theories of Americanization: A Critical Study, With Special Reference to the Jewish Group*. New York, 1920.
Bernard, L. L., ed., *The Fields and Methods of Sociology*. New York, 1934.
Bernstein, Irving, "The Growth of American Unions," *American Historical Review*. June, 1954.
Berthoff, Rowland, *British Immigrants in Industrial America, 1790–1950*. Cambridge, 1953.

Bigger, Richard, and James D. Kitchen, *How the Cities Grew*. Los Angeles, 1952.

Blake, Nelson M., *Water for the Cities*. Syracuse, 1956.

Blegen, Theodore C., *Norwegian Migration to America*. Northfield, Minn., 1940.

Blesh, Rudi, *Shining Trumpets, A History of Jazz*. New York, 1946.

Bliven, Bruce, *The Wonderful Writing Machine*. New York, 1954.

Blouet, Paul [Max O'Rell], *A Frenchman in America*. New York, 1891.

Bocock, John P., "The Irish Conquest of Our Cities," *Forum*, XVII: 186–195. April, 1894.

Bode, Carl, *The American Lyceum, Town Meeting of the Mind*. New York, 1956.

Bodein, Vernon P., *The Social Gospel of Walter Rauschenbusch and Its Relation to Religious Education*. New Haven, 1944.

Bogen, Boris D., *Jewish Philanthropy*. New York, 1917.

Bogue, Donald J., *The Structure of Metropolitan Communities*. Ann Arbor, 1939.

Boies, Henry M., *Prisoners and Paupers*. New York, 1893.

Bonnett, Clarence E., *Employers' Associations in the United States*. New York, 1922.

Bostwick, Arthur E., *The American Public Library*. New York, 1929.

Bowditch, Henry I., *Public Hygiene in America*. Boston, 1877.

Bowen, Croswell, *The Elegant Oakey*. New York, 1956.

Bowen, Frank C., *A Century of Atlantic Travel, 1830–1930*. Boston, 1930.

Bowen, Louise de Koven, *Growing Up With a City*. New York, 1926.

Bragdon, Claude, *More Lives Than One*. New York, 1938.

Brandeis, Louis, *Other People's Money, and How the Bankers Use It*. New York, 1914.

Bremner, Robert H., "The Civic Revival in Ohio," *American Journal of Economics and Sociology*, X: 1951, 185–206, 301–312, 417–429; XI: 99–110.

Bremner, Robert H., *From the Depths: The Discovery of Poverty in the United States*. New York, 1956.

Bridenbaugh, Carl, *Cities in the Wilderness*. New York, 1938.

Bridenbaugh, Carl, *Cities in Revolt*. New York, 1955.

Briggs, Warren R., *Modern American School Buildings*. New York, 1909.

Brooks, Robert C., *Bryce's American Commonwealth: Fiftieth Anniversary*, New York, 1939.

Brown, A. Theodore, *The History of Kansas City to 1870*. [Forthcoming.]

Brown, Henry C., *Brownstone Fronts and Saratoga Trunks*. New York, 1935.

Brown, Henry C., *In the Golden Nineties*. New York, 1928.

Brown, Ralph H., *Historical Geography of the United States*. New York, 1948.

Brownell, Emery A., *Legal Aid in the United States*. Rochester, N. Y., 1951.

Brunger, Eric, "Dairying and Urban Development in New York State: 1850–1900," *Agricultural History*, 29, pp. 169–174.

Bryant, Henry F., "Underground Tunnels for Wires," *Cosmopolitan*, XXVI: 439–446, 1899.

Bryce, James, *The American Commonwealth*. 2 volumes. New York, 1927 ed.

Buck, Solon J., *The Agrarian Crusade*. Chronicles of American Series, 45. New Haven, 1920.

Buck, Solon J., *The Granger Movement, 1870–1880*. Cambridge, 1913.

Buel, James W., *Mysteries and Miseries of America's Great Cities*. San Francisco, 1883.

Burchard, John, and Albert Bush-Brown, *The Architecture of America, A Social and Cultural History*. Boston, 1961.

Burgess, Ernest W., ed., *The Urban Community*. Chicago, 1926.

Burlingame, Roger, *Engines of Democracy*. New York, 1940.

Burns, James A., and B. J. Kohlbrenner, *A History of Catholic Education in the United States*. New York, 1937.

Butler, Nicholas M., ed., *Education in the United States*. New York, 1910.

Byington, Margaret F., *Homestead: The Households of a Mill Town*. New York, 1910.

Byrn, Edward W., *The Progress of Invention in the Nineteenth Century*. New York, 1900.

Caffin, Charles H., *The Story of American Painting*. New York, 1907.
Cahill, Marion C., *Shorter Hours: A Study of the Movement Since the Civil War*. New York, 1952.
Cahn, William, *Mill Town*. New York, 1954.
Calhoun, Arthur W., *A Social History of the American Family from Colonial Times to the Present*, III. Cleveland, 1919.
Calkins, Raymond, *Substitutes for the Saloon*. Boston, 1901.
Calverton, V. F., *The Liberation of American Literature*. New York, 1932.
Campbell, E. G., *The Reorganization of the American Railroad System, 1893–1900*. New York, 1938.
Campbell, Helen, T. W. Knox and Thomas Byrnes, *Darkness and Daylight; or, Lights and Shadows of New York Life*. Hartford, Conn., 1897.
Capers, Gerald M., Jr., *The Biography of a River Town, Memphis: Its Heroic Age*. Chapel Hill, 1939.
Carnovsky, Leon, and Lowell Martin, eds., *The Library in the Community*. Chicago, 1944.
Carpenter, Frances, ed., *Carp's Washington*. New York, 1960.
Carpenter, Niles, *Immigrants and Their Children, 1920*. U. S. Census Monograph, VII. Washington, 1927.
Carpenter, Niles, "Migration Between City and County in the Buffalo Metropolitan Area," chapter in N. E. Himes, *Economics, Sociology and the Modern World*. Cambridge, 1935.
Carter, Paul A., *The Decline and Revival of the Social Gospel: Social and Political Liberalism in American Protestant Churches, 1920–1940*. Ithaca, 1956.
Casson, Herbert N., *The History of the Telephone*. Chicago, 1910.
Catlin, George B., *The Story of Detroit*. Detroit, 1923.
Chapin, Anna A., *Greenwich Village*. New York, 1917.
Chapin, Charles V., *Municipal Sanitation in the United States*. Providence, 1901.
Chase, Gilbert, *American Music from the Pilgrims to the Present*. New York, 1955.
Childs, Harwood L., *Labor and Capital in National Politics*. Columbus, 1930.
Childs, Richard S., *Civic Victories*. New York, 1952.
Chinitz, Benjamin, *Freight and the Metropolis, The Impact of American Transport Revolution on the New York Region*. Cambridge, 1960.
Christian, W. Asbury, *Richmond: Her Past and Present*. Richmond, 1912.
Christie, Robert A., *Empire in Wood, A History of the Carpenters' Union*. Ithaca, 1956.
Churchill, Allen, *The Improper Bohemians, A Recreation of Greenwich Village in Its Heyday*. New York, 1959.
Claghorn, Kate H., "The Foreign Immigrant in New York City," U. S. Industrial Commission *Report*, XV: 449–492, 1901.
Clapesattle, Helen, *The Doctors Mayo*. Minneapolis, 1954.
Clark, Colin, *The Conditions of Economic Progress*. London, 1940.
Clark, Edna M., *Ohio Art and Artists*. Richmond, 1932.
Clark, Eliot, *History of the National Academy of Design: 1825–1953*. New York, 1954.
Clark, Victor S., *History of Manufactures in the United States*. 3 volumes. New York, 1929 ed.
Clark, W. C., and J. S. Kingston, *The Skyscraper*. New York, 1930.
Clarke, Isaac E., *Education in the Industrial and Fine Arts in the United States*. U. S. Bureau of Education. Washington, 1885.
Clarke, T. Wood, *Utica for a Century and a Half*. Utica, 1952.
Clawson, Marion, R. B. Held, and C. H. Stoddard, *Land for the Future*. Baltimore, 1960.
Clemens, Samuel L., *Mark Twain's Travels with Mr. Brown*. New York, 1940.
Closson, Carlos C., Jr., "The Unemployed in American Cities," *Quarterly Journal of Economics*, pp. 168–217, 1894.
Clow, Frederick R., *A Comparative Study of the Administration of City Finances in the United States*. Publication of the American Economic Association, 3rd Series II: 670–910. New York, 1901.

Coad, Oral S., and Edwin Mims, Jr., *The American Stage*. Pageant of America, XIV. New Haven, 1929.

Cochran, Thomas C., and William Miller, *The Age of Enterprise, A Social History of Industrial America*. New York, 1942.

Cochran, Thomas C., "Did the Civil War Retard Industrialization?" *Mississippi Valley Historical Review*, XLVIII: 197–210. September, 1961.

Cochran, Thomas C., *Railroad Leaders, 1845–1890: The Business Mind in Action*. Cambridge, 1953.

Cohen, Alfred, *Statistical Analysis of American Divorce*. New York, 1932.

Cohen, Isidor, *Historical Sketches and Sidelights of Miami, Florida*. Miami, 1925.

Cole, Robert D., *Private Secondary Education for Boys in the United States*. Philadelphia, 1928.

Coleman, Laurence V., *The Museum in America*. 3 volumes. Washington, 1939.

Coleman, Laurence V., *Museum Buildings*. Washington, 1950.

Coleman, Sidney H., *Humane Society Leaders in the United States*. Albany, 1924.

Commons, John R., ed., *A Documentary History of the American Industrial Society*. Cleveland, 1910.

Commons, John R., *et al.*, *History of Labour in the United States*. 4 volumes. New York, 1918–35.

Conant, Charles A., *A History of Modern Banks of Issue*. New York, 1927.

Conant, James B., *Slums and Suburbs: A Commentary on Schools in Metropolitan Areas*. New York, 1961.

Condit, Carl W., *The Rise of the Skyscraper*. Chicago, 1952.

Conference for Good City Government, *Proceedings, 1894–1900.*

Conference on Research in Income and Wealth, *Problems of Capital Formation*. Princeton, 1957.

Conklin, Alfred R., *City Government in the United States*. New York, 1894.

Connery, Robert H., and Richard H. Leach, *The Federal Government and Metropolitan Areas*. Cambridge, 1960.

Coolidge, John, *Mill and Mansion*. New York, 1942.

Coolidge, Mrs. Mary R., *Chinese Immigration*. New York, 1909.

Copeland, Melvin T., *The Cotton Manufacturing Industry of the United States*. Cambridge, 1923.

Cornick, Philip, *A Report to the State Planning Council of New York on Problems Created by the Premature Subdivision of Urban Lands in Selected Metropolitan Districts in the State of New York*. New York, 1938.

Cost of Living in American Towns. Report of an inquiry by the Board of Trade into working class rents, housing and retail prices together with the rates of wages in the (28) principal industrial towns of the United States of America. U. S. Senate Document No. 22, 62nd Congress, 1st Session, 1911.

Cotterill, Roland, "The Parks, Playgrounds and Boulevards of Seattle," *American City*, VII: 204–207, 1912.

Cottrell, Edwin A., and Helen L. Jones, *Characteristics of the Metropolis*. Metropolitan Los Angeles, I. Los Angeles, 1952.

Coulter E. Merton, *The Confederate States of America: 1861–1865*. St. Louis, 1950.

Coulter, E. Merton, *The South During Reconstruction, 1865–1877*. A History of the South, VIII. Baton Rouge, La., 1947.

Crabb, Alfred L., *Nashville, Personality and Biography of a City*. Bobbs-Merrill. 1960.

Crawford, Mary C., *The Romance of the American Theatre*. Boston, 1925.

Cremin, Lawrence A., *The Transformation of the School*. New York, 1961.

Cressey, Paul G., *The Taxi-Dance Hall*. Chicago, 1932.

Croly, Herbert, *The Promise of American Life*. New York, 1914.

Croly, Mrs. J. C., *The History of the Woman's Club Movement in America*. New York, 1898.

Cross, Robert D., *The Emergence of Liberal Catholicism in America*. Cambridge, 1958.

Crow, Carl, *The City of Flint Grows Up*. New York, 1945.

Cubberley, Ellwood P., *Public Education in the United States*. Boston, 1934.

Cummings, Richard O., *The American and His Food*. Chicago, 1940.
Cunliffie, Marcus, "Stephen Crane and the American Background for *Maggie*," *American Quarterly*, pp. 31–44. Spring, 1955.
Curti, Merle, ed. *American Scholarship in the Twentieth Century*. Cambridge, 1953.
Curti, Merle, *The Making of an American Community: A Case Study of Democracy in a Frontier County*. Stanford, Cal., 1959.
Curti, Merle, *The Social Ideas of American Educators*. New York, 1935.
Curti, Merle, and Vernon Carstensen, *The University of Wisconsin*. Madison, 1949.
Cushman, Robert E., *The Independent Regulatory Commissions*. New York, 1941.
Daniels, Morris S., *The Story of Ocean Grove Related in the Year of Its Golden Jubilee, 1869–1919*. New York, 1919.
Daniels, W. H., ed., *The Temperance Reform and Its Great Reformers*. New York, 1878.
Davenport, F. Garvin, *Cultural Life in Nashville on the Eve of the Civil War*. Chapel Hill, 1941.
Davidson, John W., ed., *A Crossroads of Freedom: The 1912 Campaign Speeches of Woodrow Wilson*. New Haven, 1956.
Davidson, Thomas, *The Education of the Wage-Earners*. Boston, 1904.
Davis, Horace B., *Shoes: The Workers and the Industry*. New York, 1940.
Davis, John P., *Corporations: A Study of the Origin and Development of Great Business Combinations and of Their Relation to the Authority of the State*. 2 volumes. New York, 1905.
Davis, Kingsley, ed., *The World's Metropolitan Areas*. International Urban Research, Institute of International Studies. Berkeley, 1959.
Debo, Angie, *Prairie City*. New York, 1944.
Debo, Angie, *Tulsa: From Creek Town to Oil Capital*. Norman, Okla., 1943.
De Forest, Robert W., "A Brief History of the Housing Movement in America," *Annals*, LI: 8–16. January, 1914.
De Forest, Robert W., and Lawrence Veiller, eds., *The Tenement House Problem*. 2 volumes. New York, 1903.
Degler, Carl N., *Out of Our Past*. New York, 1959.
Delvin, Thomas C., *Municipal Reform in the United States*. New York, 1896.
Denison, Merrill, *The Power to Go: The Story of the Automotive Industry*. New York, 1956.
Depew, Charles M., *100 Years of American Commerce*. New York, 1895.
Desmond, H. J., *The A. P. A. Movement*. Washington, 1912.
Destler, Chester M., *American Radicalism; 1865–1901, Essays and Documents*. New London, 1946.
D'Estournelles, Paul H. B., *America and Her Problem*. New York, 1915.
Detweiler, Frederick G., *The Negro Press in the United States*. Chicago, 1922.
Dewey, Davis R., *Financial History of the United States*. New York, 1931.
Dewing, Arthur S., *Corporate Promotions and Reorganizations*. Cambridge, 1914.
Dexter, E. G., *A History of Education in the United States*. New York, 1904.
Diamond, William, *The Economic Thought of Woodrow Wilson*. Baltimore, 1943.
Diamond, William, "On the Dangers of an Urban Interpretation of History," in Goldman, ed., *Historiography and Urbanization*. Baltimore, 1941.
Dickason, David H., *The Daring Young Men: The Story of the American Pre-Raphaelites*. New York, 1953.
Dickinson, Robert E., *City Region and Regionalism*. London, 1947.
Dickinson, Robert E., *The West European City, A Geographical Interpretation*. London, 1951.
Disbrow, Donald W., "The Progressive Movement in Philadelphia, 1910–1916," Ph.D. Thesis, University of Rochester, 1956.
Ditzon, Sidney, *Arsenals of a Democratic Culture: A Social History of the American Public Library Movement in New England and the Middle States from 1850 to 1900*. Chicago, 1947.
Doell, Charles E., and Gerald B. Fitzgerald, *A Brief History of Parks and Recreation in the United States*. Chicago, 1954.

Dombrowski, James, *The Early Days of Christian Socialism in America.* New York, 1936.

Doonan, George W., "Commercial Organizations in Southern and Western Cities," U. S. Bureau of Foreign and Domestic Commerce, *Special Agents Series,* No. 79, 1914.

Doran, Herbert B., and A. G. Hinman, *Urban Land Economics.* New York, 1928.

Douglas, Paul H., *Real Wages in the United States, 1890–1926.* New York, 1930.

Douglass, Harlan P., *The Suburban Trend.* New York, 1925.

Downes, Alan S., *Fifty Years of American Drama, 1900–1950.* Chicago, 1951.

Downes, Randolph C., *Lake Port.* Toledo, 1951.

Drake, Leonard A., and Carrie Glasser, *Trends in the New York Clothing Industry.* New York, 1942.

Drake, St. Clair, and Horace R. Clayton, *Black Metropolis: A Study of Negro Life in a Northern City.* New York, 1945.

Drake, William E., *The American School in Transition.* New York, 1955.

Dreiser, Theodore, *The Color of a Great City.* New York, 1923.

Dresslar, Fletcher B., *American Schoolhouses,* U. S. Bureau of Education, Bulletin 444, 1910.

Duffey, Bernard, *The Chicago Renaissance in American Letters.* East Lansing, 1954.

Duffus, R. L., *Lillian Wald, Neighbor and Crusader.* New York, 1938.

Dulles, Foster R., *America Learns to Play: A History of Popular Recreation, 1607–1940.* New York, 1940.

Dumke, Glenn S., *The Boom of the Eighties in Southern California.* San Marino, Cal., 1944.

Dunbar, Willis F., *Kalamazoo and How It Grew.* Western Michigan University School of Graduate Studies. Kalamazoo, 1959.

Duncan, Otis D., William R. Scott, Stanley Lieberson, Beverly D. Duncan, and Hal H. Winsborough, *Metropolis and Region.* Resources for the Future, Inc., Baltimore, 1960.

Duncan, Otis D., and Albert J. Reiss, Jr., *Social Characteristics of Urban and Rural Communities, 1950.* U. S. Census Monograph Series. New York, 1956.

Dunlap, George A., *The City in the American Novel, 1789–1900.* Philadelphia, 1934.

Dwing, Arthur S., *Corporate Promotions and Reorganizations.* Cambridge, 1914.

Dyer, Frank L., and T. C. Martin, *Edison, His Life and Inventions.* 2 volumes. New York, 1910.

Dyer, John, *Ivory Towers in the Market Place: The Evening College in American Education.* Indianapolis, 1956.

Eastman, Linda A., *Portrait of a Librarian, William Howard Brett.* Chicago, 1940.

Eaton, Allen, ed., *A Bibliography of Social Surveys.* Russell Sage Foundation. New York, 1930.

Eaton, Clement, *A History of the Southern Confederacy.* New York, 1954.

Eckelberry, R. H., "The History of the Municipal University in the United States," U. S. Bureau of Education, Bulletin 2, pp. 7–126, 1932.

Economic Development and Cultural Change, the University of Chicago Research Center, Vol. III, Nos. 1–4, 1955.

Edwards, George W., *The Evolution of Finance Capitalism.* New York, London, 1938.

Eldridge, Seba, ed., *Development of Collective Enterprise; Dynamics of an Emergent Economy.* Lawrence, Kan., 1943.

Ellis, Amanda M., *The Strange Uncertain Years* [of Denver and neighboring Colorado communities]. Hamden, Conn., 1959.

Ellis, David M., "Albany and Troy—Commercial Rivals," *New York History,* XLI, 1943.

Ellis, Roy, *A Civic History of Kansas City, Missouri.* Springfield, Mo., 1930.

Ellis, William T., *Billy Sunday, The Man and His Message.* Philadelphia, 1936.

Ellwood, Charles A., "Has Crime Increased in the United States Since 1880?" *American Institute of Criminal Law,* I: 378–385, 1910.

Elson, Louis C., *The History of American Music.* New York, 1925.

Ely, R. T., "Pullman," *Harper's Magazine*, 70: 453–465, 1885.
Epstein, Ralph C. *The Automobile Industry: Its Economic and Commercial Development.* New York, 1928.
Erickson, Charlotte, *American Industry and the European Immigrant, 1860–1885.* Cambridge, 1957.
Erickson, E. Gordon, *Urban Behavior.* New York, 1954.
Ernst, Robert, *Immigrant Life in New York City: 1825–1865.* New York, 1949.
Ewen, David, *The Story of America's Musical Theater.* Philadelphia, 1961.
Fairlie, John A., *Municipal Administration.* New York, 1922 ed.
Faithfull, Emily, *Three Visits to America.* New York, 1884.
Fargo, Lucile F., *Spokane Story.* New York, 1950.
Fassett, Charles M., *Assets of the Ideal City.* New York, 1922.
Faught, Millard C., *Falmouth, Massachusetts: Problems of a Resort Community.* New York, 1945.
Faulkner, Harold U., *The Decline of Laissez Faire: 1897–1917.* New York, 1951.
Faulkner, Harold U., *The Quest for Social Justice: 1898–1914.* A History of American Life, XI. New York, 1937.
Faust, Albert B., *The German Element in the United States with Special Reference to Its Political, Moral, Social, and Educational Influence.* New York, 1927.
Feder, L. H., *Unemployment Relief in Periods of Depression.* New York, 1936.
Federal Housing Administration, *The Structure and Growth of Residential Neighborhoods in American Cities.* Washington, 1939.
Fehrenbacher, Don E., *Chicago Giant; A Biography of "Long John" Wentworth.* American Historical Research Center. Madison, Wis., 1957.
Feiler, Arthur, *America Seen Through German Eyes.* New York, 1928.
Ferguson, Charles W., *Fifty Million Brothers; A Panorama of American Lodges and Clubs.* New York, 1937.
Fergusson, Erna, *Albuquerque.* Albuquerque, 1947.
Ferry, John W., *A History of the Department Store.* New York, 1960.
Fess, Margaret R., *The Grosvenor Library and Its Times.* Buffalo, 1956.
Filler, Louis, *Crusaders for American Liberalism.* New York, 1939.
Fine, Sidney, *Laissez Faire and the General-Welfare State.* Ann Arbor, 1956.
Fisher, Robert M., ed., *The Metropolis in Modern Life.* New York, 1955.
Fitch, James M., *American Building: The Forces That Shape It.* Boston, 1948.
Fitch, James M., *Architecture and the Esthetics of Plenty.* New York, 1961.
Fite, Emerson D., *Social and Industrial Conditions in the North During the Civil War.* New York, 1910.
Flagler, J. M., "Onward and Upward with the Arts," *The New Yorker*, pp. 113–129. April 14, 1956.
Ford, George B., "The Park System of Kansas City, Mo.," *Architectural Record*, 40: 499–504. December, 1916.
Ford, James, *et al.*, *Slums and Housing, With Special Reference to New York City; History, Conditions, Policy.* 2 volumes. Cambridge, 1936.
Fosdick, Raymond B., *American Police Systems.* New York, 1920.
Frankfurter, Felix, *The Public and Its Government.* New Haven, 1930.
Franklin, Fabian, *The Life of Daniel Coit Gilman.* New York, 1910.
Freidel, Frank, *America in the Twentieth Century.* New York, 1960.
French, John C., *A History of the University Founded by Johns Hopkins.* Baltimore, 1946.
Garland, Hamlin, *A Son of the Middle Border.* New York, 1923 ed.
Garner, Frederic B., F. M. Boddy, and A. J. Nixon, *The Location of Manufactures in the United States: 1899–1929.* University of Minnesota Bulletin of Employment Stabilization Research Institute, Vol. II, No. 6. Minneapolis, 1933.
Garvan, Anthony N. B., *Architecture and Town Planning in Colonial Connecticut.* New Haven, 1957.
Geddes, Patrick, *Cities in Evolution,* new and revised ed. London, 1949.
Gelfant, Blanche H., *The American City Novel.* Norman, Okla., 1954.
Gemmill, William N., "Chicago Court of Domestic Relations," *Annals,* 51: 115–123. January, 1914.

George, Henry, *Progress and Poverty*. San Francisco, 1879.

Gephart, William F., *Transportation and Industrial Development in the Middle West*. Columbia University Studies in History, Economics, and Public Law, XXXIV, No. 1. New York, 1909.

Giedion, Sigfried, *Space, Time and Architecture; The Growth of a New Tradition*. Cambridge, 1954.

Gilbert, Douglas, *American Vaudeville, Its Life and Times*. New York, 1940.

Gill, N. N., *Municipal Research Bureaus*. Washington, 1944.

Gilman, Nicholas P., *Profit Sharing Between Employer and Employee*. New York, 1889.

Gilmore, Harlan W., *Transportation and the Growth of Cities*. Glencoe, 1953.

Ginger, Ray, *Altgeld's America*, "1892–1905, The Lincoln Ideal vs. Changing Realities." New York, 1958.

Gist, Noel P., *Secret Societies: A Cultural Study of Fraternalism in the United States*. University of Missouri Studies. Columbia, Mo., 1940.

Glaab, Charles N., "Visions of Metropolis: William Gilpin and Theories of City Growth in the American West," *Wisconsin Magazine of History*. Autumn, 1961.

Gladden, Washington, *Recollections*. Boston, 1909.

Glass, Carter, *An Adventure in Constructive Finance*. New York, 1927.

Glazier, Willard, *Peculiarities of American Cities*. Philadelphia, 1886.

Glenn, John M., Lillian Brandt, and F. E. Andrews, *Russell Sage Foundation: 1907–1946*, I. New York, 1947.

Glover, John G., and William B. Cornell, eds., *The Development of American Industries, Their Economic Significance*. New York, 1951 ed.

Goldberg, Arthur, *The Buffalo Public Library*. Buffalo, 1937.

Goldberg, Isaac, *Tin Pan Alley*. New York, 1930.

Goldman, Eric F., ed., *Historiography and Urbanization*. Baltimore, 1941.

Goldman, Eric F., *Rendezvous with Destiny; A History of Modern American Reform*. New York, 1952.

Goldmark, Josephine, *Impatient Crusader; Florence Kelley's Life Story*. Urbana, 1953.

Goldsmith, Raymond W., *A Study of Saving in the United States*. 3 volumes. Princeton, 1955.

Goldstein, Sidney, "Migration: Dynamic of the American City," *American Quarterly*. Winter, 1954.

Goldstein, Sidney, "Repeated Migration as a Factor in High Mobility," *American Sociology Review*. October, 1954.

Good, H. G., *A History of American Education*. New York, 1956.

Goode, George B., "Museum History and Museums of History," Smithsonian Institution, *Annual Report*, 1897.

Goodrich, Carter, *et al.*, *Migration and Economic Opportunity*. Philadelphia, 1936.

Gottmann, Jean, *Megalopolis: The Urbanized Northeastern Seaboard of the United States*. New York, 1961.

Graham, Lloyd, and Frank H. Severance, *The First Hundred Years of the Buffalo Chamber of Commerce*. Buffalo, 1945.

Gras, N. S. B., and H. M. Larson, *Casebook in American Business History*. New York, 1939.

Gras, N. S. B., *An Introduction to Economic History*. New York, 1922.

Grattan, C. Hartley, *In Quest of Knowledge; A Historical Perspective on Adult Education*. New York, 1955.

Grebler, Leo, David M. Blank, and Louis Winnick, *Capital Formation in Residential Real Estate*. Princeton, 1956.

Green, Constance M., *American Cities in the Growth of the Nation*. London, 1957.

Green, Constance M., *History of Naugatuck, Connecticut*. New Haven, 1949.

Green, Constance M., *Holyoke, Massachusetts*. New Haven, 1939.

Green, Constance M., *Washington, Village and Capital, 1800–1878*. Princeton, 1962.

Green, Marguerite, *The National Civic Federation and the American Labor Movement, 1900–1925*. Washington, 1956.

Green, Samuel S., *The Public Library Movement in the United States, 1853–1893*. Boston, 1913.

Greenbie, Marjorie B., *Lincoln's Daughters of Mercy*. New York, 1944.

Greenwood, Thomas, *A Tour of the States and Canada*. London, 1883.

Greer, Thomas H., *American Social Reform Movements; Their Pattern Since 1865*. New York, 1949.

Grierson, Ronald, *Electric Elevator Equipment for Modern Buildings*. New York, 1924.

Griffith, Ernest S., *The Modern Development of City Government in the United Kingdom and the United States*, I. London, 1927.

Grob, Gerald N., *Workers and Utopia: A Study of Ideological Conflict in the American Labor Movement, 1865–1900*. Northwestern University Studies in History, II.

Gropius, Walter, *Rebuilding Our Communities*. Chicago, 1945.

Grossman, Jonathan, *William Sylvis, Pioneer of American Labor*. New York, 1945.

Groves, Ernest R., *The American Woman*. New York, 1944.

Hales, Charles A., *The Baltimore Clearing House*. Johns Hopkins University Studies, New Series 27. Baltimore, 1940.

Hall, Clayton C., ed., *Baltimore, Its History and Its People*. 2 volumes. New York, 1912.

Halsey, Elizabeth, *The Development of Public Recreation in Metropolitan Chicago*. Chicago Recreation Commission. Chicago, 1940.

Hamlin, A. D. F., "Twenty-five Years of American Architecture," *The Architectural Record*, Vol. 44, 1916.

Hamlin, T. F., *The American Spirit in Architecture*. Pageant of American Series, XIII. New Haven, 1926.

Handlin, Oscar, *Boston's Immigrants, 1790–1865*. Cambridge, 1941.

Handlin, Oscar, ed., *Immigration as a Factor in American History*. Englewood Cliffs, N. J., 1959.

Handlin, Oscar, *The Newcomers: Negroes and Puerto Ricans in a Changing Metropolis*. Cambridge, 1959.

Handlin, Oscar, *This Was America*. Cambridge, 1949.

Handlin, Oscar, *The Uprooted*. Boston, 1951.

Hansen, Alvin H., "Factors Affecting the Trend of Real Wages," *American Economic Review*, XV: 27–42, 1925.

Hansen, Harry, *Scarsdale, From Colonial Manor to Modern Community*. New York, 1954.

Hansen, Marcus L., *The Immigrant in American History*. Cambridge, 1940.

Hapgood, Norman, *The Stage in America, 1897–1900*. New York, 1901.

Hardy, Edward R., *The Making of the Fire Insurance Rate*. New York, 1927.

Harlow, Alvin F., *The Serene Cincinnatians*. New York, 1950.

Harris, Chauncey D., "A Functional Classification of Cities in the United States," *Geographic Review*, 33: 86–99. January, 1943.

Harrison, Shelby M., *Bibliography of Social Surveys*. New York, 1930.

Harrison, Shelby M., *Social Conditions in an American City* [Springfield, Ill.]. New York, 1920.

Harrison, Ward, O. F. Haas, and Kirk M. Reid, *Street Lighting Practice*. New York, 1930.

Hartmann, Sadakichi, *A History of American Art*. 2 volumes. New York, 1901, 1932.

Hartsough, Mildred L., *The Twin Cities as a Metropolitan Market*. Research Publication of the University of Minnesota Social Science Series, No. 18. Minneapolis, 1925.

Haskell, Henry C., Jr., and R. B. Fowler, *City of the Future; A Narrative History of Kansas City, 1850–1950*. Kansas City, Mo., 1950.

Hatcher, Harlan, *The Western Reserve*. Indianapolis, 1949.

Hatton, Joseph, *Henry Irving's Impressions of America*. London, 1884.

Hauser, Philip M., "Ecological Aspects of Urban Research," in Leonard D. White, ed., *The State of the Social Science*, pp. 229–254. Chicago, 1956.

Hawkins, Layton S., C. A. Prosser, and J. C. Wright, *Development of Vocational Education*. Chicago, 1951.

Hawley, Amos H., *The Changing Shape of Metropolitan America: Deconcentration Since 1920*. Glencoe, 1956.

Hawley, Amos H., *Human Ecology, A Theory of Community Structure*. New York, 1950.

Haynes, Frederick E., *Social Politics in the United States*. New York, 1924.

Haynes, Rowland, *Recreation Survey*. Milwaukee Bureau of Economy and Efficiency. Bulletin, 17. Milwaukee, 1912.

Hays, Samuel P., *The Response to Industrialism: 1885–1914*. Chicago, 1957.

Hedges, James B., *Henry Villard and the Railways of the Northwest*. New Haven, 1930.

Henderson, Charles R., *Industrial Insurance in the United States*. 2nd ed. Chicago, 1911.

Henderson, Charles R., *Social Settlements*. New York, 1899.

Henderson, Charles R., *The Social Spirit in America*. New York, 1897.

Henderson, Helen W., *The Pennsylvania Academy of Fine Arts*. Boston, 1911.

Hendrick, Burton J., *The Age of Big Business*. Chronicles of America Series, Vol. 39. New Haven, 1919.

Hendrick, Burton J., *The Life of Andrew Carnegie*. New York, 1932.

Henry, Alice, *The Trade Union Woman*. New York, 1915.

Herrick, John P., *Empire Oil, The Story of Oil in New York State*. New York, 1949.

Herring, Harriet L., *Welfare Work in Mill Villages; The Story of Extra-Mill Activities in North Carolina*. Chapel Hill, 1929.

Higham, John, *Strangers in the Land; Patterns of American Nativism, 1860–1925*. New Brunswick, N. J., 1955.

Hill, Joseph A., *Women in Gainful Occupations, 1870 to 1920*. U. S. Census Monograph IX. Washington, 1929.

Hilton, George W., and John F. Due, *The Electric Interurban Railways in America*. Stanford, Cal., 1960.

Hirschfeld, Charles, *Baltimore, 1870–1900: Studies in Social History*. Johns Hopkins University Studies in Historical and Political Science, 59, No. 2. Baltimore, 1941.

Hoffman, Frederick J., Charles Allen, and C. F. Ulrich, *The Little Magazine; A History and a Bibliography*. Princeton, 1946.

Hofstadter, Richard, *The Age of Reform; From Bryan to F. D. R.* New York, 1955.

Hofstadter, Richard, and C. De Witt Hardy, *The Development and Scope of Higher Education in the United States*. New York, 1952.

Hofstadter, Richard, and W. P. Metzger, *The Development of Academic Freedom in the United States*. New York, 1955.

Hofstadter, Richard, *Social Darwinism in American Thought, 1860–1915*. Philadelphia, 1944.

Holbrook, Stewart H., *The Story of American Railroads*. New York, 1947.

Holcombe, Arthur N., *State Government in the United States*. New York, 1931.

Holdsworth, J. T., *Report of the Economic Survey of Pittsburgh*. Pittsburgh, 1912.

Hole, S. Reynolds, *A Little Tour in America*. London, 1895.

Hollingshead, A. B., "Community Research," *American Sociology Review*, pp. 136–140. April, 1948.

Hollis, Andrew P., *The Contribution of the Oswego Normal School to Educational Progress in the United States*. Boston, 1898.

Hollis, Ernest V., and Alice L. Taylor, *Social Work Education in the United States*. New York, 1951.

Hoogenboom, Ari, *Outlawing the Spoils: A History of the Civil Service Reform Movement, 1865–1883*. Urbana, 1961.

Hoover, Edgar M., Jr., *The Location of Economic Activity*. New York, 1948.

Hoover, Edgar M., Jr., *Location Theory and the Shoe and Leather Industries*. Cambridge, 1937.

Hopkins, Charles H., *History of the Y.M.C.A. in North America.* New York, 1951.
Hopkins, Charles H., *The Rise of the Social Gospel in American Protestantism, 1865–1915.* New Haven, 1940.
Hornblow, Arthur, *A History of the Theatre in America from Its Beginnings to the Present Time.* 2 volumes. Philadelphia, 1919.
Horner, Charles F., *The Life of James Redpath and the Development of the Modern Lyceum.* New York, 1926.
Horton, John T., *Old Erie—The Growth of An American Community.* Vol. I of *History of Northwestern New York.* New York, 1947.
Hourwich, Isaac A., *Immigration and Labor; The Economic Aspects of European Immigration to the United States,* 2nd ed. New York, 1922.
Howard, John T., *Our American Music, Three Hundred Years of It.* New York, 1954.
Howe, Frederic C., *The City, The Hope of Democracy.* New York, 1909 ed.
Howe, Frederic C., *The Confessions of a Reformer.* New York, 1925.
Howe, Frederic C., *The Modern City and Its Problems.* New York, 1915.
Howe, Winifred E., *A History of the Metropolitan Museum of Art.* 2 volumes. New York, 1946.
Howells, William D., *Literary Friends and Acquaintance.* New York, 1902.
Hower, Ralph M., *History of Ayer & Son.* Cambridge, 1949.
Hower, Ralph M., *History of Macy's of New York, 1858–1919.* Cambridge, 1943.
Hoyt, Harlowe R., *Town Hall Tonight.* Englewood Cliffs, N. J., 1955.
Hoyt, Homer, *One Hundred Years of Land Values in Chicago.* Chicago, 1933.
Hoyt, Homer, *The Structure and Growth of Residential Neighborhoods in American Cities.* Washington, 1939.
Hudnut, Joseph, *Architecture and the Spirit of Man.* Cambridge, 1949.
Hughes, Everett C., "The Cultural Aspect of Urban Research," in Leonard D. White, ed., *The State of the Social Sciences,* pp. 255–268. Chicago, 1956.
Hughes, Glenn, *A History of the American Theatre, 1700–1950.* New York, 1951.
Hull-House, Maps and Papers, *Bulletin.* Chicago, 1895.
Hungerford, Edward, *The Personality of American Cities.* New York, 1913.
Hunker, Henry L., *Industrial Evolution of Columbus, Ohio.* Columbus, 1958.
Hunter, Floyd, *Community Power Structure; A Study of Decision Makers.* Chapel Hill, 1953.
Hutchinson, William T., *Cyrus Hall McCormick.* 2 volumes. New York, 1935.
Illson, James C., *J. Sterling Morton.* Lincoln, Neb., 1942.
Isham, Samuel, *The History of American Painting,* 2nd ed. New York, 1927.
Jacobs, Jane, *The Death and Life of Great American Cities.* New York, 1961.
Jallings, John H., *Elevators.* Chicago, 1919.
Janowitz, Morris, *The Community Press in an Urban Setting.* Glencoe, Ill., 1952.
Jerome, Harry, *Migration and Business Cycles.* New York, 1926.
Johnson, Arthur M., *The Development of American Petroleum Pipelines; A Study in Private Enterprise and Public Policy, 1862–1906.* Ithaca, 1956.
Johnson, Emory R., *et al., History of Domestic and Foreign Commerce of the United States.* 2 volumes. Washington, 1915.
Johnson, Robert U., *Remembered Yesterdays.* Boston, 1923.
Johnson, Tom L., *My Story.* New York, 1913.
Johnstone, Paul H., "Old Ideals Versus New Ideas," *Farmers in a Changing World.* U. S. Department of Agriculture, Year Book. Washington, 1940.
Jones, Cranston, *Architecture Today and Tomorrow.* New York, 1961.
Jones, Thomas J., *The Sociology of a New York City Block.* Columbia University Studies in History, Economics, and Public Law, 21, No. 2. New York, 1904.
Jordan, Philip D., *Ohio Comes of Age: 1873–1900.* Vol. V of Carl Wittke, ed., *The History of the State of Ohio.* Columbus, 1943.
Joseph, Samuel, *History of the Baron de Hirsch Fund; The Americanization of the Jewish Immigrant.* New York, 1935.
Kaempffert, Waldemar, ed., *A Popular History of American Invention.* 2 volumes. New York, 1924.
Kane, Joseph N., *Famous First Facts.* New York, 1950.

Kazin, Alfred, *On Native Grounds.* New York, 1942.

Kazin, Alfred, and Charles Shapiro, *The Stature of Theodore Dreiser.* New York, 1955.

Keating, Paul W., *Lamps for a Brighter America.* New York, 1954.

Kellogg, Paul U., *Pittsburgh Survey.* 6 volumes. New York, 1909–14.

Kelly, Edmond, *The Elimination of the Tramp.* New York, 1908.

Kelso, Robert W., *The Science of Public Welfare.* New York, 1928.

Kennaday, Paul, "New York's Hundred Lodging Houses," *Charities,* Feb. 18, 1905.

Kenngott, George F., *The Record of a City.* Social Survey of Lowell, Mass. New York, 1912.

Kimball, S. Fiske, *American Architecture.* New York, 1928.

King, Clyde L., *The History of the Government of Denver . . . and Its Relations with Public Service Corporations.* Denver, 1911.

King, Dick, *Ghost Towns of Texas.* San Antonio, 1953.

King, Grace, *Creole Families of New Orleans.* New York, 1921.

King, Grace, *New Orleans: The Place and the People.* 1902.

Kingsbury, F. J., "The Tendency of Men to Live in Cities," U. S. Commissioner of Education, *Report,* II: 1282, 1894–95.

Kipnis, Ira, *The American Socialist Movement, 1897–1912.* New York, 1952.

Kirkland, Edward C., *Dream and Thought in the Business Community, 1860–1900.* Ithaca, 1956.

Kirkland, Edward C., *Industry Comes of Age, 1860–1897.* The Economic History of the United States, Vol. V. New York, 1961.

Kirkland, Edward C., *Men, Cities, and Transportation: A Study of New England History: 1820–1900.* Cambridge, 1948.

Klein, Alexander, ed., *The Empire City; A Treasury of New York.* New York, 1955.

Knight, Edgar W., *Public Education in the South.* Boston, 1922.

Knight, Grant C., *The Critical Period in American Literature.* Chapel Hill, 1951.

Knight, Grant C., *The Strenuous Age in American Literature.* Chapel Hill, 1954.

Koch, Theodore W., *A Book of Carnegie Libraries.* New York, 1917.

Kouwenhoven, John A., *Adventures of America, 1857–1900; A Pictorial Record from Harper's Weekly.* New York, 1938.

Kouwenhoven, John A., *The Beer Can by the Highway.* New York, 1961.

Kouwenhoven, John A., *The Columbia Historical Portrait of New York.* New York, 1953.

Krout, John A., *Annals of American Sport.* Pageant of America, Vol. 15. New Haven, 1929.

La Farge, Oliver, *Santa Fe: The Autobiography of a Southwestern Town.* Norman, Okla., 1959.

Lahee, Henry C., *Annals of Music in America.* Boston, 1922.

Lahne, Herbert J., *The Cotton Mill Worker.* New York, 1944.

Lampard, Eric E., "The History of Cities in the Economically Advanced Areas," *Economic Development and Cultural Change,* University of Chicago Research Center in Economic Development and Cultural Change, III, No. 2. January, 1955.

Lampard, Eric E., "The Study of Urbanization," *American Historical Review,* pp. 49–61. October, 1961.

Landgren, Marchal E., *Years of Art; The Story of the Art Students League of New York.* New York, 1940.

Landis, Paul H., *Three Iron Mining Towns; A Study in Cultural Change.* Ann Arbor, 1938.

Larkin, Oliver W., *Art and Life in America.* New York, 1949.

Larson, Henrietta M., *The Wheat Market and the Farmer in Minnesota, 1858–1900.* New York, 1926.

Laughlin, J. Laurence, *The Federal Reserve Act, Its Origin and Problems.* New York, 1933.

Lee, Alfred M., *The Daily Newspaper in America.* New York, 1937.

Lee, Everett S., and Anne S. Lee, "Internal Migration Statistics for the United

States," *Journal of the American Statistical Association,* Vol. 55, No. 292, pp. 664–697. December, 1960.

Lee, James M., *History of American Journalism.* Boston, 1923.

Lee, Joseph, *Constructive and Preventive Philanthropy.* New York, 1902.

Leech, Margaret, *Reveille in Washington, 1860–1865.* New York, 1941.

Leiffer, Murray H., *City and Church in Transition.* Chicago, 1938.

Leighton, George R., *America's Growing Pains.* New York, 1939.

Lengyel, Emil, *Americans from Hungary.* New York, 1948.

Levine, Louis [L. L. Lorwin], *The Women's Garment Workers, A History of the International Ladies' Garment Workers Union.* New York, 1924.

Lewis, Lloyd, and Henry J. Smith, *Chicago, The History of Its Reputation.* New York, 1929.

Lewis, Nelson P., "Modern City Roadways," *Popular Science Monthly,* Vol. 56, pp. 524–536, 1900.

Lewisohn, Ludwig, *Expression in America.* New York, 1932.

Lief, Alfred, *Brandeis.* New York, 1936.

Lightner, Otto C., *The History of Business Depressions.* New York, 1922.

Lincoln, Jonathan T., *The City of the Dinner-Pail.* Boston, 1909.

Lindsey, Ben B., and Rube Borough, *The Dangerous Life.* New York, 1931.

Link, Arthur S., *Wilson: The New Freedom.* Princeton, 1956.

Link, Arthur S., *Wilson: The Road to the White House.* Princeton, 1947.

Link, Arthur S., *Woodrow Wilson and the Progressive Era: 1910–1917.* New York, 1954.

Linn, James W., *Jane Addams; A Biography.* New York, 1935.

Lipset, Seymour M., and Reinhard Bendix, *Social Mobility in Industrial Society.* Berkeley, 1959.

The Literary Club of Cincinnati: 1849–1949. Centennial Book. Cincinnati, 1949.

Livingood, J. W., *Philadelphia-Baltimore Trade Rivalry: 1780–1860.* Harrisburg, 1947.

Lloyd, Henry D., *Wealth Against Commonwealth.* Washington, 1936 ed.

The Location of Reserve Districts in the United States. U. S. Senate Documents, 63rd Congress, 2nd Session, Vol. 16. Washington, 1914.

Logie, Gordon, *The Urban Scene.* London, n. d.

Lombroso, Cesar, "Why Homicide Has Increased in the United States," *North American Review,* 165: 641–648, 1897.

Loomis, Samuel L., *Modern Cities and Their Religious Problems.* New York, 1887.

Lorwin, Lewis L., *The American Federation of Labor; History, Policies, and Prospects.* Brookings Institute. Washington, 1933.

Lou, Herbert H., *Juvenile Courts in the United States.* Chapel Hill, 1927.

Lovett, William P., *Detroit Rules Itself.* Boston, 1930.

Low, A. M., "Washington, City of Leisure," *Atlantic Monthly,* 86: 767–778, 1900.

Lundberg, George A., Mirra Komarovsky, and Mary A. McInerny, *Leisure: A Suburban Study.* New York, 1934.

Lundberg, George A., Read Bain, and Nels Anderson, eds., *Trends in American Sociology.* New York, 1929.

Lyman, George D., *The Saga of the Comstock Lode: Boom Days in Virginia City.* New York, 1934.

McAdoo, William, *Guarding a Great City.* New York, 1906.

McBain, Howard L., *The Law and the Practice of Municipal Home Rule.* New York, 1916.

McCarty, Harold H., *Industrial Migration in the United States, 1914–1927.* Iowa Studies in Business, No. VII. Iowa City, March, 1930.

McCarty, John L., *Maverick Town, The Story of Old Tascosa.* Norman, Okla., 1946.

McCrea, Roswell C., *The Humane Movement.* New York, 1910.

McCulloch, O. C., "History of Charity Organizations," National Conference of Charities, *Proceedings,* pp. 123–126, 1880.

McCullough, Edo, *Good Old Coney Island, A Sentimental Journey Into the Past.* New York, 1957.

MacElwee, Roy S., *Port Development.* New York, 1926.

Mack, Raymond, Linton Freeman, and Seymour Yellin, *Social Mobility: Thirty Years of Research and Theory.* Syracuse, 1957.

Mackay, Constance D., *The Little Theatre in the United States.* New York, 1917.

McKelvey, Blake, "American Urban History Today," *American Historical Review,* LVII: 919–929. July, 1952.

McKelvey, Blake, *Rochester: The Water-Power City, 1812–1854.* Cambridge, 1945. Cited as *Rochester,* I.

McKelvey, Blake, *Rochester: The Flower City, 1855–1890.* Cambridge, 1949. Cited as *Rochester,* II.

McKelvey, Blake, *Rochester: The Quest for Quality, 1890–1925.* Cambridge, 1956. Cited as *Rochester,* III.

McKenzie, R. D., "The Rise of Metropolitan Communities," *Recent Social Trends.* New York, 1934.

McLaughlin, Glenn E., *The Growth of American Manufacturing Areas.* Pittsburgh, 1938.

McLean, Francis H., *The Charities of Springfield, Illinois.* New York, 1915.

MacLean, J. Arthur, "Fifty Years of Toledo Art," *Northwest Ohio Quarterly,* XXIV, No. 1, pp. 13–25, 1951–52.

McMurry, Donald L., *Coxey's Army.* Boston, 1929.

McSpadden, J. Walker, *Opera and Musical Comedies.* New York, 1954.

McWilliams, Carey, *Southern California Country.* New York, 1936.

Magee, Mabel A., *Trends in Location of the Women's Clothing Industry.* Chicago, 1930.

Magnusson, Leifur, *Housing by Employers in the United States.* Bureau of Labor Statistics Bulletin, No. 263. October, 1920.

Mandel, Irving A., "Attitude of the American Jewish Community Toward East-European Immigration," *American Jewish Archives,* III: 11–36. June, 1950.

Mangun, Vernon L., *The American Normal School, Its Rise and Development in Massachusetts.* Baltimore, 1928.

Mann, Arthur, *Yankee Reformers in the Urban Age.* Cambridge, 1954.

Marshall, Walter G., *Through America.* London, 1882.

Martin, Edgar W., *The Standard of Living in 1860.* Chicago, 1942.

Martin, Walter T., *The Rural-Urban Fringe; A Study of Adjustment to Residence Location.* Eugene, Ore., 1953.

Mason, Alpheus T., *Brandeis: A Free Man's Life.* New York, 1946.

Masters, D. C., *The Rise of Toronto, 1850–1890.* Toronto, 1947.

Mathews, J. M., "Municipal Representation in State Legislatures," *National Municipal Review,* XII: 135–141, 1923.

Maxwell, Robert S., *La Follette and the Rise of the Progressives in Wisconsin.* State Historical Society of Wisconsin, 1956.

Maxwell, William Q., *Lincoln's Fifth Wheel.* New York, 1956.

May, Henry F., *The End of American Innocence; The First Years of Our Own Time, 1912–1917.* New York, 1959.

May, Henry F., *Protestant Churches and Industrial America.* New York, 1949.

May, Henry F., "The Rebellion of the Intellectuals, 1912–1917," *American Quarterly,* pp. 114–126. Summer, 1956.

Mayfield, Frank M., *The Department Store Story.* New York, 1949.

Maynard, Theodore, *The Story of American Catholicism.* New York, 1941.

Mayo-Smith, Richmond, *Emigration and Immigration.* New York, 1890.

Mead, David, *Yankee Eloquence in the Middle West; The Ohio Lyceum, 1850–1870.* East Lansing, 1951.

Menke, Frank G., *Encyclopedia of Sports,* Chicago, 1939.

Merriam, Charles E., *Chicago: A More Intimate View of Urban Politics.* New York, 1929.

Merz, Charles, *The Dry Decade.* New York, 1931.

Meyer, Balthasar H., *Railway Legislation in the United States.* New York, 1909.

Meyer, E. B., *Underground Transmission and Distribution for Electric Light and Power.* New York, 1916.

Miller, George H., "The Granger Laws: A Study of the Origin of State Railway

Control in the Upper Mississippi Valley," Ph.D. Thesis, University of Michigan, 1951.

Miller, Robert M., *American Protestantism and Social Issues: 1919–1939*. Chapel Hill, 1958.

Miller, William, "American Historians and Business Elite," *Journal of Economic History*, IX: 184–208, 1949.

Miller, William, *History of Kansas City*. Kansas City, 1881.

Miller, William, ed., *Men in Business*. Cambridge, 1952.

Miller, William D., *Memphis During the Progressive Era: 1900–1917*. Memphis, 1957.

Mills, C. Wright, "The American Business Elite: A Collective Portrait," *Journal of Economic History*, V: Supplement, 1945.

Mills, C. Wright, *The Power Elite*. New York, 1956.

Mitchell, Broadus, and George S. Mitchell, *The Industrial Revolution in the South*. Baltimore, 1930.

Mitchell, Wesley C., *Business Cycles*. New York, 1927.

Mitchell, Wesley C., *History of the Greenbacks*. Chicago, 1903.

Monroe, Joel H., *Schenectady, Ancient and Modern*. Schenectady, 1914.

Moody, John, *The Masters of Capital*. The Chronicles of America Series, 41. New Haven, 1919.

Moody, John, *The Railroad Builders*. The Chronicles of America Series, 38. New Haven, 1919.

Moody, Joseph N., ed., *Church and Society*. New York, 1953.

Moody, Walter D., *Wacker's Manual of the Plan of Chicago*. Chicago, 1924 ed.

Moore, Charles, *Daniel H. Burnham, Architect, Planner of Cities*. 2 volumes. Boston, 1921.

Morgan, Arthur E., *The Community of the Future and the Future of the Community*. Community Service, Inc. Yellow Springs, O., 1957.

Morgan, Murray, *Skid Road: An Informal Portrait of Seattle*. New York, revised ed., 1960.

Morris, John V., *Fires and Firefighters*. Boston, 1955.

Morris, Lloyd, *Curtain Time*. New York, 1953.

Morris, Lloyd, *Not So Long Ago*. New York, 1949.

Morrison, Hugh, *Louis Sullivan, Prophet of Modern Architecture*. New York, 1935.

Morse, William F., *The Collection and Disposal of Municipal Waste*. New York, 1908.

Morton, John R., *University Extension in the United States*. Birmingham, Ala., 1953.

Moses, Montrose J., *The American Dramatist*. Boston, 1925.

Mosher, Frederick C., *et al.*, *City Manager Government in Seven Cities*. Chicago, 1940.

Mott, Frank L., *American Journalism*. New York, 1941.

Mott, Frank L., *A History of American Magazines*. 4 volumes. Cambridge, 1938–47.

Mowry, George E., *The California Progressives*. Berkeley, 1951.

Mowry, George E., *Theodore Roosevelt and the Progressive Movement*. Madison, 1946.

Mueller, John H., *The American Symphony Orchestra*. Bloomington, 1951.

Muirhead, James F., *America, the Land of Contrasts*. New York, 1911.

Mumford, Lewis, *City Development*. New York, 1945.

Mumford, Lewis, *The City in History*. New York, 1961.

Municipal Affairs. Published quarterly by the Reform Club of New York, Committee of Municipal Information. March, 1897–February, 1903.

Münsterberg, Hugo, *The Americans*. London, 1905.

Murphy, Edgar G., *Problems of the Present South*. New York, 1904.

Myers, Margaret G., *The New York Money Market*. Vol. I: Origins and Development. New York, 1931.

Myrdal, Gunnar, *An American Dilemma*. New York, 1944.

Nadeau, Remi, *City-Makers; The Men Who Transformed Los Angeles from Vil-*

lage to Metropolis During the First Great Boom, 1868–1876. Garden City, 1948.

Nadeau, Remi, *Los Angeles, From Mission to Modern City.* New York, 1960.

Nadworny, Milton J., *Scientific Management and the Union.* Cambridge, 1955.

National American Woman Suffrage Association, *Victory, How Women Won It.* New York, 1940.

National Anti-Trust Conference, *Official Report of, at Chicago, 1900.* Chicago, 1900.

National Civic Federation, Commission on Public Ownership and Operation, *Municipal and Private Operation of Public Utilities.* 3 volumes. New York, 1907.

National Conference of City Planning, *Proceedings,* 1909.

National Municipal League, *A Municipal Program.* New York, 1900.

National Municipal League, *Proceedings,* 1901–1910.

National Municipal League, Committee on Metropolitan Government, *The Government of Metropolitan Areas in the United States.* New York, 1930.

National Park Service, *Municipal and County Parks in the United States.* Washington, 1937.

National Resources Committee, *Interim Report of Research Committee on Urbanism.* Mimeographed, July, 1936.

National Resources Committee, *Our Cities.* Washington, 1937.

National Resources Committee, *Population Statistics,* No. 3, Urban Data. Washington, 1937

National Resources Committee, *Urban Government.* Washington, 1939.

National Resources Committee, *Urban Planning and Land Policies.* Washington, 1939.

Nevins, Allan, *The Emergence of Modern America, 1865–1878.* History of American Life Series, VIII. New York, 1927.

Nevins, Allan, and J. A. Krout, eds., *The Greater City: New York, 1898–1948.* New York, 1948.

Newcomer, Mabel, *The Big Business Executive.* New York, 1955.

Newhall, Beaumont, *The History of Photography.* New York, 1949.

Noyes, Alexander D., *Forty Years of American Finance . . . 1865–1907.* New York, 1909.

Nutter, G. Warren, *The Extent of Enterprise Monopoly in the United States: 1899–1939.* Chicago, 1951.

Nye, Russel B., *Midwestern Progressive Politics* [1870–1958]. East Lansing, 1959.

O'Connor, William V., *An Age of Criticism: 1900–1950.* Chicago, 1952.

Ogburn, William F., "Inventions of Local Transportation and the Patterns of Cities," *Social Forces,* 24: 273–279. May, 1946.

O'Grady, John, *Catholic Charities in the United States, History and Problems.* Washington, 1930.

Olds, Mrs. Fremont, *San Francisco.* San Francisco, 1961.

Oliver, John W., *History of American Technology.* New York, 1956.

Olmsted, F. L., "The Town Planning Movement in America," *Annals of American Academy of Political and Social Science,* 51: 172–181. January, 1914.

Olmsted, F. L., Jr., and Theodora Kimball, *Frederick Law Olmsted, Landscape Architect, 1822–1903.* 2 volumes. New York, 1922.

Olson, James C., *J. Sterling Morton.* Lincoln, Neb., 1942.

O'Neill, George E., ed., *The Labor Movement: The Problem of Today.* Boston, 1887.

Osterweis, Rollin G., *Three Centuries of New Haven, 1638–1938.* New Haven, 1953.

Otte, Herman F., *Industrial Opportunity in the Tennessee Valley of Northwestern Alabama.* New York, 1940.

Oursler, William C., *The Boy Scout Story.* New York, 1955.

Overton, Richard C., *Gulf to Rockies; The Heritage of the Fort Worth and Denver-Colorado and Southern Railways, 1861–1898.* Austin, 1953.

Oviatt, F. C., "Historical Study of Fire Insurance in the United States," *Annals,* XXVI: 352–375, 1906.

Owen, Wilfred, *Cities in the Motor Age.* New York, 1959.
Owen, Wilfred, *The Metropolitan Transportation Problem.* Brookings Institute. Washington, 1956.
Pacey, Lorene M., *Readings in the Development of Settlement Work.* New York, 1950.
Pach, Walter, *The Art Museum in America.* New York, 1948.
Park, Robert E., *Human Communities: The City and Human Ecology.* Glencoe, 1952.
Park, Robert E., and Herbert A. Miller, *Old World Traits Transplanted.* New York, 1921.
Parker, Margaret T., *Lowell: A Study of Industrial Development.* New York, 1940.
Parkhurst, Charles H., *My Forty Years in New York.* New York, 1923.
Parkhurst, Charles H., *Our Fight With Tammany.* New York, 1895.
Parsons, Frank, *The City for the People,* Philadelphia, 1901.
Pasdermadjian, H., *The Department Store, Its Origins, Evolution, and Economics.* London, 1954.
Passer, Harold C., *The Electrical Manufacturers, 1875–1900.* Cambridge, 1953.
Pattee, Fred L., *The New American Literature, 1890–1930.* New York, 1930.
Patton, Clifford W., *The Battle for Municipal Reform . . . 1875–1900.* Washington, 1940.
Paullin, Charles O., *Atlas of the Historical Geography of the United States.* Carnegie Institution of Washington. Washington, 1932.
Perine, Edward, *The Story of the Trust Companies.* New York, 1916.
Perloff, Harvey S., *Education for Planning: City, State and Regional.* Baltimore, 1957.
Perloff, Harvey S., and associates, *Regions, Resources, and Economic Growth.* Baltimore, 1960.
Perrigo, Lynn I., "Law and Order in Early Colorado Mining Camps," *Mississippi Valley Historical Review,* XXVIII: 41–62. June, 1941.
Perry, Clarence A., *Housing for the Machine Age.* New York, 1939.
Perry, Clarence A., *Wider Use of the School Plant.* Russell Sage Foundation. New York, 1913.
Perry, George S., *Cities of America.* New York, 1947.
Peterson, Lorin, *The Day of the Mugwump.* New York, 1961.
Peterson, Virgil W., *Barbarians in Our Midst.* New York, 1952.
Phillips, Wilbur C., *Adventuring for Democracy.* New York, 1940.
Pierce, Bessie L., *A History of Chicago.* 3 volumes. New York, 1937–57. Cited as *Chicago,* I, II, III.
Pierce, Harry H., *Railroads of New York: A Study of Government Aid, 1826–1875.* Cambridge, 1953.
Pinkerton, Allan, *Strikes, Communists, Tramps and Detectives.* New York, 1878.
Pirtle, T. R., *History of the Dairy Industry.* Chicago, 1926.
Pollock, Horatio M., *Modern Cities.* New York, 1913.
Pomeroy, Earl, *In Search of the Golden West: The Tourist in Western America.* New York, 1957.
Pope, Jesse E., *The Clothing Industry in New York.* University of Missouri Studies in Social Science, Vol. I. St. Louis, 1905.
Popper, Samuel H., *Individualized Justice: Fifty Years of Juvenile Court and Probation Services in Ramsey County, Minnesota.* St. Paul, 1956.
Potter, David M., *People of Plenty; Economic Abundance and the American Character.* Chicago, 1954.
Pound, Roscoe, *Criminal Justice in the American City.* Part VII of Criminal Justice in Cleveland. Cleveland, 1922.
Powderly, T. V., *The Path I Trod.* New York, 1940.
Pratt, Edward E., *Industrial Causes of Congestion of Population in New York City.* New York, 1911.
Presbrey, Frank S., *The History and Development of Advertising.* New York, 1929.
Pringle, Henry F., *Theodore Roosevelt, A Biography.* New York, 1931.
Purcell, Ralph, *Government and Art.* Washington, 1956.

Pusey, Merlo J., *Charles Evans Hughes.* New York, 1951.
Quiett, Glenn C., *They Built the West: An Epic of Rails and Cities.* New York, 1934.
Quinn, Arthur H., *A History of the American Drama from the Civil War to the Present Day.* 2 volumes. New York, 1927.
Rafter, George W., and M. N. Baker, *Sewage Disposal in the United States.* New York, 1894.
Rainwater, Clarence E., *The Play Movement in the United States: A Study of Community Recreation.* Chicago, 1922.
Ramsey, Grace F., *Educational Work in Museums of the United States.* New York, 1938.
Ratner, Sidney, *New Light on the History of Great American Fortunes.* New York, 1953.
Rauschenbusch, Walter, *Christianizing the Social Order.* New York, 1912.
Ravenel, Mazyck P., ed., *A Half Century of Public Health.* New York, 1921.
Recent Social Trends in the United States. New York, 1939.
Reckless, Walter C., *Vice in Chicago.* Chicago, 1933.
Rees, Gwendolen, *Libraries for Children: A History and a Bibliography.* London, 1924.
Regier, C. C., *The Era of the Muckrakers.* Chapel Hill, 1932.
Reiser, Catherine E., *Pittsburgh's Commercial Development: 1800–1850.* Harrisburg, 1951.
Reynolds, George M., *Machine Politics in New Orleans, 1897–1926.* New York, 1936.
Reynolds, Marcus T., *The Housing of the Poor in American Cities. American Economic Association Publication,* VIII: 135–262. Baltimore, 1893.
Rezneck, Samuel, "Patterns of Thought and Action in an American Depression, 1882–1886," *American Historical Review,* pp. 284–307. January, 1956.
Richards, Charles R., *Industrial Art and the Museum.* New York, 1927.
Richmond, Mary E., *The Good Neighbor in the Modern City.* Philadelphia, 1907.
Richmond, Mary E., *The Long View: Papers and Addresses by Mary E. Richmond.* Selected and edited with biographical notes by Joanna C. Colcord and Ruth Z. S. Mann. Russell Sage Foundation. New York, 1930.
Rightor, Chester E., and others, *City Manager in Dayton.* New York, 1919.
Rickard, T. A., *A History of American Mining.* New York, 1932.
Riis, Jacob A., *How the Other Half Lives: Studies Among the Tenements of New York, 1919.* New York, 1919.
Ripley, William Z., *Railroads, Rates and Regulation.* New York, 1923.
Rischin, Moses, *The Promised City: New York's Jews, 1870–1914.* Cambridge, 1962.
Rister, Carl C., *The Southwestern Frontier—1865–1881.* Cleveland, 1928.
Robbins, Sidney M., and N. E. Terlockyj, *Money Metropolis.* Cambridge, 1960.
Roberts, Mary M., *American Nursing History and Interpretation.* New York, 1954.
Roberts, Peter, *Anthracite Coal Communities.* New York, 1904.
Robinson, Charles M., *The Improvement of Towns and Cities.* New York, 1901.
Robinson, Charles M., *Modern Civic Art, or, The City Made Beautiful.* New York, 1903.
Robinson, Louis N., and Rolf Nugent, *Regulation of the Small Loan Business.* Russell Sage Foundation, Small Loan Series. New York, 1935.
Rodgers, Cleveland, and Rebecca B. Rankin, *New York: The World's Capital City.* New York, 1948.
Rodwin, Lloyd, ed., *The Future Metropolis.* New York, 1961.
Rogers, John W., *The Lusty Texans of Dallas.* New York, 1951.
Roosevelt, Theodore, *An Autobiography.* New York, 1913.
Rose, William G., *Cleveland, the Making of a City.* Cleveland, 1950.
Rosenau, Helen, *The Ideal City: In Its Architectural Evolution.* London, 1959.
Roth, Lawrence V., "The Growth of American Cities," *Geographical Review,* V: 384–398. May, 1918.
Rubinow, I. M., *Social Insurance.* New York, 1916.

Rusk, Ralph S., *The Literature of the Middle Western Frontier*. New York, 1926.

Ryan, Frederick L., *Industrial Relations in the San Francisco Building Trades*. Norman, 1936.

Ryan, John A., *Social Doctrine in Action, A Personal History*. New York, 1941.

Ryan, W. Carson, *Studies in Early Graduate Education, the Johns Hopkins, Clark University, the University of Chicago*. Carnegie Foundation for the Advancement of Teaching, Bulletin No. 30. New York, 1939.

Saarinen, Aline B., *The Proud Possessors*. New York, 1958.

Sala, George A., *America Revisited*. London, 1883.

Sargent, P., *Handbook of Summer Camps*. Boston, 1925.

Saulnier, Raymond J., *Industrial Banking Companies and Their Credit Practices*. New York, 1940.

Schlesinger, Arthur M., *The Rise of the City. A History of American Life*, Vol. X. New York, 1933.

Schmeckebier, Laurence F., *The Customs Service: Its History, Activities and Organization*. Baltimore, 1924.

Schmid, Calvin F., *Social Trends in Seattle*. Seattle, 1944.

Schmidt, Emerson P., *Industrial Relations in Urban Transportation*. Minneapolis, 1937.

Schneider, David M., and Albert Deutsch, *The History of Public Welfare in New York State: 1867–1940*. Chicago, 1941.

Schneider, Herbert W., *Religion in Twentieth Century America*. Cambridge, 1952.

Schnore, Leo F., "The Timing of Metropolitan Decentralization," *Journal of the American Institute of Planning*, Vol. 25, No. 4, pp. 200–206. November, 1959.

Schroeder, Henry, "History of Electric Light," *Smithsonian Miscellaneous Collection*, Vol. 76, No. 2, 1923.

Schwartz, H. W., *Bands of America*. Garden City, 1957.

Scudder, Vida D., *On Journey*. New York, 1937.

Seager, Henry R., and Charles A. Gulick, Jr., *Trust and Corporation Problems*. New York, 1929.

Sears, Jesse B., "Philanthropy in the History of American Higher Education," U. S. Bureau of Education Bulletin, No. 26, pp. 53–80, 1922.

Shadwell, Arthur, *Industrial Efficiency*. London, 1909.

Shannon, David A., "A Social Gospel Minister and His Bishop: An Incident in the History of Intellectual Freedom," *New York History*, pp. 64–79. January, 1956.

Shannon, David A., *The Socialist Party of America, A History*. New York, 1955.

Shannon, James P. *Catholic Colonization on the Western Frontier*. New Haven, 1957.

Sharfman, Isaiah L., *The Interstate Commerce Commission; A Study in Administrative Law and Procedure*. 5 volumes. New York, 1931.

Shaw, Clifford R., and Henry D. McKay, *Juvenile Delinquency and Urban Areas*. Chicago, 1942.

Shaw, Frederick, *The History of the New York City Legislature*. New York, 1954.

Shepard, Mrs. F. J., "The Women's Educational and Industrial Union," Buffalo Historical Society *Publications*, XXII: 147–187.

Sheppard, Muriel E., *Cloud by Day: The Story of Coal and Coke and People*. Chapel Hill, 1947.

Shlakman, Vera, *Economic History of a Factory Town; A Study of Chicopee, Massachusetts*. Smith College Studies in History, Vol. XX, Nos. 1–4. Northampton, 1935.

Shryock, Richard H., *The Development of Modern Medicine*. New York, 1947.

Simpson, William H., *Life in Mill Communities*. Clinton, S. C., 1943.

Sims, Mary S., *The Natural History of a Social Institution—the Young Women's Christian Association*. New York, 1936.

Sinclair, Andrew, *Prohibition, the Era of Excess*. Boston, 1962.

Sizer, Theodore, "The American Academy of Fine Arts," *New York Historical Society Collection*, 76, 1943.

Sjoberg, Gideon, *The Preindustrial City: Past and Present.* Glencoe, Ill., 1960.

Slosson, Edwin E., *The American Spirit in Education.* New Haven, 1921.

Small, A. W., "Fifty Years of Sociology in the United States (1865–1915)," *American Journal of Sociology,* XXI: 734–768, 1916.

Smith, Cecil, *Musical Comedy in America.* New York, 1950.

Smith, Cecil, *Worlds of Music.* New York, 1952.

Smith, Stephen, *The City That Was.* New York, 1911.

Smith, T. V., and Leonard D. White, eds., *Chicago, An Experiment in Social Science Research.* Chicago, 1929.

Smith, Thomas R., *The Cotton Textile Industry of Fall River, Massachusetts; A Study of Industrial Localization.* New York, 1944.

Smith, Timothy L., *Revivalism and Social Reform in Mid-Nineteenth-Century America.* New York, Nashville, 1957.

Solomon, Barbara M., *Ancestors and Immigrants, A Changing New England Tradition.* Cambridge, 1956.

Solomon, Barbara M., *Pioneers in Service.* Boston, 1956.

Spahr, Walter E., *The Clearing and Collection of Checks.* New York, 1926.

Spectorsky, Auguste C., *The Exurbanites.* New York, 1955.

Spencer, Gwladys, *The Chicago Public Library; Origins and Backgrounds.* Chicago, 1943.

Sprague, Marshall, *Newport in the Rockies.* Denver, 1961.

Sprague, O. M. W., *History of Crises Under the National Banking System.* National Monetary Commission. Washington, 1910.

Stearns, Marshall W., *The Story of Jazz.* New York, 1956.

Steevens, G. W., *The Land of the Dollar.* New York, 1897.

Steffens, Lincoln, *The Autobiography of . . .* New York, 1931.

Steffens, Lincoln, *The Shame of the Cities.* New York, 1904.

Steffens, Lincoln, *The Struggle for Self-Government.* New York, 1906.

Steiner, Jesse F., *The American Community in Action.* New York, 1928.

Steiner, Jesse F., *Americans at Play,* New York, 1933.

Steiner, Jesse F., "An Appraisal of the Community Movement," *Publication of the American Social Society,* XXIII: 15–29, 1929.

Stelzle, Charles, *American Social and Religious Conditions.* New York, 1912.

Stelzle, Charles, *A Son of the Bowery.* New York, 1926.

Stevens, Edward F., *The American Hospital of the Twentieth Century,* 3rd ed. New York, 1928.

Stewart, Frank M., *A Half-Century of Municipal Reform.* Berkeley, 1950.

Stewart, Frank M., *The National Civil Service Reform League.* Austin, 1929.

Stewart, William R., *The Philanthropic Work of Josephine Shaw Lowell.* New York, 1911.

Still, Bayrd, *Milwaukee, The History of a City.* Madison, 1948.

Still, Bayrd, *Mirror for Gotham.* New York, 1956.

Still, Bayrd, "Patterns of Mid-Nineteenth Century Urbanization in the Middle West," *Mississippi Valley Historical Review,* XXVIII: 187, 206.

Stimson, Grace H., *Rise of the Labor Movement in Los Angeles.* Berkeley, 1955.

Stockton, Frank T., "The Closed Shop in American Trade Unions," Johns Hopkins University Studies, XXIX, No. 3, 1911.

Stokes, A. P., *Church and State in the United States.* New York, 1950.

Stone, Harold A., D. K. Price, and K. H. Stone, *City Manager Government in the United States.* Chicago, 1940.

Stone, Walter L., *The Development of Boys' Work in the United States.* Nashville, 1935.

Stout, John E., *The Development of High-School Curricula in the North Central States from 1860 to 1918.* Chicago, 1921.

Stover, John F., *The Railroads of the South, 1865–1900.* Chapel Hill, 1955.

Strauss, Anselm, *Images of the American City.* Glencoe, 1961.

Strong, Josiah, *The Challenge of the City.* New York, 1907.

Strong, Josiah, *Our Country: Its Possible Future and Its Present Crisis.* New York, 1891.

Strong, Josiah, *The Twentieth Century City*. New York, 1898.

Sturges, Kenneth, *American Chambers of Commerce*. New York, 1915.

Syrett, Harold C., *The City of Brooklyn, 1865–1898*. New York, 1944.

Taber, Martha Van Hoesen, *A History of the Cutlery Industry in the Connecticut Valley*. Smith College Studies in History, XLI. Northampton, Mass., 1955.

Tang, Anthony M., *Economic Development in the Southern Piedmont: 1860–1950*. Chapel Hill, 1958.

Tarbell, Ida M., *New Ideals in Business*. New York, 1916.

Tarbell, Ida M., *The Nationalization of Business*. History of American Life, XI. New York, 1936.

Tatum, George B., *Penn's Great Town: 250 Years of Philadelphia Architecture Illustrated in Prints and Drawings*. Philadelphia, 1961.

Taylor, Francis H., *Babel's Tower*. New York, 1945.

Taylor, George R., and Irene D. Neu, *The American Railroad Network, 1861–1890*. Cambridge, 1956.

Taylor, Graham R., *Satellite Cities*. New York, 1915.

Tebbel, John, *The Marshall Fields*. New York, 1947.

Thomas, Dorothy S., *Research Memorandum on Migration Differentials*. Bulletin 43 of the Social Science Research Council. New York, 1938.

Thomas, William I., and F. Znaniecki, *The Polish Peasant in Europe and America*. 2 volumes. New York, 1927.

Thompson, Carl D., *Public Ownership*. New York, 1925.

Thompson, Clarence B., *Scientific Management*. Cambridge, 1914.

Thompson, John G., *Urbanization: Its Effects on Government and Society*. New York, 1927.

Thompson, Slason, *A Short History of American Railways*. New York, 1925.

Thompson, Warren S., *Population, The Growth of Metropolitan Districts in the United States: 1900–1940*. Washington, 1948.

Thompson, Warren S., and P. K. Whelpton, *Population Trends in the United States*. New York, 1933.

Thornthwaite, C. Warren, *Internal Migration in the United States*. Washington, 1934.

Thorp, Willard L., *The Integration of Industrial Operation*. U. S. Census Monograph III. Washington, 1924.

Thrasher, Frederic M., *The Gang*. Chicago, 1936 ed.

Thwing, Charles F., *A History of Education in the United States Since the Civil War*. New York, 1910.

Thwing, Charles F., *A History of Higher Education in America*. New York, 1906.

Tisdale, Hope, "The Process of Urbanization," *Social Forces*, XX: 311–316.

Tolman, William H., *Municipal Reform Movements in the United States*. New York, 1895.

Trollope, Anthony, *North America*. New York, 1951 ed.

Truesdell, Leon E., *The Canadian Born in the United States,* "An Analysis of the Statistics of the Canadian Element in the Population of the United States, 1850–1930." New Haven, 1943.

Tryon, Rolla M., *Household Manufactures in the United States; 1640–1860*. Chicago, 1917.

Tunnard, Christopher, and Henry H. Reed, *American Skyline; The Growth and Form of Our Cities and Towns*. Boston, 1955.

Tunnard, Christopher, *The City of Man*. New York, 1953.

Twentieth Century Fund, *The Security Market*. New York, 1935.

Twyman, Robert W., *History of Marshall Field & Co., 1852–1906*. Philadelphia, 1954.

Tyrrell, Henry G., *History of Bridge Engineering*. Chicago, 1911.

Ulanov, Barry, *A History of Jazz in America*. New York, 1954.

U. S. Agriculture Department, *Year Book,* 1940.

U. S. Bureau of the Census, *Current Population Reports, Population Characteristics*. Series P-23, No. 1, Aug. 5, 1949.

U. S. Bureau of the Census, *Immigrants and Their Children, 1920*. Census Monograph VII, 1927.
U. S. Bureau of the Census, "The Integration of Industrial Operations," by W. S. Thorp. Monograph III (1924).
U. S. Bureau of the Census, *Social Statistics of Cities* (1880). Parts I and II.
U. S. Bureau of the Census, *Statistics of Cities* (1906).
U. S. Bureau of the Census, *Street and Electric Railways* (1907). Special Report.
U. S. Bureau of the Census, *Telephones and Telegraphs* (1902). Special Report.
U. S. Bureau of Education, *Public Libraries in the United States*. Special Report I, 1876.
U. S. Bureau of Labor Statistics, *History of Wages in the United States from Colonial Times to 1928*. Bulletin No. 499. Washington, 1929.
U. S. Census of Manufacturing, Part III, 1929.
U. S. Commissioner of Education, *Reports*, 1870–1915.
U. S. Industrial Commission, *Reports* (1900–01).
U. S. Senate Documents, *Location of Reserve Districts in the United States*. 63rd Congress, 2nd Session, Vol. 16. Washington, 1914.
Unwin, Raymond, *Town Planning in Practice*, 4th ed. London, 1914.
Usher, Abbott P., *A History of Mechanical Inventions*. Cambridge, 1954 ed.
Valentine, Alan, *1913: America Between Two Worlds*. New York, 1962.
Vance, Rupert B., with Nadia Danielevsky, *All These People: The Nation's Human Resources in the South*. Chapel Hill, 1945.
Vance, Rupert B., and N. J. Demerath, eds., *The Urban South*. Chapel Hill, 1954.
Van Cleef, Eugene, *Trade Centers and Trade Routes*. New York, 1937.
Van Dyke, John C., *The New New York*. New York, 1909.
Van Rensselaer, Mrs. John K., and F. Van De Water, *The Social Ladder*. New York, 1924.
Vickers, George, *The Fall of Bossism: A History of the Committee of One Hundred*. Philadelphia, 1883.
Vigman, Fred K., *Crisis of the Cities*. Washington, 1955.
Vincent, George E., "Summer Schools and University Extension," in Nicholas M. Butler, *Education in the United States*, 2nd ed. New York, 1910.
Vincent, John H., *The Chautauqua Movement*. Boston, 1886.
Wade, Louise, "Graham Taylor, Social Pioneer: 1851–1938," Ph.D. Thesis, University of Rochester, 1954.
Wade, Richard C., *The Urban Frontier*. Cambridge, 1959.
Walker, Charles R., *American City*. New York, 1937.
Walker, Franklin, *A Literary History of Southern California*. Berkeley, 1950.
Walker, Franklin, *San Francisco's Literary Frontier*. New York, 1939.
Walker, James B., *Fifty Years of Rapid Transit, 1864–1917*. New York, 1918.
Walker, Robert, *The Planning Function in Urban Government*. Chicago, 1941.
Walker, Robert, "The Poet and the Rise of the City," *Mississippi Valley Historical Review*, IL: 85–99. June, 1962.
Wallace, Schuyler C., *State Administrative Supervision Over Cities in the United States*. New York, 1928.
Walling, George W., *Recollections of a New York Chief of Police*. New York, 1888.
Wann, Louis, ed., *The Rise of Realism; American Literature from 1860 to 1900*. New York, 1949.
Warburg, Paul M., *The Federal Reserve System, Its Origin and Growth*. New York, 1930.
Ward, Edward J., *Rochester Social Centers and Civic Clubs*. Rochester, 1909.
Ware, Caroline F., ed., *The Cultural Approach to History*. New York, 1940.
Ware, Caroline F., *The Early New England Cotton Manufacture*. Boston, 1931.
Ware, Caroline F., *Greenwich Village, 1920–1930*. Boston, 1935.
Ware, Louise, *Jacob A. Riis, Police Reporter, Reformer, Useful Citizen*. New York, 1938.
Ware, Norman J., *The Labor Movement in the United States, 1860–1895*. New York, 1929.

Waring, George E., Jr., *Modern Methods of Sewage Disposal, 1894*. New York, 1903.

Waring, George E., Jr., *Street-Cleaning and the Disposal of a City's Wastes*. New York, 1898.

Warner, Amos G., Stuart A. Queen, and Ernest B. Harper, *American Charities and Social Work*, 4th ed. New York, 1935.

Warner, John D., "Civic Centers," *Municipal Affairs*, pp. 1–23. March, 1902.

Warner, Sam B. Jr., *Streetcar Suburbs: The Process of Growth in Boston, 1870–1900*. Cambridge, 1962.

Warner, W. Lloyd, *Big Business Leaders in America*. New York, 1955.

Warner, W. Lloyd, Marchia Meeker, and Kenneth Eells, *Social Class in America*. Chicago, 1949.

Watkins, Edgar, "Geography, Railroads and Men Made Atlanta," *The Atlanta Historical Bulletin*. October, 1948.

Watson, Frank D., *The Charity Organization Movement in the United States*. New York, 1922.

Watson, Richard L., Jr., "Woodrow Wilson and His Interpreters: 1947–1957," *Mississippi Valley Historical Review*, pp. 212–219. September, 1957.

Weber, Adna F., *The Growth of Cities in the Nineteenth Century*. New York, 1899.

Weber, Adna F., "Rapid Transit and the Housing Problem," *Municipal Affairs*, VI: 409–417, 1903.

Weber, Alfred, *Theory of Location of Industry*. Chicago, 1929. Translation by Carl J. Friedrich.

Weber, Max, *The City*. Edited and translated by Don Martindale and Gertrude Neuwirth. Glencoe, 1958.

Wecter, Dixon, *The Saga of American Society; A Record of Social Aspiration, 1607–1937*. New York, 1937.

Weld, Ralph F., *Brooklyn Village, 1816–1834*. New York, 1938.

Werner, M. R., *Tammany Hall*. New York, 1928.

Wertenbaker, T. J., *Norfolk; Historic Southern Port*. Durham, 1931.

Wesley, Edgar B., *Owatonna; The Social Development of a Minnesota Community*. Minneapolis, 1938.

West, Ray B., Jr., *Rocky Mountain Cities*. New York, 1949.

Wheeler, Cyrenus, Jr., "Sewers Ancient and Modern, with an Appendix (on the Auburn, N. Y., sewers)," Cayuga County, N. Y., Historical Society *Collections*, V: 15–108, 1887.

White, Morton and Lucia, *The Intellectual Versus the City: From Thomas Jefferson to Frank Lloyd Wright*. Cambridge, 1962.

White, William A., *The Old Order Changeth*. New York, 1910.

Whitehill, Walter M., *Boston, A Topographical History*. Cambridge, 1959.

Whiteside, William, *The Boston Y. M. C. A. and Community Need; A Century's Evolution, 1851–1951*. New York, 1951.

Whitlock, Brand, *Forty Years of It*. New York, 1914.

Whitney, Carrie W., *Kansas City, Missouri*. Chicago, 1908.

Wiebe, Robert H., "Business Disunity and the Progressive Movement, 1901–1914," *Mississippi Valley Historical Review*, XLIV: 664–685, No. 4. March, 1958.

Wiernik, Peter, *History of the Jews in America*. New York, 1912.

Wilcox, Delos F., *The American City; A Problem in Democracy*, 3rd ed. New York, 1909.

Wilcox, Delos F., *Great Cities in America*. New York, 1910.

Wilcox, Delos F., *Municipal Franchises*. 2 volumes. New York, 1911.

Willis, Henry P., *The Federal Reserve System*. New York, 1923.

Wilson, Howard E., *Mary McDowell, Neighbor*. Chicago, 1928.

Wilson, Rufus R., and O. E. Wilson, *New York in Literature*. Elmira, 1947.

Winters, O. O., "Rise of Metropolitan Los Angeles," *Huntington Library Journal*, X: 391–405, 1947.

Wirth, Louis, *Community Life and Social Policy*. Edited by Elizabeth W. Marvick and A. J. Reiss, Jr. Chicago, 1956.

Wisbey, Herbert A., Jr., *Soldiers Without Swords, A History of the Salvation Army in the United States.* New York, 1955.
Wittke, Carl, *The Irish in America.* Baton Rouge, 1956.
Wittke, Carl, *We Who Built America.* New York, 1940.
Wittlin, Alma S., *The Museum, Its History and Its Tasks in Education.* London, 1949.
Wolfe, Albert B., *The Lodging House Problem in Boston.* Cambridge, 1913.
Wolman, Leo, *The Growth of American Trade Unions, 1880–1923.* A National Bureau of Economic Research Publication. New York, 1924.
Wood, Edith E., *The Housing of the Unskilled Wage Earner.* New York, 1919.
Wood, Edith E., *Slums and Blighted Areas in the United States.* Housing Division Bulletin I. Washington, 1935.
Wood, F. E., *The Louisville Story.* Louisville, 1951.
Wood, James P., *Magazines in the United States,* 2nd ed. New York, 1956.
Wood, Mary I., *The History of the General Federation of Women's Clubs.* New York, 1912.
Woods, Robert A., ed., *Americans in Process.* Boston, 1902.
Woods, Robert A., ed., *The City Wilderness.* Boston, 1898.
Woods, Robert A., and A. J. Kennedy, *The Settlement Horizon.* New York, 1922.
Woodward, C. Vann, *Origins of the New South: 1877–1913.* Vol. IX of A History of the South. Baton Rouge, 1951.
Woodworth, G. Walter, *The Detroit Money Market.* Ann Arbor, 1932.
Woody, Thomas, *A History of Women's Education in the United States.* 2 volumes. New York, 1929.
Woofter, T. J., Jr., ed., *Negro Problems in Cities.* Institute of Social and Religious Research. New York, 1928.
Woolley, John G., and William E. Johnson, *Temperance Progress in the Century.* Philadelphia, 1903.
Woolston, Howard B., *Metropolis: A Study of Urban Communities.* New York, 1938.
Woolston, Howard B., *A Study of the Population of Manhattanville.* Columbia University Studies in History, Economics, and Public Law, 35, No. 2. New York, 1909.
Wright, Carroll D., *The Slums of Baltimore, Chicago, New York and Philadelphia.* Commissioner of Labor, Special Report No. 7. Washington, 1894.
Wright, Frank L., *When Democracy Builds.* Chicago, 1945.
Wright, Henry, *Rehousing Urban America.* New York, 1935.
Wytrwal, Joseph A., *America's Polish Heritage.* Detroit, 1961.
Young, Kimball, John L. Gillin, and Calvert L. Dedrick, *The Madison Community.* University of Wisconsin Studies in the Social Sciences and History, No. 21. Madison, 1934.
Zink, Harold, *City Bosses in the United States.* Durham, 1930.
Zorbaugh, H. W., *Gold Coast and Slum.* Chicago, 1929.
Zueblin, Charles, *American Municipal Progress.* New York, 1916.

Index